IFIP Advances in Information and Communication Technology 619

Editor-in-Chief

Kai Rannenberg, Goethe University Frankfurt, Germany

Editorial Board Members

IFIP – The International Federation for Information Processing

IFIP was founded in 1960 under the auspices of UNESCO, following the first World Computer Congress held in Paris the previous year. A federation for societies working in information processing, IFIP's aim is two-fold: to support information processing in the countries of its members and to encourage technology transfer to developing nations. As its mission statement clearly states:

IFIP is the global non-profit federation of societies of ICT professionals that aims at achieving a worldwide professional and socially responsible development and application of information and communication technologies.

IFIP is a non-profit-making organization, run almost solely by 2500 volunteers. It operates through a number of technical committees and working groups, which organize events and publications. IFIP's events range from large international open conferences to working conferences and local seminars.

The flagship event is the IFIP World Computer Congress, at which both invited and contributed papers are presented. Contributed papers are rigorously refereed and the rejection rate is high.

As with the Congress, participation in the open conferences is open to all and papers may be invited or submitted. Again, submitted papers are stringently refereed.

The working conferences are structured differently. They are usually run by a working group and attendance is generally smaller and occasionally by invitation only. Their purpose is to create an atmosphere conducive to innovation and development. Refereeing is also rigorous and papers are subjected to extensive group discussion.

Publications arising from IFIP events vary. The papers presented at the IFIP World Computer Congress and at open conferences are published as conference proceedings, while the results of the working conferences are often published as collections of selected and edited papers.

IFIP distinguishes three types of institutional membership: Country Representative Members, Members at Large, and Associate Members. The type of organization that can apply for membership is a wide variety and includes national or international societies of individual computer scientists/ICT professionals, associations or federations of such societies, government institutions/government related organizations, national or international research institutes or consortia, universities, academies of sciences, companies, national or international associations or federations of companies.

More information about this series at http://www.springer.com/series/6102

Michael Friedewald · Stefan Schiffner ·
Stephan Krenn (Eds.)

Privacy and Identity Management

15th IFIP WG 9.2, 9.6/11.7, 11.6/SIG 9.2.2
International Summer School
Maribor, Slovenia, September 21–23, 2020
Revised Selected Papers

 Springer

Editors
Michael Friedewald (iD)
Fraunhofer Institute for Systems
and Innovation Research ISI
Karlsruhe, Germany

Stefan Schiffner
Université du Luxembourg
Esch-sur-Alzette, Luxembourg

Stephan Krenn (iD)
AIT Austrian Institute of Technology
Vienna, Austria

ISSN 1868-4238   ISSN 1868-422X (electronic)
IFIP Advances in Information and Communication Technology
ISBN 978-3-030-72467-2   ISBN 978-3-030-72465-8 (eBook)
https://doi.org/10.1007/978-3-030-72465-8

This Springer imprint is published by the registered company Springer Nature Switzerland AG
The registered company address is: Gewerbestrasse 11, 6330 Cham, Switzerland

Preface

This volume contains the proceedings of the 15th IFIP Summer School on Privacy and Identity Management, which took place during September 21–23, 2020. Originally planned to be held in Brno, Czech Republic, the summer school had to be moved to Maribor, Slovenia, and was finally held as a fully virtual event, due to the COVID-19 pandemic. The summer school was co-located with IFIP Sec 2020 and WISE 13.

The 15th IFIP Summer School was a joint effort among IFIP Working Groups 9.2, 9.6/11.7, 11.6, and Special Interest Group 9.2.2, in co-operation with the European Union's cybersecurity competence network pilot projects CyberSec4Europe[1], SPARTA[2] and CONCORDIA[3].

This IFIP Summer School brought together more than 40 junior and senior researchers and practitioners from different parts of the world from many disciplines, including many young entrants to the field. They met to share their ideas, build a network, gain experience in presenting their research, and have the opportunity to publish a paper through these proceedings.

As in previous years, one of the goals of the IFIP Summer School was to encourage the publication of thorough research papers by students and emerging scholars. To this end, it had a three-phase review process for submitted papers. In the first phase, authors were invited to submit short abstracts of their work. Abstracts within the scope of the call were selected for presentation at the school. After the school, authors were encouraged to submit full papers of their work and received two to three reviews by members of the Program Committee. They were then given time to revise and resubmit their papers for inclusion in these proceedings.

In total, 21 abstracts were submitted, out of which 17 were presented at the virtual conference, and 13 were finally accepted for publication. In addition, Marit Hansen (State Data Protection Commissioner of Land Schleswig-Holstein, Germany) gave a keynote lecture on "Privacy-Enhancing Technologies—where are we after 25 years?", and Sandra Schmitz and Stefan Schiffner (University of Luxembourg) gave a tutorial entitled "Don't Put the Cart Before the Horse – Effective Incident Handling Under GDPR and NIS Directive". A summary of the latter is also included in this volume.

We are grateful to all contributors of the summer school and especially to the Program Committee for reviewing the abstracts and papers as well as advising the

---

[1] https://www.cybersec4europe.eu/.

[2] https://www.sparta.eu/.

[3] https://www.concordia-h2020.eu/.

authors on their revisions. Our thanks also go to all supporting projects, the organizers of IFIP Sec, the Steering Committee for their guidance and support, and all participants and presenters.

January 2021

Michael Friedewald
Stefan Schiffner
Stephan Krenn

Organization

General Chair

Stephan Krenn   AIT Austrian Institute of Technology, Austria

Program Chairs

Michael Friedewald   Fraunhofer ISI, Germany
Stefan Schiffner   University of Luxembourg, Luxembourg

Organizing Committee

Gloria González Fuster   Vrije Universiteit Brussel, Belgium
Vášhek Matyáš   Masaryk University, Czech Republic

Program Committee

Florian Adamsky   University of Applied Sciences Hof, Germany
Daniel Bachlechner   Fraunhofer Austria, Austria
Felix Bieker   Independent Centre for Privacy Protection
       Schleswig-Holstein, Germany
Mauro Brignoli   Vitrociset S.p.A., Italy
Sonja Buchegger   KTH Royal Institute of Technology, Sweden
Sébastien Canard   Orange Labs, France
Pavel Čeleda   Masaryk University, Czech Republic
Josep Domingo-Ferrer   Universitat Rovira i Virgili, Spain
Orhan Ermiş   Eurecom, France
Simone Fischer-Hübner   Karlstad University, Sweden
Pedro Freitas   University of Minho, Portugal
Michael Friedewald   Fraunhofer ISI, Germany
Lothar Fritsch   Karlstad University, Sweden
Gloria González Fuster   Vrije Universiteit Brussel, Belgium
Jan Hajný   Brno University of Technology, Czech Republic
Dominik Herrmann   University of Bamberg, Germany
Meiko Jensen   Kiel University of Applied Sciences, Germany
Stefan Katzenbeisser   University of Passau, Germany
Kai Kimppa   University of Turku, Finland
Stephan Krenn   AIT Austrian Institute of Technology, Austria
Eva Lievens   Ghent University, Belgium
Lukáš Malina   Brno University of Technology, Czech Republic
Ninja Marnau   CISPA Helmholtz Center for Information Security,
       Germany

Váshek Matyáš	Masaryk University, Czech Republic
Joachim Meyer	Tel Aviv University, Israel
Andreas Nautsch	Eurecom, France
Sebastian Pape	Goethe University Frankfurt, Germany
Aljosa Pasic	Atos Research & Innovation, Spain
Robin Pierce	Tilburg University, The Netherlands
Jo Pierson	Vrije Universiteit Brussel, Belgium
Tobias Pulls	Karlstad University, Sweden
Kjetil Rommetveit	University of Bergen, Norway
Arnold Roosendaal	The Privacy Company, The Netherlands
Ina Schiering	Ostfalia University of Applied Sciences, Germany
Stefan Schiffner	University of Luxembourg, Luxembourg
Valerie Verdoodt	London School of Economics, UK
Diane Whitehouse	The Castlegate Consultancy, UK
Marc van Lieshout	Radboud University, The Netherlands
Simone van der Hof	Leiden University, The Netherlands
Rose-Mharie Åhlfeldt	University of Skövde, Sweden
Melek Önen	Eurecom, France

Additional Reviewers

Tsany Ratna Dewi	University of Luxembourg, Luxembourg
Dara Hallinan	Leibniz Institute for Information Infrastructure, Germany
Amirhossein Adavoudi Jolfaei	University of Luxembourg, Luxembourg
Thomas Lorünser	AIT Austrian Institute of Technology, Austria
Ana Pop Stefanija	Vrije Universiteit Brussel, Belgium
Sandra Schmitz-Berndt	University of Luxembourg, Luxembourg

Contents

Tutorial Paper

Don't Put the Cart Before the Horse – Effective Incident Handling Under GDPR and NIS Directive

Sandra Schmitz-Berndt and Stefan Schiffner[(✉)]

Université du Luxembourg, Esch sur Alzette, Luxembourg
{Sandra.Schmitz,Stefan.Schiffner}@uni.lu

Abstract. This paper serves as notes to a lecture given at the IFIP summer school of privacy and identity management 2020. We discussed notification requirements in the NIS directive and the GDPR in the case of security and privacy incidents form legal and technical perspective. In particular, we discuss timing. While a need to mitigate an immediate risk of damage for an individual would call for prompt communication with data subjects, there are scenarios which may justify a delay in communication to a wider public, e.g. a large user base. This might be advisable, for instance, where a service provider needs to analyse the current attack to prevent further attacks and assess the full impact. In the latter, any delay in communication should fulfil the requirement of "without undue delay". Further, we discuss why the concurrent reporting under both regimes is needed and conclude with a call for more cooperation of the respective competent authorities.

1 Introduction

This paper contains work in progress and reflects a snap shoot of our research taken at the time of the lecture. The final results of our work are under publication and will appear later this year [1].

The field of cybersecurity in 2016 saw two important legal instruments adopted: the omnipresent General Data Protection Regulation[1], and the under-appreciated Network and Information Systems Directive[2]. The objective of both instruments is to ensure appropriate security of information technology (IT) systems and the data processed by those.

---

[1] Regulation (EU) 2016/679 of the European Parliament and of the Council of 27 April 2016 on the protection of natural persons with regard to the processing of personal data and on the free movement of such data, and repealing Directive 95/46/EC (General Data Protection Regulation), OJ L 119, 04.05.2016, pp. 1–88.

[2] Directive (EU) 2016/1148 of the European Parliament and of the Council of 6 July 2016 concerning measures for a high common level of security of network and information systems across the Union.

Both authors are supported by the Luxembourg National Research Fund as part of EnCaViBS project, grant number C18/IS/12639666/EnCaViBS/Cole.

M. Friedewald et al. (Eds.): Privacy and Identity 2020, IFIP AICT 619, pp. 3–17, 2021.
https://doi.org/10.1007/978-3-030-72465-8_1

While both instruments are largely in alignment, particularly with their risk-based approach to security measures, they have distinct interests: the GDPR covers privacy rights concerning personal data of individuals, while the NIS Directive encompasses the information security, i.e. the confidentiality, integrity and availability (CIA), of the services covered and the underlying information technology infrastructure. In many cases, the latter does include personal data, meaning that the NIS Directive can be regarded as a complementary law to the GDPR. While the NIS Directive is broader in terms of the subject matter covered, i.e. digital data including any data relating to network and information systems and its provision and continuity, it is more restrictive as regards addressees, which only include operators of essential services (OES) and digital service providers (DSP).

Both instruments introduce similar notification obligations based on the assumption that security threats can only be eliminated if security risks and data breaches are communicated to public authorities. The NIS Directive requires OES' and DSPs to notify, without undue delay, the competent national authorities of security incidents having a significant impact on the continuity of the services they provide. Where an incident simultaneously constitutes, or becomes, a personal data breach, the provider needs to inform the data protection regulator separately under the GDPR without undue delay and within 72 h. In practice, two separate regulators may have to be informed about the same incident.

In addition, under Art. 34 (1) GDPR, the provider shall communicate a personal data breach without undue delay to the data subject if the personal data breach is likely to result in a high risk to the rights and freedoms of natural persons. However, Art. 34 (3) GDPR foresees exceptions to the notification obligations and enlists conditions under which the communication to the data subject shall not be required. Member States may provide for further derogations to Art. 34 (1) GDPR, of which some will be outlined.

The reminder of this paper is organized as flows: First we map the notification obligations and the roles of the regulators. Second from an interdisciplinary perspective, we will present dilemma scenarios in which none of the exceptions for immediate notification applies, but nevertheless the provider has a prevailing and legitimate interest in suspending end user notifications. Taking the incidence response cycle as guide, we discuss, when the "clock starts to tick" for notification without undue delay.

2   Background

2.1   Information Security vs Privacy

Information security and privacy interact in a complex fashion: A breach in one might lead to an incident in the other field. While it might be obvious that unauthorized access to a data base (IT-Security incident) containing, e.g., VISA card information, is a privacy breach, the other way around might be less obvious. However, personal information leaked, might be used in spearfishing attack, e.g., the attacker might learn that a targeted person is client of a specific bank, given this information a more convincing spearfishing email can be tailored changing significantly the chances that the victim is tricked into revealing sensitive information such as logins or passphrases.

So, this backdrop set: what is the difference between privacy and security? In short, the difference is the protection goals, i.e. which assets need to be protected from whom and who are the risk takers. Traditionally in information security, we distinguish three dimensions: CIA, i.e. Confidentiality, Integrity, and Availability. Note, any practical system requires always all three dimensions to a certain extent. Moreover to describe a protection goal for a given application, one needs to describe the stakeholders and the adversary (assumptions and capabilities).

Example I. Consider the IT security of a power plant. The plant can be controlled remotely in order to adjust its output coordinated with neighbouring plants to the market needs. An adversary might attempt to falsify messages that lead to an unwanted reduction of power production. Which in turn would reduce the revenue of this plant (assuming it's a single attack and other power providers step in to avoid a blackout). Hence, in this scenario, the operator of the plant is the main risk taker, the main protection goal is availability and the main adversary is an external attack that attempts to modify messages.

Example II. Consider a hotel booking platform. Users need to provide payment details as collateral for their bookings, which are stored in a database. An adversary might attempt to access this database with the aim to use this payment data for fraudulent payments. This would at first have an impact on the users of the booking service, who are the main risk takers here. The main protection goal is thus confidentiality to prevent an external attack from the abuse of personal data, e.g. in an identity theft scheme.

Hence, CIA is relevant for information security and personal data protection, though with some differences in emphasize of the dimensions. For privacy, the literature further distinguishes 3 more protection goals: unlikability, transparency and intervenability [2]. Here unlikability means that 2 artifacts concerning the same context, cannot be related to this context by an unauthorized party. Hence this could be seen as confidentiality of meta data; transparency requires technical measures that allow a data subject to investigate how data is processed, and intervenability measures allow subjects to change the way of processing (correct data, retract consent etc.).

Both norms, GDPR and NIS Directive, reflect these protection goals; w.r.t. the notification obligations. For the first these obligations concern mainly confidentiality and unlikability breaches, while for the latter the main concern is disruptions of service, hence availability breaches.

2.2   Incident Handling Under NIS Directive and GDPR

A key element of data security is prevention and if nevertheless a data breach occurs, to be able to react in a timely manner. If a breach of personal data or a security incident occurs, the GDPR and the NIS Directive both introduce the requirement for said incident to be notified to the competent national authority. Similar notification obligations of security incidents exist under other EU legal instruments, such as Art. 19(2) Regulation (EU) 910/2014 (eIDAS Regulation)[3], Art. 96 Directive 2015/2366/EU (PSD2)[4] and Art. 40(2) Directive (EU) 2018/1972 (EECC)[5]. As regards personal data breaches Art. 4 Directive 2002/58/EC (ePrivacy Directive) contains a notification obligation limited to providers of publicly available electronic communications services.[6] The following sections outline the notification procedures under NIS Directive and GDPR.

The NIS Directive Incident Notification Scheme: Notification Obligation for OESs and DSPs. The NIS Directive is the first instrument to introduce an IT security incident notification regime across different sectors at European level. The notion of "incident" is defined in Art. 4 NIS Directive as "any event having an actual adverse effect on the security of network and information systems" with network and information systems being "interconnected systems that process, transmit and store data".

As regards the obligation to report an incident, the NIS Directive differentiates between operators of essential services (OESs) and digital service providers (DSPs). Art. 4(4) NIS Directive defines an OES as a public or private entity within one of the sectors enlisted in Annex II, which meets the criteria laid down in Article 5(2). These criteria resemble the definition of "critical infrastructure" in Art. 2(1) ECI Directive[7] with the difference that only entities depending on network and information systems may qualify as OESs and thus fall within the scope of the NIS Directive. Member States are supposed to define essential services and identify OES mwithin their territories. In contrast, Annex III of the NIS Directive enlists as DSPs to which the NIS Directive applies only three types of services: cloud services, online market places and search engines.

According to Art. 14(3) and Art. 16(3) NIS Directive, Member States shall ensure that OESs and DSPs notify, without undue delay, the competent authority or the computer security incident response team (CSIRT) of incidents having a significant impact on the continuity of the essential services they provide

---

[3] Regulation (EU) 910/2014 on electronic identification and trust services for electronic transactions in the internal market.

[4] Directive (EU) of the European Parliament and of the Council of 25 November 2015 on payment services in the internal market, amending Directives 2002/65/EC, 2009/110/EC and 2013/36/EU and Regulation (EU) No 1093/2010, and repealing Directive 2007/64/EC, OJ L 337, 23.12.2015, pp. 35–127.

[5] Directive (EU) 2018/1972 of the European Parliament and of the Council of 11 December 2018 establishing the European Electronic Communications Code, OJ L 321, 17.12.2018, pp. 36–214.

[6] Directive 2002/58/EC of the European Parliament and of the Council of 12 July 2002 concerning the processing of personal data and the protection of privacy in the electronic communications sector (Directive on privacy and electronic communications), OJ L 201, 31.07.2002, pp. 37–47.

[7] Council Directive 2008/114/EC of 8 December 2008 on the identification and designation of European critical infrastructures and the assessment of the need to improve their protection, OJ L 345, 23.12.2008, pp. 75–82.

(in case of an OES), or incidents having a substantial impact on the provision of a digital service encompassed (in case of a DSP).

The NIS Directive provides limited guidance as to what constitutes a "significant" or "substantial" impact. As regards OES, the sample parameter listed in Art. 14(4) NIS Directive to determine the significance of an impact, are of a very general nature. They for instance include the number of users affected by the disruption of the essential service, the duration of the incident, or the geographical spread without setting any thresholds. The amount of leeway as to the exact rules to be adopted in Member States may result in various notification requirements which do not only vary from Member State to Member State, but also from sector to sector. Thus, a Member State may also refrain from setting any specific requirements, leaving the service concerned to determine whether an incident had a substantial or significant impact. Considering the legal nature of a Directive, Member States are also free to impose stricter reporting requirements than those laid down in the Directive. As a result, Germany for instance obliges OESs to also notify larger "near misses".[8] Guidance at EU level is provided for the determination of "substantial impact" with regard to DSPs by the Commission Implementing Regulation (EU) 2018/151[9]. The Implementing Regulation accepts that an incident has a substantial impact where for instance the service provided by a digital service provider was unavailable for more than 5,000,000 user-hours whereby the term user-hour refers to the number of affected users in the Union for a duration of 60 min, or the incident has resulted in a loss of integrity, authenticity or confidentiality of stored or transmitted or processed data or the related services offered by, or accessible via a network and information system of the digital service provider affecting more than 100,000 users in the Union.[10] Failure to comply with the notification obligation is sanctioned via an "effective, proportionate and dissuasive" administrative fine.[11] Of relevance for this paper is the timeframe within which an incident must be reported and the addressee of said notification. Although from the Directive as such, the addressee seems clear, it has to be noted, that a variety of competent authorities exist. This is due to the fact, that almost half of all Member States opted for a

---

[8] § 8(4)(2) BSIG.

[9] Commission Implementing Regulation (EU) 2018/151 of 30 January 2018 laying down rules for application of Directive (EU) 2016/1148 of the European Parliament and of the Council as regards further specification of the elements to be taken into account by digital service providers for managing the risks posed to the security of network and information systems and of the parameters for determining whether an incident has a substantial impact, OJ L26, 31.01.208, pp. 48–51.

[10] Further where (c) the incident has created a risk to public safety, public security or of loss of life; (d) the incident has caused material damage to at least one user in the Union where the damage caused to that user exceeds EUR 1,000,000, see Art. 4 Implementing Regulation (EU) 2018/151.

[11] What is considered "effective, proportionate and dissuasive" varies significantly between Member States, with administrative fines of up to EUR 50,000 in Germany (§ 14(2) BSIG) and fines of up to GBP 17,000,000 in the UK (Art. 18(6)(d) Network and Information Systems Regulations 2018).

decentralised approach in regulation, meaning that potentially each sector has its own competent authority. In practice, there is a fragmentation of competent authorities across the EU. As regards the timeframe, the NIS Directive only refers to the indefinite concept of "without undue delay". Again, considering the amount of leeway given to Member States, a fragmentation of reporting time-lines exists with a tendency to replicate the indefinite concept of "undue delay" of the Directive. Ultimately, Art. 14(6) and 16(6) NIS Directive further foresee (after consulting the notifying entity), that the competent authority or CSIRT may inform the public about individual incidents, where public awareness is necessary in order to prevent an incident or to deal with an ongoing incident.

The GDPR Data Breach Notification Scheme: Notification Obligation for Data Controllers. Under the GDPR, data controllers must notify a personal data breach to the supervisory authority (DPA) within 72 h after becoming aware of it and communicate the personal data breach to the data subject without undue delay. The GDPR defines a personal data breach in Art. 4(12) as "a breach of security leading to the accidental or unlawful destruction, loss, alteration, unauthorised disclosure of, or access to, personal data transmitted, stored or otherwise processed". The test whether a breach occurred and has to be reported is a mere objective test [3], marginal no. 16a. The main difference to the NIS Directive is, that the GDPR only applies to security incidents that concern personal data.

The WP 29 categorises data breaches according to the following information security principles: (1) confidentiality breach, where there is an unauthorised or accidental disclosure of, or access to, personal data; (2) integrity breach, where there is an unauthorised or accidental alteration of personal data; (3) availability breach, where there is an accidental or unauthorised loss of access to, or destruction of, personal data [4].

Notification is not required where a data breach is unlikely to result in a risk to the rights and freedoms of natural persons; for instance, where the personal data is already publicly available [4] or unintelligible to unauthorised parties (e.g. encrypted data)[12] and a disclosure of such data does not pose a risk to the individual. The same applies where the controller has taken steps to ensure that the high risk posed to individuals' rights and freedoms is no longer likely to materialise.[13] Potential damage may be discrimination, identity theft or fraud, financial loss, reputational damage, and loss of confidentiality of personal data protected by professional secrecy. According to Art. 33(3) GDPR requires the controller to provide detailed information to the DPA including measures to mitigate possible adverse effects of the breach. Legal responsibility to notify the DPA rests with controllers as does the overall responsibility for the protection of personal data. Accordingly, Art. 33(2) requires data processors solely to notify controllers of a personal data breach. Relevant for this paper is the timeframe, within which the controller has to notify the DPA of a data breach. Unlike

---

[12] Art. 34(3)(a) GDPR.
[13] Art. 34(3)(b) GDPR.

the NIS Directive, the GDPS concretices the notion "without undue delay" by specifying that, where feasible, notification is required not later than 72 h after having come beware of the data breach. A controller can be considered to have become "aware" of an incident when he has "a reasonable degree of certainty that a security incident has occurred that has led to personal data being compromised" [4]. Recital 85 clarifies that where notification of the DPA cannot be achieved within 72 h, information may be provided in phases without undue further delay. In this case, the reasons for the delay must be communicated to the DPA. In addition to the required notification of the DPA, Art. 34 GDPR also requires the controller to communicate the breach to the affected individual without undue delay, where the data breach is likely to result in a high risk to the rights and freedoms of natural persons. Other than with regard to the notification of the DPA, the notion of "undue delay" is not further concretised. Undue delay is rather considered as "as soon as reasonably feasible".[14] Art. 34(3) GDPR lists derogations from the mandatory communication to the data subject. These include protection measures by the controller, that render the personal data unintelligible to any person who is not authorised to access it, such as encryption. The exceptions are rather vague and the conditions for exemption from a notification obligation are indefinite. It has to be noted that Art. 34(3) GDPR is not conclusive as Art. 23(1) GDPR, a so-called opening clause, allows further restrictions, when such restrictions respect the essence of fundamental rights and freedoms and are a necessary and proportionate measure in a democratic society to safeguard the interests enlisted in Art. 23(1) GDPR such as national or public security. Germany for instance made use of this opening clause and included further exceptions in the German federal data protection Act ("Bundesdatenschutzgesetz – BDSG"): § 29(1)(3) BDSG sets forth that the obligation to inform the data subject of a personal data breach according to Art. 34 GDPR shall not apply as far as meeting this obligation would disclose information which by law or by its nature must be kept secret, in particular because of overriding legitimate interests of a third party.[15] Failure to report a breach without undue delay may trigger an appropriate administrative fine of

---

[14] Recital 86.

[15] The exception distinguishes between two types of information: information which by law must be kept secret and information which by its nature must be kept secret. Information which by law must be kept secret relates to professional obligations to secrecy which build on a special position and usually relate to psychologists, notaries or lawyers as long as their professional associations have issued binding rules on secrecy. Special official obligations to maintain secrecy relate to obligations that are linked to the exercise of a public office. In assessing whether an information must be kept secret by its nature, due consideration has to be paid to the purpose of the data as such and the purpose of the data processing operation; the obligation to "secrecy" must stem directly from the type of the information [5], marginal no. 8. Also, there may be an interest to keep the source of information secret. This exception further requires a balancing of interest of the data subject concerned on being informed about the data breach and the interest to keep the information secret.

up to 10,000,000 EUR, or in the case of an undertaking, of up to 2% of the total worldwide annual turnover of the preceding financial year, whichever is higher.[16]

Coexistence of the Notification Regimes. While the NIS Directive and the GDPR introduce notification regimes that are in practice very similar, the obligations are not identical and do not exclude one another. The GDPR does not constitute a lex specialis to the NIS Directive in the sense of Art. 1(7) NIS Directive, which would exclude the application of the NIS Directive.

The GDPR requires breach notification only where personal data is at stake; the NIS Directive, on the other hand, requires incident notification if there is a significant disruption to the provision of the service. While, in theory, one may distinguish between incidents falling under the GDPR and such falling under the NIS Directive, in practice, most security incidents will involve some personal data, meaning that OESs and DSPs will have to report these incidents to two different competent authorities. As DSPs typically operate as data processors, conflicts and confusion could arise between authorities, if the same incident was notified by two different entities to two different authorities, namely, the DSP under the NIS Directive and the data controller (using a service provided by the DSP) under the GDPR. Considering that format, content and timeframe are not necessarily identical, there is a likelihood that the authorities will receive information with regard to one incident, that is not identical and as a consequence, one incident can potentially be treated as two separate incidents.

The notification schemes also differ in so far as they require notification of the individuals concerned. If a security incident constitutes a data breach, the data controller has to notify the data subjects concerned if the data breach is likely to result in a high risk to the rights and freedoms of natural persons in order to allow him or her to take the necessary precautions. The data subject should be put in a position to prevent the risk from materialising. Other than protecting the rights and freedoms of a natural person, publicity of incidents under the NIS Directive aims at (re-)establishing information security, i.e. confidentiality, integrity, and availability of network and information systems. As a consequence, the individual affected by a mere security incident may only gain knowledge of the incident, where public awareness is necessary in order to prevent an incident, to deal with an ongoing incident, or, limited to DSPs, disclosure is in the public interest (cf. Arts. 14(6) and 16(7) NIS Directive).

3   The Dilemma: When Immediate Notification of the Data Subject Contradicts the General Interest of Information Security

While the data subject should be in a position to take necessary precautions to prevent potential harm from materialising or limit the effects of the data breach, communication to the data subject means in any case, that the service

---

[16] Art. 83(4)(a) GDPR. See also [6].

provider has to "go public" about a security incident. In practice, it is unlikely that data subjects will keep the information confidential and even if some might obey a confidentiality clause in the notification, the adversary might be among the affected users anyway. Thus, as soon as the first notification is out to a data subject, the adversary is likely to become aware that his attack has been identified.

Now any reasonable adversary will start covering its tracks. However, they might not cease from further interferences at this point; it is more likely that the adversary changes its attack vector. This makes it particularly harder for the service provider, as well as law-enforcement, to identify the attacker or to understand the vulnerabilities of a certain technology that has been used to mount the attack. Hence, it is often in the interest of all honest parties to delay data subject notification. On the other hand, a less honest OES or DSP might use this argument to delay notifications unreasonable long.

The following section outlines responses to security incidents highlighting the dilemma of the service provider of notification without undue delay. The different stages of the incident response cycle are presented, while pointing out the different stages at which notifications might be due. Notably, these points in time are easy to identify in a post hoc analysis, but hard to recognize during an active attack.

Incident Response Cycle. Among the organizational measures for informa-tion security, a structured handling of computer incidents is crucial. NIST is providing guidance introducing an incidence response cycle with four phases, each feeding its results into the next and the last phase is feeding its lessons learned into the first again: (1) Preparation, (2) Detection and Analysis, (3) Containment and Recovery, and (4) Lessons learned [7].

During Preparation general organizational measures are taken, in particular responsibilities and lines of report and command are established, most notably system owners for each subsystem are identified. This structure is then used for a risk assessment; hence assets and their owners are identified, valued and the probability of loss are evaluated. For the latter attack vectors need to be identified and appreciated if they can be a threat. Finally, prevention and pro-tection measurements are put in place answering the potential threats, that help to either reduce the value of an asset or lower the probability of loss.

Detection and Analysis. This phase is hopefully the state of normal operation. System owners are the continuously monitoring the before identified attack vec-tors, signals, and indicators to assess the current state of the IT system. Detected anomalies are assessed, documented and trigger notifications to the incident response team of the OES or DSP, which in turn will run its assessment and inform other system owners.

Containment and Recovery. After an attack was detected its analysis needs to result in a containment strategy. The first goal is to identify effected systems and to avoid further spread and damage caused by the attack. Next evidence is collected about the mechanisms and effects of the attack this is used to repair systems, and to attribute the attack to an adversary. The latter might help to take legal steps against them, but also helps to take technical protection measures against attacks from the same source.

Lessons Learned. In the last phase of the cycle, evidence is archived and recommendations are compiled. These recommendations will be used as feedback to improve the preparedness for future attacks, so the response cycle starts anew.

Two notes: There might be back tracking within one run of the cycle if new evidence is making this necessary. Moreover, Attacks might run in parallel which leads to parallel running responses. Corollary, 2 initially independently started responses might turn out to be caused by the same attack.

Mapping of the Scenario: When Does the Countdown Start? Besides a technical response to the attack, legal responses need to be prepared. This includes steps to ensure legal compliance with the respective norms. To the end that this concerns the paper at hand, the question is if end users need to be notified or not, and if so when.

For the GDPR, data subjects need to be notified if the leaked data "is likely to result in a high risk to the rights and freedoms of natural persons"[17] and none of exceptions to refrain from data subject/general public notification applies, i.e. data was not unintelligible or the controller has not taken subsequent action to mitigate the risk for rights and freedom of data subject. Awareness of an attack requires notification without "undue delay", i.e. according to Recital 86, GDPR "as soon as reasonably feasible".

However, this leaves the data controller with the question which phase in the response cycle triggers a "reasonable" obligation to inform under Art. 34 GDPR. Beside the obvious desire to delay or even avoid to inform users about a breach, such as reputational loss, risk of liability claims by users, there are good technical reasons to delay to go public with information about a security breach.

Time Line of an Attack. An attack starts with probing a system to understand exploitable vulnerabilities. Second, the attacker choses its tools and takes preparations in its owns systems. Now the attacker can actually mount the attack and if successful, a security breach happens. This might lead to the leakage of data or to disturbance or interruption of the attacked service. Depending on the attackers aims, it might continue to run the attack until stopped or it might assess that it reached its goal (or the attack gets too dangerous for itself) and stop. In the latter case it might take action to remove evidence from the system.

These attack phases match roughly with the following phases of the response cycle: Information that can be learned by potential probing should be analysed during preparation w.r.t. to its attack potential. Moreover, probes might be detectable and should be detected during detection. Since the mere probing

---

[17] Art 34(1) GDPR.

does not establish a security breach, notifications to supervisors are debatably at most: if large scale probing is observed, it might help to prevent attacks on other similar systems. However, while this might be very desirable, there is little to no evidence to the outside if a system was probed and an attack was successful prevented.

Given the attack is actually successful mounted. It should be detected during Phase 2. However, a single attack most certainly will trigger several indicators. So analysis in phase 3 is needed. This in turn might lead to the discovery of further indicators, which makes back tracking necessary. So the open question is: how long would the back and forth between 2 and 3 be acceptable until the response team moves to phase 4 which certainly needs to include informing users and authorities if the attack fulfils the conditions for notification requirements.

No Undue Delay: Prevailing and Legitimate Interest in Suspending Data Subject Notification. The scenario highlighted that a service provider may have a legitimate interest to delay the notification of individuals as required under Art. 34 GDPR, and hence go public about an incident. Any delay in communication, however, interferes with the obligation to inform "without undue delay", i.e. to inform "as soon as reasonably feasible". What can be considered as reasonable feasible is hardly addressed in the GDPR or the NIS Directive insofar as the interplay of these instruments is concerned.

The NIS Directive addresses the necessity to suspend notification of the public in Recital 59, which requires that publicity of incidents should duly balance the interest of the public in being informed about threats against possible reputational and commercial damage for OESs and DSPs reporting incidents. This brings a further aspect into play, namely core business interests of the service providers, that deserve equal protection as the interest of the public to be informed about security incidents. Recital 59 further states that "in the implementation of the notification obligations, competent authorities and the CSIRTs should pay particular attention to the need to keep information about product vulnerabilities strictly confidential, prior to the release of appropriate security fixtures". This, however, requires that the response cycle outlined above has been fully completed, meaning that incident publicity can be delayed until technical protection measures addressing the vulnerability are in place.

Following this conclusion, the NIS Directive is obviously conflicting with Art. 34 GDPR, where the risk to the rights and freedoms of a natural persona would call for prompt communication with data subjects to mitigate potential adverse effects. Recital 86 GDPR recognises the need to respond to an attack as a justification to delay such prompt communication: "the need to mitigate an immediate risk of damage would call for prompt communication with data subjects whereas the need to implement appropriate measures against continuing or similar personal data breaches may justify more time for communication". This justification is however limited to continuing and ongoing data breaches and does not encompass ongoing security incidents as such. Hence it would fall short in an incident which incidentally compromised consumer data, but leads to an ongoing attack targeted at other vital systems of the OES or DSP. Although the legislator recognised a reasonable interest to suspend notification as such, an explicit exception is lacking.

Considering that the data controller needs to analyse the attack in order to device an appropriate containment strategy, delaying the publicity of incidents has been referred to as "responsible disclosure" [8], marginal no. 10 with further references. "Responsible disclosure" has been ignored by the legislator, as the recitals only consider suspension of notification in the interests of law-enforcement. Accordingly, Recital 88 sets forth that in setting detailed rules concerning the format and procedures applicable to the notification of personal data breaches, such rules and procedures should "take into account the legitimate interests of law-enforcement authorities where early disclosure could unnecessarily hamper the investigation of the circumstances of a personal data breach". Hence, it is accepted that a delay can be justified in the interests of law-enforcement authorities, i.e. the execution of criminal investigations. This requires that law enforcement authorities are involved in the incident response conducted by the service provider. In that regard, Art. 8(6) and recital 62 NIS Directive encourages the consultation and cooperation of competent authorities, single point of contacts and respectively the providers concerned with the relevant national law-enforcement authorities and national DPAs. Member States should encourage OESs and DSPs "to report incidents of a suspected serious criminal nature to the relevant law-enforcement authorities".[18] Hence, severe incidents are very likely to be reported to national law-enforcement authorities, either by the provider or a supervisory authority. Illegal access and illegal interception of non-public transmissions of computer data as well as data and system interferences constitute crimes under the Convention on Cybercrime of the Council of Europe,[19] However, in the beginning of an incident, it is often not clear if an actual attack is ongoing or if the incident was caused by human error or natural causes (disaster, failing material). In the case of a criminal investigation, personal data will also be processed by law-enforcement authorities for the purposes of the prevention, investigation, detection, or prosecution of criminal offences, resulting in the application of the Police Directive[20], which explicitly allows for national legislative measures delaying, restricting or omitting the provision of information to the data subject to the extent that, and for as long as, such a measure constitutes a necessary and proportionate measure in a democratic society with due regard for the fundamental rights and the legitimate interests of the natural person concerned, in order to inter alia avoid obstructing

---

[18] Recital 62 NIS Directive.

[19] Council of Europe, Convention on Cybercrime (CETS No. 185).

[20] Directive (EU) 2016/680 of the European Parliament and of the Council of 27 April 2016 on the protection of natural persons with regard to the processing of personal data by competent authorities for the purposes of the prevention, investigation, detection, or prosecution of criminal offences or the execution of criminal penalties, and on the free movement of such data, and repealing Council Framework Decision 2008/977/JHA (Police Directive), (2016) OJ L 119, 04.05.2016, pp. 89–131.

official or legal inquiries or investigations.[21] It would contravene the ratio of said norm and hamper investigations, if a data controller was obliged to inform the public of an incident.

However, where an incident does not trigger the involvement of law-enforcement authorities, the data controller still has to determine, whether suspending notification can be legitimate. While for the competent authority under the NIS Directive the aforementioned "responsible disclosure" is a necessity of an appropriate response cycle, the DPA, prioritising the rights of the data subject, may not share this technical viewpoint. A uniform approach would require cooperation of the authorities; otherwise contravening decisions are likely. As regards cooperation of the competent authorities, Art. 15(4) NIS Directive foresees that the competent NIS authority shall work in close cooperation with DPAs when addressing incidents resulting in personal data breaches.

Recital 63 specifies that in the context of compromised personal data, said authorities "should cooperate and exchange information on all relevant matters to tackle any personal data breaches resulting from incidents". This recital highlights the need to mitigate the impact of personal data breaches, while recognizing that such mitigation requires the cooperation of national authorities which have different expertise. Expertise in the field of information security does not necessarily mean that the national NIS authority may pay the necessary regard to the mitigation of personal data breaches. Vice versa, national DPAs may lack the understanding of the different stages of an incident response cycle. Hence, "responsible disclosure" can only be put in practice if the competent authorities communicate and advise the data controller concerned together: a lack of cooperation between the authorities would result in the data controller being left in limbo. Not only may the incident response be hampered, he may also be exposed to fines under one regime for non-compliance.

The dilemma may even be worse, where an OES relies on a service provided by a DSP, for instance cloud computing: in this scenario, the OES would be obliged to notify a security incident to the DPA as he remains the data controller, whereas the DSP would have to notify the competent NIS authority. Hence, one incident would be reported under two different regimes, by two different actors, very likely with non-identical yet similar information. With a lack of cooperation and information exchange between the different competent authorities, the incident may not be identified as one single incident, and thus, even be treated differently with early disclosure very likely. If cooperation does not become mandatory in such scenarios, coherence could only be achieved by implementing a joint reporting scheme. Ultimately, it is up to the national legislators to introduce cooperation mechanisms and requirements for security incidents in which personal data are compromised. These mechanisms need to be based on a certain level of liaison competence in all relevant authorities.

---

[21] See Art. 13(3) Police Directive.

4   Conclusion and Lessons Learned

Privacy and security in information technology of vital infrastructures are intertwined concepts where incidents in one domain most often have effects in the other. Moreover, the core technology to protect both are the same and need to achieve the same three core protection goals: confidentiality, integrity and availability. It is important to emphasise that in no case any of these three core goals can be omitted.

However, privacy and IT security do differ substantially when considering which assets need to be protected form which kind of threat and attacker: while privacy often boils down to confidentiality of certain types of data (personal information or metadata of usage at foremost), IT security, especially in the context of vital infrastructures, often focuses on the integrity of operational data and the availability of the service.

The above difference is reflected in the legal framework and has effects of the incident reporting obligations in the GDPR and NIS Directive. In particular, we observe variance in when to inform and who to inform. This differences can lead to tricky situations if reporting duties in both frameworks concern the same technical incident. Since neither of the legal instruments supersedes the other, there is no defined processing order. Security and privacy teams need to decide on a case by case basis how to report incidents in a coordinated fashion. A legal obligation of this coordination is currently missing but would be desirable.

While coordination on premise of the service provider/data processor can be expected without new policy, the cooperation of the competent authorities might lack behind expectations. Currently, a general willingness to cooperate might be expressed, but there is no detailed legal obligation nor evidence for a systematic approach to cooperation. Moreover, the different cultures and expertise in the data protection and incident response communities make a coordinated approach to joint incidents harder. Here mutual education is needed.

Failing in cooperation might have a negative impact on the goals of both sides: On the one hand, informing the general public about incidents prematurely, might tip off criminals that run the attack helping them to either destroy evidence or adopt the attack. On the other hand, informing victims for a privacy breach too late might leave their assets at risk for longer than necessary. Hence, optimal timing needs to consider to the inner workings of the attack and the assets of all stakeholders at risk.

While handling security and privacy incidents, the general advice should be: Lawyers: find a tech-geek for help; Computer Scientists: find a law-buff for help.

References

1. Schmitz-Berndt, S., Schiffner, S.: Don't tell them now (or at all) – responsible disclosure of security incidents under NIS Directive and GDPR. Int. Rev. Law Comput. Technol. (2021). https://doi.org/10.1080/13600869.2021.1885103
2. Hansen, M., Jensen, M., Rost, M.: Protection goals for privacy engineering. In: 2015 IEEE Security and Privacy Workshops, pp. 159–166. IEEE (2015)

3. Martini, M.: Art. 33 DSGVO. In: Paal, B., Pauly, D. (eds.) Beck'sche Kompakt-Kommentare, Datenschutz-Grundverordnung Bundesdatenschutzgesetz. C.H. Beck, München (2018)
4. WP Art 29: Guidelines on personal data breach notification under regulation 2016/679, WP250 rev.01 (2018)
5. Uwer, D.: §29 BDSG. In: Brink, S., Wolff, H.A. (eds.) Beck'sche Beck'scher Online-Kommentar Datenschutzrecht. C.H. Beck, München (2018)
6. WP Art 29: Guidelines for identifying a controller or processor's lead supervisory authority, WP 244 rev.01 (2017)
7. Cichonski, P., Millar, T., Grance, T., Scarfone, K.: Revision 2: Computer security incident handling guide recommendations. NIST Special Publication 800-61 (2012)
8. Laue, P.: Art. 34 DSGVO. In: Spindler, G., Schuster, F. (eds.) Recht der elektronischen Medien. C.H. Beck, München (2019)

Selected Student Papers

Ethical Principles for Designing Responsible Offensive Cyber Security Training

Fredrik Heiding$^{(\boxtimes)}$ and Robert Lagerström

KTH Royal Institute of Technology, 100 44 Stockholm, Sweden
fheiding@kth.se
https://www.kth.se/

Abstract. In this paper we present five principles for designing ethically responsible offensive cyber security training. The principles can be implemented in existing or new study plans and target both academic and non-academic courses. Subject matter experts within various cyber security domains were consulted to validate and fine tune the principles, together with a literature review of ethical studies in related domains. The background for designing the principles is the continuous popularity of offensive cyber security (penetration testing, ethical hacking). Offensive cyber security means actively trying to break or compromise a system in order to find its vulnerabilities. If this expertise is placed in the wrong hands, the person can cause severe damage to organizations, civilians and society at large. The proposed ethical principles are created in order to mitigate these risks while maintaining the upsides of offensive cyber security. This is achieved by incorporating the ethical principles in offensive cyber security training, in order to facilitate the practitioners with ethical knowledge of how and when to use their acquired expertise.

Keywords: Ethical principles · Offensive cyber security training · Ethical hacking · Penetration testing · Privacy · Security training · Ethical guideline · Ethical framework

1 Introduction

The world is continuously becoming more digital and the digitalization brings a plethora of advantages such as increased connectivity, improved societal functions, and more accessible information [5,11]. However, the rapid digitalization is followed by an increase in digital threats [15,26]. Things that historically have been analogue are getting connected to networks and thus becoming exposed to malicious tampering. In 2017 the WannaCry malware caused damages estimated to more than 4b$ and soon after, the NotPetya malware caused damages estimated to over 10b$ [8].

© IFIP International Federation for Information Processing 2021
Published by Springer Nature Switzerland AG 2021
M. Friedewald et al. (Eds.): Privacy and Identity 2020, IFIP AICT 619, pp. 21–39, 2021.
https://doi.org/10.1007/978-3-030-72465-8_2

The increased exposure is equally true for information as for physical machines and devices. Since personal information is often just as exposed (or even more exposed) as organizational information, our relation to privacy has been severely hurt during the last decades. This is further amplified by the rapid increase of information gathering performed by both organizations and states [23]. The rapid growth of data breaches and privacy infringements are likely to keep increasing in line with the continued digitalization, so we must act to stop or at least mitigate the situation [4].

As a response to the general increase in digital threats, offensive cyber security is becoming more popular. Offensive cyber security aims to increase the security of a system by actively trying to compromise and break the system. By doing this we can find the weaknesses of the system before an attacker has time to exploit them. This can help us stay ahead of attackers and create more secure environments. However, by educating people in offensive cyber security, we help them gain expertise and knowledge that could be used to break system. If placed in the wrong hands this information can cause severe damage. It is possible that we mistakenly train a person with malicious intentions, or that we train a person with good intentions, whose motivations later become malevolent due to some circumstance of life. Company layoffs, disputes, personal grudges or a number of other reasons may motivate a person to cause harm, and with the right technical education, it is possible for the hostile person to succeed. The weapons we are discussing is knowledge which is more elusive than a traditional firearm, but as recent history shows it is more than enough to cause severe damage, both to privacy and physical safety [8].

In order to mitigate these risks, we propose five principles for designing ethically responsible offensive cyber security training. The principles can be implemented by cyber security educators and officials, in order to create the best possible outcome of offensive cyber security training, maximizing the benefits while minimizing potential harm. The rest of the article describes the creation, foundation and finalization of these principles.

Throughout the article the terms security and cyber security are used synonymously. If the authors just write "security" the reader can assume they mean cyber security, if the context does not specifically state otherwise. Further, there is no clear consensus on what differentiates an ethical guideline and an ethical framework. For simplicity, we name the ethical suggestions proposed in this article as "principles" and consider them to be, to a large part, a building block for both ethical guidelines and ethical frameworks.

1.1 Outline

The remaining article is structured as follows: Sect. 2 analyzes ethical principles from other technical domains and those available within cyber security. Section 3 describes the creation of the principles, focusing on consulting subject matter experts and drawing conclusions from relating ethical principles. Section 4 presents the result from the consultations with the subject matter experts and Sect. 5 presents the five principles in detail. Section 6 discuss surrounding thoughts on the principles and future possibilities for continued work, and Sect. 7 concludes the article.

2 Literature Review

A literature review was done to analyze the use of ethical studies in cyber security and other technical domains. A number of different search queries were used in five major databases *(Scopus, Web of Science, IEEE Xplore, ACM Digital Library and Google Scholar)*. Initially we searched in the abstract, title, and keywords of the articles. Some selected queries were later expanded to search in the entire article, in order to capture a wider range relevant papers. In addition, some papers were found via snowballing (reading references and cited works of the current related work) and by modifying the search phrases to include more general words such as "ethics" and "technology". When searching the full text of the article or when searching with the more general keywords such as "security", the resulting matches contained several false positives and were manually scanned for relevant articles. The queries are further described in Table 1 and Table 2.

The literature review is categorized in three parts: *ethical studies in other domains, ethical studies on cyber security,* and *ethical studies on offensive cyber security.*

Table 1. Searches made in the abstract, title and keywords of the articles.

Search phrase	Scopus	WoS	IEEE	ACM	GS
"ethical framework" AND "cyber security"	6	2	0	0	2
"ethical guidelines" AND "cyber security"	16	1	0	0	1
"ethical framework" AND "it security"	0	0	0	0	1
"ethical framework" AND ("Artificial intelligence" OR "AI")	54	18	0	0	32
"ethical framework" AND "technology"	291	118	19	2	44
ethics AND "cyber security"	103	60	44	5	68

Table 2. Searches made in the entire article, include its full length text.

Search phrase	Scopus	WoS	IEEE	ACM	GS
"ethical framework" AND "cyber security"	30	2	10	6	459
"ethical guidelines" AND "cyber security"	16	1	1	12	650

2.1   Ethical Studies in Other Domains

Ethical challenges are not isolated to cyber security or offensive cyber security, nor is the challenge of educating people in potentially dangerous techniques. New knowledge can be dangerous whether it is acquired in cyber security [20], artificial intelligence [21], CBRNE subjects (chemical, biological, radiological, nuclear or explosive) [12], and many other domains. Some frameworks exist within these areas as explained below, we have studied a number of them in order to gain a better understand of how to construct our principles on offensive cyber security education.

Before creating an ethical guideline it is good to investigate what problems the guideline can help solving. For example, if the guideline treats how to digitalize health care in an ethically responsible way, it should be clear what problems may arise from digitalizing health care [18]. This provides a reason for why the guideline is needed, which should recur as a common theme throughout the different parts of the guideline [18]. In the case of health care, problems that may arise when digitalizing it include reduction of autonomy, independence, quality of life, beneficence, non-maleficence, and justice of the patients. More specific issues of cyber security includes privacy and confidentiality as well as general cyber security in itself. With that background, a guideline for ethical digitalization of health care should aspire to mitigate these given problems [18]. This line of thinking is not directly targeting the ethics of offensive cyber security training, but it presents a foundation for how ethical guidelines can be designed. Parts of this methodology will inspire our ethical principles on offensive cyber security, as shown in Sect. 3.

The actual deliverable of an ethical guideline may be a set of principles that policy-makers can use in order to evaluate decisions and processes. The principles should be easy to interpret and apply, and clearly work for the benefit of the population as a whole [3].

When dealing with human subjects in cyber security research we should use three ethical hallmarks to ensure that the subjects are treated fairly. The study should always possess the consent of the studied part, debrief the subjects of the actual impacts of the study, and when it is not possible to gain consent from the actual participants, we must gain consent from so called surrogate participants who can represent the participant [2].

There exists a number of studies that create ethical guidelines for various technical domains, such as a guideline for biofuels [3], a guideline for bioprinting human organs [25] or guidelines for CBRNE subjects (chemical, biological, radiological, nuclear or explosive) as described above [12]. A substantial portion of the found guidelines target the ethics of artificial intelligence. Searching for *"ethical framework" AND ("Artificial intelligence" OR "AI")* gave 53 results, containing articles that discuss different takes on the ethics of implementing artificial intelligence. One noteworthy study also mentions possible ways to compensate for damages caused by artificial intelligence [14]. The study also discusses the ethics of cyber security but the main focus is given to artificial intelligence and the paper does not treat offensive cyber security nor the training of new security employees. Compensation of damages caused by AI is an interesting topic that can be extended to compensation for damages caused by offensive cyber security. If it becomes evident that a hacker who caused injury has been trained at a certain university or educator, it can be asked whether the educator should take part in the responsibility (legally or ethically) of compensation.

The responsibility of damages can be further distinguished in different categories, such as accountability, liability, and culpability. In order to present a solid ethical guideline one must take note of the precautions from not following the suggested actions [21]. This can be hard since ethical values and even legal obligations vary between cultures and countries. An offensive cyber security course may host students from different origins, with different opinions of what is ethical, or even different experiences of what is legal. This problem is further described in Sect. 6.

Another set of ethical principles for artificial intelligence aims to be implemented and interpreted in machines, rather than used by humans. In order to make the framework machine readable its structure is adapted to machine answerable questions, often resulting in two-folded decision trees [24]. This offers some insight to our principles on offensive cyber security and could give rise to interesting future use cases in the area. When making frameworks for human interpretation, they often focus on offering assistance in difficult questions, rather than stating definite answers. The target audience could be any decision maker or leader, and the intended outcome is often to assist and incentivize them to choose ethical ways to deal with AI [6]. Although both of the above frameworks deal with ethics towards artificial intelligence, some of the concepts can be used as inspiration when designing ethical principles for offensive security.

2.2   Ethical Studies on Cyber Security

Ethical guidelines for cyber security can target organizations, individuals, or researchers [13]. An ethical question that has been debated in cyber security research is the collection and usage of research data. Several studies have used data from controversial sources, such as exposed data from embedded devices that has collected user data without consent, and later been exposed. These types of publicly available "found data" presents a foundation for research that is ambiguous and not necessarily ethical nor legal [13,23]. In addition to finding data one may ask the ethical validity of entering other systems (even hostile ones) without consent. It is possible to argue that unlawfully entering or compromising devices of criminal systems, such as an illegal botnet, is similar to enter the house of criminal without a search warrant [13].

When an ethical guideline is created, the subsequent task is to determine how to spread it and to whom it shall be offered. This is not necessarily a straight forward task and it can be determined in different ways depending on the guideline. Some guidelines even target this meta question, analyzing what types of leadership is most feasible for cyber security. Cyber security leadership can be divided in three branches depending on the how cyber security is being used. One branch for groups that implement cyber security and work with it practically. This could be divisions in organizations (an IT security department) or entire organizations (dedicated security companies). The second branch is people who innovate and research cyber security. This could be cyber security companies (innovating their products) or cyber security researchers. The third branch is people who regulate cyber security, this could be governmental agencies or ethical review boards [13].

Some parties question the capacity of institutions, governments or even ethical review boards to lead the progress of cyber security ethics, and rather propose more distributed and decentralized peer groups [13]. This is interesting to consider when creating an ethical foundation for offensive cyber security education. Especially regarding questions on how to spread and implement the guideline. If decentralized ethical regulators are more trusted than a unified regulating body, the guideline must be adapted for this cause, being flexible and adaptable to different nuances.

It is often said that the most susceptible part of an organization is its employees. The list of social cyber attacks is long and there are several ways to exploit the people of an organization in order to perform a cyber attack [1]. Therefore, it is not surprising that organizations are spending resources to test and train their employees on cyber security. This training is often valuable, but it can be ethically questionable, especially if the employees suffer consequences from failing a test. A test could be sending intentional phishing emails to ensure that employees do not press suspicious links or hiring physical testers who aspire to tailgate (follow someone who just entered a locked door) an employee into the office. In order to ensure these tests are ethically justified, we should keep the tests legal, always consider the consequences of our actions towards the employee, business owners, and clients, avoid actions that could cause productivity loss, and keep the tests confidential and honest [1].

2.3   Ethical Studies on Offensive Cyber Security

Searching for *"ethical framework" AND "cyber security"'* gave scarce results from all major databases. Scopus only resulted in six matching articles, of which [14] and [21] were more focused on the ethics of artificial intelligence, as mentioned above. However, some studies exist from which we can learn something useful.

When assessing the ethics of offensive cyber security it is good to start by defining which actions are acceptable and which are to be denounced, as well as defining how to categorize different hostile actions [9]. Some say a hostile cyber activity should be considered as an act of crime [10], others see it more as an act of warfare, which could justify a military response [20].

A problem with the legal approach is that countries tend to have their own laws, which makes global reinforcement of laws problematic. Although international laws and treaties have been conducted on several occasions, aligning such works from global leaders on cyber security may be challenging [10]. This could be an argument for making the ethical guideline on cyber security adaptable, allowing local variations in its implementation.

Of all the reviewed literature, one paper was found targeting how to ethically conduct offensive cyber security education [22]. The paper struggles to find relevant information from research databases, so the authors used three senior information security professionals as experts on the matter, and took their input on how to conduct ethically responsible offensive cyber security education. The interviews focused on analyzing how to make students more inclined to apply the ethics they already knew (and the ethics they learned) to hacking tasks. The questions focused solely on college students and did not try to analyze other education sources such as employers or online courses. Four areas were identified as important for making offensive cyber security education more ethical: social interaction/support system, competition, recognition, and ongoing skills development. In addition, three smaller areas were chosen to be of further importance for keeping students ethical: interaction with cyber security-related law enforcement, cyber security internships and student attendance at meetings and conferences of professional cyber security organizations [22].

The questions posed by the related studies are challenging and relevant. They offer some inspiration for how an ethical framework on offensive cyber security education can be created, but they also present a research gap for an up to date paper, specifically written on the ethics of offensive cyber security education.

2.4 Hacker Motivations

Peter Grabonsky's book *Computer Crime: A Criminological Overview* states that computer criminals are driven by a large number of different motivators depending on each individual case. The main motivators are believed to be the same as for regular criminals (and individuals), namely: greed, lust, power, revenge, adventure, and a desire to try forbidden technologies [7].

Schwartz's Theory of Motivational points out that human behavior can be motivated by three human requirements: *"biological needs (for organic survival), social interaction (for interpersonal coordination), and social institutional demands (for group survival)"* [17]. The human requirements can be translated into values such as striving for world peace in order to ensure survival of the species. The value thus refers to ideals about how we are supposed to act or how the world is supposed to be, these beliefs are what determines our actions. Ten main values of motivation are further determined: *Universalism, Benevolence, Conformity, Tradition, security, power, achievement, hedonism, stimulation and self direction*. These motivational factors were studied in combination with hacking activities in order to determine the most prominent motivators for hackers. The result suggested that the correlation between motivational factors and hacking activities is not always straightforward. The most relevant motivators for hackers were determined as intellectual challenge and curiosity [17].

3 Methodology

In this section we describe how the ethical principles were created. It was primarily done by gathering information from subject matter experts and performing a literature review on related ethical guidelines.

3.1 Literature Review

In order to create the ethical framework a systematic literature review was conducted to analyze ethical guidelines in related domains, as further explained in Sect. 2. The combined search results received a total of 2074 articles. However, a large number of these came from the Google Scholar full text searches (1059 papers) or the more general searches on "ethical framework" AND "technology" (474 papers) or ethics AND "cyber security" (280 papers). For these more general searches the search results were sorted for relevancy and the first pages were manually scanned to include relevant papers. The inclusion and exclusion criteria were thus intentionally flexible and based on the article's connection to ethics, ethical principles, and offensive cyber security education. An article with a clear and well planned ethical principle was considered relevant even though it came from another field than offensive cyber security, such as the ethical principles posed by the UN peace keeping unit discussed in Sect. 3.4. More information of the searches are found in Table 1, Table 2 and Sect. 2. The more specific search phrases generated a smaller set of matching articles so these were scanned more thoroughly, as further described in Sect. 2.

3.2 Ethical Guidelines from Computer Science Societies

There exist a number of ethical guidelines proposed by computer science societies, such as those from the Association for Computing Machinery (ACM) and the Institute of Electrical and Electronics Engineers (IEEE). These were analyzed in order to gain a better understanding of ethical principles in related areas and to gain inspiration for the principles on offensive cyber security education.

The ACM Code of Ethics and Professional Conduct targets general computer science practitioners and does not have specific information about offensive cyber security nor cyber security education. As described on the web page of the ethical code *"the code is designed to inspire and guide the ethical conduct of all computing professionals, including current and aspiring practitioners, instructors, students, influencers, and anyone who uses computing technology in an impactful way"*[1].

Some of the principles in the code is highly relevant for our principles on offensive cyber security education. Principle 1.1 (*Contribute to society and to human well-being, acknowledging that all people are stakeholders in computing.*), 1.2 (*Avoid harm.*), 1.3 (*Be honest and trustworthy.*) and 1.6 (*Respect privacy.*)

---

[1] https://www.acm.org/code-of-ethics.

concerns topics that should be treated during offensive cyber security education. Point 1.1 and 1.2 can be especially linked to principles 5 of our proposed ethical framework.

The IEEE Computer Society Code of Ethics consists of eight ethical principles for software engineer professional. Similarly to the above principles from ACM, these principles have a high level of abstractions and target general computer science rather than cyber security or offensive cyber security education. Three principles were found especially relevant for our study and used as inspiration for the created ethical principles: principle 1 (*Software engineers shall act consistently with the public interest.*), principle 6 (*Software engineers shall advance the integrity and reputation of the profession consistent with the public interest.*), and principle 4 (*Software engineers shall maintain integrity and independence in their professional judgment.*)[2].

3.3   Ethical Principles from Standardization Bodies - NIST

The authors could not locate a clear set of ethical principles or a code of conduct from the National Institute of Standards and Technology (NIST). Some documents containing information to employees were found and contained minor parts with ethical instructions, but nothing that was concrete for computer science or cyber security. A document regarding the ethical conduct for employees of the executive branch states the importance of acting in a way that serves society, which is in line with main takeaways from other frameworks [19].

3.4   Ethical Principles Within the Military, Using Violence to Keep Peace

The United Nations (UN) has an ethical code of conduct for its military peace keeping forces. There exists an interesting connections between this and offensive cyber security since both fields use (some form of) violence in order to reduce violence. There is a further similarity since UN forces operate in different nations and the peace keeper is not necessarily familiar with the laws and customs of the country they assist. Of the UN rules of conduct for UN peace keepers, rule 2 (*Respect the law of the land of the host country, their local culture, traditions, customs and practices*) and 5 (*Respect and regard the human rights of all*) are especially related to our work on offensive cyber security education. It is not uncommon for operations within offensive cyber security to cross many digital borders (such as a server or a cloud service being located in another country than that of the target), it is not always clear whether to follow the laws of the country where the target company is located or the laws of other countries encountered on the way, it is especially difficult if different laws contradict one another [16].

---

[2] https://www.computer.org/education/code-of-ethics.

3.5   Ethical Principles Within Professional Offensive Security Courses

A number of professional offensive security courses exists such as the Certified Ethical Hacking course[3] and the Certified Penetration Testing course[4] offered by the EC Council, the Global Information Assurance Certification offered by the SANS institute[5], and the Offensive Security Certified Professional course[6]. None of these seemed to contain substantial information about ethical principles so they were not investigated further. However, since only parts of the content can be viewed without purchasing the courses, it is possible that the complete material contains ethical principles or similar instructions for how to use the hacking material.

3.6   Subject Matter Experts

In order to solidify the ethical principles, expert opinions were gathered from security professionals and educators within cyber security. These sessions were partly constructed as semi-structured interviews, direct interviews or surveys based on seven questions, as displayed below. In total 24 people with various positions in cyber security were questioned in order to design and validate the ethical guidelines. The prearranged questions were created in order to give the interviews the right direction, while still being open enough to let the participants come with their own ideas and suggestions to the framework. The result of the consultations is explained in Sect. 4 and the complete list of questions are shown below.

Interview questions

1. Q1: Do you think there is a need to include offensive security training in the curriculum of cyber security education?
2. Q2: Do you think there is a need to incorporate ethics in offensive security education?
3. Q3: What do you think is the best way to incorporate ethics in offensive security education?
4. Q4: What do you think is the most influencing factor in making students use their knowledge for good, such as regular penetration testing work (several points can be selected if desired)?
   (a) Moral values.
   (b) Reputation.
   (c) Ideological gains.
   (d) Fear of repercussions from doing something illegal.

---

[3] https://www.eccouncil.org/programs/.
[4] https://www.eccouncil.org/programs/certified-penetration-testing-professional-cpent/.
[5] https://www.giac.org/.
[6] https://www.offensive-security.com/pwk-oscp/.

(e) Their past education.
(f) Their current peers or social group.
(g) Other (feel free to specify any motivator not listed above).
5. Q5: What do you think is the most influencing factor in making students use their knowledge for illegal purposes (several points can be selected if desired)?
   (a) Curiosity.
   (b) Financial gains.
   (c) Ideological gains.
   (d) Reputation.
   (e) Their past education.
   (f) Their current peers or social group.
   (g) Other (feel free to specify any motivator not listed above).
6. Q6: What do you think is the best way to ensure that students maintain their ethical mentality and use their knowledge for good, years after they have finished their training?
7. Q7: If you have any other feedback or points you wish to share, please feel free to do so here.

4   Result

In this section the proposed ethical principles are explained. Each principle of the guideline is described in detail, and the findings of the expert consultations are visualized.

4.1   Result from the Expert Consultations

The answers to the questions were categorized in different segments, in order to better classify and arrange them. The sections for each question, and their corresponding answer percentages can be seen in Table 3. For some questions more than one answer could be selected, the displayed percentage is then the fraction of votes from all consulted parts, on this question.

In general we can see a strong trend towards the belief that a peer group with solid ethical values is important to make the students stay within legal bounds. Furthermore it was common to believe that a stable job market for white hat penetration testing reduced the risk of students turning to illegal actions. Developing sound ethical values were also considered important, as well as giving the students a chance to earn positive reputation by legal means. It was deemed important to have strict application criteria, both to ensure the students remain ethical during the training and during their own time after they had graduated. This makes sense since the course can not replace all the students past experiences and if they are too far down an unwanted path, such as having a strong criminal record, it may not be feasible to change their ethical values during the time of the course. Some interesting suggestions appeared in the open discussions such as the idea to keep track of students after they have graduated and hold alumni gatherings where they can meet and share their past experiences (hopefully earning positive reputation from their legal penetration testing work).

Table 3. Result from interviews with Subject Matter Experts.

Question	Answer segments
Q1: Shall we include offensive security training in the cyber security courses?	Yes: 88% No: 4% Maybe: 8%
Q2: Shall we include ethics in offensive security training?	Yes: 96% No: 0% Other/don't know: 4%
Q3: What is the best way to incorporate ethics in offensive security education?	Working with practical cases: 25% Discussions and reflections: 25% Integrate ethics in ordinary coursework: 38% Informative material (legal, ethical etc.): 8% Other/don't know: 4%
Q4: What makes students use their knowledge for good causes?	Moral values: 30% Reputation: 25% Ideological gains: 8% Fear of repercussions: 25% Their past education: 21% Their current peers or social group: 46% Other: 21%
Q5: What makes students use their knowledge for malicious causes?	Curiosity: 42% Financial gains: 42% Ideological gains: 8% Reputation: 13% Their past education: 4% Their current peers or social group: 38% Challenge/amusement: 13%
Q6: What is the best way to ensure that students maintain their ethical mentality	Teach students to always consider and know the consequences of their actions: 25% Help the students develop a solid reasoning (ethical and otherwise) about the actions they do: 29% Have a good white hat job market, help the students develop a professional network and help them prepare to get a legal pentesting job: 17% Other/don't know: 21%
Q7: Other points	Incorporate bug bounty programs in the education Show how ethics can used to grow professionally

5   Ethical Principles for Offensive Cyber Security Education

The final five principles are designed to assist in creating more ethically responsible offensive cyber security training. The principles are motivated by the information gathered during the literature review of related ethical principles and from analyzing other ethical codes, such as *The ACM Code of Ethics and Professional Conduct* and the military principles for ethical behavior proposed by the UN peace keeping unit, as described in Sect. 3. The principles were further validated and fine tuned by the input obtained in the consultations with subject matter experts. Together the principles serves to minimize the harm while maximizing the benefits of offensive cyber security education. The principles are:

1. Include ethics in offensive cyber security education.
2. Inform the students of lucrative and legal ways of applying their hacking knowledge.
3. Introduce ways for students to earn positive reputation from their hacking skills.
4. Have selective application criteria for joining an offensive cyber security course.
5. Offensive cyber security should rarely teach hacking tools that can threaten people's essential rights.

In the following subsection the principles are explained in more detail. Each principle is described with the intent of the principle, a potential use case of how the principle can be implemented, and possible criticism against the principle.

5.1 Principle 1 - Include Ethics in Offensive Cyber Security Education

Intent. It seems clear that hacking knowledge can be used for destructive purposes. However, it is equally clear that offensive cyber security is becoming an important tool within cyber security. Thus, we ought to educate students in offensive cyber security but the education must incorporate ethics and teach students how to use their knowledge in an ethically responsible way.

Implementation. Ethical material of how to use ones hacking skills should be included in the study plan of the course. The education of ethics can for example be incorporated in the normal education slides, discussed in dedicated seminars, practiced in case studies or practically displayed by letting students use their knowledge for bug bounty hunting or other legal hacking activities.

Potential Criticism. Educational programs may be more incentivized to focus the course on raw hacking skills. Being forced to incorporate ethics can take time away from this practical hacking. Incorporating the ethical material may present additional costs for the educators and if this principle is not legally enforced, actors may ignore it. If the principle is legally enforced, it will take freedom away from course administrators and it will create bureaucratic costs for controlling the organizations.

5.2 Principle 2 - Inform the Students of Lucrative and Legal Ways of Applying Their Hacking Knowledge

Intent. In order to help the students develop an ethical compass and use their knowledge for good, it is important to demonstrate how the knowledge could be used for good, and give plenty of opportunities for them to do so. This includes capitalizing on their hacking skills by earning money, but it can also include non-monetary benefits such as ideal causes. One student may be driven by income, another may be driven by an ethical cause such as protecting the privacy of citizens. We want to teach the students how they can achieve what they want within a legal and ethical context.

Implementation. The principle can be implemented in a number of ways, one example is to make bug bounty programs part of the education. The students could even be taught how to capitalize from bug bounty challenges and earn money during the course. This principle also encourages courses to use realistic and stimulating hacking infrastructures, so the students can get practical hands on hacking experience without needing to look for challenges outside the classroom.

The implementation of this principle also includes the legal aspects of offensive cyber security. The course should inform students of the legal boundaries of offensive cyber security and how these can differ across countries and what they should keep in mind to stay legal while they perform penetration tests.

Potential Criticism. Introducing bug bounty programs and monetizing may act as a double edged sword. It is possible that this could motivate the students curiosity to keep searching for ways to earn money from hacking, which could lead them to the black market. This is especially the case if the black market offers larger monetary rewards for similar tasks.

5.3   Principle 3 - Introduce Ways for Students to Earn Positive Reputation from Their Hacking Skills

Intent. Reputation appears to be a major motivator for hackers. Educators can benefit from this by letting the students use their hacking knowledge to earn reputation in legally and ethically responsible ways. This can help the students develop a healthy attitude towards applying their hacking knowledge.

Implementation. An ethical hacking course may introduce scoreboards where the top students get a prize (the honor of being seen in top can be prize enough). It is probably best to only show the score for the top students. Publicly displaying the worst students can create resentment from those with slower learning curves.

Capture the flag (CTF) competitions is another good way to help students earn positive hacking reputation in an ethically responsible way. In these competitions the participants solve computer security problems in order to obtain "flags", the flags are often a sequence of characters. Many of the competitions are public and open for everyone to participate in. CTF competitions can be integrated in the standard curriculum of the course or shown as a place where the students can apply their skills after the course is completed.

Potential Criticism. If some students are far better than their peers (perhaps from earlier experience), they may seek new scoreboards or challenges with more equal competition. It is important that the teachers are attentive to this and present further material, such as online communities. If not, the student may be inspired to seek fame from less ethical challenges, such as tasks found on the black market. Also, in order to implement the scoreboards or ranking systems educators will have to take time and energy away from developing the raw hacking material.

5.4 Principle 4 - Have Selective Application Criteria for Joining an Offensive Cyber Security Course

Intent. Hacking knowledge can be used for malicious causes. If someone has ethical warning flags such as an extensive criminal record, it may not be suitable to accept them to a hacking course.

Implementation. Ethical hacking courses can perform a background check on the applicants, the same way one usually goes through a number of tests in order to purchase a weapon, open a bank account, apply for a job, or apply for many other courses. It is possible that a person has malicious intentions, even if the person does not have a criminal record or other ethical warning flags. Because of this, it may be relevant to do some personality assessment before accepting students to an offensive cyber security course.

Potential Criticism. From an organizational point of view it may be difficult or even impossible to grant the teacher/course responsible mandate to determine who can join the course. If it would be possible to implement, the selection can give rise to discrimination if each educator is allowed to create their own admission rules. If the admissions are instead determined by a global standard, the educators will loose freedom and bureaucratic costs will arise from controlling the admissions and arranging potential assessment tests. Furthermore, equal information can often be found online. A banned student may be fueled with stronger motivation to learn the material on their own. If that happens, anger from not being admitted may place the student at an even larger risk of using the knowledge for destructive causes.

5.5 Principle 5 - Offensive Cyber Security Courses Should Avoid Techniques for Hacking Critical Infrastructures and Other Industries that Are Crucial for Society to Function

Intent. Critical infrastructures are getting more connected and thus more susceptible to cyber attacks. It is essential to maximize the cyber security of these industries and offensive cyber security is a great tool to do so. However, since penetration testing of power plants and similar industries are sensitive and must be done with care, it is best to treat this information in dedicated and highly controlled offensiveness security courses.

Implementation. General hacking courses can avoid teaching material that is especially used for targeting critical industries. Specific hacking courses can be arranged for penetration testing targets within sensitive areas, such as power plants or hospitals.

Potential Criticism. Much of the information acquired from general hacking courses can be used for attacks against critical infrastructures as well.

6 Discussion

We have presented a set of ethical principles for offensive cyber security education. The principles aim to mitigate the risks of educating many new practitioners in offensive cyber security. In order to fully gage the usefulness of the principles, they must be implemented and used in a real life scenario. After its implementation the result must be validated. A method of validation would be to analyze actions of students who has taken an offensive cyber security courses that follow the ethical principles. These students could then be compared with students who took regular offensive cyber security courses (courses that does not actively follow the ethical principles) and the two groups would then be compared. This comparison will not take place for some time, since we first need to implement the principles and let them run for an evaluation period. However, this article serves as the first step, designing principles that are now ready to be implemented.

The results showed that a peer group with strong ethical values is important for the student to develop healthy ethical values of their own and a strong job market further increase the chance that students remain legal. This makes sense since we often tend to be influenced by our peers, and a healthy job market will reduce the risk of students turning to the black market for monetary reasons.

Another discussion is whether to have static or dynamic principles. Currently the principles are not built to be dynamic but nor are they built to be unchangeable. As briefly discussed in previous sections, it may not be feasible to implement global laws and regulations for cyber security, due to cultural and legal differences between countries and regions. This speaks in favor of having a adaptable principles that can be tweaked for different regions. Although the principles do not currently have built in support for being adjusted, they should be relatively straight forward to change in order to meet local requirements. The obvious benefit of having customizable principles is an easier integration in different organizations and cultures, since it can be adapted to suit specific requirements. A downside is that alterations may tamper with the underlying ethical values and standard of the principles. Allowing alterations would also make it more difficult to oversee the principles, if it became a legal demand to use them. Local adaptations could be made to make the principles easier to implement and use while reducing its ethical impact. This could potentially undermine the value of the principles and each investigator would need to make a manual analysis, to judge if the principles meets the standard. This problem could be mitigated by having cornerstones that could not be tampered with, but dynamic principles would still create more complicated enforcements and supervisions.

Cultural differences in ethics can also cause problems when people from different backgrounds participate in the same course. It is possible that an offensive cyber security course hosts students from a range of different cultures, these cultures may have different ethical values as well as different laws. This makes it important for the teacher to be attentive to each student in order to make sure they understand and agree with the ethical principles described. The educator should also make sure that students with different ethical views get the chance to describe and communicate their individual views.

With this said, it is not easy to ensure that students of offensive cyber security courses will use their knowledge for ethical and legal purposes. Including ethical principles in the education is no guarantee that students will behave accordingly, but it may increase the chances. The result of the interviews and literature reviews gives reason to believe that ethical principles can have a positive impact on the behavior of the students, but it is hard if not impossible to eliminate the risk of future criminal acts altogether. In light of this we must judge whether the potential benefit of educating people in the area outweighs the potential risks. Since cyber security expertise is in high demand the benefits appears to be strong enough for the trend to continue in the near future.

6.1   Future Work

The study has given rise to a number of ideas for future research in the area. One such area is adapting the principles to target offensive cyber security education for critical infrastructures. Certain requirements should be fulfilled when auditing systems that can cause severe damage to society.

Another research area of interest is the motivations of illegal hacking. There seems to be a research gap for analyzing what motivates hackers to use their knowledge for illegal causes. This could be expanded to target ethical hackers as well, analyzing if they are incentivized by certain causes such as money/career, ideological gains, reputation etc. Then a comparison could be made between the motivations for legal and illegal hacking.

A third area of future interest is how to compensate for damages caused by offensive cyber security. This includes investigating if the educator is responsibility for damages caused by the hacker and if so, how to legally reprimand the educators if the hacker commits a crime.

It would also be relevant to research adaptation of the principles. We need to assess how to best implement them and how to best guide others on how to implement them. This includes further research on whether the principles should be customizable or static.

Perhaps the most pressing future task is to implement the principles in actual offensive cyber security courses. This will provide the valuable feedback to fine tune and adjust the principles according to their practical usability.

7   Conclusion

Offensive cyber security is becoming an important part of making systems more resilient. Training people in offensive cyber security introduces a problem since it enables people to break systems, which could be used for illegitimate causes. In order to mitigate the risks associated with offensive cyber security training we propose a set of ethical principles describing how to conduct ethically responsible offensive cyber security training. The principles work to minimize the potential harm from offensive cyber security education, while maximizing its potential benefits. This article presents the background for the principles and describes each principle in detail, validated by a systematic literature review and consultations with subject matter experts. Subsequent research will implement the principles and fine tune them for real life applications.

Acknowledgments. This work has received funding from the Swedish Centre for Smart Grids and Energy Storage (SweGRIDS).

References

1. Archibald, J.M., Renaud, K.: Refining the pointer "human firewall" pentesting framework. Inf. Comput. Secur. **26**(4) (2019)
2. Bravo-Lillo, C., Egelman, S., Herley, C., Schechter, S., Tsai, J.Y.: You needn't build that: reusable ethics-compliance infrastructure for human subjects research. In: Cyber-Security Research Ethics Dialog and Strategy Workshop (2013)
3. Buyx, A., Tait, J.: Ethical framework for biofuels. Science **332**(6029), 540 (2011)
4. Durnell, E., Okabe-Miyamoto, K., Howell, R.T., Zizi, M.: Online privacy breaches, offline consequences: construction and validation of the concerns with the protection of informational privacy scale. Int. J. Hum.-Comput. Interaction **36**, 1834 (2020)
5. Eichhorst, W., Hinte, H., Rinne, U., Tobsch, V.: How big is the gig? assessing the preliminary evidence on the effects of digitalization on the labor market. Manag. Revue **28**(3), 298 (2017)
6. Floridi, L., et al.: AI4people-an ethical framework for a good AI society: opportunities, risks, principles, and recommendations. Minds Mach. **28**(4), 689 (2018)
7. Grabosky, P.: Computer crime: a criminological overview. In: Tenth United Nations Congress on the Prevention of Crime and the Treatment of Offenders (2000)
8. Greenberg, A.: Sandworm: A New Era of Cyberwar and the Hunt for the Kremlin's Most Dangerous Hackers, Doubleday (2019)
9. Holzer, C.T., Lerums, J.E.: The ethics of hacking back. In: 2016 IEEE Symposium on Technologies for Homeland Security, HST 2016 (2016)
10. Iasiello, E.: Hacking back: not the right solution. Parameters **44**, 105 (2014)
11. Jeske, T., Weber, M.-A., Würfels, M., Lennings, F., Stowasser, S.: Opportunities of digitalization for productivity management. In: Nunes, I.L. (ed.) AHFE 2018. AISC, vol. 781, pp. 321–331. Springer, Cham (2019). https://doi.org/10.1007/978-3-319-94334-3_32

12. Jillson, I.A.: Ethical frameworks for CBRNE crises: toward shared concepts and their practical application. In: O'Mathúna, D.P., de Miguel Beriain, I. (eds.) Ethics and Law for Chemical, Biological, Radiological, Nuclear & Explosive Crises. TILELT, vol. 20, pp. 53–64. Springer, Cham (2019). https://doi.org/10.1007/978-3-030-11977-5_5

13. Kenneally, E., Bailey, M.: Cyber-security research ethics dialogue and strategy workshop. Comput. Commun. Rev. **44**, 76 (2014)

14. Khisamova, Z.I., Begishev, I.R., Sidorenko, E.L.: Artificial intelligence and problems of ensuring cyber security. Int. J. Cyber Criminol. **13**(2), 564 (2019)

15. Kolias, C., Kambourakis, G., Stavrou, A., Voas, J.: DDoS in the IoT: Mirai and other botnets. Computer **50**(7), 80 (2017)

16. Langholtz, H.J.: Ethics in peace operations. In: Peace Operations Training Institute (2008)

17. Madarie, R.: Hackers' motivations: testing Schwartz's theory of motivational types of values in a sample of hackers. Int. J. Cyber Criminol. **11** (2017)

18. Magnusson, L., Hanson, E.J.: Ethical issues arising from a research, technology and development project to support frail older people and their family carers at home. Health Soc. Care Community **11**(5), 431 (2003)

19. U.S. Office of Government Ethics. Standards of ethical conduct for employees of the executive branch. J. Int. Technol. Inf. Manag. (2001)

20. O'Connell, M.E.: Cyber security without cyber war. J. Conflict Secur. Law **17**(2), 187 (2012)

21. O'Sullivan, S., et al.: Legal, regulatory and ethical frameworks or standards for AI and autonomous robotic surgery. Int. J. Med. Robot. Comput. Assisted Surg. (2018)

22. Pike, R.E.: The "ethics" of teaching ethical hacking. J. Int. Technol. Inf. Manag. **22**(4), 4 (2013)

23. Schrittwieser, S., Mulazzani, M., Weippl, E.: Ethics in security research which lines should not be crossed? In: 2013 IEEE Security and Privacy Workshops (2013)

24. Tonkens, R.: A challenge for machine ethics. Minds Mach. **19**(3), 421 (2009)

25. Vermeulen, N., Haddow, G., Seymour, T., Faulkner-Jones, A., Shu, W.: 3D bioprint me: a socio ethical view of bioprinting human organs and tissues. J. Med. Ethics **43**(9), 618 (2017)

26. Zhou, J., Cao, Z., Dong, X., Vasilakos, A.V.: Security and privacy for cloud-based IoT: challenges. IEEE Commun. Mag. **55**(1), 26 (2017)

Longitudinal Collection and Analysis of Mobile Phone Data with Local Differential Privacy

Héber H. Arcolezi[1]([✉])[ID], Jean-François Couchot[1][ID], Bechara Al Bouna[2][ID], and Xiaokui Xiao[3][ID]

[1] Femto-ST Institute, Univ. Bourg. Franche -Comté, UBFC, CNRS, Belfort, France
{heber.hwang_arcolezi,jean-francois.couchot}@univ-fcomte.fr
[2] TICKET Lab., Antonine University, Hadat-Baabda, Lebanon
bechara.albouna@UA.EDU.LB
[3] School of Computing, National University of Singapore, Singapore, Singapore
xkxiao@nus.edu.sg

Abstract. Longitudinal studies of human mobility could allow an understanding of human behavior on a vast scale. Mobile phone data call detail records (CDRs) have emerged as a prospective data source for such an important task. Nevertheless, there are significant risks when it comes to collecting this type of data, as human mobility has proven to be quite unique. Because CDRs are produced through the connection of mobile phones with mobile network operators' (MNOs) antennas, it means that users cannot sanitize their data. Once MNOs intend to use such a data source for human mobility analysis, data protection authorities such as the CNIL (in France) recommends that data be sanitized on the fly instead of collecting raw data and publishing private output at the end of the analysis. Local differential privacy (LDP) mechanisms are currently applied during the process of data collection to preserve the privacy of users. In this paper, we propose an efficient privacy-preserving LDP-based methodology to collect and analyze multi-dimensional data longitudinally through mobile connections. In our proposal, rather than regarding users as unique IDs, we propose a generic scenario where one directly collects users' sensitive data with LDP. The intuition behind this is collecting generic values, which can be generated by many users (*e.g.*, gender), allowing a longitudinal study. As we show in the results, our methodology is very appropriate for this scenario, achieving accurate frequency estimation in a multi-dimensional setting while respecting some major recommendations of data protection authorities such as the GDPR and CNIL.

This work was supported by the Region of Bourgogne Franche-Comté CADRAN Project and by the EIPHI-BFC Graduate School (contract "ANR-17-EURE-0002"). The authors would also like to thank the Orange Application for Business team for their useful feedback and comments. Computations have been performed on the supercomputer facilities of "Mésocentre de Calcul de Franche-Comté".

© IFIP International Federation for Information Processing 2021
Published by Springer Nature Switzerland AG 2021
M. Friedewald et al. (Eds.): Privacy and Identity 2020, IFIP AICT 619, pp. 40–57, 2021.
https://doi.org/10.1007/978-3-030-72465-8_3

Keywords: Local differential privacy · Call detail records · Mobility analytics · Multi-dimensional data · Mobile phone data

1   Introduction

Currently, with the increasing of massive data generated by mobile phones, the acquisition of these data has attracted considerable attention. When users make a call, send SMS, or connect to the internet, a call detail record (CDR) is generated with information on users' ID, the antennas that handled the communication service (coarse level location), and the duration and type of communication, for example. CDRs are stored by mobile network operators (MNOs) for billing and legal purposes, which implies an offline, archived, and constant update of the data without changing nor deleting old records. In other words, CDRs are of easy access and, therefore, have become one of the most used data for research [6, 10,17], *e.g.*, on human mobility.

In addition to CDRs, MNOs store subscription data from clients such as gender, date of birth (age), and invoice address. Such a combination of personal data makes mobile phone CDRs a rich source of information [6], which could allow research progress and improve individuals' life. For instance, CDRs can be used to model human mobility for tourism [16], to improve urban planning, and to help governmental decisions, which could be in the short-term, *e.g.*., response to natural disasters [21], the spread of new diseases/pandemics [26,28,36] like the ongoing COVID-19 outbreak [31]. Or to the long-term, to building new hospitals, schools, and improving transportation systems [17,23,27]. CDRs are also the type of data that we focus on in this paper, which will be used equivalently when mentioning mobile phone data.

1.1   Context of the Problem

However, mobility data are quite sensitive as human mobility has proven to be highly unique and predictable [24]. If users can be tracked away by their presence or location, in some cases the users' home/work addresses, their religion, and habits can be disclosed. Additionally, even though MNOs have the right and duty to store CDRs, according to some privacy legislation, such as the GDPR (General Data Protection Regulation) [14], it does not mean MNOs have the right to use those data for other purposes. Therefore, once MNOs intend to use such a data source for human mobility analysis, these data must be properly sanitized. Therefore, *it is vital to improving privacy-preserving techniques to collect mobile phone data* [23,38].

For instance, one could think of a straightforward solution to publishing mobility analysis according to all CDRs collected in a given time interval (*e.g.*, a day) using k-anonymity [30] or differential privacy (DP) [11,12], which are two well-known privacy models. On the one hand, k-anonymity assumes that a trusted curator holds users' raw data and relies on hiding each released record in a crowd of $k-1$ other similar ones. However, k-anonymity might not be sufficient to guarantee users' privacy [38] since it does not offer strong guarantees and may be vulnerable to intersecting and/or homogeneity attacks, for example. On the other hand, DP assumes that a trusted curator holds the raw data from users and adds noise to output private queries. By 'trusted', we mean that curators do not misuse or leak private information from individuals. However, this assumption does not always hold in real-life. To address non-trusted services in DP, authors in [19] introduced the concept of local differential privacy (LDP), which proposes to sanitize each individual's data independently during the process of data collection.

Indeed, DP- or k-anonymity-based approaches normally require the entire dataset of raw CDRs, which is not in accordance with recommendations of data protection authorities such as the CNIL (National Commission on Informatics and Liberty, in English) [8], in France, which requires that data be sanitized on the fly. More specifically, according to CNIL and GDPR, there are some important recommendations to be respected once MNOs aims to collect CDR-based data for analyzing human mobility. These recommendations are briefly described in the following: (i) CDRs are produced through the connection of mobile phones with carrier networks (*e.g.*, receiving or making calls). This means that users cannot sanitize their data via a built-in application, for example. Hence, all sanitization procedures must be done on the fly instead of collecting raw data and publishing private output at the end of the analysis. (ii) MNOs cannot store or work with data containing users' unique identifiers (IDs) or a hashed version of it as they are still unique IDs. For instance, if one can detect the same *hash(ID)* for many days, it violates the privacy of this user as s/he can be easily tracked away. And (iii), as a longitudinal study, users can generate multiple data points (*e.g.*, they can receive/make calls every day for a month). In the literature, this problem is referred to as *continuous observation* [9,13], and it must be addressed to avoid 'averaging' attacks.

1.2   Purpose and Contributions

In summary, we describe the targeted problem of this work as follows. *How can MNOs, which store CDRs for billing purposes, also collect longitudinal and multi-dimensional data based on mobile connections to publish high-utility analysis of human mobility?* To this end, the privacy-preserving methodology must comply with the three (i)-(iii) aforementioned recommendations according to the GDPR and CNIL.

We describe our system model in the following. The first entity, namely *users*, refers to n clients $\mathcal{U} = \{u_1, u_2, ..., u_n\}$ of the MNO. The second entity is the MNOs themselves, which legally store the signature data of their clients (date of birth, gender, invoice address, ...) and billing data (CDRs) into a data server. In order to avoid data breaches and to be compliant with privacy legislation such as the GDPR, these data must be stored in a secure environment. Therefore, in the data privacy context, when users connect to the MNO's antennas, there is a need for an efficient approach for privately 'exporting' (collecting) data for high-utility mobility analytics.

Without loss of generality, we assume that all the data MNOs will extract from this data server, *for publishing human mobility analysis*, is categorical. That is, in this paper, we aim to address the aforementioned problem as a *general frequency estimation in categorical data*. The reason behind this is the collection of generic values on a population through mobile connections in a given time interval to produce flows and mobility indicators based on socio-demographic data (*e.g.*, such as in [5,27]). Indeed, multi-dimensional human mobility analyses would provide more insights into people's mobility behavior by attribute values (*e.g.*, gender, origin, age-ranges). For instance, local authorities and/or organizations could take advantage of such knowledge to identify strategies to propose better decision-making solutions to society, *e.g.*, the spread of diseases, urban planning, natural disasters, and so on [10,20,21,26,28,29,36].

Therefore, in this paper, we introduce an LDP-based privacy-preserving methodology to sanitize each CDR-based data on the fly. The main reason behind our choice to use the local model is because neither MNOs nor 'trusted curators' (*e.g.*, researchers) can analyze human mobility through raw CDRs data, according to privacy legislation such as the GDPR and CNIL (in France). Figure 1 illustrates an overview of our system model, which includes our proposed LDP-based methodology as a solution to collecting data through mobile connections.

Fig. 1. Overview of our system model with an LDP-based privacy-preserving solution to sanitize users' data on the fly.

Each time a user makes a call, or sends SMS, or connects to the internet, a CDR is generated and is stored offline for billing and legal purposes in a secure data server. Notice that the secure environment is also responsible for applying the LDP sanitization to all users' data with ϵ-LDP, where ϵ is a public parameter, before sending them to a sanitized data server. Therefore, the sanitized data server can store and aggregate this data for producing statistics through frequency estimation, which depends on the LDP algorithm and public parameter ϵ. In this scenario, both users and MNOs are safeguarded as no raw data will be collected for the purpose of human mobility analysis. On the one hand, ϵ-LDP values are robust to post-processing and can be stored and shared with 'trusted' curators for studying human mobility. However, ϵ-LDP values must not be regarded as unique identifiers. In a worst-case scenario, if one can detect a unique ϵ-LDP value for many days, it would violate the privacy of this user as s/he could be easily tracked away. In this case, we propose to use the generalized randomized response (GRR) [18,33,34] LDP mechanism, which corresponds to the situation where no particular encoding is chosen. In other words, with GRR, ϵ-LDP private reports are generic to many users (*e.g.*, feminine or masculine, for the gender attribute), which could have been generated by any user u_1 or u_2 and, therefore, allowing a longitudinal collection of data. To summarize, this paper makes the following contributions:

- We introduce an LDP-based privacy-preserving methodology to sanitize multi-dimensional CDR-based data on the fly for two longitudinal data collection scenarios:

  I *Frequency estimates:* In this case, MNOs initialize a single server to collect sanitized data for each time interval. This allows MNOs to publish the frequency of users per d attributes. For example, the frequency of users in a given city and day per gender, location (antenna coverage areas), age-ranges, and so on.

  II *Cumulative frequency estimates:* In addition to point *1.*, MNOs can privately extend the analysis to include users data on different sanitized data servers. This would allow MNOs to estimate the number of users at the intersection or union of different time intervals. In this paper, we only focus on this scenario as the *Frequency estimates* scenario is already part of the latter.

- We extended the analytical analysis of GRR for multi-dimensional studies where we prove that sending only $r = 1$ attribute out of d possible ones provides *much higher utility*.

- We present extensive experiments with a 7-days, multi-dimensional, and real-world mobility dataset (CDR-driven) from [5] to validate our proposals.

Roadmap. The remainder of this paper is organized as follows. In Sect. 2 we review related work. In Sect. 3, we briefly describe the privacy notions that we are considering, *i.e.*, LDP and the GRR mechanism with its extension for multi-dimensional data. Next, we explain our proposed methodology in Sect. 4. In Sect. 5, we present our results and its discussions. Last, in Sect. 6 we present the concluding remarks and future directions.

2   Related Work

Numerous previous [16,20,21,36] and current studies [10,26–29] have shown the validity and benefits of mobility studies based on CDRs. Although event-based (*i.e.*, data are only available when using the MNOs' services) and with coarse location (*i.e.*, antennas that handled the service), CDRs are a real marker of human presence. Such a data source has been proven as a prominent way to analyze large-scale human mobility due to the high penetration rates of cell phones and low collection costs [6,10,17].

Regarding human mobility, some studies have shown that humans follow particular patterns with a high probability of predictability. This motivates, even more, a conscientious use of mobile phone data for allowing research progress, which could benefit individuals and society [23,24]. Indeed, in recent contexts, Oliver et al. [26] highlight the importance of mobile phone data like CDRs for fighting the current COVID-19 pandemic [31], and [10] review and discuss applications, opportunities, and some key challenges to use CDRs for urban climate change adaption.

Concerning CDRs sanitization, the authors in [1] describe a differentially private scheme to release the spatio-temporal density of Paris regions using CDRs of about 2 million users over one week. The authors propose data pre-processing techniques such as sub-sampling and clustering, which aims at enhancing the utility of the DP mechanism. Zang and Bolot [38] have performed extensive experiments showing that the anonymization of location data from CDRs using k-anonymity leads to privacy risks. Mir et al. [22] extended a framework namely WHERE and proposed DP-WHERE, which produces synthetic CDRs to model mobility patterns of metropolitan populations respecting DP guarantees. In [3], the authors applied a DP mechanism namely BLIP (Bloom-than-fLIP) on a CDRs dataset. Each BLIP stores the users' ID, and in the end, each bit is flipped with a given probability to guarantee DP for each user. Afterward, in [2], authors proposed an upgraded version of BLIP namely Pan-Private BLIP (PP-BLIP), which guarantees privacy protection to the internal state while the BLIP is being built as well as to its output. The authors applied PP-BLIP to human mobility modeling via wi-fi connections while highlighting its extension to CDR-based data.

Notice that the aforementioned works provide a means to model human mobility through CDRs. However, when using DP, these works collect raw data and sanitize it in the end. Secondly, using BLIP or PP-BLIP would require an unbounded privacy budget as each Bloom Filter (*e.g.*, per day) uses ϵ-DP. By the sequential composition theorem [12,39], it is clear that these methods do not allow a long-term analysis. Last, these approaches collect users' ID or a hashed version of it and do not allow collecting other data rather than the presence of users itself. In this paper, we introduce a way to address these concerns with LDP, which allows a longitudinal collection of data with high privacy guarantees to each user. The local DP model has received considerable attention in both academia [4,15,19,25,32–34] and practical deployment [9,13] since it does not rely on sharing raw data anymore, which has a clear connection to the concept of randomized response [35]. We refer the interested reader to the survey work on LDP from Xiong et al. [37] for more insights about this approach.

3   Background

In this section, we briefly present the privacy concepts considered in this work, *i.e.*, local differential privacy (Subsect. 3.1). Further, we describe the generalized randomized response LDP mechanism (Subsect. 3.2), and its extension to a multi-dimensional setting based on random sampling (Subsect. 3.3).

3.1 Local Differential Privacy (LDP)

The centralized DP outlined in the introduction assumes trusted data collectors. By 'trusted', it means that they do not steal or leak private information from individuals. However, this assumption does not always hold in real-life. To address non-trusted services, local differential privacy [19] was proposed to preserve users' privacy in the process of data collection. Rather than trusting in a trusted curator to have the raw data and sanitize it to output queries, LDP allows users to sanitize their data before sending it to the data collector server. A randomized algorithm $\mathcal{A}$ is said to provide ϵ-local differential privacy if, for any two input values $v_1, v_2 \in Domain(\mathcal{A})$ and any possible output y of $\mathcal{A}$:

$$\Pr[\mathcal{A}(v_1) = y] \leq e^\epsilon \cdot \Pr[\mathcal{A}(v_2) = y]. \tag{1}$$

Intuitively, ϵ-LDP guarantees that an attacker can not distinguish whether the true value is $v1$ or $v2$ (input) with high confidence (controlled by ϵ) irrespective of the background knowledge one has. That is because both have approximately the same probability to generate the same sanitized output.

3.2 Generalized Randomized Response (GRR)

Randomized response (RR) was proposed by Warner [35] in 1965 to collect statistics on sensitive topics while guaranteeing the survey respondents with strong deniability. The RR model was designed for binary attributes ($v = 2$ values). Further, an LDP mechanism was introduced as a general version of the RR technique to be used for $v \geq 2$ values. This LDP mechanism is referred to as k-RR in [18], as GRR in [34], and direct encoding protocol in [33]. In this paper, we refer to this LDP mechanism as GRR.

Let $V = \{v_1, v_2, ..., v_j\}$ be a set of j values of the personal data in consideration (*e.g.*, age ranges) and ϵ be the privacy budget. Given a value v_i, $GRR(v_i)$ outputs the true value v_i with probability $p = \frac{e^\epsilon}{e^\epsilon + j - 1}$, and any other value v_k for $k \neq i$ with probability $q = \frac{1-p}{j-1} = \frac{1}{e^\epsilon + j - 1}$, where $j = |V|$. A statistical-based (SB) approach for estimating the number of times $\hat{T}$ that a value v_i occurs for $i \in [1, j]$, is computed as:

$$\hat{T}(v_i) = \frac{N_i - nq}{p - q}, \tag{2}$$

where N_i is the number of times the value v_i has been reported and n is the total number of users. Wang et al. [33,34] proved that this estimator is unbiased and its variance is computed as:

$$Var[\hat{T}_{GRR}(i)] = n \cdot \frac{e^\epsilon + j - 2}{(e^\epsilon - 1)^2}, \tag{3}$$

where [33,34] remark that this variance is linear in n and j. That is, if an attribute has too many values the accuracy of using GRR decreases. Indeed, as j increases the probability p of reporting the true value decreases. Moreover, in [33], the authors have proven that if $j < 3e^{\epsilon} + 2$, the GRR mechanism presents higher utility in comparison with many other state-of-the-art LDP mechanisms, e.g., Basic One-time RAPPOR [13] and optimized unary encoding [33] (OUE).

3.3   Collecting Multi-dimensional Data with GRR

There are few works for collecting multi-dimensional data with LDP based on random sampling [25,32,33], which mainly focused on numerical data [37]. This technique reduces both dimensionality and communication costs, which will also be the focus of this paper by extending the analysis to the GRR mechanism. Suppose there are $d \geq 2$ attributes, n users, and a privacy budget $\epsilon > 0$. A naive solution is splitting the privacy budget ($M1$), i.e., assigning ϵ/d for each attribute. The other solution is based on randomly sampling (without replacement) only r attribute(s) out of d possible ones ($M2$), i.e., assigning ϵ/r per attribute. Notice that both solutions satisfy ϵ-LDP according to the sequential composition theorem [12,39].

As the number of users n differs (n and rn/d) in the two solutions, we normalize the estimator $\hat{T}$ in Eq. (2) to the range 0 to 1. The GRR variance in Eq. (3) is now described as $Var[\hat{T}_{GRR}(i)/n] = \frac{1}{n} \cdot \frac{e^{\epsilon}+j-2}{(e^{\epsilon}-1)^2}$. For the first case ($M1$), the GRR variance is $Var_1 = \frac{1}{n} \cdot \frac{e^{\epsilon/d}+j-2}{(e^{\epsilon/d}-1)^2}$ and for the second case ($M2$), the GRR variance is $Var_2 = \frac{d}{nr} \cdot \frac{e^{\epsilon/r}+j-2}{(e^{\epsilon/r}-1)^2}$. The objective is finding r, which minimizes Var_2 and guarantees that $Var_2 < Var_1$.

Following the work in [32], we multiply Var_2 by ϵ. Next, let $x = r/\epsilon$ be the independent variable and Var_2 rewritten as $y = \frac{1}{x} \cdot \frac{e^{1/x}}{(e^{1/x}-1)^2}$ be the dependent one; d/n and $j - 2$ are omitted as they are simply summing or multiplication factors. Since y is an increasing function, i.e., y increases as the x value increases, we then have a minimum and optimal when $r = 1$. The remaining question is if $Var_1 - Var_2 > 0$. Since

$$Var_1 - Var_2 = \frac{1}{n} \left(\frac{e^{\epsilon/d}}{(e^{\epsilon/d}-1)^2} - \frac{d \cdot e^{\epsilon}}{(e^{\epsilon}-1)^2} \right), \qquad (4)$$

omitting $j - 2$, it has been proven in [33] that $Var_1 - Var_2$ is always positive, and hence, the proof ends.

In this multi-dimensional setting ($M2$), one can see our solution as applying the GRR mechanism only once in d times ($1/d$) and reporting nothing $1 - 1/d$ times. In short, Algorithm 1 shows the pseudocode of using GRR for multi-dimensional data collection, which will be referred to as GRR-$M2$ for the rest of this paper. Given the set $A = \{A_1, ..., A_d\}$ of all d attributes and a tuple $t = [v_1, ..., v_d]$ with the user's true values, the GRR-$M2$ algorithm returns a tuple $t^* = \langle r, GRR(v_r) \rangle$, i.e., with the sampled attribute r and its ϵ-LDP value. Notice that, to ensure (strengthen) users' privacy over time, each user must always report the same unique attribute r. On the server-side, the SB estimator in Eq. (2) to the number of times $\hat{T}$ that a value v_i occurs for $i \in [1, j]$ has to be scaled d times.

Algorithm 1. GRR for multi-dimensional data collection (GRR-$M2$)

1: **Input:** tuple $t = [v_1, ..., v_d]$, set $A = \{A_1, ..., A_d\}$, and ϵ.
2: **Output:** tuple $t^* = \langle r, GRR(v_r) \rangle$.
3: $r \leftarrow Uniform(\{1, 2, ..., d\})$
4: $B \leftarrow t[r] = v_r$
5: $b \leftarrow Bern\left(e^\epsilon / (e^\epsilon + |A_r| - 1)\right)$
6: **if** $b = 1$:
7: $\quad B' = v_r$
8: **else:**
9: $\quad B' \leftarrow Uniform(\{A_r/v_r\})$
10: **return :** $t^* = \langle r, B' \rangle$

---

4   LDP-Based Privacy-Preserving Longitudinal Data Collection Through Mobile Connections

In this section, according to the system overview in Fig. 1, we detail our LDP-based solution (Subsect. 4.1) regarding the *Cumulative frequency estimates* scenario outlined in the introduction and its limitations (Subsect. 4.2). Notice that the *Frequency estimates* scenario of collecting data only per single time intervals is part of the *Cumulative frequency estimates* scenario, and one can intuitively simplify some steps to apply only it.

4.1   Proposed Methodology

Figure 2 illustrates the overview of our methodology applied to collect users' data for days and union of days in a flow chart. Without loss of generality, we present our methodology for days, but it can be extended to any timestamp one desires as users' LDP data are generic to many users by using the GRR mechanism.

1. **Initialization.** According to the left side of Fig. 2, the secure-server defines the privacy guarantee ϵ, which is uniform for all users. Let Nb be the whole period of analysis (*e.g.*, total number of days), the MNOs' sanitized data server initializes $Nb(Nb + 1)/2$ empty databases. For instance, if $Nb = 3$ one will have $set_{db} = \{D_1, D_2, D_2 \cup D_1, D_3, D_3 \cup D_2, D_3 \cup D_2 \cup D_1\}$.
2. **LDP-based sanitization on the fly.** The MNOs' secure-server is responsible to applying the LDP-based sanitization model on the fly (*cf.* Fig. 1). This process uses our GRR-$M2$ solution (Algorithm 1). Because LDP is applied on the secure server of MNOs, there are a few issues to be taken into account. To ensure and strengthen privacy over time using GRR-$M2$, users must always report the same unique attribute r. To solve this issue, we suggest that MNOs generate a random seed that will be associated with each user for a cryptographically secure pseudorandom number generator. Thanks to this, the same memorized and sanitized B' can always be assigned for each user, according to the same and unique sampled attribute r. Indeed, if different values B' were

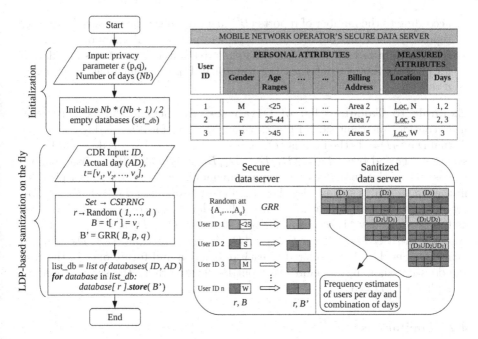

Fig. 2. Overview of our LDP-based privacy-preserving methodology to collecting data through mobile connections for days and union of days.

to be sent in each day, in the long-term, attackers who can isolate reports from a single user could infer with high confidence the true sensitive value by averaging attacks [9,13]. Also, in the real world, it is noteworthy noticing that in a given time interval between ts_{ini} to ts_{end}, the same user can generate multiple connections to MNOs' antennas. This de-duplication issue can be simply solved by the MNO's secure-server via Bloom filters [7], for example.

3. **Private data collection.** Each time a user connects to MNO's antennas, a CDR is generated, which contains the user's identifier (ID) and timestamp (actual day - AD), for example. CDRs are stored offline in a data server, which contains subscription data of users such as gender, date of birth, origin (invoice address), for example. Hence, without loss of generality, each user u_i ($1 \leq i \leq n$) has a discrete-encoded tuple record $t = [v_1, v_2, ..., v_d]$, which contains d categorical attributes $A = \{A_1, A_2, ..., A_d\}$. Therefore, the MNO's secure-server consistently uses the memoized sanitized data B' of users to send for storage according to the users' list of databases $list_{db}$. That is, by knowing the days this user "was present" (by CDRs), it allows calculating $list_{db}$, which is a list of databases (days and union of days) to store the private report of the user. We later explain in an example how to calculate $list_{db}$.

4. **Generating statistics.** At the end of the analysis period, the MNO's sanitized data server should have $Nb(Nb + 1)/2$ databases with only ϵ-LDP reports. On the one hand, MNOs can publish an accurate mobility scenario

according to the number of reports (B') in each sanitized database. The latter represents the *exact* number of users present per day and union of days. Last, for each sanitized database, one can estimate the frequency of this population for all d attributes using the SB estimator in Eq. (2), which has to be scaled d times.

Example to Calculate list of Databases. To calculate the $list_{db}$ for each user, consider the right side of Fig. 2, which has data for $Nb = 3$ days. First, let Actual Day $AD = 1$ (the first day of analysis). So, user $ID = 1$ is detected by the secure-server and his $list_{db} = \{D_1, D_2 \cup D_1, D_3 \cup D_2 \cup D_1\}$. The reason behind this is that if this user does not appear anymore, we have considered his data in the whole analysis. Next, let $AD = 2$. For the same user $ID = 1$, the secure-server knows he was present in both two days, hence, his $list_{db} = \{D_2, D_3 \cup D_2\}$ as the previous day his data was already stored in $D_2 \cup D_1$ and $D_3 \cup D_2 \cup D_1$. And, for the user $ID = 2$, her $list_{db} = \{D_2, D_2 \cup D_1, D_3 \cup D_2, D_3 \cup D_2 \cup D_1\}$ to guarantee her data is considered in each past union and future ones in the case she does not show up anymore. Without loss of generality the same procedure is applied in $AD = 3$.

4.2　Limitations

The first key limitation we see in our methodology is the storage factor, which is specifically related to the *Cumulative frequency estimates* scenario, *i.e.*, collecting users' data per day and union of days. For instance, MNOs need to initialize $Nb(Nb + 1)/2$ empty databases where if one wishes to analyze an enhanced detailed scenario, it grows up very fast (*i.e.*, with at least an $Nb^2/2$ factor). However, this scenario is only intended in special mobility analytics cases, *e.g.*, tourism events, natural disasters, following up spread of diseases, etc. In addition, there is high power for computation and powerful tools to deal with big data nowadays. One way to smooth this problem in, *e.g.*, daily scenarios, is to exclude the stored data after retrieving statistics.

Further, there is an important loss of information by not calculating the intersection of users through days. That is, we propose to compute the number of users per union of days as it may have very few users per intersection. The latter would not produce accurate frequency estimations due to the LDP formulation, which is data-hungry. At first glance, one can surely compute the pair-wise intersection for any two days in the analysis period using $|A \cap B| = |A| + |B| - |A \cup B|$. One possibility of solving the whole problem is to use the methodology from [5], which models our proposed mobility scenario (days and union of days) as a linear program to find a solution for all intersections. Besides, for the case where one can have sufficient data samples per pair-, triple-, ..., and Nb-wise intersections, one can easily extend our methodology for such a case. However, the storage factor is even bigger as MNOs would have to initialize $2^{Nb} - 1$ empty databases (all combinations of days).

Last, the *memorization* step of always reporting the same sanitized value for the unique sampled attribute can be effective to the cases where the true client's data does not vary (static) [9,13]. On the other hand, a measured attribute such as location is dynamic. As highlighted in the literature [24], humans mobility is very predictable, which means that they follow well-defined patterns, *e.g.*, alternating between $l1$ (home), $l2$ (work), and $l3$ (*e.g.*, hobby). Yet, in our privacy-preserving architecture (Fig. 1), the collected/stored sanitized data are 'uncorrelated' from users, as no ID will be stored. Therefore, under the worst-case scenario where attackers can isolate reports from a single user whose random dimension is location, they could learn the $l = 3$ memoized ϵ-LDP values. But, they can hardly (controlled by ϵ-LDP) identify these real locations thanks to memoization.

5   Results and Discussion

In this section, we report the results obtained by applying our proposed methodology in a real-world open dataset (Subsect. 5.1) and its discussions (Subsect. 5.2). The codes we developed and used for all experiments are available in a Github repository[1].

Dataset. This is a longitudinal and multi-dimensional dataset of VHs [5] resulted by inferring several statistics of human mobility; as stated by the authors, statistics were generated through sanitized mobile connections (CDR-driven). We excluded the data from 'Foreign tourist' users regarding the 'Visitor category' attribute. Hence, our filtered dataset aggregates a population of $87,098$ French users per seven days with approximately $26,700$ unique users on average per day. There are $d = 6$ attributes we are interested in, which are described in the following. *Gender* is masculine or feminine. *Age* has 7 age ranges. *GeoLife* has 12 socio-professional categories. *Region* has 22 regions in France that users are billed. *Sleeping Area* represents 11 areas that users spent the night (location). And, *Visit Duration* has 10 time-ranges in which visitors were detected each day. The two last attributes are measured ones where *Sleeping Area* is static and *Visit Duration* is dynamic.

Evaluation and Metrics. We vary the *total* privacy budget ϵ in the range $[0.5, 1, 2, 3, 4, 5, 6]$ to evaluate the privacy-utility trade-off. We use the root mean square error (RMSE) metric to measure our results.

Setup: Let $Nb = 7$ days to be the whole analysis period, we then have $Nb(Nb+1)/2 = 28$ databases considering each day and union of days combination as $set_{db} = \{D_1, ..., D_3 \cup D_2 \cup D_1, ..., D_7 \cup D_6 \cup ... \cup D_1\}$. Notice that, at the same time, we can empirically evaluate the privacy-utility trade-off according to data size, *i.e.*, each day has around $26,700$ unique users, while the last union of days $D_7 \cup D_6 \cup ... \cup D_1$ has all $87,098$ users.

Comparing Methodologies. We consider for evaluation the following approaches:

---

[1] https://github.com/hharcolezi/ldp-protocols-mobility-cdrs.

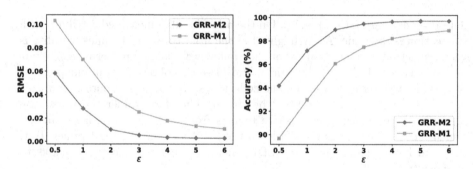

Fig. 3. Average RMSE and accuracy (y-axis) VS privacy budget ϵ (x-axis) analysis for our GRR-*M2* solution and the GRR-*M1* naive one.

- Our GRR-*M2* solution of using GRR in a multi-dimensional setting, which samples a unique attribute r and assigns the whole privacy budget ϵ to it;
- A naive solution of using GRR in a multi-dimensional setting, which splits the privacy budget among d attribute, *i.e.*, ϵ/d (GRR-*M1*).

5.1 Cumulative Frequency Estimates Results

Figure 3 illustrates the average RMSE values (y-axis) varying the privacy budget ϵ (x-axis) regarding all databases in set_{db} for our GRR-*M2* solution and the GRR-*M1* naive one (left-side); and, the corresponding $accuracy = 1 - RMSE$, which is rather intuitive of how much privacy budget to use for achieving a given "accuracy" (right-side). In more detail, Fig. 4 illustrates for both methods the RMSE results (y-axis) according to the privacy budget ϵ for each day and union of days (x-axis), *e.g.*, '321' refers to $D_3 \cup D_2 \cup D_1$. Without loss of generality, we excluded $\epsilon = 0.5$ in Fig. 4 to improve the visibility of the other curves. Finally, for the sake of illustration, Fig. 5 exhibits the frequency estimation results for a single day (D_7) and for the union of all days ($D_7 \cup D_6 \cup ... \cup D_1$) using our GRR-*M2* and $\epsilon = 1$.

5.2 Discussion

As one can notice in the results, our LDP-based methodology can be well applied to the longitudinal collection and analysis of multi-dimensional data for human mobility modeling. It is worthy noticing that we selected the GRR mechanism because the set of possible values in a given attribute is kept at j. If one-hot-encoding is used as in the Basic One-time RAPPOR mechanism [13] or OUE [33], each bit can be either 0 or 1, which means that the set of possible reports for an attribute with j values has now 2^j possibilities. This is highly important to take into account, as, for a longitudinal collection of data as we proposed, one has to try to ensure that ϵ-LDP values are not indirect unique identifiers. Moreover, high-utility mobility indicators can be achieved by generalizing attributes to a

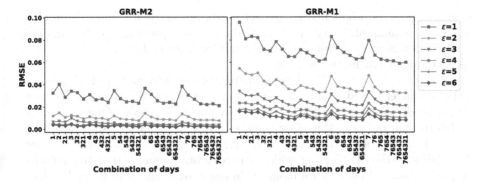

Fig. 4. RMSE (y-axis) analysis varying the privacy budget ϵ considering each combination of days (x-axis). Notice that these are discrete values. However, curves are drawn to ease interpretation.

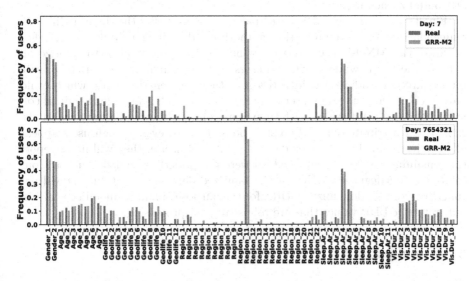

Fig. 5. Comparison between real and estimated frequencies for a single day and to the union of all days using our GRR-*M2* solution and $\epsilon = 1$.

well-defined set of values. That is, aiming to respect $j < 3e^{\epsilon} + 2$ or at least not being too far, as GRRs' utility, depends on [33].

Overall, our GRR-*M2* consistently and considerably outperforms the baseline GRR-*M1*. In Fig. 4, except for $\epsilon = 1$, our GRR-*M2* curves are under even to the best one of GRR-*M1* using the highest privacy budget $\epsilon = 6$. As also highlighted in the literature [25,32,33], privacy budget splitting is sub-optimal, which leads to higher estimation error. Indeed, in a multi-dimensional setting, the combination of privacy budget splitting and high numbers of values j in a given attribute (*e.g.*, *Region* with 22 values) leads to lower data utility even for high privacy regimes. On the other hand, our GRR-*M2* solution based on random sampling uses the whole privacy budget to a single attribute, and this problem is, hence, minimized. However, there is also an error provided by the sampling technique, which is reduced by correctly choosing the number of attributes $r < d$ as we did for GRR in Subsect. 3.3.

More precisely, our GRR-*M2* solution presents an 'accuracy' over 94% for any privacy budget tested. In Fig. 3, with $\epsilon = 1$ that is considered a good privacy-utility trade-off, while our GRR-*M2* already approaches 98% of 'accuracy', the GRR-*M1* can only get this close when $\epsilon \geq 3$ approximately. Additionally, in Figs. 4 and 5, it is noteworthy that the RMSE decreases as the data size increases. This is due to the LDP setting, which requires a big amount of data to guarantee a good balance of noise (data-hungry). In our case, single days (*e.g.*, D_7) have less data points comparing to the union of all days (*e.g.*, $D_7 \cup D_6 \cup ... \cup D_1$), and hence they are generally the peak-values in Fig. 4. However, these peak values are smoothed using our GRR-*M2*, which induce less error by sampling a single attribute for each user.

Finally, our proposed LDP-based methodology satisfies the three (i)-(iii) recommendations of data protection authorities, described in Subsect. 1.1. For instance, the MNOs' secure-server applies an LDP mechanism to sanitize all data on the fly (i) while storing no users' ID (ii). Furthermore, ϵ-LDP private reports are not (indirect) unique IDs, *i.e.*, they are generic values, which could have been generated by any user u_1 or u_2 and, thus, allowing a longitudinal collection of data (iii). Besides, each time users connect, they will always report the same $r = 1$ attribute out of d possible ones. That is, even though users appear all days in the analysis (in this dataset $\sim 0.2\%$ of users), they will never report the remaining $d - 1$ attributes, which were not directly sampled. And last, our solution also safeguards MNOs as the sanitized data server (*cf.* Fig. 1) will not collect raw or pseudonymized CDRs, for the purpose of human mobility analysis, but, rather, ϵ-LDP values that are robust to post-processing.

6   Conclusion

This work investigates the problem of longitudinally collecting and analyzing human mobility data through mobile connections. Following some major recommendations from data authorities such as the GDPR and CNIL (in France), we proposed an LDP-based privacy-preserving methodology for collecting data, on the fly, through mobile connections while providing high privacy guarantees for users. More precisely, such a privacy-preserving methodology would allow MNOs to use and/or share the sanitized data, as LDP is robust to post-processing, for publishing mobility indicators while protecting the privacy of their clients. To this end, we extended the analysis of a state-of-the-art LDP protocol named GRR [18,33,34] for multi-dimensional studies, referred to as GRR-*M2* in this paper.

As shown in the results, the proposed LDP-based methodology using our GRR-*M2* solution is capable of collecting and calculating accurate multi-dimensional frequency estimates (*cf.* Fig. 5, for example) for human mobility modeling. Indeed, in the mobility scenario we propose, the number of users per day and union of days is exactly the number of ϵ-LDP collected reports. For future work, we suggest and intend the following directions: to experimentally validate our proposed methodology using actual data from an MNO; to investigate inference attacks to check whether individuals who report dynamic attributes, such as location, are more endangered than others who report, *e.g.*, gender; and, to design LDP mechanisms for this longitudinal and multi-dimensional task considering both numerical and categorical data.

References

1. Acs, G., Castelluccia, C.: A case study: privacy preserving release of spatio-temporal density in Paris. In: Proceedings of the 20th ACM SIGKDD International Conference on Knowledge Discovery and Data Mining - KDD. ACM Press (2014). https://doi.org/10.1145/2623330.2623361
2. Alaggan, M., Cunche, M., Gambs, S.: Privacy-preserving wi-fi analytics. Proc. Priv. Enhancing Technol. **2018**(2), 4–26 (2018). https://doi.org/10.1515/popets-2018-0010
3. Alaggan, M., Gambs, S., Matwin, S., Tuhin, M.: Sanitization of call detail records via differentially-private bloom filters. In: Samarati, P. (ed.) DBSec 2015. LNCS, vol. 9149, pp. 223–230. Springer, Cham (2015). https://doi.org/10.1007/978-3-319-20810-7_15
4. Alvim, M., Chatzikokolakis, K., Palamidessi, C., Pazii, A.: Invited paper: Local differential privacy on metric spaces: Optimizing the trade-off with utility. In: 2018 IEEE 31st Computer Security Foundations Symposium (CSF). IEEE (Jul 2018). https://doi.org/10.1109/csf.2018.00026
5. Arcolezi, H.H., Couchot, J.F., Baala, O., Contet, J.M., Bouna, B.A., Xiao, X.: Mobility modeling through mobile data: generating an optimized and open dataset respecting privacy. In: 2020 International Wireless Communications and Mobile Computing (IWCMC). IEEE (2020). https://doi.org/10.1109/iwcmc48107.2020.9148138
6. Blondel, V.D., Decuyper, A., Krings, G.: A survey of results on mobile phone datasets analysis. EPJ Data Sci. **4**(1), 1–55 (2015). https://doi.org/10.1140/epjds/s13688-015-0046-0
7. Broder, A., Mitzenmacher, M.: Network applications of bloom filters: a survey. Internet Math. **1**(4), 485–509 (2004). https://doi.org/10.1080/15427951.2004.10129096
8. CNIL: Commission nationale de l'informatique et des libertés (1978). https://www.cnil.fr/en/home. Accessed 10 May 2020
9. Ding, B., Kulkarni, J., Yekhanin, S.: Collecting telemetry data privately. In: Guyon, I., Luxburg, U.V., Bengio, S., Wallach, H., Fergus, R., Vishwanathan, S., Garnett, R. (eds.) Advances in Neural Information Processing Systems, vol. 30, pp. 3571–3580. Curran Associates, Inc., (2017)
10. Dujardin, S., Jacques, D., Steele, J., Linard, C.: Mobile phone data for urban climate change adaptation: reviewing applications, opportunities and key challenges. Sustainability **12**(4), 1501 (2020). https://doi.org/10.3390/su12041501
11. Dwork, C.: Differential privacy. In: Bugliesi, M., Preneel, B., Sassone, V., Wegener, I. (eds.) ICALP 2006. LNCS, vol. 4052, pp. 1–12. Springer, Heidelberg (2006). https://doi.org/10.1007/11787006_1

12. Dwork, C., Roth, A., et al.: The algorithmic foundations of differential privacy. Found. Trends® Theoretical Comput. Sci. **9**(3–4), 211–407 (2014)
13. Erlingsson, U., Pihur, V., Korolova, A.: Rappor: randomized aggregatable privacy-preserving ordinal response. In: Proceedings of the 2014 ACM SIGSAC Conference on Computer and Communications Security. ACM, New York, NY, USA (2014)
14. European-Commission: 2018 reform of EU data protection rules (2018). https://gdpr-info.eu/. Accessed 10 Apr 2020
15. Fernandes, N., Lefki, K., Palamidessi, C.: Utility-preserving privacy mechanisms for counting queries. In: Boreale, M., Corradini, F., Loreti, M., Pugliese, R. (eds.) Models, Languages, and Tools for Concurrent and Distributed Programming. LNCS, vol. 11665, pp. 487–495. Springer, Cham (2019). https://doi.org/10.1007/978-3-030-21485-2_27
16. Heerschap, N., Ortega, S., Priem, A., Offermans, M.: Innovation of tourism statistics through the use of new big data sources. In: 12th Global Forum on Tourism Statistics, vol. 716, Prague, CZ (2014)
17. Jacques, D.C.: Mobile phone metadata for development. arXiv preprint arXiv:1806.03086 (2018)
18. Kairouz, P., Bonawitz, K., Ramage, D.: Discrete distribution estimation under local privacy. arXiv preprint arXiv:1602.07387 (2016)
19. Kasiviswanathan, S.P., Lee, H.K., Nissim, K., Raskhodnikova, S., Smith, A.: What can we learn privately? In: 2008 49th Annual IEEE Symposium on Foundations of Computer Science. IEEE (2008). https://doi.org/10.1109/focs.2008.27
20. Kishore, N., et al.: Flying, phones and flu: Anonymized call records suggest that keflavik international airport introduced pandemic H1N1 into iceland in 2009. Influenza Other Respir. Viruses **14**(1), 37–45 (2019). https://doi.org/10.1111/irv.12690
21. Lu, X., Bengtsson, L., Holme, P.: Predictability of population displacement after the 2010 Haiti earthquake. Proc. Nat. Acad. Sci. **109**(29), 11576–11581 (2012). https://doi.org/10.1073/pnas.1203882109
22. Mir, D.J., Isaacman, S., Caceres, R., Martonosi, M., Wright, R.N.: DP-WHERE: Differentially private modeling of human mobility. In: 2013 IEEE International Conference on Big Data. IEEE (2013). https://doi.org/10.1109/bigdata.2013.6691626
23. de Montjoye, Y.A., et al.: On the privacy-conscientious use of mobile phone data. Sci. Data **5**(1), 1–6 (2018). https://doi.org/10.1038/sdata.2018.286
24. de Montjoye, Y.A., Hidalgo, C.A., Verleysen, M., Blondel, V.D.: Unique in the crowd: The privacy bounds of human mobility. Sci. Rep. **3**(1), 1–5 (2013). https://doi.org/10.1038/srep01376
25. Nguyên, T.T., Xiao, X., Yang, Y., Hui, S.C., Shin, H., Shin, J.: Collecting and analyzing data from smart device users with local differential privacy. arXiv abs/1606.05053 (2016)
26. Oliver, N., et al.: Mobile phone data for informing public health actions across the COVID-19 pandemic life cycle. Sci. Adv. **6**(23), eabc0764 (2020). https://doi.org/10.1126/sciadv.abc0764
27. Orange-Business-Services: Flux vision: real time statistics on mobility patterns (2013). https://www.orange-business.com/en/products/flux-vision. Accessed 1 July 2020
28. Pollina, E., Busvine, D.: European mobile operators share data for coronavirus fight (2013). https://www.reuters.com/article/us-health-coronavirus-europe-telecoms-idUSKBN2152C2. Accessed 1 Dec 2020

29. Rhoads, D., Serrano, I., Borge-Holthoefer, J., Solé-Ribalta, A.: Measuring and mitigating behavioural segregation using call detail records. EPJ Data Sci. **9**(1), 1–17 (2020). https://doi.org/10.1140/epjds/s13688-020-00222-1
30. Sweeney, L.: k-anonymity: a model for protecting privacy. Int. J. Uncertainty, Fuzziness Knowl.-Based Syst. **10**(05), 557–570 (2002). https://doi.org/10.1142/s0218488502001648
31. Wang, C., Horby, P.W., Hayden, F.G., Gao, G.F.: A novel coronavirus outbreak of global health concern. The Lancet **395**(10223), 470–473 (2020). https://doi.org/10.1016/s0140-6736(20)30185-9
32. Wang, N., et al.: Collecting and analyzing multidimensional data with local differential privacy. In: 2019 IEEE 35th International Conference on Data Engineering (ICDE). IEEE (2019)
33. Wang, T., Blocki, J., Li, N., Jha, S.: Locally differentially private protocols for frequency estimation. In: 26th USENIX Security Symposium (USENIX Security 17), pp. 729–745. USENIX Association, Vancouver, BC (2017)
34. Wang, T., Li, N., Jha, S.: Locally differentially private frequent itemset mining. In: 2018 IEEE Symposium on Security and Privacy (SP). IEEE (2018). https://doi.org/10.1109/sp.2018.00035
35. Warner, S.L.: Randomized response: a survey technique for eliminating evasive answer bias. J. Am. Stat. Assoc. **60**(309), 63–69 (1965). https://doi.org/10.1080/01621459.1965.10480775
36. Wesolowski, A., Buckee, C.O., Bengtsson, L., Wetter, E., Lu, X., Tatem, A.J.: Commentary: containing the ebola outbreak - the potential and challenge of mobile network data. PLoS Currents (2014). https://doi.org/10.1371/currents.outbreaks.0177e7fcf52217b8b634376e2f3efc5e
37. Xiong, X., Liu, S., Li, D., Cai, Z., Niu, X.: A comprehensive survey on local differential privacy. Secur. Commun. Networks **2020**, 1–29 (2020). https://doi.org/10.1155/2020/8829523
38. Zang, H., Bolot, J.: Anonymization of location data does not work. In: Proceedings of the 17th Annual International Conference on Mobile Computing And Networking - MobiCom. ACM Press (2011). https://doi.org/10.1145/2030613.2030630
39. Zhu, T., Li, G., Zhou, W., Yu, P.S.: Differential Privacy and Applications. AIS, vol. 69. Springer, Cham (2017). https://doi.org/10.1007/978-3-319-62004-6

Privacy-Preserving IDS for In-Vehicle Networks with Local Differential Privacy

Peter Franke[1], Michael Kreutzer[2], and Hervais Simo[2(✉)]

[1] Technische Universität Darmstadt, Darmstadt, Germany
[2] Fraunhofer Institute for Secure Information Technology, Darmstadt, Germany
hervais.simo@sit.fraunhofer.de

Abstract. Intrusion Detection Systems (IDS) for In-Vehicle Networks routinely collect and transfer data about attacks to remote servers. However, the analysis of such data enables the inference of sensitive details about the driver's identity and daily routine, violating privacy expectations. In this work, we explore the possibilities of applying Local Differential Privacy to In-Vehicle Network data and propose a new privacy-preserving IDS for In-Vehicle Networks. We have designed and conducted various experiments, with promising results, showing that useful information about detected attacks can be inferred from anonymized CAN Bus logs, while preserving privacy.

Keywords: In-Vehicle Networks · Privacy · Data protection · Cybersecurity

1 Introduction and Motivation

Modern vehicles contain a large and increasing amount of electronic components. These components are commonly integrated into so-called *In-Vehicle Networks* (IVN) and are referred to as ECUs (Electronic Control Units). ECUs usually consist of a controller and a transceiver for sending and receiving messages on the network and a small processing unit to fulfill specific functions. Protocols used in modern In-Vehicle Networks include the CAN [25], FlexRay (ISO 17458), LIN (ISO 17987), MOST (ISO 21806-1), and automotive ethernet. The most used and important protocol is CAN, which is why will focus on it further on. With the development of connected cars, an even wider range of features, e.g. entertainment and connectivity found their way into vehicles through the addition of more communication interfaces. The latter include conventional interfaces like Bluetooth and USB that have been enhanced by applications like Android Auto [13] or Apple CarPlay [1], but also WiFi as another mean of short-range communication. Additionally, many present-day vehicles offer long-range communication via cellular networks like GSM, UMTS or LTE by using embedded SIM cards. These new interfaces enable a new range of applications for entertainment, like streaming of music and videos or live map data. Connected Cars also offer great

© IFIP International Federation for Information Processing 2021
Published by Springer Nature Switzerland AG 2021
M. Friedewald et al. (Eds.): Privacy and Identity 2020, IFIP AICT 619, pp. 58–77, 2021.
https://doi.org/10.1007/978-3-030-72465-8_4

maintenance possibilities, e.g. by transferring diagnostic data to vehicle manu-facturers or receiving over-the-air (OTA) updates for the vehicle. Convenience functions like control of the vehicle via a mobile phone [30] are also enabled, just like safety features like automatic emergency calling [10]. Data gathered from connected cars (we use the terms car and vehicle interchangeably) also enable a growing number of business models, e.g. for usage-based individual insurance, taxation or car sharing [6]. However, the newly added interfaces come with new attack surfaces, which might be exploited from a distance. This is problematic, because IVN protocols, especially CAN, often provide little or no security fea-tures. Thus, an insecure remote access to the IVN might lead to an attacker taking control over the vehicle [20]. An increasingly popular approach to thwart such attacks is to rely on *Intrusion Detection Systems* (IDS) to detect ongoing attacks while also being adaptive to newly occurring attacks. Current uses of IDS in vehicles involve extensive collection of data that flows on the CAN Bus. Collected data about attacks is typically sent to remote servers for an in-depth analysis. This guarantees high detection rates, but also allows many sensitive conclusions about the car and the passengers [8,12,18]. In particular, it might allow to create profiles with details about the identification of a driver, driving behaviour, habits or where and when someone drove. Such in-depth data collec-tion and analysis collides with the German Basic Law (Grundgesetz) Art. (1)(1), Art. (2)(1) and Art. 8 (1) of the Charter of Fundamental Rights of the European Union (CFR).

Contributions. This motivates our research into i) highlighting the tension between cybersecurity for IVN and privacy; and ii) developing privacy-preserving IDS for IVN, i.e., new IVN-tailored IT-solutions aiming to lessen the tension between cybersecurity and privacy. In this work, we explore the possibilities of applying Local Differential Privacy (LDP) [17,32,34] to In-Vehicle data collected by IDS and propose a privacy-preserving IDS. LDP offers strong, formal privacy guarantees when used. The key advantage of LDP from the users' perspective is that no trust in the data collector is needed. We especially highlight the challenge of applying LDP to raw CAN data, which has, to our knowledge, not been considered before.

We propose an extension of a generic In-Vehicle IDS leveraging LDP tech-niques. We consider different forms of logs about detected intrusions ("anomaly logs"). For each form, we evaluate the perturbation induced by applying LDP methods to the logs. We evaluate if valuable information about the detected attacks can still be recovered from the logs, while protecting sensitive details about affected individuals, with promising results.

Outline. The remainder of this paper is organized as follows: In Sect. 2, we introduce the CAN protocol, related security flaws, attacks and countermeasures as well as Local Differential Privacy in a more detailed fashion. In Sect. 3, we present a generic model of an IDS for IVN and its privacy limitations. In Sect. 4, we propose an extended IDS model leveraging LDP and consider three concrete scenarios of anomaly log transmission with LDP. In Sect. 5, we describe our evaluation and its results.

2 Background

The CAN Protocol (ISO 11898). The CAN (Controller Area Network) protocol was first specified by Robert Bosch GmbH in 1983. The latest version (CAN 2.0) was published in 1991 [25]. CAN allows multiple ECUs connected to a bus to communicate reliably with low latency while avoiding collisions. On a CAN network, messages are sent in the form of CAN frames. Any CAN frame sent on the bus is received by all connected ECUs. The transmission rate of a CAN Bus network is preconfigured and can vary depending on use cases. CAN networks can be in two states: The *recessive* state (logic 1) and the *dominant* state (logic 0). By default, the bus floats towards the recessive state. If two bits are transmitted at the same time, a dominant bit will always succeed. There are four different formats of CAN frames. The most important *data frame* (see Fig. 1), which is used for actual message transmission, contains the Arbitration ID (or CAN ID) field, which determines the content and priority of a message (not to be confused with the Vehicle Identification Number that is unique per vehicle and used when communicating with the manufacturer). Also, it contains a DATA field of up to 8 bytes and some further fields.

Fig. 1. Structure of a CAN 2.0 data frame. Image taken from Cho and Shin [5].

Security Flaws in In-Vehicle Networks (IVN) and CAN. IVN are used to fulfill critical vehicle functions, and failures and misbehaviour may lead to dramatic consequences for the passengers, possibly injuries or even loss of life. Security flaws may allow attacks that lead to such failures to take place. Thus, the topic of security is of high importance for IVN. CAN and similar protocols for IVN were designed in a time when the internet was still in an early phase. It was never considered or intended that such an IVN would be connected to the outside world, opening attack surfaces. Thus, there were no security considerations in the design of early IVN and especially CAN. Instead, they were primarily designed to offer safety and reliability, which obviously are sought after properties in vehicle development [35]. A concrete flaw in the CAN protocol is the lack of any authentication of the sender of messages or encrypted communication. Because messages are received by all participants on the network, any malicious party can read and use all information that is being sent. Furthermore, any participant is able to send messages with any CAN ID. This gives attackers the possibility to greatly disturb the vehicle's operation or even control its behaviour once access to the CAN Bus has been gained [15,35]. This can be established by physical access to the vehicle, e.g. by adding an additional, malicious ECU.

In the case of connected vehicles however, wireless communication interfaces and entertainment systems may contain additional vulnerabilities. When exploited, these vulnerabilities may give an attacker access to critical parts of the IVN from a distance [20].

Attacks Against In-Vehicle Networks. The mentioned problems have already led to concrete attacks being performed on vehicles: Checkoway et al. [4] showed several attacks on vehicles. Using a CD with a specially prepared WMA file, they managed to achieve full control of the CAN Bus. In 2015, Miller and Valasek [20] managed to gain access to the CAN Bus of a Jeep Cherokee car by exploiting weaknesses in the infotainment system, and remotely controlled it. Particularly, they manipulated the functions of steering and braking, being able to stop the car or force it off the road. Researchers of the Tencent Keen Security Lab managed to remotely exploit weaknesses in Tesla [21] and BMW [3] vehicles. In both cases, they gained access to the CAN Bus and were thus able to control the vehicle.

Existing Countermeasures. Due to the usually long life span of vehicles, during which many new vulnerabilities may be found, offering an appropriate protection is a challenging task [2,27]. To fix vulnerabilities, a long maintenance of vehicle types and the used software is needed. In order to secure In-Vehicle Networks and the CAN Bus in particular, several measures have been tried. To increase the difficulty of attacks, a thoughtful design of the network topology is important. The strict separation of critical and non-critical components into several network segments can stop attacks from compromising the entire IVN. For CAN in particular, there have been attempts to introduce MAC (Message Authentication Code) schemes to ensure integrity [23,24]. However, these attempts suffer from the low amount of space (8 bytes) available in the data frame in which the MAC could be transmitted. The usage of the MAC might also result in a higher latency due to increased computation effort. The CAN FD protocol that was presented in 2012 [26] and is now slowly being introduced into vehicles might provide better possibilities for MAC, as it offers 64 bytes of payload in each frame. To increase security of the CAN Bus and the entire IVN, *Intrusion Detection Systems* (IDS) [5,22,31] are gaining increasing interest among researchers and practitioners. These systems attempt to detect ongoing attacks, enabling the development of countermeasures or immediate reactions. This detection can either be provided by simple signatures of known attacks, or by complex algorithms based on machine learning to detect anomalies. In addition, with the usage of Intrusion Prevention Systems (IPS), which allow active reactions on attacks detected by an IDS, attacks may also be prevented directly.

Local Differential Privacy. *Local Differential Privacy* (LDP) is a so-called *noise-based* privacy model. Here, privacy protection is achieved by the addition of random noise to user data. The noise is added by each user individually before sending data to the collector. The collector can then aggregate multiple user responses to receive analysis results. LDP uses a *privacy parameter* or *privacy budget* ϵ that determines the level of privacy protection, where a lower ϵ means higher privacy protection, but also more required noise. LDP can be seen as an adaptation of the central model of Differential Privacy, where the noise is added by the collector to the analysis results of the collected data [7]. The advantage of LDP is that users no longer need to trust the data collector: Because the collector only receives noisy data, true data of individuals can not be abused or lost. Formally, LDP is defined as follows:

Definition 1 (ϵ-Local Differential Privacy [11]). *A randomized algorithm $\mathcal{A}$ satisfies ϵ-differential Privacy if for all pairs of client's values v_1 and v_2 and for all $R \subseteq Range(\mathcal{A})$, where $Range(\mathcal{A})$ denotes the image of $\mathcal{A}$,*

$$P[\mathcal{A}(v_1) \in R] \leq e^\epsilon \cdot P[\mathcal{A}(v_2) \in R].$$

Intuitively, this means that nobody can conclude with high confidence that a user has a specific value and not any other value - from the data this user reported. A convenient property of LDP is *composability*. It means that multiple releases of the same or correlated data result in limited and quantifiable loss of privacy protection. The *Sequential Composition* theorem states that the combination of a release with ϵ_1-LDP and one with ϵ_2-LDP still satisfies $(\epsilon_1 + \epsilon_2)$-LDP.

3   Privacy Limitations in Generic In-Vehicle IDS

Based mainly on the IDS ecosystems of ESCRYPT [9] and Argus Cybersecurity [36], we derived a model of the architecture of a generic In-Vehicle IDS, see Fig. 2. It entails the following components: 1) the Vehicle with a CAN Bus and a security system; 2) a Signature- and Specification-based IDPS component in the security system; 3) an Anomaly-based IDS component in the security system; and 4) a Backend Server performing the analysis. Processes and features provided by such a generic In-Vehicle IDS can be summarized in these steps:

1. Signature- and specification-based detection on the CAN data and blocking of known malicious traffic and attacks.
2. Anomaly detection for unknown attacks using the Anomaly-based IDS component on the data that have not been blocked in the previous step.
3. Transfer of anomaly data (logs and circumstances of the anomaly) about the anomalies detected by the Anomaly-based IDS to the Backend component.
4. Analysis of the collected anomaly data in the Backend.
5. Reaction: Deployment of Over-The-Air-Updates to the vehicle, containing updates of the detection rules for the ID(P)S.

In our generic in-vehicle IDS model, the detection of attacks takes place mainly inside the vehicle using the signature-based and anomaly-based ID(P)S. However, there is one step in which data transfer to a remote party occurs. This is Step 3, in which logs of detected anomalies are transmitted to a backend server

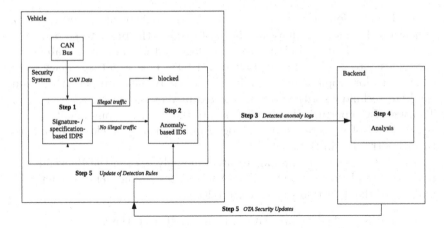

Fig. 2. Scheme of a generic IDS system.

belonging to the vehicle manufacturer or the provider of the IDS solution. The user's control over the transmitted anomaly logs is lost as soon as they leave the vehicle, resulting in potential privacy issues.

4 Our Approach

4.1 Generic IVN IDS with LDP

Our aim is to ensure privacy protection even if sensitive anomaly logs are processed outside of the vehicle (in Step 3 and 4 of our model). Because sensitive data is no longer protected as soon as it leaves the vehicle, the proposed privacy protection measures need to be applied before any data is sent to the backend. For this purpose, we propose the use of a LDP technique. This means that the anomaly logs that are sent in Step 3 need to be transformed to ensure privacy protection while they are still in the vehicle. Therefore, we modify our generic In-Vehicle IDS model, by adding a new component in the vehicle that perturbs anomaly logs in order to achieve LDP. This component is used in a new step between the anomaly detection and the transfer of the anomaly data to the backend. In this step, LDP techniques with the personal privacy budget ϵ_p are applied to the anomaly log. The selection of ϵ_p can be done by each vehicle, resp. the owner, individually, so that each vehicle v has an own budget ϵ_{pv}. In this way, each individual can choose their own minimum privacy level. To analyze the data, another new component is needed in the backend that aggregates the anomaly logs perturbed with LDP. So, we propose a new model of a generic in-vehicle IDS system that uses LDP for privacy protection, incorporating the previously mentioned new components. It is illustrated in Fig. 3 from the viewpoint of a single vehicle v. These are the steps taken in the new model:

1. Signature- and specification-based detection on the CAN data and blocking of known malicious traffic and attacks.

2. Anomaly detection for unknown attacks using the Anomaly-based IDS component on the data that have not been blocked in the previous step.
3. Application of LDP techniques to data (logs and circumstances) about the anomalies detected by the Anomaly-based IDS. This step takes place in the component for Application of LDP. The anomaly data are perturbed using the LDP techniques with the user-selected privacy parameter ϵ_{pv}.
4. Transfer of the perturbed anomaly data to the Backend component.
5. Aggregation of collected anomaly logs from multiple vehicles that are perturbed with LDP in the Backend.
6. Analysis of the collected and aggregated anomaly data in the Backend.
7. Reaction: Deployment of Over-The-Air-Updates to the vehicle, containing updates of the detection rules for the ID(P)S.

Because LDP is applied before data is transferred from the vehicle, privacy is protected during transfer and analysis of the data (Step 4 and 5). In this way, the driver can be confident that his privacy is protected without relying on the manufacturer of the vehicle or the provider of the IDS solution.

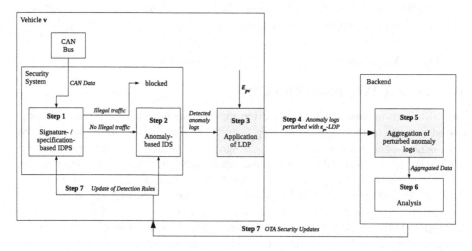

Fig. 3. Illustration of privacy protection using LDP in our scheme of a generic IDS system from the viewpoint of a vehicle.

4.2   Modelling Anomaly Logs

After introducing the model of the generic IVN IDS with LDP, we now elaborate on the form of anomaly logs, their content and how to apply LDP to them. We provide a formal model of an anomaly log and LDP for anomaly logs, as well as possible data types and their privacy sensitivity. These are used in Sect. 4.3 to give concrete scenarios of anomaly log transmission.

LDP for Anomaly Logs. We will now provide a formal definition of Local Differential Privacy for anomaly logs. We assume that an anomaly log consists of multiple, insensitive or sensitive parts, among which the privacy budget ϵ_p is distributed. We define an anomaly log and LDP for Vehicle Anomaly Data:

Definition 2 (Anomaly Log). *An anomaly log is a tuple* $L = (v, w)$*. The tuple* $v = (v_1, v_2, ..., v_j)$ *consists of* j *attributes that are privacy sensitive. The tuple* $w = (w_1, w_2, ..., w_k)$ *consists of the* k *attributes that are privacy insensitive.*

Definition 3 (LDP for Vehicle Anomaly Data). *Let* $L = (v, w)$ *be an anomaly log,* $v = (v_1, v_2, ..., v_j)$ *be the privacy sensitive attributes of the log and* $w = (w_1, w_2, ..., w_k)$ *be the privacy insensitive attributes. Let* V_i *be the domain from which the attribute* v_i *comes. Let* $\epsilon_p \in \mathbb{R}$ *be the personal privacy parameter that is selected by the user. Let* $\epsilon = (\epsilon_1, \epsilon_2, ..., \epsilon_j) \in \mathbb{R}^j$ *such that* $\epsilon_i \geq 0$ *for all* i*. Let* $A = (A_1, A_2, ..., A_j)$ *be a tuple of algorithms. LDP for Anomaly Data is satisfied if:*

1. $\sum_{i=1}^{j} \epsilon_i \leq \epsilon_p$
2. *For every* $i \in [1, j]$*, every* $v_{i1}, v_{i2} \in V_i$ *and every* $R \subseteq Range(A_i)$*:*
   $Pr[A_i(v_{i1}) \in R] \leq exp(\epsilon_i) \cdot Pr[A_i(v_{i2}) \in R]$

This means that we select an algorithm for each individual part. Each algorithm must satisfy ϵ_i-LDP for its own part. Due to the sequential composition of LDP, the sum of all used partial budgets ϵ_i must not surpass the privacy budget ϵ_p to guarantee ϵ_p-LDP in total. This definition is general enough to be applicable to various scenarios of anomaly log transmission regarding the actual content, data types and algorithms used. In order to apply this definition in practice, we further specify possible contents of an anomaly log and their sensitivity.

Content and Data Types in an Anomaly Log. First, we consider data types that may be useful for an anomaly log of an IDS on the CAN Bus. We call these data types "abstract" data types and their concrete, mathematical representation the "basic" data type. The relevant abstract data types are these:

- *CAN Frame*: Under the assumption that the anomaly-based IDS that detected the anomaly operates on CAN data, CAN frames are relevant to give information about the anomaly. The relevant parts of a CAN frame are the CAN ID and the DATA field. The CAN DATA field has the basic data type of "general binary data", as it is a bit vector with a length of up to 64, and we can not assume anything about the content or structure. The CAN ID field can also be seen as general binary data, but it is known that it contains a numeric identifier value. Thus, it should be viewed as discrete numeric or categorical data. For the purpose of logging, we assume that each CAN frame is paired with a timestamp, which can be viewed as continuous numeric data.
- *High level data*: This type of data respects the semantics of CAN Bus messages and can be directly derived from CAN frames. Usually, information proprietary to vehicle manufacturers is needed for this task. This abstract data type can consist of various different basic data types. These types are single bits, continuous numeric data, discrete numerical or categorical data.

- *Metadata about the anomaly*: It is reasonable to assume that metainformation about the anomalies benefits the analysis. For example, the IDS could differentiate different types of anomalies/attacks and send this information. This metainformation can consist of any basic type.
- *Metadata about driving situation*: There are several more types of metainformation that don't directly concern the anomaly, but the situation in which it occurred and are collected additionally. Examples are the time of detection, the location at which the anomaly was detected, information about the driver and more. This abstract type can also contain any of the basic types.

Sensitive and Insensitive Data Types. Based on the information that they contain, we classify the abstract data types into sensitive and insensitive data types. The LDP techniques are applied only to the sensitive data types for privacy protection. In order to not jeopardize the privacy protection efforts, only a very limited amount of information should be classified as insensitive and transmitted without the application of LDP. Thus, we assume that only timestamps (relative to the start of the anomaly log) and metainformation about the anomaly should be considered insensitive, since other data can be used to deduce locations, driving behaviour, usage of vehicle features and more.

4.3   Scenarios of Anomaly Log Transmission

Based on our knowledge of the possible data types, we now illustrate possible scenarios of anomaly log transmission such that our definition of LDP for anomaly logs is satisfied. We give three concrete instantiations of such a scenario.

Scenario 1: Transmission of a whole log of CAN frames: In this scenario, a log of all CAN Bus traffic surrounding the anomaly is constructed. This means that a certain number of messages n around the detection of the anomaly are included. Additionally, metainformation about the anomaly type is transmitted. An anomaly log (v, w) is created in the following way: v contains all the CAN frames divided into ID and DATA fields. w contains timestamps and the type of the anomaly determined by the IDS. Using one algorithm suitable for reporting CAN ID values with LDP and one for CAN DATA fields, the log is perturbed. The privacy budget is divided equally among the CAN frames, and a fixed ratio is used to divide the budget per frame between the ID and DATA field.

Scenario 2: Transmission of a single random CAN frame: Since the transmission of large amounts of data requires adding a high amount of noise, in this scenario, only a single CAN frame is randomly selected from the CAN traffic log and transmitted to the backend. This allows using less privacy budget or sending less, but more accurate information with the same budget. Additionally, metainformation about the anomaly type is transmitted. The anomaly log (v, w) consists of the following components: v contains the single CAN ID and DATA field, w contains the anomaly type. The algorithms are selected as in Scenario 1. The privacy budget is divided between ID and DATA field with a fixed ratio.

Scenario 3: Transmission of only CAN frames that have been classified as anomalous: Here, it is assumed that the IDS is able to determine which frame caused the detected anomaly. Then, only one CAN frame that was classified as anomalous is transmitted to the backend, again with metainformation about the anomaly and timestamps. Else, this scenario is equivalent to Scenario 2.

Further scenarios are possible, e.g. including high level data, which were not in the focus of this work and the evaluation.

5 Evaluation

We performed an evaluation of our approach in the described scenarios. In this section, we describe the used dataset, our methodology and the results.

5.1 Dataset

For the evaluation, we obtained the *"Car-Hacking Dataset"* [14] created by the Hacking and Countermeasures Research Lab (HCRL) at Korea University. The labelled dataset contains 5 parts of CAN traffic, each lasting about 30–40 min: "DoS", "Fuzzy", "Spoofing gear", "Spoofing RPM" and attack-free data. The message counts for each part can be seen in Fig. 4. Each attack was performed for 3–5 s and every part contains 300 attacks. For the DoS attack, a message with the ID 0x000 was injected at high frequency. For the Fuzzy attack, a message with a random ID and payload was injected. In the two spoofing attacks, a message was injected with the CAN ID for gear (0×316) respectively RPM $(0 \times 43f)$ information. The attributes collected are the timestamp, CAN ID, DLC (Data Length Code), the DATA field, and the label (injected or normal message). The dataset was created for and first used by Seo et al. in [28]. It is also used in [29]. It is available at https://sites.google.com/a/hksecurity.net/ocslab/Datasets/CAN-intrusion-dataset.

Attack Type	# of messages	# of normal messages	# of injected messages
DoS Attack	3,665,771	3,078,250	587,521
Fuzzy Attack	3,838,860	3,347,013	491,847
Spoofing the drive gear	4,443,142	3,845,890	597,252
Spoofing the RPM gauze	4,621,702	3,966,805	654,897
GIDS: Attack-free (normal)	988,987	988,872	-

Fig. 4. Message counts for each part of the HCRL Car-Hacking Dataset [14].

5.2 Methodology

Here, we will describe the methodology and setup of our evaluation. We evaluate *Scenario 1* (Transmission of a whole log of CAN frames), *Scenario 2* (Transmission of a random frame from the log) and *Scenario 3* (Transmission of a frame that is marked as anomalous). In each scenario, we evaluate various population sizes, where the population size is the number of users reporting at a time, LDP algorithms and values of the privacy parameter ϵ_p. In every configuration, we run the evaluation 5 times. We first describe the values we use for the mentioned parameters, then the evaluation procedure and finally the analysis of the results.

Parameters

LDP Algorithms. For the transmission of CAN IDs, we assume the existence of two cases that influence the algorithm choices: In the first case, only CAN IDs occurring in normal traffic are allowed on the bus, and all other IDs are filtered out by the Signature-/specification-based IDPS component (see Fig. 3). In our dataset, there are 27 normal IDs if the ID of $0x000$ is considered a normal ID, whereas the maximum number of IDs is 2048 (11-bit CAN IDs are used in the dataset). Such a reduced domain size is of advantage for processing times and the utility of the produced data. However, the Fuzzy attack can not be evaluated in this case, as all possible IDs occur in this part. In the second case, the anomaly logs can contain any of the 2048 possible IDs. The LDP algorithms we use are:

CAN ID Field (Only Normal IDs Allowed): Exponential Mechanism (EM) [19] (originally used for central DP), Optimized Unary Encoding (OUE) [34]. These algorithms can estimate the frequency of all possible values. Due to the small domain of 27 elements, Unary Encoding techniques (bit vector with 1 digit for every possible value is reported) can be efficiently used here. For the EM, which needs a utility function for user values, we encode each ID into an integer number corresponding to the order of IDs, i.e. the lowest ID is encoded to 0 and the highest to 26. The distance between numbers is the utility function.

CAN ID Field (All IDs Allowed): Optimized Local Hashing (OLH) [34]. Because of the larger domain (2048 elements), we use OLH, which uses hash functions to reduce communication cost while requiring more computation during aggregation. We did not evaluate the EM in this case because of poor results even with the normal IDs. We did not include OUE here because of its large communication cost (a vector of 2048 bits for each report).

CAN DATA Field/Payload: Our choices were guided by the large domain size of 2^{64} for 64-bit long DATA fields, making it impossible to estimate frequencies for every value. We use Parallel Randomized Response (PRR), which estimates the mean of each individual bit. Also, we use the Prefix Extending Method (PEM) [32]. It can identify the most common values and their frequencies (heavy hitters). It divides users into groups that report prefixes of increasing length using OLH. With PEM, we identify the top 4 heavy hitters. For a DATA field of 64 bits, we use 6 groups with prefix lengths of 12, 22, 32, 42, 53 and 64.

These choices support fast computation times, as the needed time is exponential in the prefix length extension per group. By using less groups, one may improve the accuracy while increasing the computation time.

Population Sizes. Population size in this context refers to the amount of reports on an anomaly that can be aggregated at once. The maximum population size that can be used is limited by the number of attacks in the dataset. We assume that one anomaly log in Scenario 1 contains 10 CAN frames in our evaluation. We construct the logs by choosing one attack frame and the 9 frames following it, ensuring at least one attack frame (but usually more) in each log. Using this approach, the maximum amount of anomaly logs that can be constructed from the DoS dataset is 103180. Thus, we limit the maximum population size to 100000 and consider the following population sizes: $[1000, 10000, 25000, 50000, 100000]$.

Privacy Parameter Settings. While we created our model to be as general as possible by allowing each user to choose their own privacy parameter ϵ_p, we will assume that all users choose the same privacy parameter in this evaluation. The privacy parameter indicates the available privacy budget *per anomaly log* in this context. We evaluate the integer values in the range $[1, 10]$ as privacy parameters per anomaly log. Further, we use 70% of the privacy budget available for one frame for the DATA field and 30% for the ID field.

Anomaly Labels by the IDS. For the sake of simplicity, we assume that the IDS is able to perfectly tell apart the different attack types occurring in our dataset. In our scenarios (Sect. 4.3), we assume that the anomaly type is sent unperturbed in the anomaly log by each user. Thus, the aggregator is also able to distinguish anomaly logs originating from different anomalies. This allows us to perform the evaluation on each part of the dataset individually.

Used Hardware and Software. The evaluation was conducted on a machine with an AMD Ryzen 7 3700X and 16 GB of RAM and a machine with an AMD FX-6300 and 8 GB of RAM. Both machines used Windows 10. Python 3 was used for the implementation. The used third-party packages were diffprivlib, numpy, xxhash and matplotlib (pyplot). For the Exponential Mechanism, we used the implementation in the "DiffPrivLib" package by IBM [16]. For OLH, we took inspiration from the implementation by Wang available at [33].

Evaluation Procedure. Here, we describe the steps taken in our evaluation. These are Data Preprocessing, Perturbation, Aggregation and Analysis.

Data Preprocessing. For each of the attack datasets, we create the anomaly logs for each population size in Scenario 1 by finding a frame labelled as malicious and extracting this and the following 9 frames. From each of these anomaly logs, an anomaly log for Scenario 2 is created by choosing a random frame from the log and one for Scenario 3 by choosing the first frame from the log. Further, we use the attack-free part in the dataset to create a histogram of the normally occurring CAN IDs and DATA field values, which is used in the analysis step.

Perturbation. For each combination of population size, privacy parameter ϵ_p, dataset part and scenario, the corresponding input dataset D is loaded. Let ϵ_f be the privacy budget per CAN frame ($0.1 \cdot \epsilon_p$ in Scenario 1). We run each algorithm $A_I \in \{EM, OUE, OLH\}$ on D with the privacy budget $\epsilon_i = \epsilon_f \cdot 0.3$ to create perturbed CAN ID data. On the Fuzzy dataset, perturbed data are only created for the case of 2048 allowed IDs (using OLH). We run each algorithm $A_D \in \{PRR, PEM\}$ on D with the privacy budget $\epsilon_d = \epsilon_f * 0.7$ to create perturbed CAN DATA field data. In Scenario 1, the algorithms are run on all 10 frames in each anomaly log individually.

Aggregation and Analysis. For each scenario, population size, privacy parameter and dataset part, we aggregate the perturbed data in the following way: For each algorithm $A_I \in \{EM, OUE, OLH\}$, we aggregate the perturbed ID data into a histogram of ID frequencies. For the PEM algorithm, we aggregate the perturbed DATA field data to identify the $k = 4$ top heavy hitters and their frequencies. For the PRR algorithm, we use the perturbed DATA field data to estimate the frequency (which is also the mean) of every bit individually. The aggregated data are analyzed dependent on the dataset part used and thus the anomaly label: For the DoS Attack, we use the ID data to infer the CAN ID used in the attack. For the Gear spoofing and RPM spoofing attacks, we try to both identify CAN ID and DATA values used in the attack. Because the Fuzzy attack in our dataset uses completely random IDs and payloads, it is impossible to identify a single or few IDs and payloads responsible for the attack. In order to find out malicious CAN IDs and DATA field values, we use the histogram of ID values that was created from the aggregated anomaly logs respectively the heavy hitter DATA fields estimated by PEM. Frequencies of IDs and DATA fields that are smaller than 5% are considered insignificant and set to 0. The frequencies of IDs and DATA fields are then compared to a histogram of normal CAN traffic. Any value that is more than 3 times as frequent as in the normal data is pointed out as possible cause of the anomaly. If the PRR algorithm was used, only one DATA field value is always identified using the frequencies estimated for each bit: If the estimated frequency of a bit is higher than 0.5, it is set to 1, else to 0. The bit vector constructed in this way is pointed out as a malicious payload.

Evaluation of the Analysis Results. We evaluate the analysis results in two ways: First, we compare the empirical error (Mean Absolute Error (MAE) averaged over the 5 runs) induced by the perturbation when compared with the same aggregation on unperturbed data. For the CAN ID algorithms, we create a histogram of the used IDs in the unperturbed input dataset and compare it with the estimated histogram (before post-processing). We compute the MAE between the two histograms. For the PRR algorithm, we compute the mean of each bit in the unperturbed data and use the MAE between the estimated mean values and the true values. For the PEM algorithm, we compare the up to 4 estimated heavy hitters and their frequencies with the true heavy hitters computed from the unperturbed data. We again use MAE between the estimated and the true frequencies. If a true heavy hitter is not identified, or an identified heavy hitter is not a true heavy hitter, the frequency of this heavy hitter is added to the error sum before the mean is taken. If CAN ID or DATA field values that caused the anomaly are inferred, we count one inference as successful detection if the inferred value actually caused the anomaly. If a value that was not the cause of the anomaly was inferred, we count this as a false positive. We compute the detection rate and precision over the 5 runs of each evaluation setup.

5.3 Results

We now describe the findings of our evaluation. We illustrate the findings using plots, where one plot shows the performance (w.r.t. quality of results, not computing performance) of one algorithm in one scenario for all ϵ values and population sizes. Each plot contains 3 subplots containing empirical error, detection rate or precision for all ϵ values with one graph for each population size. We found that the obtained results for the DoS, RPM and Gear datasets were almost identical across all scenarios, which is why we only show plots for the RPM dataset for brevity. Throughout the experiments, it is a common feature that the incurred error drops when the privacy parameter ϵ is increased, as well as when the population size is increased. In the same way, the detection rate and precision rise. This is the expected behaviour, as larger samples decrease variance and a larger ϵ allows for more accurate information in one report. For the population size of 1000, the performance was inferior to the other population sizes. The MAE was a lot higher than the error for other population sizes, which is also manifested in a slower rise of the detection rate and precision with ϵ. This leads us to the conclusion that a population size of 1000 is not sufficient for our use case in all of the tested scenarios. With larger population sizes, especially 25000 and upwards, meaningful results can be obtained while using smaller ϵ. While the population size of 100000 led to the best performance, the improvement over 50000 was very small in most cases. In a real world scenario, it is obviously best to use the largest available population size that can still be processed in an appropriate time.

An interesting observation is that the performance in Scenario 1, in which a log of 10 CAN frames is transmitted in each report, was inferior to the performance in the Scenarios 2 and 3, where one CAN frame is transmitted. Even though the largest amount of data is collected in Scenario 1, the MAE was typically about 3 to 5 times as high as the Error of the same algorithm run on the same dataset part, but under Scenario 2 or 3. The achieved detection rates and precision in Scenario 1 also rose slower than in Scenario 2 and 3. We show this using OUE as an example, illustrated using Fig. 5, which shows the performance of OUE on the RPM dataset in Scenario 1 and 2. When using OUE in Scenario 1, the error was consistently big: For any population size, the MAE was always larger than 0.3, which is a large amount when remembering that the true value is a histogram of ID Frequencies where the sum of all frequencies is 1, which means that most individual frequencies are a lot smaller than 0.3. While the detection rate was 1 for all population sizes and ϵ values, meaning that the malicious ID could always be identified, the precision increased noticeably smaller than in Scenario 2 and 3, where a precision of 1 was achieved for every population size greater than 1000 even with $\epsilon = 1$. Because ϵ designates the privacy budget available per log, the budget that is available per CAN frame in Scenario 1 is only $\frac{1}{10}$ of ϵ. Thus, every single frame needs to be perturbed a lot more to achieve ϵ-LDP for the whole log. In Scenario 2 and 3, only one frame is contained in the anomaly logs, and the whole ϵ can be used for this frame. Thus, each individual frame is perturbed much less than each frame in Scenario 1. The errors show that sending a small amount of data with low perturbation per data unit is better for the utility of the analysis results than sending a large amount of data among which the privacy budget needs to be divided, leading to high perturbation per data unit. Thus, the transmission of anomaly logs with LDP should take place in Scenario 2 or 3 and not Scenario 1.

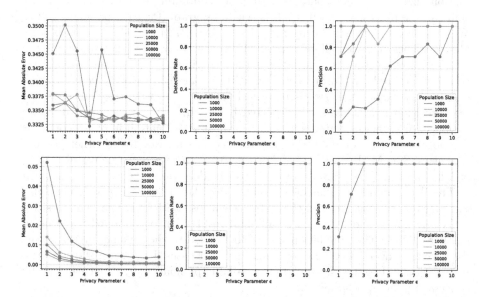

Fig. 5. Performance of the Optimized Unary Encoding on the RPM dataset in Sc. 1 (top) and Sc.2 (bottom)

When viewing the effectiveness of detecting malicious IDs and payloads with respect to the used ϵ, very good detection rate and precision were usually obtained for most population sizes with ϵ of 3 and more per anomaly log, even in Scenario 1. This indicates that a higher privacy budget per log is not necessary in our case. Choosing a too high budget may even be counterproductive, as it may lead to a rapid decrease in the protection level if multiple reports are sent by one user. Then, that a stricter limit on the number of reports per user might need to be used. If the same information can be learned using less privacy budget, this decreases the total amount of useful information learnable by the aggregator.

An exception from the good results seen with most algorithms is the EM. It showed consistently bad performance in all scenarios, with unacceptably high error and low precision, as demonstrated in Fig. 6 for Scenario 3 with the RPM dataset. Even here, an improvement in detection rate and precision can be seen in the Scenarios 2 and 3 over Scenario 1. The bad results with normal IDs were the main reason why we did not evaluate the EM with the full ID range. Because of its bad performance, not the EM should be used to infer malicious CAN IDs, but OUE and OLH. These two algorithms showed a good performance in all scenarios even with low ϵ values and small population sizes as seen in Fig. 5 and 6 in Scenario 2.

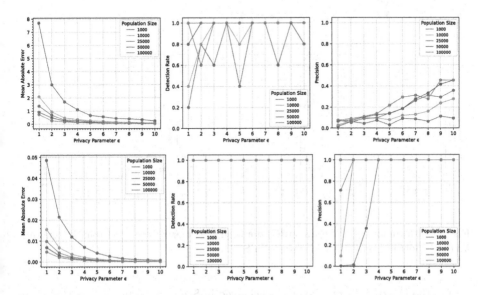

Fig. 6. Performance of the Exponential Mechanism in Sc.3 (top) and Optimized Local Hashing in Sc.2 (bottom) on the RPM dataset

An appealing property of using PRR for the DATA field is its simplicity. However, the identification of a suspicious payload value using the mean of each individual bit can only succeed if the malicious payload dominates all other payloads: Even when using unperturbed data, the frequency of the malicious payload needs to be above 0.5 in order to be able to identify it in any case. Even one estimation that is on the wrong side of 0.5 makes the identified heavy hitter a false positive. Thus, PRR in the way it is used here is not a robust way to identify a malicious payload. This is also reflected by our experimental results, as PRR was not able to identify any malicious payload in Scenario 1 and 2. Only in Scenario 3, where *all* frames contain the malicious payload, this payload could be identified. Still, the identification with our proposed upper bound of $\epsilon = 3$ only had a good success rate for a population size of 25000 and more. Even in Scenario 3, the PRR algorithm would have almost no chance in identifying a malicious payload if multiple payloads are part of the attack. Thus, we do not recommend using PRR for the DATA field, but PEM, which showed a consistently good performance in all Scenarios. PEM is more robust, can detect multiple values and determine frequencies while outperforming PRR in all scenarios. The performance in Scenario 2 can be compared in Fig. 7.

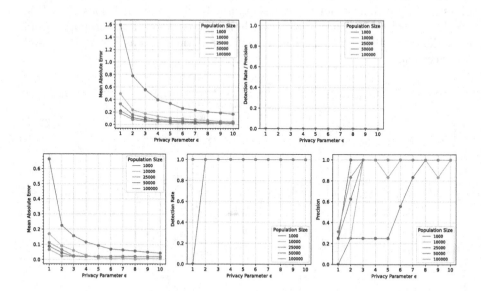

Fig. 7. Performance of the Parallel Randomized Response (top) and Prefix Extending Method (bottom) on the RPM dataset in Sc. 2

On the Fuzzy dataset, the errors achieved in Scenario 2 and 3 show that it is still possible to closely estimate the frequencies of IDs and payload values even if random data are injected into the anomaly logs. However, these results do not carry much more information than the fact that a fuzzy attack is going on.

Limitations. The main limitation of our results is that the attacks and thus the identification tasks that are associated with the dataset parts "DoS", "Gear" and "RPM" are relatively simple and similar: In each of these attacks, messages with one single CAN ID are injected, and each injected message carries the same payload. This likely is the reason why the performance of the algorithms was extremely similar on these three dataset parts. Thus, the performance of the used algorithms in more complicated situations, for example if the input data are mixed from multiple datasets is of interest. In a trial on a mix of 25% data from the RPM part, 25% of the Gear part and 50% of the Fuzzy part in Scenario 3 with a population size of 10000 and $\epsilon = 3$, PEM correctly identified both malicious payloads associated with the RPM and Gear parts. Two other payload values were identified with frequencies below 5% and would thus be discarded in our analysis. This result indicates the effective applicability of our approach even if data from different attacks are mixed up at the aggregator. However, this needs to be evaluated more thoroughly to be confirmed. Overall, the results show that it is indeed possible to transmit anomaly logs to a backend while using LDP algorithms to provide privacy guarantees. It is possible to recover relevant information about the attacks that caused the creation of the transmitted anomaly logs from the aggregated data. In particular, promising results were achieved with OUE, OLH and PEM. We showed possibility of the effective recovery of basic pieces of information about the anomalies from the perturbed anomaly data, namely the CAN IDs and payloads used in the attacks.

6   Conclusion

In this work, we highlight the tension between cybersecurity for In-Vehicle Networks (IVN) and privacy implications of transferring CAN logs to remote server for further analysis. We propose applying Local Differential Privacy (LDP) techniques to CAN anomaly logs as a means to lessen such a tension. LDP techniques perturbe IVN data before transfer to a remote collector and provide strong, formal privacy guarantees. The underlying architecture here is an adaptation of a generic deployment of an In-Vehicle IDS that ressembles approaches from the industry. In contrast to the widespread In-Vehicle IDS deployment model, our architecture and model aim to protect the privacy of individuals even if IVN data is transferred to the backend. The proposed model includes the perturbation of the anomaly logs using LDP techniques on the vehicle side, and an aggregation step of multiple perturbed logs on the backend side. The proposed adaptations for the transfer of anomaly logs to the backend server using LDP algorithms are generic enough to cover various scenarios for In-Vehicle IDS. We performed an experimental evaluation of our proposal in three different attack scenarios. Our evaluation aimed at assessing whether it is possible to ensure privacy via LDP while preserving the ability to learn useful information about ongoing attacks from the collected IVN data. In our underlying scenarios, anomaly logs consist of varying amounts of frames from the CAN Bus. Using various LDP algorithms and a widely used CAN intrusion dataset, we showed that it is possible to recover useful information about attacks from the perturbed anomaly logs while preventing re-identification. Our results have promising implications for the possibility of privacy-preserving IDS for In-Vehicle Networks, even though they are currently limited to relatively simple pieces of information about attacks that are recovered.

6.1   Further Research

As part of future work, it may be interesting to conduct a complete evaluation of more sophisticated scenarios including mixed attacks. Another interesting topic could be a thorough investigation of the impact of continuous reporting of anomaly logs on privacy degradation and lowering this impact. Investigating how users may choose a personalized ϵ is another item for future research.

Acknowledgments. This research work has been funded in part by the German Federal Ministry of Education and Research (BMBF) and the Hessen State Ministry for Higher Education, Research and the Arts within their joint support of the National Research Center for Applied Cybersecurity ATHENE, and co-funded by the BMBF within the project "Forum Privatheit und selbstbestimmtes Leben in der Digitalen Welt".

References

1. Apple: Apple carplay. https://www.apple.com/ios/carplay
2. Boehner, M.: Security for connected vehicles throughout the entire life cycle. ATZ-electronics Worldwide **14**(1–2), 16–21 (2019)
3. Cai, Z., Wang, A., Zhang, W., Gruffke, M., Schweppe, H.: 0-days & mitigations: roadways to exploit and secure connected BMW cars. Black Hat USA (2019)
4. Checkoway, S., et al.: Comprehensive experimental analyses of automotive attack surfaces. In: USENIX Security Symposium, San Francisco, vol. 4, pp. 447–462 (2011)
5. Cho, K.T., Shin, K.G.: Fingerprinting electronic control units for vehicle intrusion detection. In: Proceedings of the 25th USENIX Conference on Security Symposium, SEC 2016, USA, pp. 911–927. USENIX Association (2016)
6. Coroama, V.: The smart tachograph - individual accounting of traffic costs and its implications, pp. 135–152, May 2006. https://doi.org/10.1007/11748625_9
7. Dwork, C.: Differential privacy: a survey of results. In: Agrawal, M., Du, D., Duan, Z., Li, A. (eds.) TAMC 2008. LNCS, vol. 4978, pp. 1–19. Springer, Heidelberg (2008). https://doi.org/10.1007/978-3-540-79228-4_1
8. Enev, M., Takakuwa, A., Koscher, K., Kohno, T.: Automobile driver fingerprinting. Proc. Priv. Enhancing Technol. **2016**(1), 34–50 (2016)
9. ESCRYPT: Flyer: intrusion detection and prevention, May 2018. https://www.escrypt.com/sites/default/files/2018-08/ESCRYPT_Flyer_IDPS_Web.pdf
10. European Commision: The interoperable EU-wide eCall. https://ec.europa.eu/transport/themes/its/road/action_plan/ecall_en
11. Fanti, G., Pihur, V., Erlingsson, Ú.: Building a rappor with the unknown: privacy-preserving learning of associations and data dictionaries. Proc. Priv. Enhancing Technol. (PoPETS) **2016**(3), 41–61 (2016)
12. Gao, X., Firner, B., Sugrim, S., Kaiser-Pendergrast, V., Yang, Y., Lindqvist, J.: Elastic pathing: your speed is enough to track you. In: Proceedings of the 2014 ACM International Joint Conference on Pervasive and Ubiquitous Computing, UbiComp 2014, pp. 975–986. Association for Computing Machinery, New York (2014). https://doi.org/10.1145/2632048.2632077
13. Google: Android auto. https://www.android.com/auto
14. Hacking and Countermeasures Research Lab: Car-hacking dataset. https://ocslab.hksecurity.net/Datasets/CAN-intrusion-dataset
15. Hoppe, T., Kiltz, S., Dittmann, J.: Security threats to automotive CAN networks – practical examples and selected short-term countermeasures. In: Harrison, M.D., Sujan, M.-A. (eds.) SAFECOMP 2008. LNCS, vol. 5219, pp. 235–248. Springer, Heidelberg (2008). https://doi.org/10.1007/978-3-540-87698-4_21
16. IBM: Diffprivlib: The IBM differential privacy library (version 0.2.1) (2020). https://github.com/IBM/differential-privacy-library
17. Kairouz, P., Oh, S., Viswanath, P.: Extremal mechanisms for local differential privacy. In: Advances in Neural Information Processing Systems, vol. 27, pp. 2879–2887 (2014)

18. Lawson, P., McPhail, B., Lawton, E.: The connected car: who is in the driver's seat? A study on privacy and onboard vehicle telematics technology (2015)
19. McSherry, F., Talwar, K.: Mechanism design via differential privacy. In: 48th Annual IEEE Symposium on Foundations of Computer Science (FOCS 2007), pp. 94–103, October 2007. https://doi.org/10.1109/FOCS.2007.66
20. Miller, C., Valasek, C.: Remote exploitation of an unaltered passenger vehicle. Black Hat USA 2015, 91 (2015)
21. Nie, S., Liu, L., Du, Y.: Free-fall: hacking tesla from wireless to can bus. Briefing, Black Hat USA, pp. 1–16 (2017)
22. Nowdehi, N., Aoudi, W., Almgren, M., Olovsson, T.: CASAD: CAN-aware stealthy-attack detection for in-vehicle networks. arXiv preprint arXiv:1909.08407 (2019)
23. Nürnberger, S., Rossow, C.: – vatiCAN – vetted, authenticated CAN bus. In: Gierlichs, B., Poschmann, A.Y. (eds.) CHES 2016. LNCS, vol. 9813, pp. 106–124. Springer, Heidelberg (2016). https://doi.org/10.1007/978-3-662-53140-2_6
24. Radu, A.-I., Garcia, F.D.: LeiA: A lightweight authentication protocol for CAN. In: Askoxylakis, I., Ioannidis, S., Katsikas, S., Meadows, C. (eds.) ESORICS 2016. LNCS, vol. 9879, pp. 283–300. Springer, Cham (2016). https://doi.org/10.1007/978-3-319-45741-3_15
25. Robert Bosch GmbH: CAN Specification, Version 2.0
26. Robert Bosch GmbH: Can with flexible data-rate, specification version 1.0
27. Schoitsch, E., Schmittner, C., Ma, Z., Gruber, T.: The need for safety and cyber-security co-engineering and standardization for highly automated automotive vehicles. In: Schulze, T., Müller, B., Meyer, G. (eds.) Advanced Microsystems for Automotive Applications 2015. LNM, pp. 251–261. Springer, Cham (2016). https://doi.org/10.1007/978-3-319-20855-8_20
28. Seo, E., Song, H.M., Kim, H.K.: GIDS: gan based intrusion detection system for in-vehicle network. In: 2018 16th Annual Conference on Privacy, Security and Trust (PST), pp. 1–6, August 2018. https://doi.org/10.1109/PST.2018.8514157
29. Song, H.M., Woo, J., Kim, H.K.: In-vehicle network intrusion detection using deep convolutional neural network. Veh. Commun. 21, 100198 (2020)
30. Tesla: Introducing software version 10.0. https://www.tesla.com/blog/introducing-software-version-10-0
31. Tomlinson, A., Bryans, J., Shaikh, S.A., Kalutarage, H.K.: Detection of automotive can cyber-attacks by identifying packet timing anomalies in time windows. In: 2018 48th Annual IEEE/IFIP International Conference on Dependable Systems and Networks Workshops (DSN-W), pp. 231–238, June 2018. https://doi.org/10.1109/DSN-W.2018.00069
32. Wang, T., Li, N., Jha, S.: Locally differentially private heavy hitter identification. IEEE Trans. Dependable Secure Comput. 18, 982–993 (2019)
33. Wang, T.: Implementation of optimized local hashing (OLH) (2019). https://github.com/vvv214/LDP_Protocols/blob/master/olh.py
34. Wang, T., Blocki, J., Li, N., Jha, S.: Locally differentially private protocols for frequency estimation. In: 26th USENIX Security Symposium (USENIX Security 17), pp. 729–745, August 2017. https://www.usenix.org/conference/usenixsecurity17/technical-sessions/presentation/wang-tianhao
35. Wolf, M., Weimerskirch, A., Paar, C.: Security in automotive bus systems. In: Proceedings Of The Workshop On Embedded Security In Cars (ESCAR) (2004)
36. Yaron Galula, M.B.: Combining the strengths of Elektrobit's SecOC with argus IDPS. Technical report Elektrobit Automotive GmbH (2017). https://www.elektrobit.com/tech-corner/combining-strengths-ebs-secoc-argus-idps/

Strong Customer Authentication in Online Payments Under GDPR and PSD2: A Case of Cumulative Application

Danaja Fabcic[✉][ID]

Centre for IT & IP Law, KU Leuven, Leuven, Belgium
danaja.fabcic@kuleuven.be
https://www.law.kuleuven.be/citip/

Abstract. Authentication is the process of confirming the user's identity before the payment can be performed. It contributes to cybersecurity by preventing access by unauthorised parties. However, in e-payments the authentication differs from traditional identity checks since it is performed online and remotely. This paper explores the relationship between two important legal instruments on authentication in payment services: General data protection regulation (Regulation 679/2016) and the Second payment services directive (Directive 2015/2366). This paper shows that while the relationship between the two instruments can be considered unclear, previous research and European soft law favour cumulative application, and not a lex specialis and lex generalis relationship. These findings are then discussed in the context of implementing authentication procedures in compliance with the rules of the GDPR, with a focus on the identity of the controller, legal basis for implementing authentication, and the security requirements under art. 32 of the GDPR. Based on the "means reasonably likely" test from the Breyer judgment, we assume that PSPs could be considered controllers even when processing pseudonymised credentials. Legal grounds to process personal data in an authentication procedure are either performance of a contract or legitimate interests of the controller, insofar as the necessity criterion is met. Relying on legal obligation is, however, more doubtful. Finally, exceptions to strong customer authentication bring their own cybersecurity considerations, since complexity of security systems can lead to more vulnerabilities. When PSD2 and GDPR are both applied, it may mean that compliance with the higher standard is required, which is enabled by the optional nature of art. 18(1) of the RTS.

Keywords: Strong customer authentication · Data protection · Payment services · Cybersecurity

Funding disclaimer. The research for this paper was carried out in the context of two Horizon 2020 projects: FENTEC (Grant agreement no. 780108) and KRAKEN (Grant agreement no. 871473).

M. Friedewald et al. (Eds.): Privacy and Identity 2020, IFIP AICT 619, pp. 78–95, 2021.
https://doi.org/10.1007/978-3-030-72465-8_5

1   Introduction

Online shopping is a growing industry in Europe – Eurostat reports that between 2009 and 2019, the number of online shoppers has doubled, and 60% of Europeans buy online at least once a year. During the first 2020 lockdown, there was an estimated 17.4% growth in online and mail orders[1,2]. Online shopping is facilitated by electronic payments, the online transfer of money through a variety of payment services providers (PSPs). However, identification of online shoppers cannot be performed in person, meaning that PSPs need to counter the risk of fraud, impersonation or unauthorized access to the device [3,11]. As the perpetrators have begun to use more complex and more successful equipment to carry out social engineering attacks, PSPs respond by adopting stronger security measures [13]. These often include authentication, a process intended to confirm the user's identity by the PSP before the payment can be performed [5].

In the European Union, authentication in online payments falls under the Second payment services directive (Directive (EU) 2015/2366, hereafter: PSD2)[3], which requires PSPs to implement strong customer authentication (SCA); or as a security measure under the General data protection regulation (Regulation (EU) 2016/679, hereafter: GDPR)[4] if personal data are processed.

The goal of this paper is to provide clarity on the interplay between GDPR and PSD2 and illustrate their cumulative application on the example of SCA in online payment services within the European Union. The knowledge can be used to help understand lawyers, engineers and computer scientists what are the legal requirements for SCA under these two frameworks. This will contribute to understanding how to best achieve compliance with authentication requirements for actors in e-payments industry, especially those who provide payment services.

The work will follow the existing doctrinal work on the interplay of PSD2 and the GDPR, taking into account applicable legislation and interpretative guidelines by expert bodies, in order to answer the following research question: "What is the relationship between the General data protection regulation and the Second payment services directive; and what is its impact on compliance of strong customer authentication processes?" Methodologically, the paper is based on doctrinal and black letter research.

---

[1] https://ec.europa.eu/eurostat/statistics-explained/index.php?title=Impact_of_Covid-19_crisis_on_retail_trade, last accessed 2020/09/12.

[2] https://ec.europa.eu/eurostat/web/products-eurostat-news/-/DDN-20200420-2, last accessed 2020/09/12.

[3] Directive (EU) 2015/2366 of the European Parliament and of the Council of 25 November 2015 on payment services in the internal market, amending Directives 2002/65/EC, 2009/110/EC and 2013/36/EU and Regulation (EU) No 1093/2010, and repealing Directive 2007/64/EC. OJ L 337.

[4] Regulation (EU) 2016/679 of the European Parliament and of the Council of 27 April 2016 on the protection of natural persons with regard to the processing of personal data and on the free movement of such data, and repealing Directive 95/46/EC (General Data Protection Regulation) (Text with EEA relevance). OJ L 119.

This paper is structured as follows. The first part is descriptive: the legal framework of authentication in EU payment services law is presented, drawing upon the analysis of legal provisions, doctrinal work and soft law documents. In the second part, the relationship between the GDPR and the PSD2 is analysed *in abstracto*, and *in concreto* on the example of authentication.

2   Strong Customer Authentication in EU Legal Framework

European Union regulation of cybersecurity started out in soft-law document: recommendations, communications and guidelines issued by institutions, especially at the political levels (e.g. European Council). Jasmontaite et al. [14] provide an overview of soft law documents issued in the period 2000–2016. The authors note that there is no holistic approach to cybersecurity at the EU level; instead, various frameworks are used, such as network and information security measures, data protection and privacy in electronic communications, and cybercrime legislation.

A possible reason is that the Union has limited competences in the area of cybersecurity under the conferral principle as set out in art. 5 of the Treaty on European Union. (TEU)[5] Under this principle, the EU can only act under the competences conferred upon it by the member states, and the member states retain the other competences. Hence, the EU is restricted to regulating cybersecurity in the context of internal market. Since it is a comparatively new legislative area, some flexibility is necessary. That is achieved by combining minimum harmonisation directives with full harmonisation regulations [12].

EU cybersecurity regulation is based on trade-offs, such as security and utility (the more secure something is, the less usable it is), or privacy against another valuable goal in the e-health, business or finance domain [28]. Authentication is a good example of usability versus security, since users typically don't like complicated passwords, and yet maintaining cybersecurity is an important objective for stakeholders involved[6].

Regulation of cybersecurity in payment services is likewise a relatively new area of EU legislative effort. The two main instruments, which impose cybersecurity obligations and safeguard data in payment services, namely the Second payment services directive (PSD2) and the General data protection regulation (GDPR), were adopted within the context of internal market regulation.

The regulation of electronic payments is layered, following the value chain of payments, (mobile) device, retail and technology, meaning that each subset is subject to a specific set of rules [16]. In this section, the legal framework on authentication in online payment services in the EU is presented.

---

[5] Treaty on European Union. Official consolidated version. OJ C 326/12.

[6] https://social.techcrunch.com/2018/12/25/cybersecurity-101-guide-two-factor/, last accessed 2020/09/12.

2.1 General Data Protection Regulation (GDPR)

The GDPR applies to processing of personal data, which are any information relating to an identified or identifiable natural person (data subject). It was adopted by the European Parliament and the Council in 2016, and has been in force since May 25, 2018. Data protection is an important objective of the European Union: the GDPR was adopted with the aim of contributing to protection of fundamental rights, the area of security, freedom and justice, as well as facilitating exchange of data in the burgeoning economic union of the internal market (recital 2 of the GDPR). The Regulation lays down a comprehensive, cross-sectoral regime for protection of personal data.

Processing is only allowed if there are valid legal grounds, exhaustively listed in art. 6. These are the consent of the data subject, or if processing is necessary for the performance of a contract, compliance with a legal obligation, to protect the vital interests of the data subject or of another natural person, for the performance of a task carried out in the public interest or in the exercise of official authority, or necessary for the purposes of the legitimate interests pursued by the controller or by a third party, unless these interests are overridden by the fundamental rights of the data subject. According to WP29, only one legal basis applies to a data processing activity, and no other legal grounds may be considered.

The central burden of compliance with the obligations contained in the GDPR lies with the data controller, the entity which, alone or jointly with others, determines the purposes and means of the processing of personal data (art. 4(7)). The controller is responsible for implementing appropriate technical and organisational measures to ensure and to be able to demonstrate that processing is performed in a compliant manner (art. 24). This includes the obligation to implement data protection by design and by default (art. 25(1) and (2)), to choose its subcontractors (data processors) with due diligence (art. 28), and to lay down appropriate security measures (art. 32).

In the payment services, the GDPR might apply to issuing and verifying credentials during the authentication process. Credentials can fall under the definition of data processing since they are on principle tied to one specific user. If the user is an identified or identifiable individual natural person, then they are a data subject with-in the meaning of art. 4(1) of the GDPR. This is especially the case if biometrics are used as the second authentication factor.

The GDPR defines biometric data in art. 4(14) as personal data resulting from specific technical processing relating to the physical, physiological or behavioural characteristics of a natural person; these data are then used for unique identification of that natural person. If these data are used for uniquely identifying a natural person, then they fall into a special category of personal data under art. 9 of the GDPR (also called sensitive personal data). Their processing is subject to a stricter regime, and is in principle not allowed unless strict conditions are met, such as explicit consent or other criteria laid down in national legislation. Mobile wallet and mobile bank providers, such as Apple Pay and Google Wallet, give their user a choice between biometric authentication or using a PIN code [11].

2.2 Second Payment Services Directive (PSD2)

PSD2 is a full harmonization directive adopted by the EU in 2015 with the objective of closing the regulatory gaps while at the same time providing more legal clarity and ensuring consistent application of the legislative framework across the Union. The instrument aims to benefit operators of payment services by opening up the market, as well as enhancing consumer protection by providing for safe and secure payment services. Among other goals, the PSD2 addresses the security challenges of ever more complex online payments. In its Recital 7, it states that safe and secure payment services constitute a vital condition for a well-functioning payment services market. Users of payment services should therefore be adequately protected against such risks.

PSD2 applies to payment services provided by payment service providers within the Union. The exhaustive list of payment services is laid down in Annex I to the directive, and includes eight different types of payment services, such as placing cash on a payment account, or execution of payment transactions, including transfers of funds on a payment account, as well as payment initiation services and account information services. A payment service provider is an entity, which falls into one of the six categories laid down in art. 1(a) of the directive, for example: credit institutions as defined in art. 4(1) of Regulation (EU) No 575/2013[7], electronic money institutions within the meaning of art. 2 of Directive 2009/110/EC[8], or payment institutions authorized under Chapter 1 of Title II of the PSD2. The PSD2 also introduces two new types of PSP: an account information service provider, and a payment initiation service provider.

An account information service provider is an online service which provides consolidated information about different payment accounts held by one user (art. 4(16) of PSD2). For example, these are apps that help with budgeting, spending monitoring and financial planning [9][9].

A payment initiation service provider is a service which initiates a payment order at the user's request (art. 4(15) of PSD2), thus providing an alternative to users not possessing or not wishing to use credit cards. For example, a payment initiative service provider is Sofort in Germany[10], and Bancontact in Belgium[11].

---

[7] Regulation (EU) No 575/2013 of the European Parliament and of the Council of 26 June 2013 on prudential requirements for credit institutions and investment firms and amending Regulation (EU) No 648/2012. OJ L 176.

[8] Directive 2009/110/EC of the European Parliament and of the Council of 16 September 2009 on the taking up, pursuit and prudential supervision of the business of electronic money institutions amending Directives 2005/60/EC and 2006/48/EC and repealing Directive 2000/46/EC. OJ L 267.

[9] https://ec.europa.eu/commission/presscorner/detail/fr/MEMO_15_5793, last accessed 2020/09/14.

[10] https://www.sofort.de/, last accessed 2020/09/14.

[11] https://www.bancontact.com/en, last accessed 2020/09/14.

The PSD2 has a dedicated chapter on cybersecurity. Its Sect. 5 is entitled 'Operational and security risks and authentication'. Under art. 95, PSPs must implement mitigation measures and control mechanisms to manage the operational and security risks (art. 95(1) of PSD2), and to report those mechanisms regularly to the competent authority (art. 95(2) of PSD2).

Under the first paragraph of the article, PSPs are required to establish a frame-work with appropriate mitigation measures and control mechanisms to manage the operational and security risks, relating to the payment services they provide. The establishment and maintenance of effective incident management procedures, including for the detection and classification of major operational and security incidents, is part of the mitigation and control framework. The second paragraph obliges PSPs to report those mechanisms to competent authorities regularly. More specifically, PSPs need to provide an updated and comprehensive assessment of the operational and security risks relating to the payment services they provide, and report on the adequacy of the mitigation measures and control mechanisms implemented in response to those risks.

The third paragraph gives EBA the mandate to issue guidelines on the establishment, implementation and monitoring of the security measures; the guidance was given in late 2019 [4].

Art. 97 lays down authentication obligations. PSD2 defines authentication in art. 4(2) as a procedure which allows the payment service provider to verify the identity of a payment service user or the validity of the use of a specific payment instrument, including the use of the user's personalised security credentials. Personalised security credentials mean personalised features provided by the payment service provider to a payment service user for the purposes of authentication (art. 4(31) of PSD2).

Strong customer authentication (SCA) is defined in art. 4(30) as an authentication based on the use of two or more elements. Those elements can be knowledge (something only the user knows), possession (something only the user possesses) or inherence (something the user is); the elements must be independent, in that the breach of one does not compromise the reliability of the others, and is designed in such a way as to protect the confidentiality of the authentication data. However, PSD2 explicitly requires PSPs to put into place only user or customer authentication, whereas authentication of other actors may fall under general requirements of art. 95. It is unclear why the legislator has taken this decision given the contribution of authentication to cybersecurity of PSPs.

PSPs are required to apply strong customer authentication in three instances, when the payer (a) accesses its payment account online; (b) initiates an electronic payment transaction; or (c) carries out any action through a remote channel which may imply a risk of payment fraud or other abuses.

2.3 Regulatory Technical Standards (RTS)

Regulatory Technical Standards (RTS) for strong customer authentication and common and secure open standards of communication were adopted by the Commission on the basis of European Banking Authority's activities (Commission delegated regulation 2018/389)[12]. While the term "standard" implies voluntary compliance, their adoption by the Commission means that the RTS are a legally binding instrument and PSPs need to comply with them as of September 2019.

One of the goals of the RTS is to specify the requirements of SCA. More specifically, SCA should be applied each time a payer accesses its payment account online, initiates an electronic payment transaction or carries out any action through a remote channel which may imply a risk of payment fraud or other abuse. To counter the risk, an authentication code which should be resistant against the forgery or disclosure, should be issued (recital 1 of RTS).

Like PSD2, the RTS describe strong customer authentication as procedure (art. 1(a) of RTS). In order to provide strong customer authentication, payment provider must ensure that authentication is based on two or more elements factors. As in the PSD2, these elements are categorised as knowledge, possession and inherence, and the characteristics of those elements described in detail in art. 6, 7 and 8 of RTS. The elements of authentication need to be independent from each other, meaning that if one of them is breached, the others are not disclosed as a result (art. 9 of the RTS).

There are some exceptions to requiring two-step factor authentication, for example for low-value transactions. These are one-off transactions below 30EUR, or transactions whose cumulative value is below 100EUR, and there can be at most five transactions until SCA is required again (art. 16, paras a-c of RTS).

3   Theoretical Overview of the Overlap Between PSD2 and GDPR

PSD2 has been understood in the context of open banking, the opening up of traditionally bank-dominated industry to new players and actors (often broadly referred to as fintech). Open banking on the one hand improves the customer experience; on the other, it forces the 'traditional' financial industry to invest significant resources in technological innovation and in the creation of new technical and compliance processes [19]. The adoption of the revised directive in 2015 was predicted to enhance harmonization, encourage growth and innovation, as well as ensure security and consumer protection, and enable the fight against payment fraud [27].

The framework contained in the PSD2 interacts with the GDPR when personal data are processed. The relationship between the two frameworks has been analysed from the perspective of security of third party access to accounts under art. 66 and 67 of the PSD2 [27], their interaction in an open banking context and the opportunities they bring to new fintechs [20], the re-use of personal data by PSPs under the purpose limitation principle [25], and finally the relationship

---

[12] Commission Delegated Regulation (EU) 2018/389 of 27 November 2017 supplementing Directive (EU) 2015/2366 of the European Parliament and of the Council with regard to regulatory technical standards for strong customer authentication and common and secure open standards of communication. C/2017/7782 OJ L 69.

was thoroughly analysed by the EDPB, with a strong focus on data protection issues [9].

In July 2020, the EDPB issued its Guidelines 06/2020 on the interplay of the PSD2 and the GDPR (hereafter: the Guidelines 06/2020) [9], which answered some of the above questions. The document was open for consultation to the public until September 2020; the final version of the guidelines has not been made available yet.

The board stresses that framework contained in the PSD2 establishes a link be-tween data protection, consumer protection and competition law, the focus is given above all to the data protection aspects. The document further analyses the position of PSPs within the context of the GDPR, explaining that depending on the context the PSPSs can act either as controllers or processors. In order to process personal data lawfully, they can invoke the legal grounds of necessity to perform a contract, legal obligation to grant access to the account under art. 66 of the PSD2, or further processing of already lawfully collected data. The Guidelines 06/2020 also tackle the notion of explicit consent, which differs under art. 94(2) of the PSD2 and arts. 6, 7 and 9 of the GDPR. The explicit consent contained in art. 94(2) of the PSD2 cannot be valid legal grounds for data processing; instead, it can play a role as an additional data protection safeguard for the data subject. More specifically, in para. 36 the board explains that the explicit consent under the PSD2 has a contractual nature, meaning that the PSPs must disclose exactly what kind of personal data will be processed, and for which specific purposes. Thus, the requirement of explicit consent under art. 94 of the PSD2 guarantees transparency and gives more control to the user of the payment service (para 38).

The Guidelines 06/2020 emphasize that the lack of appropriate security measures in a PSP may have dire consequences: financial losses for the company, loss of customer trust, and if the PSP is a bank, then the customers cannot use their cards to access their funds. For example, a recent incident in a South African bank following the theft of a master key led to the bank recalling 12 million bank cards[13]. Moreover, extensive financial records can offer a very detailed insight into an individual's life. For example, donations to political parties, annual membership fee in a labour union, frequent visits to a swingers club, or settling of medical bills for a specific health condition. Using big data techniques, payment records can also show minute behavioural pattern, all of which may lead to a higher risk of fraud [9]. Hence, the board recommends that PSP implement the principle of data minimisation as part of their data protection by design approach and to contribute to the security of personal data under art. 32 of the GDPR.

The access to data under art. 66 and 67 of the PSD2 was predicted to reduce online payment costs, and give rise to new business models, while art. 97 aims to improve client authentication and security [18, 20]. Data portability and screen

---

[13] https://www.zdnet.com/article/south-african-bank-to-replace-12m-cards-after-employees-stole-master-key/, last accessed 2020/09/12.

scraping are key measures to facilitate open banking. However, opening up the data held by banks to new players also brings cybersecurity considerations [20].

PSPs rely on computer infrastructure in order to carry out online payments. This means that a cyber-incident could jeopardise the functioning of ICT systems, pose risks to data integrity and cause other impacts stemming from cyber-incidents that go beyond financial losses on stock markets [1,4].

The cybersecurity of the payment depends on the security measures adopted by different actors throughout the payment chain ecosystem. Carrying out security risk assessments and including security measures into the general governance can con-tribute to overall security. Specifically, designing application with security in mind, as well as using high quality end-to-end encryption (SSL/TLS), are minimum security measures that can be adopted at different points in the payment chain, by the users, customers and the merchants [5,11]. Despite the recommendation for the users to adopt security measures, the ultimate responsibility for a well-designed system should not lie on the individual user [22].

Traditional financial institutions should also implement strong controls over privileged system access, meaning accounts with elevated system access entitlements, such as administrator accounts. Measures should follow the need-to-know principle based on strong authentication [4]. ENISA recommends adopting measures on the side of users as well as merchants, and the PSPs themselves should ensure secure development of the payment service [11], in accordance with the emerging principle of security by design [7].

There are two types of authentication required during a payment process: first, authentication of the device and secondly, that of the user [11]. Art. 4(29) of the PSD2 states that authentication is a procedure which "allows the payment service provider to verify the identity of a payment service user or the validity of the use of a specific payment instrument, including the use of the user's personalised security credentials" . It is not clear whether this definition includes the authentication of the device.

Poor authentication is a risk, since it can lead to unauthorized payments, as well as disclosing the underlying sensitive payment data, such as credit card information and personal credentials to unauthorized third parties. Since security of online payments relies to a large extent on the secrecy of tokens and cryptograms, strong authentication can be an effective protection measure [11]. However, while authentication is a useful counter-measure, in itself it is not sufficient and must be paired with other security measures to counter ICT and security risks [4].

Implementing strong authentication is also a motivated business decision. As the banks lose their traditional monopoly over the payment market, they also lose the control and their exclusive access to customer data. In order to prevent fraud and unauthorized access to payment data, strong authentication measures are necessary. However, under the PSD2 banks are placed in an awkward position, since they are required to ensure data protection of their customers' data, and prevent fraud, while needing to trust that the PSPs have adequate authentication mechanisms without banks being able to verify them [18,27].

4   Relationship Between GDPR and PSD2

4.1   Relationship Between the PSD2 and GDPR – Article 94 of PSD2

Data protection in payment services is discussed in Recital 89, and art. 94 of the PSD2. While other articles, especially those on access to information by payment services providers in art. 66 and 67, contain a link to data protection law [27], this is the only explicit rule on the subject.

According to art. 94, processing of personal data by payment systems and payment service providers is *permitted when necessary* to safeguard *the prevention, investigation and detection of payment fraud*. Individuals must be informed on the processing of personal data for those purposes with accordance of the GDPR (in the original text, Directive 95/46/EC). Alongside this provision, the PSD2 states that payment services shall only *access, process and retain* personal data necessary *for the provision of their payment services*, with the *explicit consent* of the payment service user (art. 94(2) of the PSD2, all emphases added by the author).

This means that the PSD2 provides two broad situations when personal data can be processed:

– The legal obligation to safeguard the prevention, investigation and detection of fraud (if the necessity criterion is met), thus providing the legal grounds for data processing as understood in art. 6(1)(c) of the GDPR; and
– In the absence of the first situation, with the user's explicit consent. However, it is not entirely clear if these two options are mutually exclusive.

4.2   The Curious Case of Explicit Consent

PSD2 and GDPR both recognise consent, and explicit consent, as important safe-guards of data protection. However, there are differences in how the two instruments understand the notion of consent, and the interpretations outlined here provide some useful insight into resolving the two frameworks' conflicts on ensuring data protection.

Under art. 6 of the GDPR, the data subject's consent is one of the six legal bases available to the controller to justify data processing. The data controller carries the burden of proving that valid consent has been obtained, meeting all the criteria contained in the GDPR, especially its art. 6 and 7, meaning that consent represents a freely given, specific, informed and unambiguous indication of the data subject's wishes. The GDPR also recognizes the notion of explicit consent, as legal grounds for processing of special categories of personal data (sensitive personal data). As explained in the previous section, biometric data for the purpose of uniquely identifying a natural person may well be used as the second factor in an authentication process, meaning that explicit consent under the GDPR is relevant legal grounds.

The clear division under the GDPR is muddled by the notion of explicit consent as understood by art. 94 of the PSD2. Here, explicit consent of the user is laid out as the second option for data processing, when the first situation (legal obligations to fight fraud) is not given. Thus, the idea of explicit consent under the two instruments does not overlap. To a large extent, it was not clear if the explicit consent under art. 94(2) of the PSD2 could be considered valid legal grounds in the sense of art. 6 of the GDPR. Initially, it was argued that obtaining explicit consent might not even be necessary. The reasoning was that if the PSP could rely on other legal grounds to process personal data, such as necessary for the fulfilment of a contract between them – i.e. to provide an authentication process, and that consent should not be asked despite the PSD2's requirement [26]. Others held the view that where PSD2 requires explicit consent, the same standards for consent as required by the GDPR should be adhered to, including the information obligations towards users who are data subjects. That means that those users should be fully aware of what they are consenting to and that their data protection rights apply [6].

The dilemma was finally resolved by the EDPB in July 2020: the explicit consent as understood by the PSD2 is not legal grounds; however, it can be considered as a safeguard under data protection law as it gives the data subject the control and transparency over their personal data. In other words, explicit consent cannot be considered extra lawful grounds alongside contract performance [9].

The question of (explicit) consent has an indirect effect on authentication. Insofar as cybersecurity involves processing of personal data, the measures need to rely on valid legal grounds. If biometrics are used as the second authentication factor, then one of the valid legal bases under art. 9 of the GDPR is explicit consent.

4.3   Lex Specialis and Lex Generalis, or Cumulative Use?

There is an overlap in scopes of application of the GDPR and PSD2, when the payment service provider processes personal data. This leads us to the question of the relationship between the two instruments. The provision of art. 94 refers to processing of personal data for the purposes of the PSD2, which shall be carried out in accordance with the data protection framework, now contained in the GDPR and relevant national data protection acts. However, it does not explain any possible conflicts between the two instruments should be resolved. As explained above, explicit consent is an example of such a conflict.

One option is to explore whether the frameworks are more specific to one another, in which case the general provision must give precedence to the more specific one. The fundamental legal principle of lex specialis derogat legi generali applies in a situation when two divergent provisions are at stake; a typical example is the relationship between the GDPR and the ePrivacy regime. If the former gave greater protection than the latter, the ePrivacy regime would nevertheless apply, as it is the more specific rule [10].

However, it is unclear if that is the case here, since PSD2 explicitly refers to the data protection regime to inform the users about the processing of their data, while at the same time, the provision clarifies conditions under which data processing can be carried out. The conditions are either that processing is necessary to safeguard the prevention, investigation and detection of payment fraud, or if the user has given its explicit consent. If both instruments regulate data processing with the aim of ensuring a high level of data protection (albeit from two different viewpoints), does that mean they are in a lex specialis and lex generalis relationship?

The position of scholars seems to be in favour of cumulative application rather than lex specialis and lex generalis relationship. Cumulative application means that both instruments apply. The reference to the application and use of GDPR is seen as an implicit need for joint application of the two – the two instruments should be read together insofar as there is an overlap in their scope of application [25]. This view has been implicitly confirmed by the EDPB in their 2020 guidelines, in which the obligations from each instrument are discussed cumulatively [9].

4.4   The Implications of Cumulative Use

How does the cumulative application of PSD2 and GDPR affect the legal regime for strong customer authentication? We provide three considerations: first, who is responsible for implementing authentication as the data controller; second, what are lawful grounds for authentication, and thirdly, what is the required security standard under either framework.

Firstly, cumulative use means that all relevant provisions of the GDPR must be complied with.

As explained above, the obligations under the GDPR centre mostly on the data controller, which is the entity determining the means and purposes of data processing. During an authentication procedure, credentials are securely processed in a pseudonymised or an encrypted form [17]. Encryption data is a form of data pseudonymisation, and pseudonymised data are considered personal data under art. 4(5) of the GDPR [8]. The decryption keys must be kept securely and separately from the identifiable personal data. Pseudonymised authentication is possible under art. 11 of the GDPR, when the purposes for which a controller processes personal data no longer require the identification of a data subject by the controller. Personalised security credentials as understood by art. 4(31) could be an example of pseudonymised authentication.

However, if a PSP only processes personalized security credentials without being able to identify the user, its position as a controller or processor is not entirely clear. In payment services, the role of controller or processor depends on the specific context [9]. In the case of encrypted data, it has long been unclear whether actual access to the decryption key is necessary to be considered a controller [23]; the question was partly answered in the Breyer case of the Court of Justice of the EU[14]. Following the reasoning of the judgment, as long as a party has the legal means which enable it to identify the data subject with additional

---

[14] Patrick Breyer v Bundesrepublik Deutschland. Case C-582/14. Judgment of the Court (Second Chamber) of 19 October 2016.

data, it can be considered a controller. This implies that as long as relevant decryption keys can be obtained by the PSP or other actors, the PSPs will likely be considered data controllers. Inter alia, that means that the controller carries the responsibility to comply with the GDPR's provisions, including ensuring that security measures are in place to protect the authentication related personal data.

Secondly, there must be valid legal grounds to process personal data in the course of an authentication procedure. As the EDPB explains in its Guidelines 06/2020, following its previous work, the six legal bases in art. 6 of the GDPR are listed exhaustively (para. 26). This means that authentication insofar as it represents processing of personal data must fall under one of these six options. The process of authentication has been confused with giving consent to processing of personal data; however, that is not correct [8]. Consent represents the freely given, specific, in-formed and unambiguous indication of the data subject's wish to agree to data processing (art. 4(11) of the GDPR), while authentication fulfils another goal – it ensures authorised access to and carrying out of the payment services. Therefore, other legal basis must be found.

Is there a conflict between the position of the EDPB on numerous clausus legal bases under the GDPR and the data protection clause of art. 94 of the PSD2? Recital 40 of the GDPR provides if a lawful basis is contained in a law outside the GDPR, the latter must contain a reference to the former. Therefore, we might assume that an-other law can only provide legitimisation for data processing when it further specifies one of the provisions of art. 6 of the GDPR, but other legal bases cannot exist. This would mean that while the data protection clause of the PSD2 provides for (at least) two situations in which processing of payment services-related personal data is lawful, those situations are specifications of the existing legal bases under art. 6 of the GDPR. The EDPB appears to corroborate this option in para. 35 of the Guidelines 06/2020 when it considers the position of explicit consent not to be an "additional" legal basis [11].

Drawing parallels with access to data under art. 66 and 67 of the PSD2, where PSPs can rely on necessity for a legal obligation under art. 6(1)(c) of the GDPR, it can be asked whether PSPs carry a legal obligation to process personal data to put into place cybersecurity measures, such as authentication. A similar obligation to be able to identify the signatory party can also be found in art. 26(b) of the Regulation 910/2014 (i.e. the eIDAS Regulation)[15].

The assumption of PSD2 seems to be that authentication relies on personalised credentials (art. 97(3) of the PSD2). If the credentials refer to an identifiable person, they are then considered personal data under art. 4(1) of the GDPR. However, even if credentials are not personalised (e.g. art. 11 of the GDPR allows for pseudonymous identification), the second authentication factor may well be. Biometric data, used for the purpose of uniquely identifying a natural person, are personal data according to art. 9 of the GDPR. The possession factor, such as a one-time password, might be sent to an email address or a

---

[15] Regulation 910/2014 on electronic identification and trust services for electronic transactions in the internal market. OJ L 257.

personal mobile device. In practice, authentication largely relies on personalised credentials, since it is difficult to assess identity otherwise [17]. Nevertheless, there does not appear to be an explicit legal obligation to process personal data for authentication purposes.

The execution of the payment relies on a contractual relationship between the user and the PSP (often by means of complying with the terms of service, or terms of use), meaning that necessity for the performance of a contract may be relevant legal basis [6,26]. Alternatively, if there is no contractual relationship, for example because a third party is carrying out the authentication procedure for the PSP, legitimate interests of the PSP as the data controller may be relevant (art. 6(1)(f) of the GDPR). In this case, processing of authentication data can be carried out if it is necessary for the purposes of the legitimate interests pursued by the controller or by a third party. However, the processing may not be carried out if the legitimate interests are overridden by the interests or fundamental rights and freedoms of the data subject which require protection of personal data, according to art. 6(1)(f) of the GDPR. Recital 49 of the GDPR suggests that processing with the aim of ensuring cybersecurity, such as preventing unauthorised access to electronic communications networks is an example of the controller's legitimate interest. Implementing security measures, such as authentication, may therefore fall under the notion of legitimate interest.

Either legal grounds must meet the necessity requirement: data processing is lawful insofar as it is necessary, either for contractual performance or achieving legitimate interests. This may be problematic in cases of screen scraping, where the PSP may have access to more user data than is strictly necessary to carry out the payment [27], which has led to the adoption of dedicated interfaces by banks when allowing non-traditional PSPs access to user data, in accordance with art. 33(4) of the Regulatory technical standards. This means that PSPs are allowed to make use of the interfaces made available to the payment service users for the authentication and communication with their account servicing payment service provider. These interfaces will be used insofar as necessity of processing remains a concern in the context of screen scraping, according to art. 32 of the RTS.

Thirdly, authentication as a cybersecurity measure contributes to security of personal data under art. 32 of the GDPR. On principle, both the GDPR and the PSD2 require high security standards. Due to various legal requirements, the security systems may become more complex. In security design, complexity may compromise security: the more devices are involved, the more likely there will be a vulnerability [21]. Exceptions likewise contribute to complexity, since the code will need to foresee more situations [2].

However, it is difficult to say whether adopting measures to comply with the authentication requirements in art. 97 of the PSD2 and Sect. 2 of the RTS would conflict with the art. 32 of the GDPR. First argument is found in art. 18(1) of RTS, which provides for voluntary compliance with this requirement. The PSPs may, but are not obliged to implement the exceptions under their art. 18(1). Therefore, if enabling the exceptions could lead to security vulnerabilities, the PSPs may decide to use strong customer authentication for all transactions.

This might meet the standard under art. 32 of the GDPR, which requires that security of personal data must take into account the level of risk of varying likelihood and severity for the rights and freedoms of natural persons. In general, PSD2 seems to favour innovation and competition over privacy and security [18,27]; however, considering that both instruments need to be applied due to cumulative use, needing to comply with the higher cybersecurity standard may mean having to implement authentication for all payments, if compliance with art. 32 cannot be guaranteed otherwise.

5   Open Questions

This paper explored the relationship between Second payment services directive (PSD2) and the General data protection regulation (GDPR), and their cumulative application to strong customer authentication. The legal regime nevertheless leaves some open questions into which future research might provide better insight. It is also worth considering whether there is a spill over effect of strong (customer) authentication into other policy areas. The rising popularity of e-commerce in the context of the Covid-19 crisis needs a safe and secure underlying payment service infrastructure, to whose compliance the understanding of cumulative use of PSD2 and GDPR may contribute.

First, given that attack vectors multiply when several authentication procedures are used, does the access to account information under art. 66 and 67 of the PSD2 jeopardise the PSD2's stated goal of improving cybersecurity in payments? Account information service providers, and payment initiation service providers are entitled to access certain information under art. 66 and 67 of the PSD2 to perform their services. This means that three authentication procedures will be put into place: the first on the side of the bank, the second to verify the identity of the customer, and the third with the payment service provider itself. However, as Wolters and Jacobs show, this regime creates more risks, since more procedures bring the multiplication of attack vectors, which can lead to more possible vulnerabilities [27]. Does cumulative use, and the need to comply with the standard of security contained in art. 32 of the GDPR respond adequately to this problem?

Secondly, since PSD2 is a directive, it must be transposed into national legal systems by the legislative bodies of member states. Given the variety and diversity of legal systems across the EU, and various options for scope exemption in the PSD2, such as art. 2(5), allowing member states to exclude credit institutions under the capital ratings regime[16] from certain PSD2 obligations, will this lead to further conflicts for different authentication requirements in different member states, based on the type of institution providing payment services?[17]

---

[16] Regulation (EU) No 575/2013 of the European Parliament and of the Council of 26 June 2013 on prudential requirements for credit institutions and investment firms and amending Regulation (EU) No 648/2012. OJ L 176.

[17] https://ec.europa.eu/info/files/psd2-member-states-options_en, last accessed 2020/10/16.

Thirdly, given the shift to online services, it is likely that the need for strong authentication might spill over into other policy areas. During the Covid-19 pandemic, many (public) service providers, including governments and healthcare, have been motivated to adapt to an online context. Socially distanced shopping and services usually require online banking, and stronger authentication may soon be necessary to improve cybersecurity. In that scenario, how will the cumulative use of PSD2 and GDPR interact with other frameworks, and what will be the impact on cybersecurity? For authentication purposes, PSPs could in some instances leverage the use of certificates issued under the eIDAS framework; however, the lack of legal clarity surrounding this possibility may have contributed to its slow spread [15,18,24]. Nonetheless, the shift to online services during the pandemic may be a strong incentive for private businesses to leverage the eIDAS framework, insofar as that is possible under the national law, for example in Belgium with the itsme application[18].

Finally, it remains to be seen whether the standards for strong customer authentication adopted by the PSD2 and its Regulatory technical standards become the benchmark in other policy areas when or if strong authentication requirements are mandated, or whether the legislators and the Commission will require different standards. This question can only be answered by careful examination of future regulation and policy-making at all relevant levels, from European Union and national legislation to initiatives by the industry, such as standard-setting.

References

1. Agrafiotis, I., Nurse, J.R.C., Goldsmith, M., Creese, S., Upton, D.: A taxonomy of cyber-harms: defining the impacts of cyber-attacks and understanding how they propagate. J. Cyber Secur. 4(1) (2018). https://doi.org/10.1093/cybsec/tyy006
2. Alenezi, M., Zarour, M.: On the Relationship between software complexity and security. ResearchGate (2020)
3. Arner, D.W., Zetzsche, D.A., Buckley, R.P., Barberis, J.N.: The identity challenge in finance: from analogue identity to digitized identification to digital KYC utilities. Eur. Bus. Organization Law Rev. 20(1), 55–80 (2019). https://doi.org/10.1007/s40804-019-00135-1
4. European Banking Authority: Guidelines on ICT and security risk management. Technical Report. https://www.eba.europa.eu/regulation-and-policy/internal-governance/guidelines-on-ict-and-security-risk-management
5. European Central Bank: Recommendations for the security of internet payments. Technical Report. https://www.ecb.europa.eu/pub/pdf/other/recommendationssecurityinternetpaymentsoutcomeofpc201301en.pdf
6. European consumer organisation: Recommendations to the EDPB on the interplay between the GDPR and PSD2. Technical Report BEUC-X-2019-021 (2019). http://www.beuc.eu/publications/beuc-x-2019-021_beuc_recommendations_to_edpb-interplay_gdpr-psd2.pdf

---

[18] https://www.itsme.be/en/, last accessed 2020/10/16.

7. European consumer organisation and European association for the coordination of consumer representation in standardisation: Keeping consumers secure: How to tackle cyber security threats through EU law (2019). https://www.beuc.eu/publications/beuc-x-2019-066_keeping_consumers_secure_how_to_tackle_cybersecurity_threats_through_eu_law.pdf

8. European Data Protection Board: Guidelines 3/2019 on processing of personal data through video devices. Technical Report. https://edpb.europa.eu/our-work-tools/public-consultations/2019/guidelines-32019-processing-personal-data-through-video_en

9. European data protection board: Guidelines 06/2020 on the interplay of the Second Payment Services Directive and the GDPR. Technical Report 06/2020 (2020). https://edpb.europa.eu/sites/edpb/files/consultation/edpb_guidelines_202006_interplaypsd2andgdpr.pdf

10. European data protection supervisor: Opinion 6/2017 on the Proposal for a Regulation on Privacy and Electronic Communications (ePrivacy Regulation). Technical Report (2017). https://edps.europa.eu/sites/edp/files/publication/17-04-24_eprivacy_en.pdf

11. European Union Agency for Cyber security: Security of Mobile Payments and Digital Wallets. Technical Report (2016). http://www.enisa.europa.eu/publications/mobile-payments-security

12. Fuster, G.G., Jasmontaite, L.: Cybersecurity regulation in the European union: the digital, the critical and fundamental rights. In: Christen, M., Gordijn, B., Loi, M. (eds.) The Ethics of Cybersecurity. TILELT, vol. 21, pp. 97–115. Springer, Cham (2020). https://doi.org/10.1007/978-3-030-29053-5_5

13. Hartl, V.M.I.A., Schmuntzsch, U.: Fraud protection for online banking. In: Tryfonas, T. (ed.) HAS 2016. LNCS, vol. 9750, pp. 37–47. Springer, Cham (2016). https://doi.org/10.1007/978-3-319-39381-0_4

14. Jasmontaite, L., González Fuster, G., Gutwirth, S., Wenger, F., Jaquet-Chiffelle, D.O., Schlehahn, E.: Canvas White Paper 2 - Cybersecurity and Law. SSRN Scholarly Paper ID 3091939, Social Science Research Network, Rochester, NY (2017). https://papers.ssrn.com/abstract=3091939

15. Jones, B.: Are eIDAS certificates sufficient for PSD2 Open Banking? https://www.finextra.com/blogposting/17379/are-eidas-certificates-sufficient-for-psd2-open-banking

16. Kemp, R.: Mobile payments: current and emerging regulatory and contracting issues. Comput. Law Secur. Rev. **29**(2), 175–179 (2013). https://doi.org/10.1016/j.clsr.2013.01.009, http://www.sciencedirect.com/science/article/pii/S0267364913000277

17. Kogetsu, A., Ogishima, S., Kato, K.: Authentication of patients and participants in health information exchange and consent for medical research: a key step for privacy protection, respect for autonomy, and trustworthiness. Front. Genetics **9** (2018). https://doi.org/10.3389/fgene.2018.00167. https://www.frontiersin.org/articles/10.3389/fgene.2018.00167/full

18. Mansfield-Devine, S.: Open banking: opportunity and danger. Comput. Fraud Secur. **2016**(10), 8–13 (2016). https://doi.org/10.1016/S1361-3723(16)30080-X. http://www.sciencedirect.com/science/article/pii/S136137231630080X

19. Passi, L.F.: An open banking ecosystem to survive the revised payment services directive: connecting international banks and FinTechs with the CBI globe platform. J. Payments Strategy Syst. **12**(4), 335–345 (2018). http://kuleuven.ezproxy.kuleuven.be/login?url=https://www.dynamed.com

20. Rousseau, H.P.: GDPR, PSD2 and open banking are creating a new dynamic in personal financial services: a note - ProQuest. J. Internet Bank. Commer. 24(1), 1–7 (2019). http://search.proquest.com/docview/2278751804?rfr_id=infonumber:1
21. Schneier, B.: News: Complexity the Worst Enemy of Security - Schneier on Security (2012). https://www.schneier.com/news/archives/2012/12/complexity_the_worst.html
22. Schneier, B.: Stop trying to fix the user. IEEE Secur. Privacy 14(5), 96 (2016). https://doi.org/10.1109/MSP.2016.101
23. Spindler, G., Schmechel, P.: Personal data and encryption in the European general data protection regulation. JIPITEC 7(2) (2016). http://www.jipitec.eu/issues/jipitec-7-2-2016/4440
24. Terziman, L.: The eIDAS Challenge for TPPs under PSD2. https://www.finextra.com/blogposting/17221/the-eidas-challenge-for-tpps-under-psd2
25. Thys, T., Van Raemdonck, S., Desmet, K.: GDPR, PSD2 and the repurposing of data: no big deal? Droit bancaire et financier - Bank- en Financieel Recht 2018(3), 144–197 (2018), https://www-jurisquare-be.kuleuven.ezproxy.kuleuven.be/en/journal/bfr/2018-3/financiele-reglementering-actualiteit-il-est-urgent-dattendre-bedenkingen-bij-het-fintech-action-pla/index.html#page/144/search/
26. Vandezande, N.: Reconciling Consent in PSD2 and GDPR (2020). https://thepaypers.com/expert-opinion/reconciling-consent-in-psd2-and-gdpr-777976
27. Wolters, P.T.J., Jacobs, B.P.F.: The security of access to accounts under the PSD2. Comput. Law Secur. Rev. 35(1), 29–41 (2019). https://doi.org/10.1016/j.clsr.2018.10.005, http://www.sciencedirect.com/science/article/pii/S0267364918302620
28. Yaghmaei, E., et al.: Canvas White Paper 1 - Cybersecurity and Ethics. SSRN Scholarly Paper ID 3091909, Social Science Research Network, Rochester, NY (2017). https://papers.ssrn.com/abstract=3091909, issue: ID 3091909

Privacy in Payment in the Age of Central Bank Digital Currency

Frédéric Tronnier(✉)

Goethe Universität Frankfurt, Frankfurt am Main, Germany
frederic.tronnier@m-chair.de

Abstract. In academia and at central banks, central bank digital currency (CBDC) is increasingly being researched due to the continuous decline in cash payments and the emergence of private stablecoins such as Libra. While CBDC offers various advantages for central banks, sensitive transaction and holdings data of individuals and users need to be protected. This paper analyses how privacy in payment is being discussed in CBDC related literature and pilot projects of central banks. Central banks rarely identify privacy as a key requirement in the development and implementation of a CBDC. Instead, anonymity is seen as one possible feature of a CBDC that could hinder know-your-customer (KYC) and anti-money laundering (AML) compliance of banks. In pilot projects, different techniques and solutions have been proposed to achieve varying levels of privacy for users. A comprehensive framework on how best to achieve privacy in retail CBDC is needed. Such a framework should consider the differing underlying design aspects of a CBDC and the use cases for which the CBDC is to be developed.

Keywords: Privacy · Payment · Central bank digital currency · CBDC · Cryptocurrency

1 Introduction

Payment systems and currencies have been subject to a multitude of significant changes over the last millennia, from shells to coins to banknotes, cheques to the current digital payment in ever-changing currencies. Today, electronic and mobile payment systems are challenging cash-based payments. For the last 400 years [1], central banks have been responsible for issuing legal tender to the population of their respective country or empire. Cash, to this day the only form of legal tender that may be owned by individuals and is issued directly through a central bank [2], grants the holder the option to carry out transactions with a high degree of privacy. With the decrease in cash payments in many parts of the world [3] and particularly in countries like Sweden [4], economies are shifting towards electronic, online, and mobile payment.

Through the introduction of Bitcoin by Nakamoto [5], cryptocurrencies were established with the intention to provide new and decentralized means of payment, units of account, and stores of value. Although cryptocurrencies have not -yet - lived up to their self-set expectations, organizations such as Facebook have started working on

M. Friedewald et al. (Eds.): Privacy and Identity 2020, IFIP AICT 619, pp. 96–114, 2021.
https://doi.org/10.1007/978-3-030-72465-8_6

their own cryptocurrencies or tokens to offer their customers a new means of transactions to increase their market dominance [6].

With the rise in cryptocurrency prices and attention towards it, the decrease in cash use, and the increased efforts of global corporations aiming to enter the currency market, the questions of whether and how central banks are going to react to these developments have arisen naturally given their central role in managing the money supply of a country. As a result, central banks worldwide have started piloting projects on central bank digital currency (CBDC), most notably in Sweden [7], China [8], South Africa [9] and the whole European Union (EU) [10]. These central bank-issued digital currencies could potentially offer central banks the possibility to effectively and efficiently oversee, track and analyse holdings and transactions much better than with cash [11]. Protecting sensitive financial and non-financial personal data in payment is therefore essential and needs to be researched in academia.

2   Aim of This Paper

"Currency cannot be private, money is a public good of sovereignty..."

- Francois Villeroy de Galhau, Governor of the Bank of France [12]

The quote by the Governor of the Bank of France, the French central bank, highlights the ongoing discussion by CBs about the introduction of a CBDC in response to decentralized or private cryptocurrencies and the need for a digital alternative to cash for individuals. Currently, CBDC as a new form of payment is discussed worldwide in academia and by central banks through research papers as well as first pilot tests and proofs-of-concepts (PoC).

However it was shown that CBDC is discussed mainly through papers that provide a general introduction to the topic, as well as work on the possible economic and monetary effects that a CBDC would have on the banking industry and the economy as a whole, while literature on the societal impact, or stakeholders who might be impacted by CBDC, is scarce [13]. Scientific papers and reports published by central banks focus on discussing the general underlying technical concept, the potential design options, and their (dis)advantages of CBDC [13]. Work with a main focus on privacy in CBDC has only been issued by the Bank of Canada [14] and the European Central Bank [15]. In this paper, information privacy follows the notion of Clarke [16] that data of individuals should not be available to other entities and that the individual must be able to execute "... a substantial degree of control over that data and its use." [16, p. 60]. Garratt and van Oordt [17] analyzed privacy in payment and argued that privacy can be viewed as a public good. The inability or failure of individuals to preserve their payment information impose a negative externality on others as it can be used for price discrimination of other individuals and therefore leads to socially suboptimal results. Privacy concerns of individuals and users have also been researched for newer payment systems such as online [18] and mobile payment [19]. In electronic payments, various methods and solutions for anonymous payment systems have been introduced in the past, from hardware tokens [20] to protocols [21] and various cryptocurrencies [22, 23].

Naturally research in CBDC, often conducted by central banks, focuses on CBDC from the perspective of a central bank. A notable exception is the work of, Leinonen [24] who highlights the requirements for a CBDC from an end-user perspective. He states that a CBDC should have more in common with currently used private (digital) payment services than with traditional cash, and mentions the possibility of market turbulence in the payments sector caused by introducing/issuing a CBDC, and suggests that this CBDC should serve as a basic payment instrument.

While currency may be a public good, the information that are generated while paying and transacting in a currency should not be public and are protected through regulation such as the General Data Protection Regulation (GDPR). Therefore, this paper aims to contribute to the growing body of literature on CBDC by exploring privacy in CBDC payments for the first time through the analysis of existing research and information published by central banks. Pilot projects from central banks and developed PoC will be examined to gain a thorough understanding of the potential impact of CBDC on users' privacy. Thus, this paper aims to assess how central banks address the topic of privacy in CBDC both theoretically, in published information, and practically, in pilot projects that implemented CBDC.

3   Central Bank Digital Currency

In order to define CBDC it is advisable to define money itself first. Greco and Thomas [25] provide the practical definition that money "… is anything that is generally accepted as a means of payment." [25, p. 27]. Money provides several functions. The three most important ones are to act as a medium of exchange, as a unit of account, and as a store of value. The concept of the Money Flower is introduced in [26], which distinguishes between different forms of money through four key properties: issuer (central bank or private institutions), form (digital or physical), accessibility (available to the general public or limited to banks), and technology (account- or token/value-based). Currently, only banknotes and coins are issued by central banks as legal tender for the general population. Bank deposits, although denominated in the same monetary unit as cash, are issued by private commercial banks and not central banks. These commercial banks also have access to central bank digital money in the form of reserves and settlement accounts, which are not accessible for the general population. Cryptocurrencies like Bitcoin and other forms of digital tokens, on the other hand, can either be widely accessible or wholesale only, but are not private and not central bank-issued. Cryptocurrencies may be defined as a virtual type of currency that "… rely on the transmission of digital information, utilizing cryptographic methods to ensure legitimate, unique transactions" [27, p. 3]. Within this framework, stablecoins form a special category. Stablecoins are private, digital tokens that are often backed by a basket of established currencies, cryptocurrencies, or other assets with the goal to generate and maintain a stable price of the coin. Libra, the proposed token of the eponymous project initiated by Facebook and other organizations [28] is one example of a stablecoin that could potentially function similarly to a CBDC.

Based on [26] and [29], three major categories of CBDC can be identified: general-purpose accounts, general-purpose tokens and wholesale tokens. While general-purpose accounts only expand on the existing reserves and settlement account systems of central banks, tokens are based on blockchain or distributed ledger technology (DLT) that may be accessible for the general public or limited to financial institutions. In this context, a token represents a digital and identifiable unit of currency that is transferred as a means of payment. This stands in contrast to an account-based model in which the owner of an account is identified, rather than the means of payment [30].

For this paper, CBDC are defined as digital, central bank-issued currencies, excluding existing central bank reserves and settlement accounts. The underlying technology, account-based CBDC or token, also called blockchain or DLT-based, may differ between the investigated research and the different pilot projects of central banks. Similarly, the use cases of central banks with a CBDC differ between general-purpose and wholesale CBDC. While a general-purpose CBDC may be used by the general public with cash-like features, a wholesale CBDC is not accessible by the general public and is used for interbank payment settlements [31]. As this paper analyses the privacy implications of a CBDC for individuals, the focus is on general-purpose CBDC.

For central banks, CBDC offers various potential advantages, including a greater market power and the ability of stronger control over monetary policy [see 32–34]. However, a CBDC also offers central banks the general possibility to effectively and efficiently oversee, track and analyze transactions much better than before, depending on the design and technical features of the CBDC. This represents a strong potential threat to user privacy and data protection [35]. Both academia and central banks themselves published various papers and articles on CBDC. Tronnier, Recker and Hamm [13] showed that the majority of research is focused on providing an initial overview of the topic, followed by research on the monetary and economic implications of a CBDC. However, research on other factors such as societal and legal implications has been scarce. Issues on privacy and anonymity of transactions in CBDC have thus far been researched only superficially. In [26] it is argued that a CBDC could have the same level of privacy as cash but note that the property of privacy in cash emerged over time out of convenience. In CBDC, the decision for anonymity as a feature would nowadays become a conscious one. Wandhöfer [11] argues that anonymity is a key property of cash and proposes to equip CBDC with a comparable level of anonymity, for instance through the identification of users at the point of conversion, without linkage to cryptographic transaction information. The author also highlights the importance of anonymous payment solutions to protect citizens against surveillance. In [36] it is argued that anonymity in CBDC would be of even greater importance in the future, should cash use continue to decline or eventually be completely replaced by CBDC. Then, a CBDC would act as the only anonymous payment method for individuals.

The close collaboration of central banks with all stakeholders in the development of a CBDC is important [31]. Although central banks already collaborate with technology service providers, financial institutions and other central banks, we argue that for retail CBDC, the end-users, the general population, is equally important for the success and adoption of a CBDC. Thus, this paper evaluates how central banks consider privacy and its importance for individuals. Several central banks are in different stages of piloting first projects on CBDC to test their hypotheses and the underlying technology of the CBDC. These pilot projects are a stark contrast to the majority of theoretical papers on the subject as first solutions are implemented and evaluated by the manufacturing central bank.

4 Methodology

To evaluate how privacy and privacy concerns are currently being discussed and considered, published research and pilot projects have to be identified first. A first literature review is provided in [13], where the authors evaluate both academic works as well as published literature by the central banks and finding that central bank papers have been published in academic journals in the past. Furthermore, the authors search multiple scientific databases, among others Web of Science, AIS eLibrary, EBSCOhost and IEEE Xplore, for the term Central Bank Digital Currency, finding 19 articles on the topic. However, their work does not encompass all central banks but only the five main central banks that issue the most important currencies worldwide by number of users and overall economic importance.

In this paper, we adapt the process of a systematic academic literature review by [37] to websites of various central banks to identify papers of academic quality and pilot projects. Additionally, a simplistic Google based search is used to identify information that could not be found directly through a central banks' website. The focus hereby lies in research and pilot projects on retail CBDC, acting as a cash equivalent, as privacy is of particular importance for individuals and end-users. While privacy can and should also be considered in wholesale CBDC, the number of stakeholders, different banks, and payment service providers is significantly lower than the number of people that would use a CBDC as a cash equivalent in everyday payments.

The work of several other authors is also used to provide a starting point in identifying pilot projects and central bank activities. The authors of [38] provide not only a comprehensive overview of CBDC but also a first list of central bank pilot projects. The authors analyze 17 retail CBDC projects from 17 countries based on the design choices architecture, infrastructure, access, and state the motivation and result of each project. In a paper provided by Bank of International Settlement [29] 63 central banks are surveyed on whether and how they are investigating CBDC. A similar survey was conducted in 2020 with 66 central banks [39]. Another very recent work also provides a comprehensive list of CBDC projects and activities of central banks [31]. The authors focus on wholesale CBDC projects for interbank settlement and payment and the underlying DLT. Political, legal and societal implications are explicitly stated to be outside of the scope of their work.

Based on the work of [13, 29, 31, 38] we identified a total of 78 CBs for initial consideration. These CBs have all participated in the surveys by the Bank of International Settlement or were previously identified to conduct research on CBDC by [31] or [38]. All CBs are listed in Table 1 and Table 2 of this work. The website of each CB was then searched for the keywords "CBDC", "Central Bank Digital Currency" and "digital currency". Only complete research publications in English that have been published by the specific central bank have been considered as "Final Hits". Several keyword hits are due to speeches, talks and news on this topic, which have not been counted in the final hits. Hits have been reviewed using the title and/or the abstract to assess their relevance to this study by covering the topic of CBDC in general.

Additionally, a Google keyword search was conducted for the keywords stated above in combination with the country of each central bank to obtain supplementary information that has or has not been published by the central banks themselves. This was especially helpful to obtain information on pilot projects of central banks, as the search engine on most central bank websites demonstrated to be less effective and expedient than expected.

5   Results of the Literature Review

Table 1 demonstrates the result of the systematic literature review on central bank websites. Due to page limitations, only findings that demonstrated hits are included. All final hits have been read and analysed to gather information on whether and how the central bank covers privacy and data protection in their analysis of CBDC.

It can be seen that for 38 (48,7%) central banks no hits could be found, while for an additional 13 central banks, no final hits were found, leaving 27 central banks for consideration. From the ones that published information on CBDC, data protection and privacy was often covered only superficially. Only the European Central Bank (ECB) and the Bank of Canada published research specifically dedicated to the topic of privacy. Table 1 covers all central banks that exhibited findings while Table 2, in the appendix, lists the central banks for which no hits could be reported through the literature review, as well as on how detailed information on privacy have been provided by the banks. As the search function provided on many central banks' websites proofed to be ineffective, an additional google search was conducted to verify the results and obtain additional information where possible. Hereby, the official name of the central bank, along with the term CBDC were used as keywords, using the Google News search mask. Supplementary information could be found particularly on the pilot projects of central banks, provided by various newspapers. In the following, selected findings will be reviewed to establish the focus of different publications and central banks.

Table 1. Hits of the Literature Review on Central Bank Websites

Central Bank	Search	Coverage	Hits	Final Hits	Privacy consideration level*
Bank Indonesia	All results	No option	10	1	1
Bank Negara Malaysia	All results	No option	9	1	1
Bank of Canada	All content types	No option	36	16	4

(continued)

Table 1. (*continued*)

Central Bank	Search	Coverage	Hits	Final Hits	Privacy consideration level*
Bank of England	Publications	All	4	4	2
Bank of France	Publications	All	5	3	3
Bank of Israel	No option	No option	10	2	2
Bank of Italy	Full site	No option	8	2	4
Bank of Japan	Contained in page	No option	22	4	1
Bank of Korea	All	No option	1	1	1
Bank of Lithuania	All	No option	5	2	2
Bank of Spain	All	No option	27	1	3
Bank of Thailand	No option	No option	77	5	3
Central Bank of Brazil	All categories	All	3	1	1
Central Bank of Iceland	All categories	All	1	1	1
Danmarks Nationalbank	No option	No option	6	2	3
De Nederlandsche Bank	No option	No option	13	3	3
European Central Bank (ECB)	No option	No option	30	5	4
Federal Reserve	Entire Site	No option	2	1	1
Hong Kong Monetary Authority	Data, Publications and Research	No option	4	1	1
Monetary Authority of Singapore	All	All	2378	2	4
Mongolbank	No option	No option	1	1	1
National Bank of Belgium	No option	No option	10	1	1
Norges Bank	Publications	No option	2	2	2
Reserve Bank of India	All	All	1	1	1
Reserve Bank of New Zealand	No option	No option	4	1	1
Sveriges Riksbank	PDF	No option	29	13	2
Swiss National Bank	Any Result Type	Any Modified Date	13	1	1

*1: not mentioned, 2: privacy mentioned superficially, 3: privacy discussed, 4: privacy as core design element or requirement

Table 1 provides the official name of the respective central bank, used search options as well as the number of hits and final hits for the keywords "CBDC" and "Central Bank Digital Currency". Additionally, a privacy consideration level is provided, depending on how much work CBs provide on privacy in CBDC. A lower score indicates that privacy issues have not, or only superficially, been discussed. This demonstrates that final hits in Table 1 may discuss CBDC without even mentioning privacy considerations or data protection. CBs with a higher score provided chapters specifically on privacy and data protection in their work, or published dedicated work with privacy as its sole focus.

Although various central banks published information and research on CBDC, many central banks covered privacy only superficially. As a possible explanation for this, the Bank of England argues that that privacy considerations do not fall directly into the area of business of a central bank but must be nonetheless taken into account [40].

The Central Bank of France discusses privacy in more detail and conducted a taskforce to document the potential benefits, issues and risks of a CBDC, taking an operational perspective on the topic [41]. Privacy and anonymity are discussed with regards to anti-money-laundering (AML) and the combating financing of terrorism (CFT) requirements as well as international legislation on privacy. The bank states that the "Regulation (EU) 2016/679 of the European Parliament and of the Council of 27 April 2016 on the protection of natural persons concerning the processing of personal data..." must be applied when creating and implementing a CBDC. Furthermore, the bank states that the Directive (EU) 2015/2366 of the European Parliament and of the Council of 25 November 2015 on payment services (PSD2) excludes central banks from being payment service providers, resulting in the question whether a central bank is legally allowed to issue a CBDC. Concerning AML/CFT requirements, the bank notes that the Directive (EU) 2015/849 of the European Parliament and of the Council of 20 May 2015 on the prevention of the use of the financial system for the purposes of money laundering or terrorist financing (amended in 2018 by Directive (EU) 2018/843) defines virtual currencies as "a digital representation of value that is not issued or guaranteed by a central bank...", wherefore a CBDC would not be treated as a virtual currency in the AML/CFT regulation. However, the central bank may be defined as a financial institution under the Directive 2013/36/EU and would, therefore, have to object to AML/CFT regulation [41].

The Bank of Japan reviews anonymity as both, a possible advantage or a disadvantage of CBDC. While anonymity ensures privacy protection in payments, cash is also used for illicit activities, money laundering and tax evasion. The authors reference the Peoples Bank of China that pointed out the prevention of such activities as one possible advantage of a CBDC [42]. Similarly, the Bank of Spain focuses on the (dis) advantages of an anonymous CBDC. The authors note that, even if a CBDC would be non-anonymous, money laundering and illicit activities would still be conducted, only using other currencies, gold, or cryptocurrencies. As a further disadvantage, a non-anonymous CBDC would require the central bank to invest heavily in IT-infrastructure to secure such a system and validate transactions [43]. According to the authors, the adaption of a decentralized validation mechanism of cryptocurrencies to a CBDC might be problematic. This would add costs and could pose a security threat if the system turns out to not be robust. However, it has to be noted that these arguments are only applicable to a token-based CBDC.

In a report for the central bank of the Netherlands, the authors of [44] note that, depending on the design of the CBDC, personal information could be obtained by non-banking operators, whereby surveys indicate that households trust non-banking operators less with their data than they trust financial institutions. As privacy is a key objective for CBDC, the authors would choose a design in which the central bank does not obtain balances and transaction information if the CBDC is used for commercial purposes. Figure 1 demonstrates the degree of privacy for users for different payment systems as evaluated by [44].

Fig. 1. Degree of privacy for users by payment system [34, p. 33]

The authors argue that a CBDC would provide a higher degree of privacy than commercial bank money and private digital currencies like Libra because the CB does not have commercial incentive to use payment data. Nonetheless, a CB might need to provide, undefined, supervisory authorities with access to payment data to investigate illegal activities such as money-laundering or the financing of terrorism. Furthermore, the authors argue that intermediaries might only need access to transaction data to initiate payments, balances could only be visible to the CB. However, Fig. 1 provides only a subjective scale and no further information on possible attack models are given.

The author of [45] from the Bank of Italy analyses the demand for CBDC and introduces a novel specification for money, the notion of money as a store of information. Here, the existence of privacy cost is assumed and linked to the demand for trustlessness [45 and 46 as cited by 47]. The loss of trust in public institutions is speculated to be one driver in the adoption of cryptocurrencies. In an economic, computer-based experiment with 80 students as participants, the author tested for design features of money that are valued by participants. The participants had to create portfolios consisting of different shares of the four currency types E-Currency -the CBDC of the experiment-, paper currency, banking currency and cryptocurrency [48]. The currency types differed on their safeness, store of value and anonymity, whereby the CBDC was chosen to be non-anonymous. The features and the building of the portfolio were described to the participants beforehand and 1440 responses were collected from the 80 participants. The preliminary results indicated that participants value liquidity and expected return in currencies while anonymity as a feature was valued less.

The Norges Bank, the central bank of Norway, discusses privacy as an aspect of consumer protection [49]. The bank notes that the country is working on incorporating the General Data Protection Regulation (GDPR) into their national legislation and state that it would be beneficial to consider guidelines on data protection by default and by design in the development of a CBDC. Further legislation that affects privacy are EEA agreements for the free flow of transactions and capital as well as the Financial Contracts Act that regulates the misuse of payments, for instance, if an authorized payment has been made by another entity than the customer. A CBDC must comply with these rules, which affects data protection.

The Bank of Canada published an analytical note on privacy in CBDC in June 2020 and provided one of the very few papers with a specific focus on privacy. The authors provide a framework to compare different retail payment solutions regarding their privacy profiles for holdings and transactions. They differentiate between stakeholders such as the government, banks or money service business (MSB) that can either act on behalf of the payee (Pe) or the payer (Pr), or other users [14]. MSB hereby legally defines non-bank financial institutions, that offer money transfers, the issuing money orders or the exchange and transfer of digital currencies to the public [50].

Figure 2 displays the results of the different payment technologies for the different stakeholders, whereby higher values indicate a higher level of privacy.

Solution	Government H: O	B	T: Pr	Pe	A	Payer MSB H: O	B	T: Pr	Pe	A	Payee MSB H: O	B	T: Pr	Pe	A	Payee T: Pr	Payment providers H: O	B	T: Pr	Pe	A	Public (other users) H: O	B	T: Pr	Pe	A
Credit card (stripe)	3	3	1	1	0	0	0	0	0	0	0	2	3	2	0	0	1	3	1	0	0	3	3	3	3	3
Credit card (EMV)	3	3	1	1	0	0	0	0	0	0	0	2	3	2	0	2	1	3	1	1	0	3	3	3	3	3
E-transfer	3	3	1	1	0	0	0	0	0	1	0	1	3	1	0	2	1	3	1	1	0	3	3	3	3	3
Debit card	3	3	1	1	0	0	0	0	0	0	0	1	3	1	0	1	1	3	1	1	0	3	3	3	3	3
Permissioned DLT	1	0	1	1	0	0	0	0	0	1	0	1	3	1	0	1	1	0	1	1	0	3	3	3	3	3
Bitcoin custodial	2	3	2	2	0	0	0	0	2	0	2	3	2	0	0	2	2	3	2	2	0	2	3	2	2	0
Bitcoin pro	3	3	2	2	0	3	3	2	2	0	3	3	2	2	0	2	3	3	2	2	0	3	3	2	2	0
Tiered ledgers	1	0	1	1	0	0	0	0	0	1	0	2	3	2	0	1	3	3	3	3	3	3	3	3	3	3
Device-based (KYC, non-transferable)	0	2	2	0	2	0	2	2	0	2	0	2	2	0	2	1	2	3	3	3	3	3	3	3	3	3
Device-based (non-KYC, transferable)	3	3	2	0	2	3	3	2	0	2	3	3	2	0	2	1	2	3	3	3	3	3	3	3	3	3
Cash	3	3	3	3	3	3	3	3	3	3	3	3	3	3	3	2	3	3	3	3	3	3	3	3	3	3

Fig. 2. Privacy profiles of payment technologies [14] of the Bank of Canada

It can be seen that DLT-based solutions provide anonymity only to certain stakeholders for specific data categories. For instance, a custodial Bitcoin payment offers a relatively high level of anonymity, as stated by the authors, for holdings data, that is information on the owner (O) and the balance (B) of a wallet. However, the transaction (T) amount (A) is always visible for all entities in all columns. A permissioned DLT, a solution that is favored by many central banks, would provide a high level of anonymity from other users or the general public. The central bank as well as the banks or non-bank financial institutions that are executing such a transaction on behalf of payer and payee have however access to most data types using such a solution. Overall, the authors demonstrate that the level of privacy a payment solution provides depends on the type of data and differs between stakeholders that may or may not view and access payments information.

The authors therefore note that a CBDCs privacy system depends on several questions that need to be considered first. Should all transactions be disclosed to the government? How much and what kind of information is necessary for merchants, banks, MSBs and law enforcement? Should Know-your-customer (KYC) regulations apply at all times? Both KYC and AML/CFT requirements need to be met, which could impact the maximum level of achievable privacy. Lastly, it is concluded that nuanced and fine-grained solutions are possible in designing a CBDC. Hereby privacy by design and several privacy-enhancing techniques such as zero-knowledge proofs, multi-party computation and differential privacy are mentioned. These concepts and techniques could be applied to a CBDC.

6 Pilot Projects on CBDC

Several findings of the literature review included not only theoretical work by the central banks but also information on pilot projects and PoCs of central banks in CBDC.

A country that has already introduced CBDC as legal tender are the Marshall Islands. As one of the smallest countries in the world, with a population of about 50.000 living on more than 1000 islands, the traditional payment system is not suitable for the geographic conditions of the country, leading to high transaction fees [51]. Thus, the country introduced the Marshallese Sovereign (SOV) in 2018, a blockchain-based cash equivalent and declared it as legal tender through the Sovereign Currency Act 2018. The declaration requires all users of the SOV to undergo KYC procedures. User data is not kept on the blockchain, and users can choose between different accredited verifiers that then issue the user a cryptographically signed ID. Additionally, users can create multiple IDs by verifying multiple accounts through multiple verifiers, thereby increasing the level of privacy. Verifiers, however, are not only responsible for IDs but analyse and monitor transactions with the ability to report suspicious activities and blacklist users [52].

The Sand Dollar of the Central Bank of the Bahamas was introduced in a whitepaper in 2019 and is being piloted on several islands of the country. The project uses an account-based solution where transactions and holdings are not anonymous but confidential. The CBDC is meant to act as both, a cash equivalent for the general population as well as a payment method for wholesale applications such as interbank settlements [53]. A key requirement for the project has been that transactions are non-anonymous while still protecting user confidentiality. The central bank itself will maintain a KYC register and monitor transactions. In the whitepaper, additional information on the KYC requirements is provided. The requirements vary for low- and medium-value personal accounts and high-value accounts for businesses. Limits are set for the maximum holding amount as well as for a maximum transaction limit per month. Depending on the account, account holders are required to provide only basic information like name and address or use official documents to activate an account. Apart from that, the project differs from other findings as stakeholder research has been conducted to assess the willingness of the country's inhabitants to adopt digital financial services. The survey, conducted among 519 randomly chosen residents of the district of Exuma, did however only assess the respondents' use of online and mobile payment behavior and did not question privacy concerns with regard to the respective technologies [53].

Sweden started working on a CBDC as early as 2017 and is one of the countries most often mentioned when it comes to digital currencies in general. The country, due to the strong decrease in cash use among its citizens, is evaluating a digital cash equivalent, the e-krona. In its second report, the central bank states that payment with e-krona will be traceable, as, regardless of whether the currency will be account- or token-based, a central register for transactions will exist [54]. The bank notes that transaction and user data can be identified, although the bank will comply with all applying regulations and ensure data protection. Interestingly, the bank mentions a prepaid e-krona card, which could be exchanged physically between users and thus would allow for anonymous transactions. Such prepaid cards, with token-based e-krona already stored on, could be anonymously bought and would comply with the respective AML regulation. This would not be possible with an account-based e-krona.

The ECB of the EU represents the only central bank that provided a document exclusively dedicated to privacy and anonymity in the PoC of a retail CBDC. In their Issue no 4/2019, titled "Exploring anonymity in central bank digital currencies" [15], they report the results of a PoC that provides users with some degree of privacy. The PoC, developed by the European System of Central Bank's (ESCB) EUROchain research network, is based on the Corda network, an open-source distributed ledger technology (DLT) platform. The solution uses "anonymity vouchers" that are issued by an AML authority at regular intervals towards users. This entity performs anti-money laundering checks, authorizes transactions and verifies users' identities. The ECB does not act as the AML authority in the PoC. Instead, the ECB itself is responsible for issuing and removing CBDC from circulation. Users can then spend anonymity vouchers, one voucher per one unit of CBDC, for anonymous transactions. The vouchers are not transferable and the amount of vouchers per user in a specific time-frame is specified by the AML authority. Figure 3 describes the transfer of CBDC with anonymity vouchers, as compared to the transfer using AML checks. The ECB itself is not involved in transfers using anonymity vouchers. The payer sends CBDC stating the amount, payee information, and the wish for an anonymous transaction to its inter-mediary. The payer's intermediary then checks if the payer has enough anonymity vouchers. Using the DLT network, the intermediary attaches the vouchers and CBDC to the transfer to prove to the payee's intermediary that the transaction can occur anonymously. If enough anonymity vouchers are provided, the payer's intermediary does not need approval by the AML authority, creating an anonymous transaction as the payee's intermediary does not have to validate the transaction with further checks.

If no or not enough vouchers, are used, the AML authority has to authorize the transaction while a notary node maintains a registry of transactions and states, without specific transaction value data or user information. The ECB concludes that it's PoC CBDC payment system can ensure users' privacy for low-value payments while still ensuring AML/CFT compliance for higher-value transactions. Nonetheless, several issues are noted that can be improved in the future. Regarding privacy preservation, intermediaries need to view past transactions to validate new transactions, which could be used to create a knowledge graph over time in the current PoC. This issue could be solved through chain snipping, meaning that the transaction history of users will be

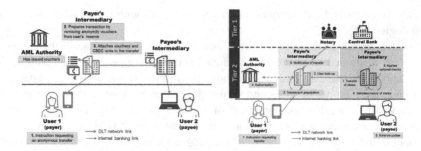

Fig. 3. CBDC transfer with (left) and without (right) anonymity vouchers [15]

reset. Privacy-enhancing techniques and technologies such as rotating public keys, zero-knowledge proof, and enclave computing may be added to increase user privacy.

7 Discussion

The systematic literature review demonstrated that privacy plays only a minor role in the information provided by central banks on CBDC. Several banks either published no information on CBDC at all or did not discuss privacy, trust, and anonymity of transactions in their work. Others discussed these topics only superficially. By investigating the literature and pilot projects of central banks directly, more information on privacy as a feature or design element of the prototypes could be found. The approach towards privacy has not been standardized and differs between the findings. In the theoretical findings, privacy is often seen as one design feature that a CBDC might possess. The advantages and disadvantages of anonymous CBDC are outlined for individuals and the central bank. For individuals, it is assumed that anonymity is a desired characteristic in a currency, although individuals attitudes towards privacy in CBDC have only been researched directly in [48]. Apart from that, only the Central Bank of the Bahamas interacted with users directly by surveying respondents on financial inclusion as a prerequisite for the introduction of a CBDC [53]. In [48], the preliminary results even indicated that anonymity seems to play a weaker role for individuals than what could reasonably be expected. Thus, additional research is necessary to establish the importance of anonymity and possible privacy concerns of individuals for novel payment methods. The concept of trust is closely connected to privacy concerns and was found to also be examined only lightly. The authors of [44] state that households trust financial institutions more with their data than non-banking operators. Such findings need to be incorporated in the design of a CBDC to ensure that only trusted entities can access privacy-sensitive information in CBDC payments and holdings.

For central banks, anonymity is not seen as a desirable feature as this could hinder compliance with AML/CFT regulation and KYC requirements and could enable illicit activities. It is noted, however, that such activities would still be possible through other (crypto)currencies even if a CBDC were to be completely non-anonymous. Additional disadvantages for the central bank would be increasing costs due to the required investments in the IT-infrastructure as well as substantial research and labor costs to create and manage such a system and to validate transactions. The concepts of privacy-by-design and privacy-by-default are only mentioned in findings that focus specifically on privacy. Similarly, privacy-enhancing technologies (PETs), such as zero-knowledge proof or other techniques that could be applied to token-based CBDC, are not discussed but merely mentioned for future research. Since the publication of the corresponding papers, blockchain platforms such as Corda have adapted such technologies, potentially changing the evaluation result of central banks of such platforms.

While CBs often cite existing regulation and the prevention of illegal activities as reasons to limit privacy in CBDC, it fails to consider regulation that requires the provision of privacy of information for individuals in a similar matter. Financial and personal information that would be stored, exchanged and created by using a CBDC is defined as personal data in Art. 4 GDPR. As this personal data would be processed, defined as the performance of operations on the data (Art. 4(2) GDPR) by CBs and other payment service providers, the GDPR would regulate and restrict how exactly personal data can be used and processed in CBDC payments. Thus, CBs need to consider how privacy can be established in CBDC payments and should not only look for compliance that is focusing on the prevention on illegal activities. The European Data Protection Board (EDPB) has recently published guidelines on the interplay of the GDPR and PSD2 [55] and reiterates the need for data protection and compliance with the GDPR in electronic payments.

The Bank of Canada [14] provides the work with the strongest focus on privacy in CBDC exhibited in this literature review. Although the authors provide an overview of privacy profiles of different payment technologies and rate these technologies on their level of privacy, distinguishing between the possible stakeholders involved, these ratings are not explained in detail. It is, for instance, unclear how the scale in this rating is derived and how exactly it was determined how well a certain technology scored. Furthermore, as was shown in the pilot projects of other central banks, different privacy-enhancing technologies and techniques can substantially improve the possible level of privacy in DLT based payment systems. Therefore, information is missing on the underlying assumptions for the payment systems and how certain technologies could affect the possible level of privacy.

The ECB used a DLT-based solution in its pilot project. The use of "anonymity vouchers" offers a solution that could potentially be independent of the underlying Corda platform solution. In this regard, it is comparable with the use of prepaid cards already loaded with CBDC, an idea introduced by the Central Bank of Sweden [54]. Although neither can function without an underlying technical solution, be it token- or account-based, both possibly provide an interesting workaround to ensure privacy for individuals, without the need for extensive technological research that is required to ensure privacy on the ledger level. Privacy is therefore not only discussed theoretically in various papers of central banks, but also in pilot projects on a technical level. As no finding provided a list or overview of the possible levels on which privacy could be applied or ensured, it is concluded that a comprehensive overview of this subject is still missing.

8 Conclusion and Future Work

This paper evaluates both, the current theoretical work and pilot projects on central bank digital currency concerning privacy and anonymity in payments. Although privacy is a fundamental right and payment and transaction data classify as sensitive information, privacy is discussed often superficially and with no real consideration towards the user or individual. Instead, privacy is discussed as a feature that could hinder central banks' obligations to comply with KYC/AML requirements. Therefore, legal requirements and possible disadvantages of an anonymous CBDC are predominantly discussed. Possible privacy concerns of users are discussed only superficially, similarly to possible technical solutions to ensure privacy. Upon further investigation, it could be shown that several pilot projects of central banks discuss privacy in CBDC in more detail and provide first solutions to foster privacy in retail CBDC.

The current work of central banks is lacking a comprehensive overview of the possible solutions to achieve privacy, grouped by different use cases and desired design choices. The analyzed papers demonstrated that several solutions exist, from de-identification techniques that can be integrated into token-based CBDC to the use of anonymity vouchers or prepaid cards that are loaded with CBDC for both, token- and account-based CBDC. Future work could furthermore focus on individuals' privacy concerns, the desire for anonymity and trust in CBDC, and the involved stakeholders in such a payment system. Existing research on privacy concerns in established payment systems could be adapted and repeated with CBDC as a new payment system. Privacy concerns and trust issues could be researched as potential factors that might influence the adoption of CBDC by the people. Privacy should not only be seen as a feature or option but rather as a requirement that needs to be met.

9 Limitations and Contributions

This paper comes with several limitations. Concerning the review of central bank activities in this domain, not every central bank worldwide has been evaluated. Additionally, not all central banks provide information or search interfaces in English, making a review of their publications and work difficult. The search engines themselves proved to be less effective than expected. As central banks are not obliged to publish their work it is also possible that significant work on CBDC has been done internally that was not communicated to the general public. By using a simple Google and Google News search we tried to mitigate these issues and obtained more information on pilot projects of central banks. Additionally, only information on retail CBDC has been discussed. Through the literature research, it became apparent that various central banks provide information on wholesale CBDC, for interbank payment and settlement, for which privacy should also be considered.

The paper contributes to the scientific body of knowledge of both privacy and payment systems through the identification of research gaps in those domains. The under-researched topic of CBDC, in general, was discussed with a particular focus on privacy. It was shown that privacy as a key design aspect of a CDBC has only been researched scarcely, which is surprising given the impact that the introduction of a

CBDC in a country would likely have on individuals. Further research on how to protect sensitive transaction and holdings information in CBDC payments is necessary. As a managerial contribution, it was shown that a multitude of options exist to create a privacy friendly CBDC. Different central banks used different techniques, both in theory and practice, to tackle the existing issue of designing a CBDC that meets both AML/CFT requirements and the fundamental rights of individuals.

Appendix

Table 2. List of Central Banks and monetary authorities for which no hits could be reported

Central Bank of Azerbaijan	Central Bank of Ecuador	Central Bank of Tunisia	Central Bank of Montenegro
National Bank of Serbia	Central Bank of Egypt	National Bank of Ukraine	Central Bank of the Islamic State of the Iran
Central Bank of Bahrain	Bank of Estonia	Banco Central de Venzuela	Banco Central del Paraguay
Bangladesh Bank	Central Bank of Eswatini	Central Reserve Bank of El Salvador	The Central Bank of the Bahamas
Central Bank of Iraq	Bank Al-Maghrib (Morocco)	National Bank of Georgia	Monetary Brunei Darussalam
National Bank of Cambodia	Central Bank of Kenya	Central Bank of Hungary	Banco Central de la Republica Dominica
Banco de Cabo Verde	Central Bank of Kuwait	Central Bank of Sri Lanka Authority	Central Bank of West African States
Cayman Islands Monetary Authority	Marshall Islands Government	Saudi Arabian Monetary Authority	National Reserve Bank of Tonga
Peoples Bank of China	Central Bank of Jordan	State Bank of Vietnam	Central Bank of the Republic of Kosovo
		Bank of Jamaica	Bank of Zambia

References

1. Quinn, S., Roberds, W.: The Bank of Amsterdam and the leap to central bank money. Am. Econ. Rev. **97**, 262–265 (2007). https://doi.org/10.1257/aer.97.2.262
2. European Commission. COMMISSION RECOMMENDATION of 22 March 2010 on the scope and effects of legal tender of euro banknotes and coins. Off J Eur Union (2010)
3. Doidge, F., Bright, I.: All aboard for the cashless society (2017)
4. Riksbank, S.: The Riksbank's E-Krona Project Report 2 (2018)
5. Nakamoto, S.: Bitcoin: A Peer-to-Peer Electronic Cash System (2008)

6. Vasudevan, R.: Libra and Facebook's Money Illusion (2020). https://doi.org/10.1080/05775132.2019.1684662
7. Skingsley, C.: Should the Riksbank issue e-krona? Speech FinTech Stock 16 (2016)
8. The Economist. China aims to launch the world's first official digital currency (2020)
9. South African Reserve Bank. South African Reserve Bank Procurement Division - Expression of Interest (2019)
10. ECB. Central bank group to assess potential cases for central bank digital currencies (2020)
11. Wandhöfer, R.: The future of digital retail payments in Europe: a place for digital cash? J. Paym. Strateg. Syst. **11**, 248–258 (2017)
12. Phillips, D.: "Digital currency cannot be private," warns Bank of France Governor (2020)
13. Tronnier, F., Recker, M., Hamm, P.: AIS Electronic Library (AISeL) Towards Central Bank Digital Currency – A Systematic Literature Review Towards Central Bank Digital Currency – A Systematic Literature Review (2020)
14. Darbha, S., Arora, R.: Privacy in CBDC technology (2020). https://www.bankofcanada.ca/2020/06/staff-analytical-note-2020-9/#table1
15. ECB. Exploring anonymity in central bank digital currencies. Focus 1–11 December 2019
16. Clarke, R.: Internet privacy concerns confirm the case for intervention. Commun. ACM **42**, 60–67 (1999)
17. Garratt, R.J., van Oordt, M.R.C.: Privacy as a public good: a case for electronic cash, Work Paper (2019). https://doi.org/10.1017/CBO9781316658888.004
18. El Haddad, G., Aimeur, E., Hage, H.: Understanding trust, privacy and financial fears in online payment. In: Proceedings of the 17th IEEE International Conference on Trust, Security and Privacy in Computing and Communications 12th IEEE International Conference on Big Data Science and Engineering Trust, pp. 28–36 (2018). https://doi.org/10.1109/TrustCom/BigDataSE.2018.00015
19. Sahnoune, Z., Aimeur, E., El Haddad, G., Sokoudjou, R.: Watch your mobile payment: an empirical study of privacy disclosure. In: Proceedings of the 14th IEEE International Conference on Trust, Security and Privacy in Computing and Communications Trust, vol. 1, pp. 934–941 (2015). https://doi.org/10.1109/Trustcom.2015.467
20. Mars, A., Adi, W.: Fair exchange and anonymous e-commerce by deploying clone-resistant tokens. In: 2019 42nd International Convention on Information and Communication Technology Electron Microelectron MIPRO 2019 – Proceedings, pp. 1226–1231 (2019). https://doi.org/10.23919/MIPRO.2019.8756734
21. Sekhar, V.C., Mrudula, S.: A complete secure customer centric anonymous payment in a digital ecosystem. In: International Conference on Electronics Communication Technologies, ICCEET 2012, pp. 1049–1054 (2012). https://doi.org/10.1109/ICCEET.2012.6203889
22. Ben-Sasson, E., Chiesa, A., Garman, C., et al.: Zerocash: decentralized anonymous payments from bitcoin. In: Proceedings of the IEEE Security and Privacy, pp. 459–474. https://doi.org/10.1109/SP.2014.36
23. Jayasinghe, D., Markantonakis, K., Mayes, K.: Optimistic fair-exchange with anonymity for bitcoin users. In: IEEE International Conference on E-Business Engineering, ICEBE 2014 - Including 10th Work Service-Oriented Applications, Integration and Collaboration SOAIC 2014, 1st Work E-Commerce Engineering, ECE 2014, pp. 44–51 (2014). https://doi.org/https://doi.org/10.1109/ICEBE.2014.20
24. Leinonen, H.: Electronic central bank cash: to be or not to be? J Paym. Strateg. Syst. **13**, 20–31 (2019)
25. Greco, J., Thomas, H.: Money. Understanding and Creating Alternatives to Legal Tender. Chelsea Green Publishing Company (2001)
26. Bech, M.L., Garratt, R.: Central bank cryptocurrencies (2017)

27. Farell, R.: An analysis of the cryptocurrency industry. Whart Res. Sch J. Pap **130**, 1–23 (2015)
28. Libra Association. Cover Letter - White Paper v2.0, pp. 1–29 (2020)
29. Barontini, C., Holdenm, H.: Proceeding with caution - a survey on central bank digital currency (2019)
30. Kahn, C.M., Rivadeneyra, F., Wong, R.: Should the central bank issue E-money? SSRN Electron. J. (2018). https://doi.org/10.2139/ssrn.3271654
31. Opare, E.A., Kim, K.: A compendium of practices for central bank digital currencies for multinational financial infrastructures. IEEE Access **8**, 110810–110847 (2020). https://doi.org/10.1109/access.2020.3001970
32. Bordo, M., Levin, A.T.: U.S. Digital Cash: Principles & Practical Steps, pp. 1–31 (2019)
33. Nabilou, H., Prüm, A.: Central Banks and Regulation of Cryptocurrencies. Rochester, New York (2019)
34. Hampl, M., Havranek, T.: Central bank equity as an instrument of monetary policy. Comp. Econ. Stud. **62**, 49–68 (2019). https://doi.org/10.1057/s41294-019-00092-1
35. Lannquist, A., World, E.F.: Central banks and distributed ledger technology: how are central banks exploring blockchain today? World Econ Forum (2019)
36. Bordo, M., Levin, A.: Central Bank Digital Currency and the Future of Monetary Policy. Universitas Nusantara PGRI Kediri (2017)
37. Vom Brocke, J., Simons, A., Niehaves, B., et al.: Reconstructing the giant: on the importance of rigour in documenting the literature search process. In: 17th European Conference on Information Systems, ECIS 2009 (2009)
38. Auer, R., Böhme, R.: The technology of retail central bank digital currency. BIS Q. Rev. 85–100 (2020)
39. Boar, C., Holden, H., Wadsworth, A.: Impending arrival - a sequel to the survey on central bank digital currency. BIS Pap 19 (2020)
40. Bank of England. Central Bank Digital Currency, Opportunities, challenges and design (2020)
41. Banque de France. Central Bank Digital Currency (2020)
42. Yanagawa, N., Yamaoka, H.: Digital Innovation, Data Revolution and Central Bank Digital Currency, pp. 1–20 (2019)
43. Nuño, G.: Monetary policy implications of central bank-issued digital currency. Econ. Bull., 1–8 (2018)
44. Wierts, P., Boven, H.: Central Bank Digital Currency, The Netherlands, Amsterdam (2020)
45. Masciandaro, D.: Central bank digital cash and cryptocurrencies: insights from a new baumol-friedman demand for money. Aust. Econ. Rev. **51** (2018). https://doi.org/10.1111/1467-8462.12304
46. Pagnotta, E., Buraschi, A.: An equilibrium valuation of Bitcoin and decentralized network assets. SSRN Electron. J. (2018). https://doi.org/10.2139/ssrn.3142022
47. Kahn, C.M.: Payment systems and privacy. Fed. Reserve Bank St Louis Rev. **100**, 337–344 (2018). https://doi.org/10.20955/r.100.337-44
48. Borgonovo, E., Cillo, A., Caselli, S., Masciandaro, D.: Between cash, deposit and Bitcoin: would we like a central bank digital currency? SSRN Money demand and experimental economics (2018). https://doi.org/10.2139/ssrn.3160752
49. BANK N. NORGES BANK PAPERS Central bank digital currencies (2018)
50. Financial Transactions and Reports Analysis Centre of Canada (2020) Money services businesses (MSBs). https://www.fintrac-canafe.gc.ca/msb-esm/msb-eng. Accessed 26 Nov 2020
51. SOV Development Foundation. The Marshall Islands (2019). https://sov.foundation/marshall-islands

52. Foundation SD. The Marshallese Sovereign (SOV): Fair, Sustainable Money (2019). https://docsend.com/view/nvi59vw
53. Central Bank of the Bahamas. Project Sand Dollar (2019)
54. Sveriges Riksbank. The Riksbank's e-krona project (2018)
55. European Data Protection Board. Guidelines 06/2020 on the interplay of the Second Payment Services Directive and the GDPR, 1–23 (2020)

Analysing Drivers' Preferences for Privacy Enhancing Car-to-Car Communication Systems
A Study from South-Africa

Lejla Islami[1]([✉]), Simone Fischer-Hübner[1], Eunice Naa Korkoi Hammond[2], and Jan Eloff[2]

[1] Karlstad University, Karlstad, Sweden
lejla.islami@kau.se
[2] University of Pretoria, Pretoria, South Africa

Abstract. While privacy-enhancing solutions for car-to-car communication are increasingly researched, end user aspects of such solutions have not been in the focus. In this paper, we present a qualitative study with 16 car drivers in South Africa for analysing their privacy perceptions and preferences for control and privacy trade-offs, which will allow to derive end user requirements for privacy and identity management for vehicular communication systems. Our results show that while the South African participants are willing to share their location data with family and close friends, they often lack trust in external entities. They perceive safety implications from criminals and hackers and therefore dispel constant location tracking. Usability, privacy and safety are top priorities, with differing privacy – usability trade-offs for different users. The results show that participants demand more control over their privacy and seek usable privacy notices, transparency and fine-grained controls.

Keywords: Vehicular communication · Privacy-enhancing technologies (PETs) · Privacy perception · Privacy preferences · Usable privacy and identity management

1 Introduction

Future vehicular communication systems can bring many benefits for society, enhancing transportation safety, efficiency and convenience for drivers [17]. However, they pose privacy challenges at the same time. Continuous collection of users' location data enables to profile the drivers' locations and to derive sensitive information, e.g. about their activities or social contacts. Driving data is expected to be a 1.2 trillion euro market by 2030 [13], and thus there is an interest to use these data for different purposes. At the same time, many users may

© IFIP International Federation for Information Processing 2021
Published by Springer Nature Switzerland AG 2021
M. Friedewald et al. (Eds.): Privacy and Identity 2020, IFIP AICT 619, pp. 115–133, 2021.
https://doi.org/10.1007/978-3-030-72465-8_7

want to benefit from the wide range of applications, from infotainment services, navigation services, collision avoidance alerts and traffic condition updates, as long as their privacy is protected. The deployment of the continuous advances in vehicular ad hoc networks (VANETs) may only become a reality after the security and privacy of users are safeguarded [21]. There have been an extensive research on enabling fundamental security and privacy building blocks for the introduction of such systems in the future (e.g., [16,17]). Focusing on achieving anonymity and unlinkability in car-to-car communication systems, most of the proposals are pseudonym-based solutions [23]. Despite the importance of the development of privacy-enhancing solutions for vehicle communication, we know little about users' perceptions about the potential trade-offs of these solutions and their preferences and requirements in regard to privacy trade-off settings. We argue that it is essential to understand users' perception and preferences and to elicit their privacy requirements for implementing usable privacy and identity management solutions for VANETs, which are based on usable configuration options offering suitable selectable privacy settings that similar-minded users share.

As privacy is a cultural construct [18], user requirements and preferences may differ culturally. For our study we decided to address the following research questions while choosing the context of South Africa:

- **RQ1:** *What privacy perceptions and preferences for data sharing and control do South African drivers have for car-to-car communication systems?*
- **RQ2:** *What are their preferences concerning trade-offs of location privacy vs. costs, safety and utility and usability?*

Within the scope of the SSF project SURPRISE and a SASUF (South Africa – Sweden University Forum) – funded project, we have the ultimate goal to conduct an intercultural comparison study by researching these questions in Sweden and South Africa. As a first step in this direction, we conducted 16 semi-structured interviews with car drivers in South Africa. This paper reports about the findings of this first study, on which we will base our future research on usable privacy and identity management for VANETs.

The remainder of this paper is structured as follows: The following Sect. 2 presents as Background the current role of privacy in South Africa and briefly explains how far privacy trade-offs need to be made for privacy-enhancing VANETs. Section 3 is then presenting the methodology that we took for conducting and evaluating the interviews. The results of the interviews are then presented in Sect. 4 followed by a discussion in Sect. 5. Section 6 is then discussing related work before final conclusions and an outlook are provided in Sect. 7.

2   Background

This section first explains the role of privacy in South Africa, and then the privacy trade-offs to be made for privacy-enhancing VANETs.

2.1   Privacy in South Africa

From social gatherings to backyard entertainment, South Africans are inevitably one of the most sociable groups of people around the world [30]. However, this may come as a contrast to the amount of value nationals and residents place on their security and safety on day to day activities and living. With the ever increasing crime rate in the country [11], many South Africans choose to invest in putting a guard on their surroundings. This has not only taken place in their physical environments, but also on various online communication streams and other interactions.

Views on privacy may be largely impacted through knowledge of the European Union's (EU) General Data Protection Regulation (GDPR) [10], yet South Africa's version of the privacy protection act, the Protection of Personal Information (POPI) Act [22], is one that may also ensure that privacy is protected and preserved. Signed into a law in late 2013, this act is targeted at the protection of personal information of individuals, with highlights on the confidentiality and integrity of this personal digital information, amongst others [8].

Privacy preferences by South Africans are more generally by preference, and one would hope that by an assurance of the safety of data and information, the average South African will likely have their hearts at rest, that is, by their data being protected (i.e. private), they will be safe. Nonetheless, this does not seem to be the case, as research shows that the gap between the expectations that people have about their privacy protection and whether or not these expectations are being met, is quite high [7]. A recent study [6] revealed that 91.8% of the participants had these high expectations concerning their privacy yet remained concerned when they have to share this information, especially online [6].

With this, it appears there is a clear contradiction as to what is stated in the POPI Act versus what many nationals actually experience, and whether this is intentional or not, this raises doubts in many hearts and minds and establishes the "concern for information privacy", as to whether or not their safety is actually guaranteed, as a result of these privacy expectations [6].

2.2   Privacy Trade-Offs

Through an interview with experts researching privacy-enhancing VANETs from the SURPRISE project, we identified privacy trade-offs that may have to be made for privacy-enhancing solutions with costs, utility, usability and safety, which are also partly discussed in [23].

We are focusing on privacy-enhancing solutions based on short-lived pseudonyms and k-anonymity as the most commonly used, especially by our partners of the SURPRISE project (e.g., [16,17]). For such solutions the privacy trade-offs can be summarised as follows: the shorter the time periods with that pseudonyms are exchanged, the lower the degree of linkability and thus the higher privacy protection. However, exchanging pseudonyms frequently implies higher costs for obtaining more signed pseudonyms from the issuing party (trade-offs with costs). Moreover, traffic collisions may be more difficult to predict the shorter the time periods are (trade-offs with traffic safety). On the other side, the more frequent traffic information is submitted, the higher the quality of traffic information. However, if pseudonyms are often reused in a period of time, the degree of linkability raises (trade-offs with quality/utility).

Another privacy-enhancing technique is using obfuscation by generalizing the spatiotemporal information related to the drivers' location information, such that the location of a driver cannot be distinguished from that of at least k-1 other drivers, thus achieving k-anonymity [28]. For PET solutions with k-anonymous location privacy, privacy trade-offs with utility, and thus with usability, arise as well, as we will illustrate below.

3   Methodology

We conducted 16 semi-structured interviews with car drivers in South Africa to analyse what privacy perceptions and preferences drivers have for car-to-car communication systems and to find out how would they trade-privacy off with other goals such as costs, usability, data quality, safety. The study was approved by Research Ethics Board at University of Pretoria and the Ethical Advisor at Karlstad University. In this section we describe the qualitative research methods employed, interview procedure and data analysis.

3.1 Participants

We recruited our participants via posting flyers around University of Pretoria's campus and asking individuals through word of mouth. In the invitation letter, we did not use the word "privacy" to avoid a bias. The invitation letter requested participants who had used any kind of car-to-car communication system, but did not place any other restrictions for participation. We asked all 16 participants that volunteered to first fill in a short questionnaire and sign a consent form for informing about data processing in compliance with POPI act and the GDPR. The questionnaire requested demographics (age group, gender, educational background) and asked them to specify the vehicular communication system they currently use or had used before. We interviewed 10 male (P1–2, 4–7, 10–11, 15–16) and 6 female (P3, 8–9, 12–14) participants in age groups ranged from 18 to 40, all from South Africa. Five participants were students (P1, 5, 9–11), 9 had a university degree (P3–4, 6–8, 13–16) and 2 had a MSc degree or higher (P2, 12). Our participants used different vehicular communication and navigation tools, most common Waze and Google Maps.

3.2 Interview Procedure

All interviews were conducted face-to-face in a semi-structured fashion, lasting for 20 min on average, and were all audio-recorded. Before we defined the catalog of interview questions, we conducted interviews with PET research experts of the field to identify the potential privacy trade-offs (see Sect. 2.2).

Privacy Perceptions and Preferences for Existing Systems. Particularly, the focus on existing systems rather than future developments was on purpose as we wanted to look at users' experience and perception on practical solutions and not on newer systems that are hardly in use or not at all. Participants were asked questions about their perceptions about existing vehicular communication systems in terms of perceived sensitivity towards location data tracking, location data linked with their identity, and if they want to manage and control the driving data or hand over the control to others. Furthermore, we asked them with whom they would share their identity/location data and with whom not, and whether the users would like that other drivers can have location privacy and under which conditions (e.g., whether accountability plays a role).

Privacy Perceptions and Preferences for PETs. To address and identify drivers' trade-off preferences of short-lived pseudonyms, we asked participants questions about their perceptions in regard to different trade-offs of location privacy with costs, data quality/utility/usability, and safety. They were asked if they perceived any advantages of PET solutions for VANETs in comparison to existing ones, and whether they would pay for obtaining more pseudonyms from an issuing party to increase pseudonymity. They were also asked whether they would like to be located for safety reasons (in case of an accident), against whom they want to be private and whether they would like to have fine-grained privacy controls for protecting and sharing personal location data.

Privacy Vs. Data Utility Preferences. We introduced participants with a use case for a privacy-enhancing solution based on obfuscation of location data. Practically they were said to imagine they were getting assistance from a navigation application on their mobile phone when searching for available parking spots in their nearby. They were shown two mock-ups consisting of two different navigation maps (see Fig. 1), where in the first one the user would receive a map with parking places in the specific street he was interested in, and in the second one, he would receive a map with parking places for a larger region. In the first case, as he is the only driver in that street at the moment, the service provider can identify the user and see his fine-grained location. In the other one, it is possible to hide his exact location so that the system would not know where he is exactly, since there are many other cars nearby (it is possible to hide within a crowd of (k) other car drivers for achieving k-anonymity). Then, in order to get in the nearby parking spot, the user zooms-in the map. We asked them how they would trade privacy vs. data utility/usability in that scenario.

Ranking of Goals. In the last part of the interview, we asked our participants to rank different goals such as: usability and data utility, costs, safety, accountability, privacy.

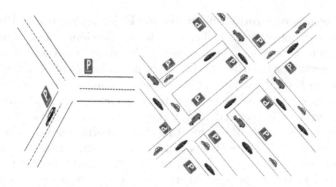

Fig. 1. Navigation maps mock-ups

3.3   Data Analysis

All interviews were audio-recorded, transcribed and coded using open, axial and selective data coding methods of grounded theory [12,26]. Thus, the themes to answer the research questions emerged from the inductive analysis of the interview transcripts. To do so, we firstly got ourselves familiar with the data by reading through the scripts multiple times. Then we performed open coding process with the help of the guidelines from the Saldaa code book [25] to develop an initial codebook. Secondly these codes and concepts derived from the data were combined into categories and that resulted in the development of core categories in the axial coding phase. After iterative discussions between two researchers, we observed and agreed on a set of findings. Over 100 unique codes emerged from the analysis, which were then assigned to several categories such as "criteria for sharing", "data control", "lack of trust", etc. The data analysis was supported by NVivo 12 software. Using a software program such as NVivo facilitated creative management of multiple data sources, enabled multiple overlapping nodes and ensured visibility of our methodological processes [24].

4   Results

In this section, we present and expand on the main categories that emerged from the evaluation of the interview transcripts, including quotes from participants labeled P1 to P16.

4.1   Privacy Perceptions About Car-to-Car Communication

This category describes participants' perceived sensitivities and concerns about data used in vehicular communication systems, positive and negative perceptions using the system, and how they perceive location tracking implications.

Comfort with Data Collection. Participants shared privacy concerns in regard to the system provider collecting personal data about them. Our analysis shows that perceived privacy and security risks of big data collection by the provider impacts their comforts. Six participants proved to be very uncomfortable with personal data being collected by the system. *"It actually scares me to know how much Google knows about me and the places I visit. There is a huge privacy issue there in terms of Google and in terms of what they actually track about the user. Cause as end users we do not necessary know what data Google is collecting and essentially what they are doing with that data"* (P2).

Ten other participants are less concerned about location data being collected, often rationalizing that it is beneficial to improve the system or the user experience. However, half of these participants (P1, 3, 9, 12, 15) are not comfortable with location data being linkable with other data, especially identity. This indicates that participants are often unaware that the user of location data can anyhow be easily identified, which means that they are anyhow concerned.

Therefore, all but five participants (P1–5, 9–10, 12–13, 15–16) would feel very uncomfortable with linking location data with name and that data being shared with third parties. *"I am on the edge about that because it is linked to my identity, that compromises my privacy"* (P10).

Furthermore, our observation demonstrates a lack of understanding of the problem of metadata that could be inferred from location data and thus, participants inadvertently believe there is no risk to privacy (P1, 8–9, 11, 13).

On the other side, P6–8, 11, 14 expressed different views on the perceived comfortability in respect to the third party the data is shared with, and the perceived benefits, as P14 argued: *"Well, I don't know. If it is insurance or somewhere I need help, then that is perfectly fine"*.

Some participants (P3, 10–11) rationalized their reluctance to take actions to protect their privacy considering themselves not important enough, as captured by the following statement by P11: *"The only concern would be if someone wants to use my location data against me in some negative way, which I can not really see a situation like that happening except if I am the American president"*.

When asked about the perceived level of sensitivity of different types of data such as: identity/location/navigation data, most participants (P1–4, 6–9, 12–14, 16) regarded them as very sensitive. *"I mean they are sensitive data, personal information so they are extremely sensitive to me"* (P12). In comparison, P5, 10–11, 15 do not really consider the data very sensitive.

Concerns about home address and identity information were among the most sensitive issues discussed, as partly mentioned due to burglary problems in South Africa. When asked if they think that someone could derive sensitive details from the location data, all participants identified home address inference concern. *"Generally no, but my house, my home yes. Like the data says I go to University of Pretoria every day that is fine but I don't want particularly people know where my house is"* (P9).

Moreover, some participants acknowledged that association of a user with a specific location can reveal sensitive details about different things: health problems, association among people, habits, etc. *"Yeah, definitely, I mean you can figure out if two people are closely related, you can figure out when did they meet up, where they meet up"* (P16).

Users Privacy Concerns in Car-to-Car Systems. Privacy risks can be conceptualized as the perceived potential loss of control in regard to data disclosure and the potential misuse of personal information [29].

Participants' privacy concerns range from fear of data misuse and worries about bad privacy practices of the data in general, to data security issues and potential leaks. Among the perceived risks they emphasized the risk of tracking, profiling, third party data sharing and impersonation attacks.

Most of the participants (twelve out of sixteen) fear that their data could be used in a way that could damage their reputation and perceive location tracking implications in terms of privacy and safety, often aggravated to fear of life. *"I do think there are implications if someone is looking to do something malicious then yeah, definitely. As I said if someone is willing, they can put in the effort and try to track me down"*(P10). On a related note, three participants (P9, P10, P13) raised the fear of stalking as a possible implication of tracking. *"I mean of course someone can find where I stay and use that against me by coming to my house or following me where I would go usually everyday, I could be stoked"* (P9).

Several other participants (P5, 11–12) identified location tracking implications in relation to car robbery crime or safety threats in South Africa. *"For instance I know criminals in South Africa especially try to keep track of when someone is at home or when they get back. If they then get my information and keep track of when I am not home to possibly go and rob, yeah"* (P11).

P12 emphasized the safety risks of kidnapping: *"Of course there is security implication, especially in South Africa, you wouldn't want anyone to know where you are living because the problem is in terms of security, is the people that know you that actually are the security risk and not the people that might not know you. To an extent for example in my home country kidnapping is a huge thing"*.

Some participants highlighted their inability to prevent location tracking by keeping the location disabled as much as possible and seem resigned against constant tracking by companies. *"I guess you just resign to the fact that Google can do this much tracking and damage to your reputation, you come to terms that being the only option that you have"* (P2). P12 has lost her trust in achieving location privacy noting: *"I know I am being tracked and I know there is no privacy so I don't. . .".*

On the other side, participants expressed concerns whether companies have the adequate technical means to protect their data, whether it is stored securely, encrypted and anonymised in the first place. Moreover, users are concerned of the purposes the driving data is being used for, as highlighted by P16. *"It would be quite intense I think because it sort of comes out to how would they use that information, that would be my biggest question"*. Regarding other factors impacting their concerns, participants (P1–2, 6) echoed issues if data leaks or gets hacked and gets into wrong hands (criminals). *"Maybe I don't want to use this because I don't want this data to be leaked to anybody"* (P1).

Managing data collection is very difficult for users because of the different collectors, which challenges the users' trust regarding intentional or unintentional collection of information that is not necessary for the service. P12 brought up the problem of the enormous data that is collected and its potential misuse from the services in South Africa. *"How much unnecessary information they would collect for every service in South Africa, the purpose that they collect it for is not what they use it for, but are trying to use it for personal gain. In such scenario I am not protecting my privacy but I feel that they are invading my space"*.

If the data is collected, it is easier for the external entities, collectors, governments, hackers to access and use the information. Especially, participants identified an increasing potential for data exploitation by government and law enforcement, hence feeling about potential privacy intrusions.

Trust on External Entities. Data disclosure means loss of privacy, hence it is translated in loss of trust by many participants (P1, 3, 4, 7, 10, 12, 16). Our results demonstrate that some participants (P4, 7, 10, 13) often perceive strong lack of trust towards service provider companies and their data collection and handling practices. *"I wouldn't trust companies, I don't know why I trust them"* (P7). Our analysis identified that participants are very concerned about the probability of data misuse by the data receiving party and previous research found out that users with high privacy concerns also mistrust the integrity of service providers to appropriately handle their data (Zhou, 2012).

Furthermore, benefit or threat to privacy depends also on the entities that gain access to personal information, thus participants perceive different division of trust level between many entities. For instance, all participants identified their trust in family and friends, but not necessarily in government as highlighted by P2 and P7. *"I think anybody or government that want to exploit data in terms of spyware or tracking users based on certain risk factors or bodies that want to sell the information to make profit"* (P2).

On the other side, some participants (P3, 8–9, 15) perceived trust in location based service provider, but do not want to release the data to the public or to share it with other third parties.

In comparison, the results could also replicate a significant negative effect of privacy concerns on trust on other drivers in regard to the location data. When asked whom would they trust in respect to location data, many participants (P1–2, 4–5, 7, 16) declared they would not trust anyone. *"I don't know whom I wouldn't trust because well, you just don't know, you just don't trust anyone in general"* (P1).

4.2 Preferences for PETs

This section describes users' privacy preferences in regard to identity management control options, it provides a detailed overview of participants' requirements in regard to collecting and sharing the driving data, conditions for being tracked, and whether they prefer other drivers to have location privacy and under which conditions.

Trust in PETs. Our interviewees (eleven out of sixteen) recognize the benefits of short-lived pseudonyms and PETs in terms of enhancing data privacy, enabling anonymity, and protecting against tracking and profiling. However, P2 and P12 indicated they would trust pseudonymity only if traceable in case of crime, if accountability is guaranteed. *"I am definitely in favour of the privacy-preserving pseudonyms however, I guess there is a case where we have to forsake some sort of trade-off to actually have some regulations and laws in place, so if certain incidents happen you should actually be able to track an attacker for instance but, it should not be overly exploited by law enforcement for spying"* (P2).

Other participants (P6–8, P10) reflected on other advantages of PETs in regard to protecting against tracking and profiling. P9, 11, 14 confirmed they would feel more secure and safe with PETs as they believe PETs can protect users (scared of being assassinated) from malicious people. P4 liked PETs but he believes they can be in conflict with transparency: *"I can see advantages like security but then also if you want to see the data they have on you, that would be very difficult if it is more security in place. You can't track your data and staff"*.

However, some participants perceive limited trust that PETs can protect location privacy. For instance, P1 had issues trusting that pseudonymity is securely implemented, and P2 stated that trust in PETs requires open source. Several other interviewees also had some questions in regard to PETs. While P14 seem to have doubts how far databases can really be secured, P16 is not sure how privacy controls can be implemented.

Privacy Preference Specification. Our qualitative analysis indicates that participants have different perceptions in relation to data control, most of them (nine participants P1, 4–5, 7–8, 11–13, 15) prefer to hand over the control to a trusted third party believing that they are not inclined to manage the data as it may be difficult, time-consuming or may hinder system's usability. Given their desire for convenience and the difficulty to configure privacy settings, participants might instead trust the service provider to protect their privacy. Previous literature has shown that users may be unwilling to manage their privacy due to the required effort to manage privacy controls and the perceived difficulty to configure them [19]. In comparison, seven participants (P2–3, 6, 9–10, 14, 16) desire full controls over the data they share, from decisions to who they share it with, data minimization to rights to deleting collected data. *"I would say the least amount of driving that being collected is the best, so I would like to have full control of my driving data or any data that is being collected"* (P2).

All but three participants (P8, P11, P15) prefer fine-grained privacy control options for protecting and sharing personal location data.

Moreover, participants want to be granted control such as the option to access, to consent or deletion of their data. Several participants (P5, 16) emphasized that users should be able to delete the data collected about them. P5, 12,

14–16 strongly seek to consent for any data processing practices and want to have their right to data traceability. P12 explained, *"I prefer to know and let me give my consent to say you can go ahead and use it for research or whatever but, let me be aware of it"*. In addition, participants (P2, 5, 12) desire to be notified and aware of location tracking. Some of them (P3, 6–8, 14) are comfortable to be tracked by insurance companies and sometimes police only if it is transparent and there is a need. When asked whether they want to be tracked for safety, in case of an accident, P2, 5, 11–13 identified the option to share location in distress through a panic button rather than being constantly tracked while driving. *"Give you the option to share that, let's say there is a button that says: Emergency, call the police"* (P5). Furthermore, P10 explained that he refuses to be tracked by companies: *"I think I don't mind being tracked by close friends and family but I don't think tracking information is necessary to big companies and stuff like that"*. Some interviewees (P2, 5, 7) noted they dispel spying by government or police. *"I wouldn't like to be tracked by the police or things like that"* P(5). Other participants (P1–2, 9, 12) stated they dispel being tracked at all, probably due to the identified safety risk in South Africa. *"I don't want anyone to track me. Nobody should track me, no one"* (P12).

Transparency. Transparency relates to the legal right of the data subject, granted by the GDPR and the POPI act, to obtain insight in regard to all processing practices of his data by the data controller. Transparency about the data collected and the purpose of the collection also influence comfort levels for data collection [2]. In light of our findings, transparency was a key concern shared by participants, both in terms of data collection, the processing and storing of it. This concern increases when data is shared with third parties as P2 elaborated: *"Sometimes is not really transparent in terms of end user knowing that this is actually happening, without reading through the long terms and conditions to find print where they say that they store some information about you. It could be sending it off to third party companies to get additional revenue profits, so there is no transparency or accountability in terms of what Google is doing with this location tracking"*.

Insights from the responses indicate that participants perceive a strong lack of service provider accountability, and several of them (P2,12) relate to the GDPR, raising an interesting point in regard to the applications often being not fully GDPR compliant with the principles of data minimization and transparency. Some interviewees also noted that while the collected data would not necessarily be misused, the uncertainty of what happens with it actually concerned them more. In principle, all but two participants identified they explicitly seek transparency for the collected data. A strong requirement that participants have is to be aware of the data that is collected about them. This includes to be informed about which kind of data are collected, who is receiving it and what is done with it. *"I would like to know who is being able to see it and why they need to see it"* (P9).

Our analysis suggests that participants (P2–5, 11–12) are particularly strict about seeking transparency of purposes of data use, as P12 put it: *"I want to know what my data is being used for, and if it is being used for what is said they want to use it for"*. P4 and P14 demand transparency not only of how data is handled, but also and if it is secured and whether it leaks. P8 also pinpointed transparency in regard to breach notifications, noting: *"I would like to know if there has been any leaks"*.

Even though participants prefer to be informed about everything, this is practically not always the case, as explained by P1–2, 4–5, 15, who complained about privacy policies often being too long, containing irrelevant information or difficult-to-understand.

Sharing Criteria. We analysed participants' preferences in regard to with whom they would like to share their identity/location data and with whom not, and whether participants would like that other drivers can have location privacy or not and under which conditions. Through the responses related to discomfort of data collection, we found out many factors of why participants do not want to share their data. Perceived risks and limited trust on external entities to protect the data, were key observations to impact participants' unwillingness towards sharing their driving data.

In contrast, most of our participants (12 out of 16) pointed out they would share location with family and friends. Noteworthy is that participants showed a high agreement in regard to the specific cases they would share the data other than their family members.

Participants mentioned safety or emergency situations as the only purposes for data sharing that they would approve of. When asked whether they want to share location or identity in case of an accident, all participants expressed willingness to share location and identity for safety reasons. Therefore, ten out of sixteen participants indicated they would share location with law enforcement or insurance for emergency services. However, they seek to share location by choice, expose it only when the need arises and not continuously while driving. *"Yes, but it would have to be a choice, I would have to say I am at this location, I would have to give consent that someone else could access it"* (P16). On the other side, the perceived limited trust to use the data appropriately would make some participants (P1–2, 15, 16) hesitant to share location or identity with external entities for safety situations. *"Yes, if I have a confidence that is what it is used for I guess. If I can guarantee that they are going to use it in a responsible way"* (P15). Our results further substantiate this, as some participants (P2, 7) seek to be private against government and law enforcement and many (P4, 7, 10, 13, 16) conveyed that they want privacy against companies.

Other participants (P1, 3, 10, 13–14, 16) expressed they want other drivers to have location privacy as well, and they also liked their family members to be locatable for safety reasons. *"As well as emergency services, yes. I have a younger brother, he is still sixteen and when it comes to certain things, you would want to know where they are"* (P13).

4.3   Privacy Trade-Off Preferences

This section reports about participants' willingness to trade privacy for data utility, safety and costs.

The wish for increasing safety and the wish for privacy and potential trade-offs, is seen in two different spectrums, safety from criminals and hackers, and traffic safety against car accidents. We found out that the higher the perception of safety risk from car accidents, the likelihood to trade privacy among participants increases. All of them agree to share location for traffic safety.

In contrast, our results exhibit significant effects of car robbery problems in South Africa on the desire for safety and protecting one's own privacy. Participants showed strong safety concerns particularly in regard to tracking for criminal purposes, kidnapping and stalking (see Sect. 4.1), thus they explicitly demand location privacy from criminals and hackers. Hence, location privacy towards the service provider and other drivers is rather perceived as an important enabler for safety against criminals. While conflicts between privacy and safety still arise in regard to the question if the drivers' location should be kept private from law enforcement, most users would still only trade-off privacy in specific emergency cases due to their limited trust, as discussed above.

Our results also indicate that many participants (P2, 7–8, 11–13) acknowledge the importance of user accountability.

The perceptions of privacy risks to personal data had considerable impact on participants that were less likely to trade privacy off with data utility. Ten out of sixteen participants precised they would not trade privacy off with data utility/usability. When asked about the use case presented to them (see Sect. 3.2), participants (P3–6, 8–10, 13–14, 16) expressed they would be interested in a more privacy-friendly solution on the cost of data utility/usability. *"I go for the second one cause my data is protected. And I think it wouldn't take much time for me to be able to zoom in and try to get my parking place that I am looking for"* (P6). P5 regarded location privacy more important than usability in the context of safety problems in South Africa. *"I think the second one, just in terms of I wouldn't want people to know where my car is and to be able to follow me because in our case in South Africa maybe it is a dangerous area where I am looking for a parking spot and they will know where I am and that I am going to be there"*.

However, not everybody perceived the map providing location generalisation as a trade-off. P8 would actually see bigger utility on the bigger map, explaining: *"I would prefer the second one actually just because it gives me an overview of..., I would like to see in my nearby region where the parkings are rather than just one specific region"*. Insights from the responses indicate that the higher the perception of convenience among the other participants (P1–2, 7, 11, 15), the likelihood to trade privacy increases. *"First of all, it makes sense, it is pretty cool. I would probably be on the convenience side and sacrifice privacy but I think the beauty of this thing is you can be on a continues spectrum, depending on how much you value privacy and the granularity of this. But for me personally I am on the convenience side"* (P15). In contrast, P11 saw it in relation to crime problems in South Africa: *"So, in terms of this, I would say, especially in South Africa, the first one, the utility is much better cause people in South Africa tend to park very close to where they want to go cause they are scared to walk"*.

Only one participant, P12 explained the trade-off between usability and privacy depending on the context: *"I am willing to trade-off if the need arises, and the trade-off for me is really important. But at any given space, the trade-off will always win: what is more important to me right now? Do I need a parking now or do I need to protect my privacy now? When I weight the options, I choose what works now. Tomorrow I may decide not to came to campus by car. I turn off the tracking and I walk, so it depends"*.

However, when asked to rank usability, cost, privacy, safety, accountability and driving assistance (data utility) as essential triggers of introducing privacy-enhancing solutions for vehicular communication in the future, there was no clear indication of their preferences, as participants showed a high variance in their rankings and also in relation to the above use case preferences. For instance, six participants (1–2, 9–11, 16) valued usability the most relevant goal, while four participants (P4, 6, 10, 13) ranked privacy the highest goal and four other participants (P3, 5, 10, 14) ranked safety against criminals on top. While three participants (P7–8, 15) qualified driving assistance (data utility) the paramount goal, interestingly, only P12 perceived accountability the most important. It is important to note, that privacy, usability and safety were perceived nearly at the same level, as participants perceived safety and privacy equally important as their second option.

In light of our findings, cost was perceived the least important goal by all participants. When asked if they would be ready to pay more for more frequently changed pseudonyms issued by a third party, we observed a split in participants' attitudes towards paying. The majority of them (9 out of 16) stated they would not pay for short-lived pseudonyms. Within the qualitative responses related to hesitance to pay for more short-lived pseudonyms, we also found explanations of why participants do not want to pay. P2 and P5 rationalized their reluctance by inferring that pseudonymity/privacy should be cost-free. *"Generally this anonymity I think shouldn't really come at the users expense because then you kind of discriminate against users in terms of - if you want to be more secure you have to pay more"* (P2). *"The thing is I wouldn't want to pay for it because that is going to send various people to be less safe because people want the free option"* (P5). While P9 (wrongly) thinks that three alternating pseudonyms would be sufficient to protect her identity, P12 anyhow does not trust pseudonyms, as she thinks that they could still be linked with her name. While most participants expressed scepticism to paying, some (P3–4, 6, 10, 13–14) noted they were willing to pay but not to a large extent.

5 Discussion

In this section, we discuss the results in terms of the cultural impact and in terms of end user and design requirements that we can derive for privacy-enhanced VANETs. Moreover, limitations of our study are briefly discussed.

Cultural Aspects: We believe that several of our findings are specific for South Africa and may not apply for users or other countries, such as especially demand for location privacy for protecting against criminals and stalkers, which is more an issue in South Africa than Sweden. In addition, also the lack of trust in Government does likely differ from Sweden, which is according to a recent Euro-barometer survey the European country with the highest trust in government in regard to handling its citizens' data [9]. Moreover, the willingness to share location information with family and close friends may be different from Sweden that has been classified as an individualist society [14] in which responsibility is taken for direct family only and in which family bounds may be less tight.

End User and Design Requirements: From our findings we can derive requirements for privacy and identity management for VANETs. Firstly, given the users' desire for transparency and control, transparency and intervenability online functions should be offered by design. Particularly, for VANETs based on short-lived pseudonyms, there should be options for the users to securely and pseudonymously exercise their transparency and interveneability rights online (e.g., by authenticating users as the pseudonym holders with zero-knowledge by using anonymous credential proofs [4]), as it is for instance also supported by Art. 11 (2) GDPR. Secondly, for meeting preferences in terms of data sharing as stated by the study participants, fine grained controls should allow to share location data with persons of trust, while restricting access for the provider and other external parties. Thirdly, different selectable profiles of privacy settings should be offered for South African users. The default setting should enforce the most privacy-friendly option for enforcing the privacy by default principle. In addition, further selectable profiles could differ in regard to different degrees of privacy trade-offs with utility/usability and costs while not compromising on traffic safety and basic privacy protection that were rated with highest priority.

Limitations: Our study may have a bias through the limited number of inter-viewees with higher educations than the average population. Also for this reason, we plan a follow-up quantitative study for analysing hypotheses derived from this study with a broader sample of participants.

6   Related Work

Previous surveys reviewing privacy-preserving solutions for IoT environments and VANETs based on pseudonyms [1,23] show that while there have been an extensive research focusing on technical aspects of PETs for vehicular communication systems, the end-user aspects of such systems, and especially usable pseudonym configurations considering privacy trade-offs, are still fairly unaddressed. Nonetheless, earlier research has treated the users' privacy perceptions and requirements for different IoT application areas, especially for smart homes, and for mobile applications, or have studied related end user aspects concerning privacy and trust for VANETs.

Previous related studies on smart homes have also focused on end user privacy perceptions and requirements. For instance, the authors in [35] examined users' attitudes regarding privacy, intimacy and trust issues for medical technology in smart homes and found privacy and trust the main requirements of users. Another work [32] explored user-centered privacy design for smart homes and identified usability, user experience, system intelligence, system modality and, similarly as we identified in our study for VANETs, also data transparency and control, security and safety, as key design factors for smart home privacy. Cottrill et al. [5] conducted a survey to examine consumers' perceptions of privacy in the mobile environment and also researched location data sharing preference factors. The results revealed that while participants responses perceive that sharing data in the mobile environments pose privacy risks, they do not take further steps to protect their privacy. Moreover, key findings were that users' privacy preferences and willingness to share location data are impacted by personal characteristics, contextual factors of the possible sharing of data (entities the data could be shared with - which is also discussed in our study), and the perceived benefits.

In the vehicular context, [31] examined the acceptance of connected vehicular services in a high-fidelity simulation environment and observed privacy perceptions to impact usage adoption. Bossauer et al. [3] qualitatively analyzed the relationship between the need for trust and privacy in peer-to-peer car-sharing from the perspective of car owners and rentees. Though, not exclusively focused on privacy and vehicular communication, a related set of research [20,33,34] have investigated users' perceptions on privacy concerns and preferences inside the smart home environments and have identified a range of findings, highlighting the importance of understanding users to be able to create usable privacy mechanisms [15]. Others have also shown in an empirical study similar findings in regard to users' perceived privacy concerns for connected cars in terms of a lack of transparency of data sharing with and use by car manufacturers [27]. This work also reports that some study participants mentioned perceived benefits in terms of safety and risks if location data are shared with the police or household members for tracking activities, without that this work is however analysing these aspects more systematically and in more detail.

Despite such previous work examining end user aspects for other IoT and mobile application areas, to the best of our knowledge, this study is the first to analyze drivers' privacy perceptions and preferences for privacy trade-offs and control for privacy-enhancing car-to-car communication systems. Moreover, we are the first to study these end user aspects for VANETs for South Africa.

7   Conclusions

In this paper, we reported on a qualitative study on privacy perceptions and preferences for deriving requirements related to privacy-enhanced car-to-car communication systems. We asked 16 drivers from South Africa about their preferences about control and trade-offs of PET solutions for vehicular communications. The main results and key observations that strike us as the most vivid and representational of the study for South African users are listed below in relation to our two research questions that they are addressing.

Recurring Themes Answering RQ1:

- The more sensitive the data are perceived, the more concerned, the less willing the users are to share.
- Participants are uncomfortable of location data being linked with their identity.
- Drivers often perceive lack of trust on external entities (government, police, ISP) to protect their privacy properly.
- Drivers perceive limited trust in the privacy protection of PETs.
- Participants want more control over their privacy and want to make privacy decisions transparent (usable privacy notices and control, transparency and fine-grained settings).
- All of them are willing to share location and identity with family and close friends.
- All participants are willing to share location in distress, they dispel being tracked all the time.
- Drivers want to remain private against other drivers.

Recurring Themes Answering RQ2:

- Safety against criminals and privacy are the primary concerns of drivers in car-to-car communication systems.
- Participants perceive safety implications (from criminals, hackers) of location tracking.
- Opinions about data sharing depend on perceived safety benefits and trust on external entities.
- Convenience (usability), privacy and safety (both traffic safety and safety against criminals, hackers) are top priorities for users.
- Some participants are willing to pay for pseudonyms, but not much.

Based on our findings, we also elicited a first set of design requirements for usable privacy and identity management for VANETs. Participants demonstrated different views on location data sharing, and hence, different selectable profiles should be offered based on different degrees of privacy-trade-offs with utility/usability and cost. Moreover, transparency and interveneability options should be offered by design, also for pseudonymous users, and fine-grained control options should be available for users.

We are currently conducting the same type of interviews in Sweden for an intercultural comparison and gaining further insights in regard to how far selectable profiles of typical preference settings should differ for South African and Swedish drivers. This will allow us also to derive hypotheses that will be tested with a quantitative study for a follow-up in-depth analysis.

Acknowledgements. This work was supported by the Swedish Foundation for Strategic Research (SSF) SURPRISE Project and the South Africa-Sweden University Forum (SASUF). We would like to thank all interview participants and our partners from the SURPRISE project that contributed with valuable background information.

References

1. Akil, M., Islami, L., Fischer-Hübner, S., Martucci, L.A., Zuccato, A.: Privacy-preserving identifiers for IoT: a systematic literature review. IEEE Access **8**, 168470–168485 (2020)
2. Bilogrevic, I., Ortlieb, M.: If you put all the pieces together... attitudes towards data combination and sharing across services and companies. In: Proceedings of the 2016 CHI Conference on Human Factors in Computing Systems, pp. 5215–5227 (2016)
3. Bossauer, P., Neifer, T., Stevens, G., Pakusch, C.: Trust versus privacy: using connected car data in peer-to-peer carsharing. In: Proceedings of the 2020 CHI Conference on Human Factors in Computing Systems, pp. 1–13 (2020)
4. Camenisch, J., Lysyanskaya, A.: An efficient system for non-transferable anonymous credentials with optional anonymity revocation. In: Pfitzmann, B. (ed.) EUROCRYPT 2001. LNCS, vol. 2045, pp. 93–118. Springer, Heidelberg (2001). https://doi.org/10.1007/3-540-44987-6_7
5. Cottrill, C.D., et al.: Location privacy preferences: a survey-based analysis of consumer awareness, trade-off and decision-making. Transp. Res. Part C: Emerg. Technol. **56**, 132–148 (2015)
6. Da Veiga, A.: An information privacy culture instrument to measure consumer privacy expectations and confidence. Inf. Comput. Secur. (Emerald) **26**(3) (2018)
7. Da Veiga, A., Ophoff, J.: Concern for information privacy: a cross-nation study of the United Kingdom and South Africa. In: Clarke, N., Furnell, S. (eds.) HAISA 2021. IAICT, vol. 593, pp. 16–29. Springer, Cham (2020). https://doi.org/10.1007/978-3-030-57404-8_2
8. Dala, P., Venter, H.S.: Understanding the level of compliance by South African institutions to the protection of personal information (POPI) act. In: Proceedings of the Annual Conference of the South African Institute of Computer Scientists and Information Technologists, pp. 1–8 (2016)
9. EU Commission: Special Eurobarometer 431 - Data Protection (2015)
10. Commission, E.U.: Regulation (EU) 2016/679 (General Data Protection Regulation). Official J. Eur. Union **L119**, 1–88 (2016)
11. Garidzirai, R., Chikuruwo, R.E.: An economic analysis of the social grant policy in South Africa. J. Adv. Res. Law Econ. **11**, 362–369 (2020)
12. Harry, B., Sturges, K.M., Klingner, J.K.: Mapping the process: an exemplar of process and challenge in grounded theory analysis. Educ. Res. **34**(2), 3–13 (2005)
13. Heid, B., Huth, C., Kempf, S., Wu, G.: Ready for inspection: the automotive aftermarket in 2030. https://www.mckinsey.com/industries/automotive-and-assembly/our-insights/ready-for-inspection-the-automotive-aftermarket-in-2030. Accessed 13 Sept 2020
14. Hofstede Insights: Country comparison. https://www.hofstede-insights.com/country-comparison/sweden/. Accessed 13 Sept 2020
15. Jacobsson, A., Davidsson, P.: Towards a model of privacy and security for smart homes. In: 2015 IEEE 2nd World Forum on Internet of Things (WF-IoT), pp. 727–732. IEEE (2015)

16. Jin, H., Papadimitratos, P.: Resilient privacy protection for location-based services through decentralization. ACM Trans. Priv. Secur. (TOPS) **22**(4), 1–36 (2019)
17. Khodaei, M., Jin, H., Papadimitratos, P.: SECMACE: scalable and robust identity and credential management infrastructure in vehicular communication systems. IEEE Trans. Intell. Transp. Syst. **19**(5), 1430–1444 (2018)
18. Lunheim, R., Sindre, G.: Privacy and computing: a cultural perspective (1994)
19. Madejski, M., Johnson, M., Bellovin, S.M.: A study of privacy settings errors in an online social network. In: 2012 IEEE International Conference on Pervasive Computing and Communications Workshops, pp. 340–345. IEEE (2012)
20. McCreary, F., Zafiroglu, A., Patterson, H.: The contextual complexity of privacy in smart homes and smart buildings. In: Nah, F.-H., Tan, C.-H. (eds.) HCIBGO 2016. LNCS, vol. 9752, pp. 67–78. Springer, Cham (2016). https://doi.org/10.1007/978-3-319-39399-5_7
21. Papadimitratos, P., Gligor, V., Hubaux, J.P.: Securing vehicular communications-assumptions, requirements, and principles (2006)
22. PARLIAMENT of the Republic of South Africa: Protection of Personal Information Act (POPI Act) (2020). https://popia.co.za/. Accessed 15 Oct 2020
23. Petit, J., Schaub, F., Feiri, M., Kargl, F.: Pseudonym schemes in vehicular networks: a survey. IEEE Commun. Surv. Tutorials **17**(1), 228–255 (2014)
24. Ryan, M.E.: Making visible the coding process: using qualitative data software in a post-structural study. Issues Educ. Res. **19**(2), 142–161 (2009)
25. Saldaña, J.: The Coding Manual for Qualitative Researchers. Sage, California (2015)
26. Strauss, A., Corbin, J.: Grounded theory methodology. Handb. Qual. Res. **17**(1), 273–285 (1994)
27. Svangren, M.K., Skov, M.B., Kjeldskov, J.: The connected car: an empirical study of electric cars as mobile digital devices. In: Proceedings of the 19th International Conference on Human-Computer Interaction with Mobile Devices and Services, pp. 1–12 (2017)
28. Sweeney, L.: k-anonymity: a model for protecting privacy. Int. J. Uncertainty Fuzziness Knowl. Based Syst. **10**(05), 557–570 (2002)
29. Tan, M., Teo, T.S.: Factors influencing the adoption of internet banking. J. Assoc. Inf. Syst. **1**(1), 5 (2000)
30. Venter, E.: The notion of ubuntu and communalism in African educational discourse. Stud. Philos. Educ. **23**(2–3), 149–160 (2004)
31. Walter, J., Abendroth, B.: On the role of informational privacy in connected vehicles: a privacy-aware acceptance modelling approach for connected vehicular services. Telematics Inform. **49**, 101361 (2020)
32. Yao, Y., Basdeo, J.R., Kaushik, S., Wang, Y.: Defending my castle: a co-design study of privacy mechanisms for smart homes. In: Proceedings of the 2019 CHI Conference on Human Factors in Computing Systems, pp. 1–12 (2019)
33. Zeng, E., Mare, S., Roesner, F.: End user security and privacy concerns with smart homes. In: Thirteenth Symposium on Usable Privacy and Security (SOUPS 2017), pp. 65–80 (2017)
34. Zheng, S., Apthorpe, N., Chetty, M., Feamster, N.: User perceptions of smart home IoT privacy. In: Proceedings of the ACM on Human-Computer Interaction, vol. 2(CSCW), pp. 1–20 (2018)
35. Ziefle, M., Rocker, C., Holzinger, A.: Medical technology in smart homes: exploring the user's perspective on privacy, intimacy and trust. In: 2011 IEEE 35th Annual Computer Software and Applications Conference Workshops, pp. 410–415. IEEE (2011)

Learning Analytics and Privacy—Respecting Privacy in Digital Learning Scenarios

Marvin Priedigkeit[1]([envelope]) [iD], Andreas Weich[1] [iD], and Ina Schiering[2] [iD]

[1] Georg Eckert Institute for International Textbook Research Member of the Leibniz Association, Braunschweig, Germany
{marvin.priedigkeit,andreas.weich}@gei.de
[2] Ostfalia University of Applied Sciences, Wolfenbüttel, Germany
i.schiering@ostfalia.de

Abstract. With the rise of digital systems in learning scenarios in recent years as learning management systems, massive open online courses, serious games, and the use of sensors and IoT devices huge amounts of personal data are generated. In the context of learning analytics, this data is used to individualize contents and exercises, predict success or dropout. Based on a meta analysis it is investigated to which extent the privacy of learners is respected. Our research found that, although surveys have shown that privacy is a concern for learners and critical to adopt to establish trust in learning analytic solutions, privacy issues are very rarely addressed in actual learning analytic setups.

Keywords: Learning analytics · Privacy · Educational datamining · MOOC · LMS · Serious games

1 Introduction

Based on the rise of digital systems in learning scenarios, the analysis of learning results and meta-data, also called learning analytics, is an area of research gaining importance. The society for Learning Analytics defines learning analytics as "the measurement, collection, analysis, and reporting of data about learners and their contexts, for purposes of understanding and optimizing learning and the environments in which it occurs" [1].

An overview about the current state of the learning analytic research field was given by Papamitsiou et al. [22]. According to them, Massive Open Online Courses (MOOCs) are leading the field of learning analysis, in addition traditional learning management systems (LMS) [21], serious games [19] and sensor-based IoT devices as e.g. stylus [28] are investigated. In this context it is stated that "At the same time, the discussion about ethics and privacy in learning analytics is not new, and is also well-grounded in theoretical frameworks, however, those frameworks are still external to the core of the field itself." [22].

© IFIP International Federation for Information Processing 2021
Published by Springer Nature Switzerland AG 2021
M. Friedewald et al. (Eds.): Privacy and Identity 2020, IFIP AICT 619, pp. 134–150, 2021.
https://doi.org/10.1007/978-3-030-72465-8_8

In this paper, a meta-analysis of research in the area of learning analytics is presented. There the consideration of privacy is investigated in the context of usage groups, technologies, and intended users. To this aim user studies, technology proposals, discussion papers, and case studies are investigated. Based on this analysis a privacy risk classification is proposed.

2 Background

A huge motivation for using learning analytics is to predict the success rate of students and to identify students at risk. To this aim besides data of MOOCs and LMS such as log-in time, log-in frequency, or video pause behavior also historical performances and demographics [3, 24] are used. Moreover, even biometric sensor data were used to analyze students learning performance [28]. In addition to MOOCs, digital serious games are commonly used to analyze students' behavior when confronted with new tasks. For example, Kaeser and Schwartz let students predict the outcome of a digital tug of war game and trained a neural network to group them into clusters according to their learning behavior [19]. The prediction of drop out rates is not only limited to education in schools or universities. Companies, such as Udacity, had also developed methods to analyze enrolled participants at risk. For example, Udacity's researchers Kim et al. developed a deep neural network to identify enrolled participants at risk of failing to complete a course [17].

Learning analytics is already used since several years especially based on existing LMS data. Arnold and Pistilli described a learning analytic solution to predict student's success based on interactions within the Purdue university's learning management system and other sources such as demographic data and historical performance [3]. They used a proprietary algorithm to compute a signal light feedback for the students and focused more on the behavior change of the students at risk. In contrast, Pelaez et al. [24] used machine learning to identify subgroups of students at risk enrolled in the Introductory Psychology course at the San Diego state university. Their goal was to enable the administration to further support this specific sub-groups.

3 Related Work

An overview about the current state of the learning analytic research field was given by Papamitsiou et al. [22]. They analyzed 627 publications, which were published between 2011 and 2019 at the Learning Analytic and Knowledge Conference and the Journal of Learning Analytics, extracted key-terms from these publications manually as well as by statistic analysis, grouped them into 14 clusters, each representing a research theme or sub-field, and sorted these into 4 categories. According to this analysis, MOOCs are leading the field of learning analysis, while "At the same time, the discussion about ethics and privacy in learning analytics is not new, and is also well-grounded in theoretical frameworks, however, those frameworks are still external to the core of the field itself." [22].

In addition to the Learning Analytics and Knowledge Conference, the Educational Data Mining conference is an popular venue for data driven education. Chen et al. analyzed and compared both of them [7]. Beside different other properties, they extracted the eleven most common topics on both conferences. The "Predictive and Descriptive Analytics" topic is at the top of their list, while privacy is none of the top eleven topics.

Privacy issues in learning analytics research are for example incorporated in interviews and questionnaires for students and other stakeholders. For example, Whitelock-Wainwright et al. asked in a survey more than 2000 students in three countries about their expectations of learning analytics, including their privacy concerns [29]. According to them: "From a student perspective, we can see that, on average, they have strong ideal expectations towards the university ensuring all data remain secure or controlling the access from third party companies. However, responses to the predicted expectation scale show students' beliefs to not be as". Tsai et al. identified, that an ethics and privacy framework, including anonymity, is key to ensure that students feel comfortable while sharing their data for learning analytics purposes [27]. Approaches to give institutions support to introduce learning analytic solutions had been made as well [8,14].

Moreover, Drachsler et al. proposed a checklist for trusted learning analytics in order to help institutions to implement learning analytics with privacy concerns in mind [10]. They conclude that ethics and privacy concerns should be on the same level as functional requirements. Others such as Siemens and Pardo analysed similar privacy issues [23]. However, reports of common practices in higher education show that privacy and ethics are rarely considered sufficiently in concrete learning scenarios [12].

4   Methodology

To investigate the consideration of privacy in the field of learning analytics a broad variety of publications as user studies, technology proposals, discussion papers, case studies are taken into account. We identified relevant literature mainly by two different approaches. First by searching based on corresponding search terms such as "learning analytic privacy study", "empirical learning analytic" on scientific search engines and databases, such as Google scholar and IEEE Xplore. The second approach was to consider proceedings from relevant conferences, i.e. the LAK conference and the EDM conference. In addition, papers identified by these two approaches were used as a starting point for further research via considering references.

For publications, selected in this first phase, the following criteria were evaluated. To this aim, we define the terms participants and audience. *Participants* are persons, which participate in a study and whose data are collected, while *audience* are people, which are addressed as the intended audience by the aim of the study. In the following, the criteria of the intended classification are explained.

Participant Type

This criterion describes which type of persons participates mainly in the study. For example typical types of participants are K-12 pupil (learners from primary to secondary education) or students enrolled in courses at a university.

Number of Participants

This criterion describes how many participants were investigated in the study. In the context of studies participants could be people, participating in a lab study, students enrolled in a online course, which will be analysed by the study or someone answering questions in a survey.

Target Audience

As described above we distinguish the terms participant and target audience. This could be the same type as the participants or a different group. A study which investigates how MOOC users interact with the system in order to develop a traffic light warning system for future MOOC users, the target audience and the participant types match, both would be MOOC user. Though, the individual participants, whose data are used to develop such a system, might not benefit from this system as they probably already finished their MOOC. If in a similar study a system collects data from a class of K-12 pupil and warns the corresponding teacher, the target audience would be teachers, while the type of participant would be pupil.

Feedback Type

This describes if a study contains a feedback system and how this feedback is provided, for example a traffic light system to warn MOOC users, that they are at risk to fail the course. The feedback system is always based on the participants data.

Context

This criterion describes in which context the participants contribute to a study. In the case of students using their university LMS to solve home work excises, which data is collected and used in context of a study, the context would be the LMS. It is not necessarily the case, that participants are aware, that they or their data contribute to a study, i.e. a learning analytics scenario. A typical example, when participants are not aware that their data is used in the context of a study are demographic data of enrolled students. We chose to integrate this criterion as transparency is an important privacy requirement and privacy concerns of participants might be influenced if they know that they contribute to a study or not.

Data Source Type

This criterion describes which type of data is used in the study. Typical data sources are LMS interactions such as login frequency, video playback behaviour or the output data of various biosensors attached to participants in a lab study. Another example of data source types are answers to a survey or demographic data.

Processing

This describes which methods are used to evaluate and analyse the collected data. A typical processing method is frequency analysis for surveys or machine learning methods such as deep neural networks.

Aim

The aim criteria describes, what the study should achieve for the target audience. For example giving the administration at a university guidance how to implement learning analytics into their institution.

Privacy

This criterion describes if and to what extent privacy is considered in the investigated research. A survey with questionnaires regarding privacy concerns or security perceptions of participants is an example, which should be identified by this criterion. Another typical example is if the study design incorporated privacy concerns upfront or if they evaluate privacy implications only afterwards based on the developed system.

In the second stage, these criteria were used to analyze the selected publication from our first stage and identify relevant publications. As we are interested in studies which actually interact with participants or are at least are addressed to a specific audience like the educational administration, publications which only presented technical solution, but had not tested them with participants were excluded. Additionally, publications that do not provide information about their target audience or aim, were excluded. As learning analytic is an emerging and adapting topic, publications published before 2012 were not considered. The extant publications form our final pool of publications. Based on these, we used the criteria to identify clusters within our pool of publications. Our findings will be described in the following section.

5   Analysis

Based on the proposed criteria in the methodology section we identified 23 research publications, which will be analyzed in this section. First, a brief overview of the publications is given grouped by different contexts. Afterward, other criteria will be analyzed. Finally, relations between publications will be described and clusters of publications will be identified and analysed.

5.1   Overview of Search Results

To gain a better understanding of the search results, for every context example publications are in the following summarized.

Table 1. Pool of publications

Index	Publication
1	Ebner, Martin, and Matthias Pronegg. "Use of Learning Analytics Applications in Mathematics with Elementary Learners." *International Journal of Academic Research in Education* 1.2 (2015): 26-39.
2	Wampfler, Rafael, et al. "Affective State Prediction in a Mobile Setting using Wearable Biometric Sensors and Stylus." *Proceedings of The 12th International Conference on Educational Data Mining (EDM 2019)*. 2019.
3	Kim, Byung-Hak, Ethan Vizitei, and Varun Ganapathi. "GritNet: Student performance prediction with deep learning." *arXiv preprint arXiv:1804.07405* (2018).
4	Sclater, Niall. "Developing a code of practice for learning analytics." *Journal of Learning Analytics* 3.1 (2016): 16-42.
5	Whitelock-Wainwright, Alexander, et al. "Assessing the validity of a learning analytics expectation instrument: A multinational study." *Journal of Computer Assisted Learning* 36.2 (2020): 209-240.
6	Pelaez, Kevin. "Using a Latent Class Forest to Identify At-Risk Students in Higher Education." *Journal of Educational Data Mining* 11.1 (2019): 18-46.
7	Tsai, Yi-Shan, Alexander Whitelock-Wainwright, and Dragan Gašević. "The privacy paradox and its implications for learning analytics." *Proceedings of the Tenth International Conference on Learning Analytics & Knowledge*. 2020.
8	Käser, Tanja, and Daniel L. Schwartz. "Exploring Neural Network Models for the Classification of Students in Highly Interactive Environments." *International Educational Data Mining Society* (2019).
9	Karumbaiah, Shamya, Ryan S. Baker, and Valerie Shute. "Predicting Quitting in Students Playing a Learning Game." *International Educational Data Mining Society* (2018).
10	Drachsler, Hendrik, and Wolfgang Greller. "Privacy and analytics: it's a DELICATE issue a checklist for trusted learning analytics." *Proceedings of the sixth international conference on learning analytics & knowledge*. 2016.
11	Hunt-Isaak, Noah, et al. "Using online textbook and in-class poll data to predict in-class performance."
12	Pirkl, Gerald, et al. "Any problems? a wearable sensor-based platform for representational learning-analytics." Proceedings of the 2016 ACM International Joint Conference on Pervasive and Ubiquitous Computing: Adjunct. 2016.
13	Hernández-García, Ángel, et al. "Applying social learning analytics to message boards in online distance learning: A case study." *Computers in Human Behavior* 47 (2015): 68-80.
14	Hernández-Lara, Ana Beatriz, Alexandre Perera-Lluna, and Enric Serradell-López. "Applying learning analytics to students' interaction in business simulation games. The usefulness of learning analytics to know what students really learn." *Computers in Human Behavior* 92 (2019): 600-612.
15	Blikstein, Paulo, et al. "Programming pluralism: Using learning analytics to detect patterns in the learning of computer programming." *Journal of the Learning Sciences* 23.4 (2014): 561-599.
16	Yu, Taeho, and Il-Hyun Jo. "Educational technology approach toward learning analytics: Relationship between student online behavior and learning performance in higher education." *Proceedings of the fourth international conference on learning analytics and knowledge*. 2014..
17	Khalil, Hanan, and Martin Ebner. ""How satisfied are you with your MOOC?"-A Research Study on Interaction in Huge Online Courses." *EdMedia+ Innovate Learning*. Association for the Advancement of Computing in Education (AACE), 2013.
18	Fianu, Eli, et al. "Factors affecting MOOC usage by students in selected Ghanaian universities." *Education Sciences* 8.2 (2018): 70.
19	Baradwaj, Brijesh Kumar, and Saurabh Pal. "Mining educational data to analyze students' performance." *arXiv preprint arXiv:1201.3417* (2012).
20	Merceron, Agathe, and Kalina Yacef. "Educational Data Mining: a Case Study." *AIED*. 2005.
21	Pigeau, Antoine, Olivier Aubert, and Yannick Prié. "Success Prediction in MOOCs: A Case Study." *International Educational Data Mining Society* (2019).
22	Whitehill, Jacob, et al. "Beyond prediction: First steps toward automatic intervention in MOOC student stopout." *Available at SSRN 2611750* (2015).
23	Mcbroom, Jessica, Irena Koprinska, and Kalina Yacef. "How does student behaviour change approaching dropout? A study of gender and school year differences." *the 13th International Conference on Educational Data Mining (Upcoming)*.

In the *biosensor context*, different approaches are investigated to attach existing commercial level sensors to learners measuring their body's signals and determining how they feel, while participating in paper equivalent exercises [25]. The identified publications in this context exclusively use students as participant type but could be applied to any kind of learner as well. As every participant needs to be attached to these sensors, the amount of participants is relatively low, compared to other contexts.

Publications from a *serious game* context let participants play specially designed games and analyze their behavior doing so. In our pool of publications, different kinds of serious games are considered. Some are designed like video games where participants need to solve multiple levels to succeed, others are designed to simulate business interactions, where a group of participants needs to decide how a fictive company should adjust its strategy [15,16]. Typically, serious games designed like video games had K-12 pupils as the type of participants while serious games designed as simulations focused on students as participants.

In addition to that, we identified publications with the context *guides and surveys* which aim to give educational administration support to implement and understand learning analytic solutions. While surveys have students as participants, guides do not have participants [26,27]. Hence for this type of publication, not all criteria could be applied.

LMSs is the most common context in our pool of publications. Publications in this context use different existing data sources such as grade books or demographic data to further understand the learning process of the learners, predict their performance, or determine groups at risk [24]. They almost exclusively have students as participants and tend to target teachers as an audience.

Finally, we identified the context of *MOOCs* which is the second commonest context in our pool. Publications in this context revolve around different types of participants, which participate in full virtual courses. Their behavior such as the time they read a text or answer a quiz is analyzed [17]. These publications focus on adult users, either students or general participants. Moreover, they are the only ones that do target general participants at all. Besides students, these general participants take part in courses e.g. for general training purposes.

5.2   Analysis of Criteria

The general findings for each criterion from the methodology section summarized as a starting point of the analyses followed by a thorough investigation of relations and correlations between different publications.

Participant Type

Publications usually had exactly one type of participant. We choose to term K-12 pupil as pupil, students enrolled in universities as students, and participants in a MOOCs, which are not exclusively for students enrolled at a university or pupil, as general participants. The most common type of participant is students. This is in line with our expectations, as students are usually of legal age (not minors), therefore it is easier to integrate them into studies. Moreover, compared to regular MOOC users, universities already collect different demographic data by enrollment. This forms a solid research basis of data and legal factors.

Number of Participants

The number of participants varies widely, from 6 participants in a biosensor based lab study to over 10000 participants in a MOOC based study. However, even within the same type of context, the number of participants varies widely. For example, in the context of LMS, the number of participants varies from about 100 to over 3000 participants.

Target Audience

We observed, that the type of participants and the target audience differ in most publications. Moreover, our research has identified, that typically different types of teachers are targeted, for example, teachers for K-12 pupils and teachers at universities. As all the different types of teachers mainly have the task to help learners achieving their individual learning targets, we choose to summarize K-12, university, and MOOC teachers as teachers in general. Other target audiences that occur, are pupils, students, and general users, which are matching the participant types. Additionally, two other target audiences occurred, education administration and research.

Feedback Type

Our research has found, that the usual type of feedback is either to inform the according type of participant or the according teacher or to deliver no direct feedback at all. It should be noted, that most publications only reported their findings, but did not take the extra step to develop a feedback system or inform at least the participants.

Context

Different contexts could be identified by our research. We summarized interaction within any kind of LMS such as forum posts, day, and time of exercise download or submission behaviour as LMS context. Different kinds of biosensors, such as eye trackers, heartbeat detectors, or stylus pressure, are also summarized as biosensors. In addition to them MOOCs, surveys, and serious games also occurred as the context of publications.

Data Source Type

Different data sources had been found. We observed an obvious correlation between the data source type and the context of the study. Studies within the context MOOC, mostly had different kinds of MOOC related data sources such as clickstreams, while publications within the context of serious games had very game-specific data sources. Although plenty of data sources, including sensitive data such as past grades and biosignals, are used in the pool of publications, data minimization approaches could not be identified.

Processing

Our research has identified different approaches concerning machine learning, such as neural networks and latent class trees [17, 19, 24]. However, we termed every machine learning approach and even linear regression as machine learning. Besides machine learning, the most common processing method were different statistic methods such as frequency analysis for the evaluation of surveys, which we termed as statistical analysis.

Aim

The aim of the publications varies as well. Some papers aim to understand participant expectations for learning analytic systems, others want to understand how participants learn or predict various aspects of their learning outcome, such as grades or their risk to fail a certain course. Though some publications aim to understand learning, this aim is limited to understanding certain easy to measure factors of this complex system.

Privacy

We observed, that privacy is rarely addressed in our pool of publications. Some surveys tackle privacy concerns in order to give guidance on how to implement learning analytics or by questionnaires in a survey but the majority do not concern them at all.

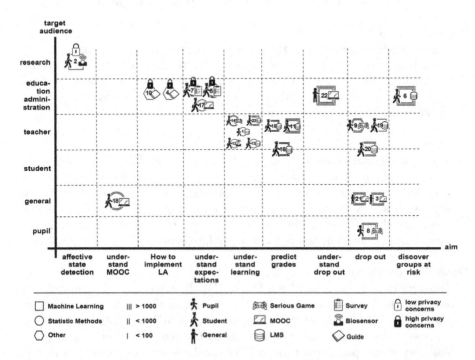

Fig. 1. Visualization of our pool of publications. The numbers refer to the entry in Table 1

An overview of our pool of publications and their according criteria is visualized in Fig. 1. The target audience and the aim are important criteria with multiple values, therefore we choose them as axis values for our visualization. They give a good overview of our pool of publications. We encoded our additional criteria by additional shapes or symbols. Therefore every study has a shape, which determines the processing criteria, whereas the size of the shape is used to visualize the number of participants. Additionally, every study can have three additional symbols. The left symbol determines the participant type, while the right symbol determines the context criterion. Finally, every study can have either a hollow or a solid lock symbol, representing low or respective high privacy concerns. The lock is not present if the study does not concern privacy at all.

Relations between different criteria could be identified and will be described in the following. We observed first of all typical relations between the type of participants and the target audience. In general, the type of participant and the target audience of a study are different. Although the main participant type of publications is students, they are almost never the target audience. This is true across all aims. To a lesser degree, the same is true for pupil, if they are the type of participants, mostly the teacher is the according target audience for them. However, in one of three publications, they are also their own target audience and therefore this is much more common compared to the student participant group. In contrast to that, if general users are participants in a study, they usually are the target audience as well.

Overall, teachers and the education administration are the most common target audience, while the combined group of actual learners, in the different contexts, are a less common target group. Therefore we identified an imbalance between the group of learners as participants, which contribute with their data, and the according target group. In most publications, the group of learners does not receive any feedback nor are they the target group.

Also, a strong relation between the aim criterion and the target audience criterion was observed. Many aims are exclusive for a certain target audience, such as *How to implement LA* and *understand expectations*. In contrast, we observed, that aims that are involved in the prediction of learners' performance such as *predict grades* and *drop out* are spread through multiple target audiences. Another observation is, that the education administrative target group is the group with the most differentiated aims.

The processing method is spread through different aims. However, we observed, a relation between machine learning-based processing and aims, that resolve around drop out of students. Almost any study that aims to understand drop out, discover groups at risk or determine drop out uses machine learning approaches to process the collected data. In contrast, aims such as *How to implement LA* and *understand expectations* obviously never uses machine learning processing methods.

Finally, relations between the context and privacy concerns have been observed. Whenever the context is either *guide* or *survey* high privacy concerns have been considered. In contrast, no privacy concerns have been taken into account in any other aims.

5.3   Proposed Clusters Based on Analysis

Beyond relations between different criteria, we were able to identify major cluster of publications, which share multiple relations with each other. These clusters will be described in the following.

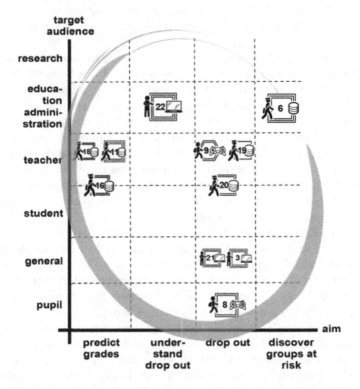

Fig. 2. Cluster of publications using machine learning to determine learners performance

The first major cluster of publications is shown in Fig. 2. Publications within this group target every type of audience involved in the actual learning process. They aim to predict the learners' performance and using machine learning as processing method. Even though the prediction of a learner's performance might influence the perception of the learners' real performance, especially by his teacher, the actual process of how the machine learning processing method determines this prediction is not transparent to the learners' nor their teachers'. Even though they use sensitive data such as past grades, none of these publications even address privacy issues at all. The next group is shown in Fig. 3.

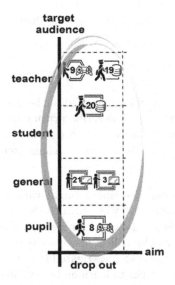

Fig. 3. Cluster of publications with a highly diverse target audience

We identified that drop out is a major aim across all types of target audience involved in the actual learning process. In contrast, most other aims are limited to a single target audience. Moreover, a mix of different contexts appears in this cluster. Though every type of participant appears in this cluster privacy is never concerned.

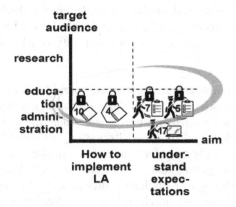

Fig. 4. Cluster of publications with high privacy concerns

Our last clusters contain publications with high privacy considered, as shown in Fig. 4. We identified that privacy is mainly addressed with surveys and guides, the target audience is education administration. Therefore the group of learners is not targeted whenever privacy is a high concern. Moreover, the contest of privacy concerning publications is almost exclusively limited to guides and surveys.

5.4 Privacy Risks

We observed that privacy is rarely concerned in the pool of publications. Therefore, in this section, we will further describe privacy threats in learning analytic systems and briefly outline measurements for them. To this aim, we will follow the six privacy protection goals to analyse learning analytic systems [13].

Confidentiality
> The observed publications describe a broad variety of contexts and therefore plenty of different data is collected in the learning analytic scenarios. In addition to regular personal data such as name, address, and so on, proposed learning analytic systems also collect very sensitive data such as learning performance and grades. Moreover investigated systems also track detailed data from log-in times and patterns to learning behaviours such as the video playback behaviour [17]. This makes the learners transparent, as very individual behaviours such as how the learner engages with the material are tracked. Moreover, contexts such as the biosensor context even track physical feats, for example, heartbeat rate [28]. Therefore the confidentiality of this data is especially important and should be limited to authorized stakeholders such as the according teacher. To achieve this goal different established solutions could be used. From a privacy model and its strict implementation of rules, roles and responsibility to data protection by encryption with well established cryptographic encryption schemes such as AES and ChaCha20 in combination with digital signature algorithm on elliptic curves like Ed25519 to prevent unauthorized interactions [4,5,9]. Although solutions exist the observed publications do not mention if or how confidentiality is achieved.

Integrity
> Data from learning analytic systems or in general learning contexts are often intertwined with grades and in the long run with graduation. Therefore it is necessary that such sensitive data is integrous and not altered by unauthorized stakeholders and at least alternations should be documented and logged. This is not only true for grades but also for the fundamental data which leads to that grade, such as engagement with learning material and submissions. Unintended or malicious alternations of learners' data such as grades, or enrolled courses could lead to serious difficulties for example falsely missing requirements for graduation. Similar to confidentiality, integrity could be provided by established cryptographic solutions, but, also similar, our pool of publications does not mention if or how they tackle integrity as a goal for their proposed systems [5].

Availability
> As data intertwined with grades and graduation stays relevant for a relatively

long time, often the learners' whole lifetime, it should be assured that key data from learning analytic systems are available for the same time. However, in most scenarios, the data availability is not very time crucial and other goals such as confidentiality are more important and therefore should have priority. However, availability could fairly easily be introduced, even into existing solutions, by the redundancy of according data and offline backup solutions.

Transparency

In the observed learning analytic publications, it is not transparent for the learner who has actual access to their data and who might get access in the future. This is especially true in complex relationships, for example, who is actually reading and correcting submissions into a MOOC? The actual teacher which was recorded for the video material, the support staff, or even an algorithm? Therefore it is necessary to inform the learners up front, who has or will become accessible to what kind of data in an understandable way. Moreover, in contrast to our observations, learning analytic systems shall also target the actual learners as the target audience. Privacy notifications can be one way to raise the learners' awareness about their data usage and provide them transparent information, like who accessed which data [20].

Unlinkability

While learners are interested in a transparent understanding of how their data is processed, it is also necessary to hinder others to link different data about the learner. In scenarios that involve real-world interactions between learners and teachers, a teacher could link individual learners with additional data, such as social media profiles. Therefore, unlinkability is very limited in these scenarios, as it is in non-digital classroom scenarios. In other learning scenarios, for example, MOOC's without real-world interactions, techniques such as data minimisation and pseudonymisation could be used and are proposed in some publications [6]. Nevertheless, the risk of reidentification is always present because of the amount and detail of data [18].

Especially in conjunction with machine learning approaches more sophisticated solutions are needed since usually a huge amount of data from LMS is used. To this aim, privacy-preserving machine learning is important, encompassing methods such as homomorphic encryption and differential privacy [2,11]. Though we observed different publications that process data with machine learning methods such solutions have not to be mentioned.

Intervenability

As the processed data consists of highly sensitive data, which is often stored for a long time, the Intervenability of learners should be taken into account as well. A learner should be able to intervene in every stage of the learning analytic system. From mistakenly clicked answers to the grading of submissions and the conclusions of the learning analytic system. However in order to intervene transparency is necessary. Though, our observed publications often target other stakeholders such as the teacher or education administration and only present them with the conclusions of the system. Therefore learners do not even know the conclusions of learning analytic systems, therefore they are unable to intervene in case of faulty data, such as wrongly calculated grades.

6   Discussion and Conclusion

In general learning, analytics has a huge potential in digital learning scenarios and the use of such approaches is gaining importance. On the other hand students' interaction with such systems provides a huge amount of personal data and at the moment privacy is rarely adequately considered.

Our study revealed that privacy issues are mostly addressed in surveys or guides, but very rarely in actual learning analytic implementations. Moreover, data usage is not transparent.

Trustfulness and privacy are key factors to successfully implemented accepted learning analytic systems [10,23]. Therefore holistic systems, which already tackle privacy concerns in the preferable participatory, design process, are needed. Even though surveys and guides for the education administration are a first step to design privacy-preserving learning analytic systems, all in the learning process involved parties and their concerns need to be address by such systems to unfold the potential slumbering inside learning analytics. Moreover, participants should always be considered as, at least secondary, audiences in order to make transparent, what happened to their data and to let them know the results.

Although pseudonymization techniques to ensure privacy is widely used in different scenarios [6], it has been shown, that pseudonymization or even minimal data collection techniques can be overcome, thus leading to reidentification [18]. Therefore more sophisticated approaches from the privacy and security community have to be included into learning analytic systems. Moreover cultural, social, political, and ethical considerations should be included in interdisciplinary projects. This is especially true, as different machine learning approaches are gaining attention within the learning analytic community in recent years. As they mostly operate on private data and pseudonymization is prone to fail, solutions for this dilemma must be found. Privacy-preserving machine learning is, among others, an approach to build learning analytic systems with privacy by design, which could solve this dilemma.

Acknowledgement. This work was supported by the Leibniz Association and the Ministry for Science and Culture of Lower Saxony as part of Leibniz ScienceCampus – Postdigital Participation – Braunschweig.

References

1. What is learning analytics. https://www.solaresearch.org/about/what-is-learning-analytics/
2. Albrecht, M., et al.: Homomorphic encryption security standard. Technical report, HomomorphicEncryption.org, Toronto, Canada, November 2018

3. Arnold, K.E., Pistilli, M.D.: Course signals at Purdue: using learning analytics to increase student success. In: Proceedings of the 2nd International Conference on Learning Analytics and Knowledge, LAK 2012, Vancouver, British Columbia, Canada, pp. 267–270. Association for Computing Machinery, April 2012. https://doi.org/10.1145/2330601.2330666
4. Bernstein, D.J.: Chacha, a variant of salsa20. In: Workshop Record of SASC, vol. 8, pp. 3–5 (2008)
5. Bernstein, D.J., Duif, N., Lange, T., Schwabe, P., Yang, B.Y.: High-speed high-security signatures. J. Cryptogr. Eng. **2**(2), 77–89 (2012). https://doi.org/10.1007/s13389-012-0027-1
6. Bosch, N., Crues, R.W., Paquette, L., Shaik, N.: "Hello, [REDACTED]": protecting student privacy in analyses of online discussion forums. EDM (2020)
7. Chen, G., Rolim, V., Mello, R.F., Gašević, D.: Let's shine together! a comparative study between learning analytics and educational data mining. In: Proceedings of the Tenth International Conference on Learning Analytics & Knowledge, LAK 2020, Frankfurt, Germany, pp. 544–553. Association for Computing Machinery, March 2020. https://doi.org/10.1145/3375462.3375500
8. Corrin, L., et al.: The ethics of learning analytics in Australian higher education (2019). https://melbourne-cshe.unimelb.edu.au/research/research-projects/edutech/the-ethical-use-of-learning-analytics
9. Daemen, J., Rijmen, V.: Reijndael: the advanced encryption standard. Dr. Dobb's J. Softw. Tools Prof. Program. **26**(3), 137–139 (2001)
10. Drachsler, H., Greller, W.: Privacy and analytics: it's a DELICATE issue a checklist for trusted learning analytics. In: Proceedings of the Sixth International Conference on Learning Analytics & Knowledge, LAK 2016, Edinburgh, United Kingdom, pp. 89–98. Association for Computing Machinery, April 2016. https://doi.org/10.1145/2883851.2883893
11. Dwork, C.: Differential privacy: a survey of results. In: Agrawal, M., Du, D., Duan, Z., Li, A. (eds.) TAMC 2008. LNCS, vol. 4978, pp. 1–19. Springer, Heidelberg (2008). https://doi.org/10.1007/978-3-540-79228-4_1
12. Flanagan, B., Ogata, H.: Integration of learning analytics research and production systems while protecting privacy. In: The 25th International Conference on Computers in Education, Christchurch, New Zealand, pp. 333–338 (2017)
13. Hansen, M., Jensen, M., Rost, M.: Protection goals for privacy engineering. In: 2015 IEEE Security and Privacy Workshops, pp. 159–166. IEEE (2015)
14. Hermann, O., Hansen, J., Rensing, C., Drachsler, H.: Verhaltenskodex für trusted learning analytics, March 2020. https://doi.org/10.13140/RG.2.2.24859.41760
15. Hernández-Lara, A.B., Perera-Lluna, A., Serradell-López, E.: Applying learning analytics to students' interaction in business simulation games. the usefulness of learning analytics to know what students really learn. Comput. Hum. Behav. **92**, 600–612 (2019)
16. Karumbaiah, S., Baker, R.S.J.D., Shute, V.J.: Predicting quitting in students playing a learning game. In: EDM (2018)
17. Kim, B.H., Vizitei, E., Ganapathi, V.: GritNet: student performance prediction with deep learning. In: EDM (2018)
18. Klose, M., Desai, V., Song, Y., Gehringer, E.: EDM and privacy: ethics and legalities of data collection, usage, and storage. In: EDM (2020)
19. Käser, T., Schwartz, D.L.: Exploring neural network models for the classification of students in highly interactive environments. In: EDM 2019, International Educational Data Mining Society, July 2019. https://eric.ed.gov/?id=ED599211

20. Murmann, P., Reinhardt, D., Fischer-Hübner, S.: To be, or not to be notified. In: Dhillon, G., Karlsson, F., Hedström, K., Zúquete, A. (eds.) SEC 2019. IAICT, vol. 562, pp. 209–222. Springer, Cham (2019). https://doi.org/10.1007/978-3-030-22312-0_15

21. Mwalumbwe, I., Mtebe, J.S.: Using learning analytics to predict students' performance in Moodle learning management system: a case of Mbeya University of Science and Technology. Electron. J. Inf. Syst. Dev. Countries **79**(1), 1–13 (2017). https://doi.org/10.1002/j.1681-4835.2017.tb00577.x

22. Papamitsiou, Z., Giannakos, M.N., Ochoa, X.: From childhood to maturity: are we there yet? Mapping the intellectual progress in learning analytics during the past decade. In: Proceedings of the Tenth International Conference on Learning Analytics & Knowledge, LAK 2020, Frankfurt, Germany, pp. 559–568. Association for Computing Machinery, March 2020. https://doi.org/10.1145/3375462.3375519

23. Pardo, A., Siemens, G.: Ethical and privacy principles for learning analytics. Br. J. Educ. Technol. **45**(3), 438–450 (2014). https://doi.org/10.1111/bjet.12152

24. Pelaez, K., Levine, R., Fan, J., Guarcello, M., Laumakis, M.: Using a latent class forest to identify at-risk students in higher education. In: EDM 2019 (2019). https://doi.org/10.5281/zenodo.3554747

25. Pirkl, G., et al.: Any problems? a wearable sensor-based platform for representational learning-analytics. In: Proceedings of the 2016 ACM International Joint Conference on Pervasive and Ubiquitous Computing: Adjunct, pp. 353–356 (2016)

26. Sclater, N.: Developing a code of practice for learning analytics. J. Learn. Anal. **3**(1), 16–42 (2016). https://doi.org/10.18608/jla.2016.31.3

27. Tsai, Y.S., Whitelock-Wainwright, A., Gašević, D.: The privacy paradox and its implications for learning analytics. In: Proceedings of the Tenth International Conference on Learning Analytics & Knowledge, LAK 2020, Frankfurt, Germany, pp. 230–239. Association for Computing Machinery, March 2020. https://doi.org/10.1145/3375462.3375536

28. Wampfler, R., Klingler, S., Solenthaler, B., Schinazi, V., Gross, M.: Affective state prediction in a mobile setting using wearable biometric sensors and stylus (2019). https://doi.org/10.3929/ethz-b-000393912

29. Whitelock-Wainwright, A., et al.: Assessing the validity of a learning analytics expectation instrument: a multinational study. J. Comput. Assist. Learn. (2020). https://doi.org/10.1111/jcal.12401

Preserving Privacy in Caller ID Applications

Tamara Stefanović$^{(\boxtimes)}$ ⓘ and Silvia Ghilezan ⓘ

University of Novi Sad, Novi Sad, Serbia
{tstefanovic,gsilvia}@uns.ac.rs

Abstract. Caller identification (or Caller ID) is a telephone service that transmits a caller's phone number to a receiving party's telephony equipment when the call is being set up. Besides the telephone number, the Caller ID service may transmit a name associated with the calling telephone number. The appearance of the first Caller ID devices caused suspicion among the users and the public because of the potential security and privacy issues that the caller identification may cause. Privacy issues apply to users of the Caller ID applications, but also to non-users whose phone numbers are stored in the database of some Caller ID application. The emergence of the data privacy laws has led discussions on the privacy policies of Caller ID applications and their compliance with the law. In this paper we investigate two Caller ID applications, Truecaller and Everybody, and compliance of their privacy policies with the data privacy laws, especially the GDPR, the ePrivacy Directive and the ePrivacy Regulation. Further, we deal in more detail with the data privacy problem of non-users and we give the connection between those problems, and the inverse privacy problem. In order to solve the privacy problem of non-users, we develop the mathematical model based on the notions of privacy variables and sensitivity function. Finally, we discussed open questions related to the identity protection of Caller ID app users and non-users, and their trust in Caller ID apps.

Keywords: Caller ID applications · Privacy policy · GDPR · Inverse privacy · Name sensitivity · Privacy variables

1 Introduction

Caller identification (or Caller ID) is a telephone service, available in analog and digital phone systems and in most Voice over Internet Protocol (VoIP) applications, that transmits a caller's phone number to a receiving party's telephony equipment when the call is being set up [17]. Besides the telephone number, the Caller ID service may transmit a name associated with the calling telephone number. Even before the proliferation of mobile phones, the appearance of the

M. Friedewald et al. (Eds.): Privacy and Identity 2020, IFIP AICT 619, pp. 151–168, 2021.
https://doi.org/10.1007/978-3-030-72465-8_9

first Caller ID devices caused suspicion among the users and the public. The New York Times asked the question whether the Caller ID was a "friend" or a "foe" back in 1992 [18]. The reason for the suspicion lies in the potential security and privacy issues that the caller identification may cause.

Since then, the invention of smartphones and the success of the first Caller ID applications have further developed the problem. Despite this, the new functionalities of Caller ID applications have attracted a large number of users and in recent years, the use of Caller ID applications is constantly increasing. Currently, some of the most commonly used Caller ID applications are Truecaller[1], Hiya[2], Everybody[3], etc. These kind of applications provide their users with the following features: identification of incoming calls from the unknown numbers, blocking calls and messages, call recording, search function and so on. There are a lot of benefits associated with caller identification. From the business perspective, it allows companies to better understand where the majority of their calls are coming from, and in that manner, they can find where most of their interested clients come from. From the perspective of an average person, caller identification is useful because it can protect from harassment. In addition to the good sides of caller identification, there are also some concerns that Caller ID leads to problems with confidentiality, privacy and individual's safety. Users and non-users of Caller ID applications are facing those problems equally. The question is whether it is possible to find a way to use these applications, but also to ensure the privacy and safety of others.

Results. In this paper, the focus is on the privacy problem of non-users in Caller ID applications. We first explore the privacy policies of two Caller ID applications, Truecaller and Everybody, and their compliance with data privacy laws such as GDPR, ePrivacy Directive and ePrivacy Regulation. We further argue that the problem of non-user privacy falls into the scope of inverse privacy. Building on this connection, we introduce the notion of name sensitivity and privacy variables and solve the problem of non-user privacy. Finally, we discuss open questions related to the identity protection of Caller ID app users and non-users, the place for storing privacy preferences about a phone number and linked data in Caller ID apps.

Paper Outline. The rest of the paper is structured as follows. Section 2 presents the main Caller ID app features and describes how the Caller ID applications violate individual's privacy. Section 3 investigates privacy policies of two Caller ID applications and their compliance with the data privacy laws. Section 4 gives a connection between the privacy problem of non-users and the inverse privacy problem. Section 5 introduces the name sensitivity and the privacy variables. Section 6 and Sect. 7 discuss and conclude the paper.

---

[1] https://www.truecaller.com/.

[2] https://hiya.com/.

[3] http://www.evrbd.com/.

2   Background and Motivation

In this section, we recall the main features of Caller ID applications and describe how they may violate individual's privacy.

2.1   Caller ID App Features

After the installation of a Caller ID app, the app creates and stores some information (user's profile) about the user. The user's profile includes his/her name, phone number, and/or e-mail address. Information from user's address book (contact names, phone numbers, e-mail addresses, etc.), call lists and messages is also included in the user's profile. The information provided by the user can change at any time (e.g., the user can change his/her name, the user can change names and phone numbers in his/her address book, and also add or delete some contacts) so the database storing this information is dynamic. Besides information provided by the user, the user's profile may include information gathered by the app itself relating to activities of the user. Such activities includes interactions and connections with other users and non-users (e.g., call frequency). A non-user is a person whose phone number is stored in the address book of a user of the Caller ID application, but he/she is not using the Caller ID app by himself/herself. The relationship between individuals is modeled by a social graph. A node of the social graph corresponds to Caller ID app user, or a non-user, while edges connecting two nodes correspond to a relationship between two individuals.

The main functionality of these applications is caller identification. To be specific, when a user receives an incoming call, the phone can display the caller's phone number and the name associated with this number if available. If the caller's phone number and a corresponding name are available in the user's address book, the phone displays the corresponding name in addition to the phone number. If the caller's phone number and a corresponding name are not available in the user's address book, the app searches its database and in case the name associated with the given number exists in the database, it forwards the name to the user. The search is based on the user's interaction with other users and non-users.

The Caller ID apps also provide a search function. Particularly, a user can access an address book stored in the Caller ID app's database, look up a contact in the address book and connect with the contact. The search can be based on the name or on the phone number.

For better functionality, Caller ID applications may require location access. Also, various applications have the additional option for interacting with a third party services, like Facebook, Twitter and so on, in which case those third party services may provide the app with additional information.

2.2   Violating Individual's Privacy

The definition of data privacy itself is notoriously complex, so we have to put it in a particular context. For further analysis, we will think of privacy in terms of transfer of personal information. The term "personal information" refers to any information related to an identified or identifiable natural person. As names and telephone contacts actually enable the adequate identification of natural individuals, there is no doubt that such information actually constitutes personal data.

Once you install a Caller ID application, it will have access to your address book, call list, messages and so on. Additional features require access to your microphone, camera, and location. During the installation, you confirm that all the persons from your address book have given their consent to share their phone number and the name under which their number is stored in your address book. The problem is that the required consent is not strictly defined, and the users are not required to provide any proof of given consent. This leads to the conclusion that non-users do not have any control over their personal data, and they are not even aware of the collection and publication of their personal data.

In addition to the fact that Caller ID apps violate individual's privacy, participating in a Caller ID app database can greatly endanger individual's safety.

Danger for Users. Nowadays using just Caller ID is not enough to prove who is the real caller since there are several ways to manipulate the caller identity. As Caller IDs are vulnerable to spoofing attacks, they have been used in a variety of misuse and fraud incidents:

- credit card frauds, when credit card companies mistakenly authenticate newly issued cards or stolen cards by phone calls of a fake credit card holder, like in [19], or when a person gets a false call from a bank in order to give personal information, like credit card number [15];
- swatting, frauds representing an attempt to trick an emergency service with false reporting of an incident, which can even end tragically [21].

There have been several attempts to detect Caller ID spoofing attacks like [13, 22].

Danger for Non-users. The applications we cherish can endanger not only us but the people around us. They are in even more dangerous situation, because they are not aware that their data is collected. The example of a journalist betrayed by an application she was not even using, can be found in [1]. Namely, she was working on sensitive TV show stories like human trafficking, drug cartels and so on. That is why she was not using social media and she did not appear on screen. It was very important for her to protect her anonymity. She traveled to a foreign country for a story. She bought a local SIM card and she was using it only for communication with her sources. The people she was investigating were just regular citizens and she didn't have to worry about state surveillance of her communications. It allowed her to be open with her sources about her name, affiliation and intentions. At some point she used her local number to order a cab, and when she entered the cab, the driver already knew the name of the TV show she worked. She could see her name and the name of the TV show she worked next to her phone number on the driver's phone. What happened to her is that one of her sources was using the same Caller ID app as the cab driver. This source tagged her phone number using her name and affiliation, and this tag became available for all the users of this particular Caller ID app. She didn't use any of Caller ID applications, but her safety was endangered by one of them. Although this example is taken from a web article, the scenario of the example is easily applicable in everyday life.

It should be mentioned that there are some practical methods for individuals to suppress their identity. One of them is prefixing a phone number with a certain code, which is usually characteristic for each country. This action suppresses the caller's number for almost all cell phones. The same can be done in the settings of the phone. Although this is one way individuals can protect themselves, it is not a global solution to the problem. The global solution should be provided by the Caller ID app.

Unlike the problems faced by Caller ID application users, the problem of non-users is insufficiently investigated. Therefore, in this paper, the emphasis will be on the problem of non-users.

3   Compliance with the Data Privacy Laws

Below we will analyze the privacy policies of Caller ID applications, as well as their compliance with the data privacy laws. Given that countries are creating their own data privacy laws, we will focus on the General Data Protection Regulation (GDPR) [5], the ePrivacy Directive [6], and the ePrivacy Regulation [4] because of their territorial scope. As examples for privacy policies of Caller ID applications, we will use Truecaller and Everybody privacy policies [7,24].

3.1   Truecaller and Everybody Privacy Policies

Truecaller. First of all, Truecaller privacy policy states that if you provide them with personal information about someone else, you confirm that they consent to use their information. Further, by enabling the Truecaller Enhanced Search Functionality, you can share with the app contact information from your address book, but only phone numbers, attached names, Google ID's and e-mail addresses. Other information from your address book is filtered away. Sharing the contact information with the Truecaller is optional, and you can make your contact information unavailable for search in the Truecaller database at any time. If you are in the Truecaller database and someone search your name, you will get a message and you may choose whether or not to share your phone number with that person. Also, if you are a non-user of Truecaller and you do not want your personal information to be in their database, you can contact them to unlist you.

Everybody. Everybody privacy policy states that the user, immediately after installation, is asked if he/she wants to share his/hers address book with the Everybody app or not. If accepted, contact information is stored on their server. Contact information includes name, surname, and phone number. The consent for sharing someone else's personal information is not mentioned. Further, contradictory with the first one, they state that non-user information will not be stored on their server. When it comes to the transfer of personal information of non-users, the Everybody app works as follows. When the non-user first calls a user who does not have his/her phone number in the address book, the application notifies the non-user via SMS and asks him/her to state whether he/she allows further processing and forwarding of his/her name. It is possible at any time to withdraw the consent for sharing information from your address book with the application, and they respect the right of deletion of your personal data from the Everybody's database.

3.2   Compliance with the GDPR, ePrivacy Directive and ePrivacy Regulation

First of all, according to the definition of personal data in the Art.4 of GDPR, there is no doubt that Caller ID applications process the personal data of both their users and non-users. When it comes to users, Caller ID applications indeed protect personal information of their users.

When it comes to users, sharing and processing of user's personal data is lawful because is based on the given consent (according to the Art.6 of GDPR), users have the right to withdraw the consent at any time (according to the Art.7 of GDPR), and also have the right of erasure of their personal data (according to the Art.17 of GDPR).

When it comes to non-users, the situation is a little more complicated. Namely, Caller ID applications obtain data of non-users from a third party, that is, the data is not obtained directly from the data subject. In that case the data subject has the right (according to the Art.14 of GDPR): to be provided with categories of personal data concerned, the purpose of processing, the recipients of the personal data, the information from which source the personal data originates and the right of erasure or restriction of processing of his/her personal data. The information referred above shall be provided at the latest when the personal data are first disclosed. The privacy policies of the mentioned applications are compliant with those requirements. They are also compliant with Art.12 of the e-Privacy Directive 2002/58/EC which requires that data controllers obtain additional consent from data subjects before including their data in directories searchable solely on the basis of telephone number. In recent years these applications have faced numerous criticisms and in the meantime have updated their privacy policies to comply with privacy laws.

The sharing of non-users' personal data by the Caller ID application is legal, but the question is whether they have the right to store this data in their database at first. Although the non-users are entitled to exclude themselves from a Caller ID app database, in order to do so, they must be aware of the existence of that particular Caller ID app. In case they want to be excluded from the databases of all Caller ID applications, they would have to be excluded from each database individually, which is practically impossible. This brings us back to the question of the consent that users should obtain from their contacts for sharing personal data. According to the Art.2 of GDPR, this regulation does not apply to the processing of personal data by a natural person in the course of a purely personal activity. Processing also includes disclosure by transmission (according to the Art.2 of GDPR). People use the Caller ID app for personal purposes, but sharing contact information that will be stored in a public database goes beyond personal purposes. In that sense, either the GDPR is not applicable in this situation or the Caller ID applications force their users to break the law while they remain clean. Then, in a legal sense, the opponent of the non-user would be the user who forwarded the non-user's personal information without his/her consent, and not the application itself. However, a problem that non-users might face when legally claiming their rights is that they would not have information on exactly which person forwarded their data to the Caller ID app. Caller ID app providers certainly have that information and according to the Art.14 of GDPR they should pass it to non-users, but this action would harm their users.

The ePrivacy Regulation [4] was proposed in 2017 and is still waiting to be adopted (up to December 2020). It would repeal ePrivacy Directive [6] and would be lex specialis to the GDPR [5]. The purpose of this regulation is protection of personal data in electronic communications. It could resolve many questions, because it could apply to all sorts of tech firms providing electronic communication services, and also protect people from unsolicited communications like marketing phone calls. Marketing callers will need to display their phone number or use a special pre-fix that indicates a marketing call. This could raise a question of the primary purposes for using Caller ID applications.

4   The Inverse Privacy Problem

In this section, we recall the notion of inverse privacy and give a connection between the inverse privacy problem and the Caller ID app privacy problem.

4.1   The Inverse Privacy

People have shared their personal data with many public and private institutions for a very long time, but over the past decades these institutions have been given a significant advantage over regular persons in terms of data collection capacity. For this reason there is more and more personal data that is not available to us. This kind of data is called **inversely private data**. Access to this data could benefit individuals and we should be entitled to access our inversely private data.

To be more specific, an item of your personal information is inversely private if some party has access to it but you do not have [10]. The inaccessibility to you of your personal data is the inverse privacy problem. A good solution of the problem should provide you with convenient accessibility to your inversely private data. In order to ensure convenient access, the following three items should be considered:

- *Large database.* On a daily basis we interact with various institutions leaving and creating new inversely private information. The database that would store our inversely private data would be large and it would be growing daily.

- *Sensitive information.* Some of our inversely private information might be too sensitive to be shared with us, and among our inversely private data there might be information that we do not want and should not see. Although it may be hard to believe, even in addition to intelligence data, there are certain scenarios in which our inversely private information should not be available to us. For example, some of our personal information could be a part of the research that examines the risks of getting a certain type of disease. This information should be available to us in many scenarios (if our doctor suspects the possibility of the disease), but not on a daily basis. Another example comes from the perspective of Caller ID apps. To be specific, Caller ID app database can contain some sexist and offensive names associated with our phone number, and it is not convenient to provide us the access to such names.
- *Privacy and Security.* Sharing back our inversely private information has to be secure, ensuring certainty provided by user identity credentials [2], differential privacy [3], multi-party computation [20], and other relevant means.

The question is where to look for a solution to the inversely private problem. The inverse privacy problem is a product of technological progress, and it can be solved only with better technology.

The Biggish Platform. Microsoft Research proposed a solution for the inverse privacy problem in [9]. The solution includes the Biggish platform, a trusted platform for storing your personal data, driven by the idea of securely storing on the cloud. Your data about finance, health, location, etc. would be consolidated on the Biggish platform, and you would access them through various analytics apps. In order to ensure customer trust, these apps should preserve user's privacy and they should not leak data. In that sense, Biggish would be useful not only to individuals, but also to software developers. One more beneficiary of Biggish would be a company or set of companies that host Biggish. The ownership of all that data would require the development of new privacy policies. Biggish is a solution proposal for the inverse privacy problem, and based on that proposal, Microsoft started testing new Bali project in 2019. The test results are not yet published [16].

4.2 Caller ID App Privacy Problem and the Inverse Privacy Problem

We claim that there is a link between the Caller ID app privacy problem and the inverse privacy problem. Our phone number is our personal information, the name under which our phone number is stored in someone's address book is also our personal information but to which we generally do not have access. This leads to the conclusion that the Caller ID app privacy problem falls into the scope of the inverse privacy problem. Nevertheless, it must be stated that in this situation the inverse privacy problem is only relevant from the perspective of the provider of the Caller ID app and it is not been caused by an individual user of the Caller ID app.

To explain the main similarities and differences between our problem and the problem of inverse privacy, we will present *infons*. The notion of infons has been introduced in [11] - an infon is defined as an item of information.

First of all, previous research on the topic of inverse privacy has been based on the assumption that certain infon is personal to only one individual. Our problem is slightly different. The name, under which the telephone number of the person A is stored in the address book of the person B, is also personal to the person B. If the person A were given access to that information, then the privacy of the person B would be also violated. Even if one did not know whose address book a particular name belonged to, it might still be possible to infer from some previous experience.

Also, as we stated before, some of our inversely private information might be too sensitive to be shared with us. Caller ID applications generally contain mechanisms that exclude offensive names, but that doesn't mean that if people have access to a database of names under which their phone number is stored somewhere, they won't see the names they don't like.

Given the link between the Caller ID app privacy problem and the inverse privacy problem, the solution for the inverse privacy problem can be used to solve the Caller ID app privacy problem. Our proposition on how to use the Biggish platform to solve privacy issues in Caller ID applications is as follows. Some part of the Biggish platform could contain a database with names under which our phone number is stored in other people's address books. Given the size of the database and the presence of sensitive data, it would be necessary to provide adequate access.

Access to the database will be two-fold. On the one hand, we will have access to the database, and on the other hand, the Caller ID applications will have access as well (Fig. 1). Also, we should not see which name belongs to which address book, in order to preserve the privacy of the owner of the particular address book. Hiding this information would protect the privacy of the address book owner in many scenarios, but not in general. There are certain scenarios in which, with the help of some additional information, it is possible to find out whose directory a certain name belongs to (for example if any characteristic nickname is in question). This leads to the conclusion that our access to the database does not have to be through the display of the list of names, but through the possibility of certain manipulations over the database. Particularly, we could set our preferences regarding the names. In the first place, we could set our phone number to be private, partially private and non-private. In that way, the information about privacy of a phone number would be stored in one place to which each Caller ID application would have access. Setting our phone number to be private at only one place is much more simple than excluding ourselves from the databases of every Caller ID application separately. It's the same thing with setting the number to be non-private. In that case, the Caller ID applications according to their mechanisms could forward any name associated with our number. The most interesting case is the partially private phone number. In order to explain partial privacy, in the next section, we introduce the notion of privacy variable.

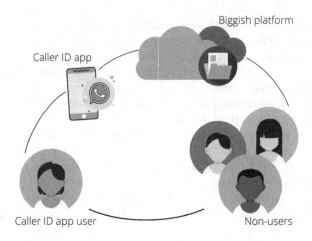

Fig. 1. The connection between users, non-users and the Biggish platform

5 Preserving Privacy in Caller ID Apps

In this section, we introduce privacy variables and name sensitivity function. We further design an algorithm for determining caller identification and providing an adequate privacy preserving name. Finally, we discuss the position of the name sensitivity function and it's use aside the use in Caller ID apps.

5.1 Name Sensitivity and Privacy Variables

As noted before, individuals and the connections between them can be represented by a social graph. Each individual is associated with a set of attributes: name, school, profession, etc. Since the Caller ID applications, in addition to the name, phone number and e-mail, filter all other data from the phonebook and pass only the name to users, we will focus below on the attribute that indicates the name. A Caller ID app social graph is then defined as follows.

Definition 1 (Caller ID App Social Graph). The Caller ID application data is modeled by a graph $G = (V, E, A, P)$, where V is a set of nodes representing users and non-users, $E \subseteq V \times V$ is a set of edges representing relations between users and non-users, A is a set of attributes associated with every node, and P is a set of privacy variables.

A *privacy variable* is a variable associated with the name attribute: name, surname, hometown, school, profession and so on. Those variables can have only two values, 0 for non-private information and 1 for private information. When setting his phone number to be partially private, the person defines values for each of the privacy variables. The motivation for introducing privacy variables is the greater sensitivity of certain names compared to other names. For the journalist mentioned before, the information about her profession is more sensitive than her name and surname. She could define that the names that include her profession are not shared with the users of Caller ID applications. Below we define a function that represents the sensitivity of a particular name, or the sensitivity of a particular value for a name attribute.

Definition 2 (Name Sensitivity Function). Let X be a name attribute and x any value of the name attribute, sensitivity of x denoted by $S(x)$ is defined by:

$$S(x) = \begin{cases} 0, & \text{if } 1° \text{or } 2° \\ \frac{n}{m}, & \text{if } 3° \\ 1, & \text{if } 4° \text{or } 5° \end{cases} \tag{1}$$

where n is a number of variables that are marked as private, and the value x matches them, m is a total number of variables that are marked as private, and

1° The phone number associated with the name x is non-private.
2° The phone number associated with the name x is partially private, but x does not match any variable that is marked as private.
3° The phone number associated with the name x is partially private and x matches some of the variables that are marked as private.
4° The phone number associated with the name x is private.
5° The phone number associated with the name x is partially private and x matches all the variables that are marked as private.

Example 1. Let the set of privacy variables be $P = \{P_1, P_2, P_3, P_4\}$ where P_1 defines name, P_2 defines town, P_3 defines profession, P_4 defines affiliation and let Alice set P_2, P_3 and P_4 to be private. The sensitivity of the following names associated with her phone number is:

- if $x_1 =$ "Alice", $S(x_1) = \frac{0}{3} = 0$;
- if $x_2 =$ "Bob", $S(x_2) = \frac{0}{3} = 0$;
- if $x_3 =$ "Alice the professor", $S(x_3) = \frac{1}{3}$;
- if $x_4 =$ "Bob Novi Sad", $S(x_4) = \frac{1}{3}$;
- if $x_5 =$ "Alice the professor Novi Sad", $S(x_5) = \frac{2}{3}$;
- if $x_6 =$ "Bob the professor Faculty of Technical Sciences", $S(x_6) = \frac{2}{3}$;
- if $x_7 =$ "Alice the professor Faculty of Technical Sciences Novi Sad", $S(x_7) = \frac{3}{3} = 1$;

Example 2. For the journalist, mentioned in Sect. 2, information about her/his profession and affiliation is more sensitive than her/his name. Given the set of privacy variables $P = \{P_1, P_2, P_3\}$ where P_1 defines name, P_2 defines profession, P_3 defines affiliation, and setting P_2 and P_3 to be private, the sensitivity of the following names associated with her/his phone number is:

- if $x_1 =$ "Alice", $S(x_1) = \frac{0}{2} = 0$;
- if $x_2 =$ "Bob", $S(x_2) = \frac{0}{2} = 0$;

- if x_3 = "Alice the journalist", $S(x_3) = \frac{1}{2}$;
- if x_4 = "Bob the journalist New York Times", $S(x_4) = \frac{2}{2} = 1$.

Each person has his/her own sensitivity function that reflects his/her preferences regarding the privacy of his/her phone number and the names associated with his/her phone number. A finer model could be obtained by defining privacy variables to take values from an interval $[0, 1]$. In this way, each person could even define a certain sensitivity threshold for each variable.

5.2   APPN Algorithm

In order to give the answer to the question when the sensitivity of the name is checked, we design the algorithm that provides adequate privacy preserving name (APPN algorithm) in Fig. 2.
Below we give a detailed description of the algorithm:

Step 1. Obtain a phone number of an incoming call.
Step 2. Check whether the phone number is stored in the user's address book. If the phone number is not stored in the user's address book, skip to the Step 3, either way skip to the Step 6.
Step 3. Check the privacy of the phone number. If the phone number is set to be non-private skip to the Step 4. If the phone number is set to be partially private, check which of the privacy variables are set to be private and skip to the Step 4. If the phone number is set to be private, skip to the Step 6.
Step 4. Single out the names associated with the given phone number from the database, and skip to the Step 5.
Step 5. Check the sensitivity of every name that has been singled out in the Step 4. Select one of the names with zero sensitivity and skip to the Step 6.
Step 6. Present the adequate name of the calling party, or inform the user that it was not possible to find an adequate name.

A problem that has not been considered is the matching of the name with a certain privacy variable. Names, professions, towns can be represented by their abbreviations. They are also characteristic of each speaking area. Further, people tend to use personal indications for labeling contacts in their address books (names like "mom", "dad", etc.). A mitigating circumstance is that Caller ID apps already have their own mechanisms that exclude names based on personal indication and such names are not passed on to their users. However, the mechanism for verifying the matching of names with privacy variables should be further investigated.

5.3   The Position of the Name Sensitivity Function

We will here discuss the position of the name sensitivity function from legal and practical aspects.

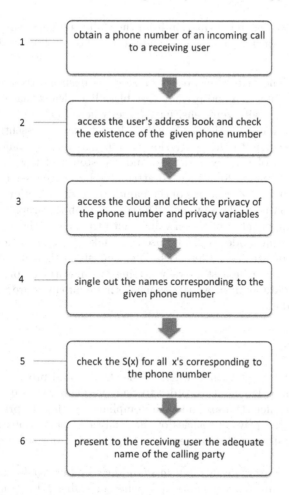

Fig. 2. An algorithm for determining caller identification and providing adequate privacy preserving name.

Legal Side. With respect to the inclusion of the Biggish platform in the solution for Caller ID app privacy problem, the question of the position of the name sensitivity function arises. There are two possibilities. The first one is to include the approach of the sensitivity function in the business model of the Caller ID app provider. The second one is to include the approach of the sensitivity function in the business model of the provider of the Biggish platform. Both business models should comply with the requirements imposed by the GDPR, and data subjects should be aware of their data being processed. In the second case, the Biggish platform becomes the controller of the personal data. The Biggish platform is then obliged to inform data subjects about the processing and to check whether providing access to this data by the Caller ID app provider is according to the data privacy laws. However, when it comes to the way in which the Biggish platform obtained name information from the Caller ID apps, the responsibility regarding the forwarding of that information is still on each individual Caller ID app.

Practical Side. The algorithm presented above is designed on the basis of the name sensitivity function and privacy variables. The idea is that Caller ID apps can use only names with zero sensitivity (cases where $S(x) = 0$). The remaining two cases of the name sensitivity function do not play an essential role in the algorithm. This leads to the conclusion that the algorithm could be designed only on the basis of privacy variables, and the step 5 of the algorithm could become "choose a name for which no attributes have been set to be private". However, the remaining two cases of the name sensitivity function are applicable in other areas related to data privacy. The social graph that represents Caller ID app data has significant application value. With the help of the name sensitivity function, the graph model could be used to make some statistical analysis of different levels of privacy preferences. The analysis is then usable in tracking down those with the highest privacy settings in a world of privacy nihilism. Companies for data analysis as well as marketing companies are very interested in this type of data.

6   Discussion

The first issue we dealt with is whether the storage and processing of data by the Caller ID apps is lawful. In order to find the answer, we analyzed privacy policies of two Caller ID apps and their compliance with data privacy laws. We concluded that the privacy policies of the analyzed applications respected the privacy of their users and non-users at a large degree, but some questions still remain unresolved.

Caller ID app users decided not to share their address books. What will happen? One of the unresolved questions is whether Caller ID app users have the right to share personal data of their contacts with the Caller ID app they use, and what would happen if users stopped sharing data from their address books. The data from the Caller ID app database mainly comes from the address books of its users (some of the data comes from public databases, from interaction with third party services like Facebook, Twitter, LinkedIn, etc.). When users would not share the data from their address books with Caller ID apps, the way these apps fundamentally work would have to be changed. That would conflict with the purpose of Caller ID apps and the interests of the Caller ID providers.

The right of deletion of your personal data. How to be sure that your personal data is actually removed from the database? The next unresolved question concerns the non-users. The privacy policies of both investigated apps respect the right of non-users to unlist themselves from the app's database and to delete their personal data. Both applications have their own websites. Assuming that you are aware of the existence of these applications, you can contact the app providers via their website in order to unlist you from their database. The questions that remain open are:

- how to be sure that your personal data is actually removed from the Caller ID app database,
- how this action prevents adding your personal data again to the app's database once another user having you as a contact on his/her address book actually allows for such access.

The Biggish platform - one more technology product to trust? Further in the paper we discuss the connection between the inverse privacy problem and the Caller ID app privacy problem. We argue that the solution for the inverse privacy problem, the Biggish platform, can resolve the privacy problem of Caller ID apps. This solution is based on a mediator between users, non-users and caller id apps. In this sense, individuals should trust not only the Caller ID applications, but also the Biggish platform, in terms of storing and processing their data and in terms of respecting their preferences (about privacy of their phone number and the names associated with their phone number). In order to achieve high level of trust, the Biggish platform should function in accordance with all GDPR requirements. In this sense, the main principles of privacy by design and privacy by default should be respected (according to the Art.25 of GDPR), which requires a deeper analysis of this problem.

The Biggish platform-failure for the Caller ID apps? The next question regarding the Biggish platform is would the existence of such platform that stores all data of all users and non-users would lead to the failure of all Caller ID apps. If the Caller ID applications had the access on the Biggish platform only to preferences and not to the complete data related to a certain phone number, they would continue to function as before. Competition between them would still be based on the fact who has a larger database and better search mechanisms. Of course, since it is not yet known how the platform will work, it is not possible to say with certainty how its existence will affect the Caller ID applications and also many other applications that operate on personal data. Caller ID was invented in the 70's and since then many of its functions have evolved due to the development of technology. There is a possibility that the Caller ID application will change their functions over time and with the discovery of new technologies.

A safe place for storing privacy preferences of a phone number. Where to find it? Another question related to the Biggish platform is what would happen if it was suddenly removed and what would it mean for the operation of the Caller ID applications. We argue that is much more simple to set preferences about privacy of a phone number at only one place than to exclude ourselves from the databases of every Caller ID application separately. That place must be protected from sudden deletion and illegal access. The solution can be found in distributed databases [23] or blockchain technology [8].

Identification of individuals. Is it possible by combining public and semi-private information? Finally in the paper we introduce the notion of privacy variables and name sensitivity. There are certain open questions on this topic. We argue that certain names have greater sensitivity compared to other names, and that allowing someone to set his/her phone number to be partially private (to set some privacy variables to be 1) can greatly increase person's security. On the other hand, we state that the Caller ID applications collect data from public databases and through the interaction with social media, in addition to the address books of their users. The question that arises is whether it is still possible to uniquely identify individuals by combination of public and semi-private information. The answer is yes, but individuals would be more aware of that possibility than they are now. At the moment the majority of the population is not sufficiently familiar with the ways in which identification of individuals can be done and in general with their rights based on the data privacy laws. Having the ability to set phone number privacy preferences would increase individuals' awareness of their rights at least in some way.

Informations from multiple sources. How should Caller ID apps treat them? The last question we will discuss relates to linked data. To be more specific, the question is how should Caller ID apps treat combined information from multiple sources while ensuring privacy protection. On the one hand, the Caller ID app has the information about privacy of our phone number collected from the Biggish platform, and on the other hand, it has many other informations about our phone number collected from their users, public databases and social media. In order to provide privacy protection in this case, a logic-based model can be implemented like in [12].

7   Conclusion and Further Work

Our aim is to give a comprehensive view on data privacy problems caused by the Caller ID applications. To this end, we first explored the privacy policies of two Caller ID applications, Truecaller and Everybody, and their compliance with data privacy laws such as GDPR, ePrivacy Directive and ePrivacy Regulation. It can be concluded that the creators of the Caller ID applications have updated their privacy policies to comply with privacy laws, but also that some issues related to the privacy of non-users have not yet been resolved. We further argue that the problem of non-user privacy falls into the scope of inverse privacy. Building on this connection, we introduce the notion of name sensitivity and privacy variables and solve the problem of non-user privacy. Finally, we discussed open questions related to the trust of the Caller ID app users, the place for storing privacy preferences about a phone number and linked data in Caller ID apps.

The above discussion motivated us to continue our research on the topic of blockchain with the intention of finding a safe way for storing privacy preferences about a phone number. We also plan to extend the mathematical model presented in [12], in order to answer the question how should Caller ID apps treat combined information from multiple sources while ensuring privacy protection.

Another direction of the further research will be the privacy problem on the server side, where the Caller ID app provider learns significant information about the social graph. Due to the fact that social graph data has significant application value, this data is increasingly being made public or sold to third parties. The data is then used for commercial and research purposes. In this paper we have seen that the data of the Caller ID applications contains private information of individuals, so the question is how to prevent individual privacy disclosure while publishing this data. The ongoing and future work will consider anonymization and privacy preserving techniques along the lines [14] and [25].

Acknowledgement. We would like to thank the referees for their careful reading of our submission. Their comments and suggestions have guided us to revise and improve the paper. Furthermore, we would like to thank the organisers and session chairs of the IFIP Summer School for the feedback of the discussions which highly broadened our research. Last but not least, we would like to thank the IFIP Summer School participants for valuable discussions during the summer school.

This work has been partially supported by the Science Fund of the Republic of Serbia under grant AI4TrustBC (6526707).

References

1. Betrayed by an app she had never heard of https://ifex.org/serious-privacy-concerns-raised-about-the-app-truecaller/. Accessed 3 Sept 2020
2. Bosworth, K., Gonzalez Lee, M.G., Jaweed, S., Wright, T.: Entities, identities, identifiers and credentials - what does it all mean? BT Technol. J. **23**(4), 25–36 (2005). https://doi.org/10.1007/s10550-006-0004-2
3. Dwork, C.: Differential privacy. In: Bugliesi, M., Preneel, B., Sassone, V., Wegener, I. (eds.) ICALP 2006. LNCS, vol. 4052, pp. 1–12. Springer, Heidelberg (2006). https://doi.org/10.1007/11787006_1
4. European Commission: Proposal for a Regulation on Privacy and Electronic Communications (ePrivacy Regulation). https://ec.europa.eu/digital-single-market/en/news/proposal-regulation-privacy-and-electronic-communications
5. European Parliament and Council of the European Union: Regulations (EU) 2016/679 of the European Parliament and of the Council - general data protection regulation (GDPR) (2016). https://eur-lex.europa.eu/eli/reg/2016/679/oj
6. European Parliament, Council of the European Union: Directive 2002/58/EC of the European parliament and of the council of 12 July 2002 concerning the processing of personal data and the protection of privacy in the electronic communications sector (directive on privacy and electronic communications) (2002). https://eur-lex.europa.eu/legal-content/EN/TXT/?uri=OJ:L:2002:201:TOC
7. Everybody privacy policy. http://www.evrbd.com/policy.html#. Accessed 5 Sept 2020
8. Ghosh, J.: The blockchain: opportunities for research in information systems and information technology. J. Global Inf. Technol. Manage. **22**(4), 235–242 (2019). https://doi.org/10.1080/1097198X.2019.1679954
9. Gurevich, Y., Haiby, N., Hudis, E., Wing, J., Ziklik, E.: Biggish: a solution for the inverse privacy problem. Technical report. MSR-TR-2016-24, Microsoft, May 2016. https://www.microsoft.com/en-us/research/publication/230-biggish-solution-inverse-privacy-problem/
10. Gurevich, Y., Hudis, E., Wing, J.M.: Inverse privacy. CoRR abs/1510.03311 (2015). http://arxiv.org/abs/1510.03311
11. Gurevich, Y., Neeman, I.: Logic of infons: the propositional case. ACM Trans. Comput. Log. **12**(2), 9:1–9:8 (2011). https://doi.org/10.1145/1877714.1877715
12. Jaksic, S., Pantovic, J., Ghilezan, S.: Linked data privacy. Math. Struct. Comput. Sci. **27**(1), 33–53 (2017). https://doi.org/10.1017/S096012951500002X

13. Mustafa, H., Xu, W., Sadeghi, A.R., Schulz, S.: You can call but you can't hide: detecting caller id spoofing attacks. In: Proceedings of the International Conference on Dependable Systems and Networks, June 2014. https://doi.org/10.1109/DSN.2014.102

14. Narayanan, A., Shmatikov, V.: De-anonymizing social networks. CoRR abs/0903.3276 (2009). http://arxiv.org/abs/0903.3276

15. News, A.: https://abcnews.go.com/GMA/Consumer/story?id=3305916. Accessed 2 Sept 2020

16. Otokiti, E.: Microsoft tests new personal data bank, project Bali. https://channels.theinnovationenterprise.com/articles/microsoft-tests-new-personal-data-bank-project-bali. Accessed 14 Oct 2020

17. Papakipos, M.N., Walkin, B.M.: Caller identification using social network information, August 2012

18. Ramirez, A.: Caller id: Consumer's friend or foe? (1992). https://www.nytimes.com/1992/04/04/news/caller-id-consumer-s-friend-or-foe.html

19. Schneier, B.: https://www.schneier.com/blog/archives/2006/03/caller_id_spoof.html. Accessed 2 Sept 2020

20. Schoenmakers, B.: Multiparty Computation, pp. 812–815. Springer, Boston (2011). https://doi.org/10.1007/978-1-4419-5906-5_7

21. Stevens, M., Chow, A.R.: https://www.nytimes.com/2018/11/13/us/barriss-swatting-wichita.html. Accessed 2 Sept 2020

22. Sukma, N., Chokngamwong, R.: One time key issuing for verification and detecting caller id spoofing attacks. In: 2017 14th International Joint Conference on Computer Science and Software Engineering (JCSSE), pp. 1–4 (2017)

23. Tan, K.L.: Distributed Database Systems, pp. 894–896. Springer, Boston (2009). https://doi.org/10.1007/978-0-387-39940-9_701

24. Truecaller privacy policy. https://www.truecaller.com/privacy-policy. Accessed 5 Sept 2020

25. Xie, Y., Zheng, M.: A differentiated anonymity algorithm for social network privacy preservation. Algorithms **9**(4), 85 (2016). https://doi.org/10.3390/a9040085

"Identity Management by Design" with a Technical Mediator Under the GDPR

Anne Steinbrück[✉]

Center of Advanced Legal Studies,
Karlsruhe Institute of Technology, Karlsruhe, Germany
anne.steinbrueck@kit.edu

Abstract. The Charter of Fundamental Rights of the European Union (CFR) and the GDPR refer to the protection of personal data and personal identities. In the General Data Protection Regulation (GDPR) the term of personal data contains the protection of the physical, physiological, genetic, psychological, economic, cultural and social identities, Art. 4 para. 1 GDPR. This legal definition introduces the understanding of "identity" in a pluralistic sense. Thus, the notion of pluralistic and dynamic identities should be translated in a *"privacy by design"* mechanism. This notion of pluralistic identities would mirror a differentiated protection for personal identities based the right of informational self-determination, Art. 7, 8 CFR. Thus, the data subject should be enabled to develop the personal identity in an online-context in the same manner as it is done in an offline-context. This includes the opportunity for the data subject to control personal identities in their static *"Idem-*part" such as the name and their dynamic *"Ipse-*part" realized by the behavior (based on the philosophical theory by *Ricœur*). These parts of the personal identity should be visualized with a "dashboard" that allows the data subject to control and manage the personal identities. This "dashboard" should include an impartial technical mediator that embodies an effective, non-discriminatory and structured process. Such a technical mediator should be specified in an *"identity management by design"* mechanism based on Art. 25 GDPR in order to achieve an effective privacy protection in the era of Big Data.

Keywords: Privacy by design · Identity protection · Human rights · Mediation · Game theory

1 Introduction

The Charter of Fundamental Rights of the European Union (CFR) and the General Data Protection Regulation (GDPR) protect personal data. At the same time, the protection of personal data in the definition of Art. 4 para. 1 GDPR embodies the notion that personal data can be factors of physical, physiological, genetic, psychological, economic, cultural and social identity. Thus, the CFR and the GDPR include the notion of pluralistic identities, because personal identities can be realized in many contexts and have to be protected as such. Comparing the protection of personal identities in an offline- and online-context, in an online-context there is a lack of transparency regarding the profiles and personal identities. In particular profiles based on user

© IFIP International Federation for Information Processing 2021
Published by Springer Nature Switzerland AG 2021
M. Friedewald et al. (Eds.): Privacy and Identity 2020, IFIP AICT 619, pp. 169–186, 2021.
https://doi.org/10.1007/978-3-030-72465-8_10

behavior in social media are the origins for advertisements or feeds and remain unknown for the data subject, as it became obvious in the *Cambridge Analytica* case [34]. These advertisements or feeds based on profiles are often the result of user behavior that is unconscious ("digital unconscious" [14]) rather than rational. The user might assume to be able to fully exercise his fundamental rights, but in fact remains unprotected with respect to the profiles created by the controller. The gap between theoretical protection of users and generated profiles requires a differentiated protection of context specific generated profiles as identities. The question should be examined, how to describe an effective protection regime for the online-specific usage of pluralistic identities for each context. Such a protection regime should fulfill the requirement of self-determination based on Art. 7, 8 CFR.

To describe a protection regime, existing legal perspectives on privacy and identity protection should be evaluated. The research from other disciplines should also be included to reflect the phenomena of identities in the online-context and define an effective mechanism for protection. First it should be shown that the concept of plural identities can be described by the term "dynamic identity" (2.). Furthermore, the dynamics of identities in each context in the GDPR should be determined, so that the *"contextual integrity"* of personal identities will be described (3.). Consequently, the protection of personal identities in an offline- and online-context and the term of dynamic identity should be included in the technological and organizational measures. This could be realized with a specific concept of *"privacy by design"* based on Art. 25 GDRP, which covers the protection of dynamic identities with a *"identity management by design"* mechanism (4.). Such a mechanism should include a "technical mediator" in order to implement ethical and human rights standard for a dynamic identity protection based on the Charter of Fundamental Rights to effectively protect personal identities in the era of Big Data (5.). Finally, the requirements for an effective protection of dynamic identities should introduce a paradigm shift towards a differentiated identity protection in the GDPR (6.).

2   The Term *"Dynamic Identities"*

2.1   The Term *"Dynamic Identities"* in the Charter of Fundamental Rights

The protection of personal data based on Art. 8 CFR contains the definition of personal data under the secondary law of the GDPR, so that the economic, physiological and psychological identities are also protectedly Art. 8 CFR [17, 24]. The "self-determination of the individual with regard to his or her data" was recognized in the deliberations of the Charter of Fundamental Rights to be protected by Art. 8 CFR [5]. To exercise self-determination is covered in data protection law by the concept of consent, Art. 6, 7 GDPR. The consent justifies the processing and that context-specific personal identities are generated. Subsequently, the control by the data subject is strengthened by the exercise of the data subject rights in accordance with Art. 8 para. 2 s. 2 CFR in order to determine the personal identities.

In particular, control includes the right to be forgotten, which is fundamental for the protection of personal identities: The right to a new beginning in the sense of a *tabula rasa*-right is decisive for a new beginning in the online-context, and is reflected in the recent decision of the German Constitutional Court on the "Right to Forget I" (German Constitutional Court, Judgment, November 09, 2019, No. 1 BvR 16/13). It was held that with regard to past crimes and the past imprisonment, there must be a chance for a new beginning. The new beginning has to include the right to forget, so that an article regarding the crime in an archive that is online available can be deleted. Consequently, the term of dynamic identities covers the right of a new beginning in an online- and offline-context.

According to Art. 7 CFR, private life and communication are protected. The protection of the private life includes that the identity shall be constituted and determined by oneself [17]. This makes clear that, in addition to identity as a name the term identity includes the dynamic part of the personality realized in online- and offline-contexts. In addition, the Convent of the Charter of Fundamental Rights discussed the inclusion of the wording "identity" in Art. 7 CFR [5]. However, since the term of identity is rarely used in the wording of the constitutions of the Member States, the Convent has distanced itself from this. So the term of identity in its "individual uniqueness" of personalities is part of the right to informational self-determination based on Art. 7, 8 CFR [5]. Thus, personal identities and the possibilities for personal development are protected for the online-context in the same way as in the offline-context. In particular the right to be forgotten allows an individual to leave past behaviors behind and to have the chance of a new beginning. Accordingly, it is inherent that the Charter of Fundamental Rights includes the protection of personal identity in a dynamic and communicative dimension [5, 17]. This applies in particular to the online-context, which is also covered with regard to new developments by the protection of Art. 7, 8 CFR [5]. Conclusively, the term of dynamic personal identities is part of the protection regime of the Charter of Fundamental Rights.

2.2 The Term Identity from an Interdisciplinary Perspective

Information Technology Perspective. The term "identity" describes the process of comparison in order to determine perfect equality between two objects. Taking the perspective of information technology into account, identity is primarily understood as the process of identification and authentication [37]. The process of identification and authentication provide access rights that are often called "digital identities" [16, 37]. These "digital identities" represent the numerical part of a personal identity during a life cycle. Thus, the term identity in the perspective of information technologies includes the numerical part of identity, which corresponds with a static understanding of identity. This static understanding of identity can be seen by calling electronic ID-cards "digital identities" [16]. With such static digital identities trust regarding the correctness of the identity can be established. A high degree of trust can be particularly applied by issuing electronic signatures. Also employee-IDs are examples for static and numeric identities that enable certain access rights.

Thus, identities from an information technological perspective include the management of access rights [37]. In conclusion the informational technology perspective embodies a static notion on identity and the concrete content of the personal identity is of secondary importance.

Philosophical Perspective. The static perspective on identity is expanded with the notion of a dynamic personal identity by the philosophical model of *Ricœur* (Fig. 1). The concept of identity is differentiated between a numerical part of equality (*Idem*) and a behavioral part of selfhood (*Ipse*) [15, 20, 31]. The *Ipse*-part is defined by the interaction with others and the *Idem*-part particularly describes the process of identification with a high degree of credibility and reputation [15]. This philosophical differentiation between the "dynamic" *Ipse*- and the "static" *Idem*-part of an identity illustrates the expressions of identity. In particular, the *Idem*-part of identity is the name and it responds to the question of "who?" [31]. The *Ipse*- and *Idem*-part of identity together constitute the character of a person that mediates both identity parts [31]. Thus, the character is the result of a dialectic relation between the static *Idem*- and dynamic *Ipse*- part of identity [31]. This character is the source of the temporary action that becomes visible for others [21]. With the temporary action the self-presentation and the communication with others the identity is subject to an iterative dialogue [21]. This dynamic of an iterative dialogue is one source for the personal development, which is taking place in an online- and offline-context equally [14]. This differentiated philosophical perspective of identity is mirrored in the definition of personal data in Art. 8 para. 1 CFR and should be subject to the technical mechanism of *"identity management by design"*.

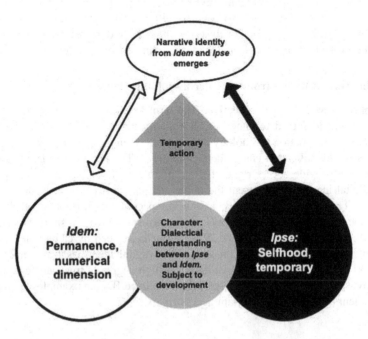

Fig. 1. Model of the term identity by *Ricœur,* "Oneself as another".

Social-Psychological Perspective. In addition, the social-psychological and the communication psychology perspective on personal identity stress the dynamic aspect of identity [22, 36]. In general the social-psychological understanding of identity depends on the current social-psychological schools. For example, the school of *Erikson* [9] assumes the formation of identity in eight phases, which can have an effect on the later personality and possible conflicts. This school understands identity as "inner capital" that is formed in the childhood and adolescence so that an "unitary identity" [18] is the result. This school is contrasted by the modern theoretical understanding of personal identity, which is characterized by a continuous identity formation in life. The identity is subject to continuous formation by internal and external social structures. Consequently, personal identity defines itself in a dialog and is in continuous construction, so that identity emerges from actions and narratives [20]. From a psychological perspective identity can be summarized as a "I am many", which is constituted by a social self, professional self, a physical self and a religious self [19, 21]. This understanding of many identities includes the different realization of identity in each context and its dependency on the communicative relationship. This allows a dynamic identity building [21], that gives the personal identity an amoeba-like character. However, these characteristics of dynamic personal identity in an offline-context should also be reflected in an online-context.

It has been observed that there is an online-specific shift in identity building. In particular, the de-territorialized internet usage has made it easier to find social contacts and to present the own identity in the desired image. One reason for this change in the individual behavior is stated to be the cognitive distortion while using the internet and that it is easy to establish virtual identities [35]. This makes identity experiments possible, which can influence the development of personal identities [35].

Conclusively, the social-psychological perspective on personal identity includes a dynamic understanding of many identities. These personal identities are realized in communicative relationships in an offline- and online-context. In an online-context the communication can be influenced by the interface design so that cognitive distortion can influence the realization of identities.

2.3   *"Dynamic Identity"* in the GDPR

The definition in Art. 4 para. 1 GDPR includes, in addition to the protection of personal data, a context-specific concept of identity that classifies economic, cultural and social identity as worthy of protection. Taking the contexts for the identities into account, it seems that the notion of many identities in a communicative relation is immanent to the GDPR. This is also visible with the definition of special categories of personal data under Art. 9 GDPR, according to which the expression of political opinions, religious, ideological beliefs, trade union membership or health data enjoy a higher level of protection. The different identities defined in Art. 4 para. 1 GDPR and the different special categories of personal data defined in Art. 9 GDPR express behavior related *Ipse*-parts of a personal identity. These *Ipse*-parts of a personal identity depend on the context and may temporarily appear and disappear.

Also profiles as defined in Art. 4 para. 4 GDPR stipulate a dynamic behavioral oriented understanding of personal identity. Such profiles are constituted out of algorithm-based deconstructions and combinations of characteristics of a personal identity. Even the use of pseudonyms (Art. 4 para. 5 GDPR) demonstrates the *Idem*-part of the identity as a static identifier, and the temporary use of the identifier establishes the dynamic *Ipse*-part of the personal identity. In conclusion the GDPR embodies the notion of a dynamic personal identity that is subject to the protection regime of the GDPR.

2.4   Protection of Dynamic Identities

The term of dynamic identities has its source in the protection of personal data and private life based on Art. 7, 8 CFR. Thus, personal identities are protected by the European Charter of Fundamental Rights not only regarding the static name, but also the dynamic part of personality and identity building behavior are covered. Taking the interdisciplinary perspective into account, in particular the model by *Ricœur* allows a clear differentiation between static *Idem*- and dynamic *Ipse*-parts of personal identity. The model by *Ricœur* reflects the protective regime of personal data and private life, Art. 7, 8 CFR. Also the social-psychological perspective includes a broad understanding of personal identity that depends on the communicative relationship that constitutes several identities. Consequently, the term of dynamic personal identities is reflecting the interdisciplinary understanding of identity and is protected by the Charter of Fundamental Rights and the GDPR. In addition, the protection of the static *Idem*- and dynamic *Ipse*-parts of personal identity also depends on the context the identity is realized.

3   Contextual Protection of Dynamic Identities in the GDPR

The GDPR explicitly differentiates between the economic, social, health and professional context, Art. 4 para. 1, Art. 88 GDPR. In addition the activities in the private and family context are out of the scope of GDPR, Art. 2 para. 2 c) GDPR. However, the processing of personal data in a private context falls within the scope of the GDPR if the context changes towards e.g. social media or a business environment. Such a change of the context can evolve gradually, making it impossible to distinguish clearly whether it falls within the scope of the GDPR. But in order to apply the protective regime of the GDPR Art. 2 para. 2 c) must be interpreted narrowly, as it was stipulated by the European Court of Justice (ECJ) in the *Linquist*-decision (ECJ, 06. November 2003 - C-101/01). In this judgment it was held that private information even though it is presented in a slightly humorous way on a website, has to be considered in scope with the Data Protection Directive.

Furthermore, the GDPR provides with Art. 88 GDPR a specific regulation for the context of employment. The requirements under Art. 88 GDPR include the phases of application, hiring, work relation and termination of the contract [25]. Therefore in the employment context several static *Idem*-parts of personal identity are required. These include the health insurance number, tax identification number, and social security number as *Idem*-parts of personal identity.

These different contexts in the GDPR illustrate that the *Idem*- and *Ipse*-parts of the identity have to be controlled by the data subject in order to make use of the right of informational self-determination. With an identity management scheme that includes both the static *Idem*- and dynamic *Ipse*-part of personal identity the integrity of the personality can be realized in each context. In order to reach a high level of identity protection the principle of data minimization (Art. 5 para. 1 c) GDPR) would be implemented by a context specific identity management. This would establish a contextual integrity of personal identities. In addition, the contextual identities would be kept separate, so that the specific needs of protection in each context would be realized. Such a mechanism is described by *Nissenbaum's* concept of "contextual integrity" [26] that differentiates between different degrees of protection and context-specific "justice". Under this concept privacy can be realized in an official, professional and private communication and the specific information depends on the definition of the context. Such a mechanism is described by *Nissenbaum's* concept of "contextual integrity" [26] that differentiates between different degrees of protection and context-specific "justice". Under this concept privacy can be realized in an official, professional and private communication and the specific information depends on the definition of the context. Thus, the concept of "contextual integrity" includes the control of the degree of publicity of the information and the access level to sensitive and confidential contexts.

Finally, the management of the dynamic *Ipse*- and static *Idem*-part of a personal identity the contextual integrity should be maintained. In order to effectively implement contextual integrity in an identity management system, the technology has to be adjusted to the concept of static *Idem*- and dynamic *Ipse*-identities. Therefore the concept of *"privacy by design"* based on Art. 25 GDPR, recital 78 s. 2 might give fundamental guidance.

4   *"Identity Management by Design"* Based on Art. 25 GDPR

The concepts of *"privacy by design"* and *"privacy by default"* are part of Art. 25 GDPR, recital 78 s. 2 and stipulate the technological implementation of the principles of data processing pursuant to Art. 5 para. 1 GDPR. This includes the application into the technical and organizational design pursuant to Art. 25, 5 para. 1 GDPR.

In order to increase the level of protection for data subjects the concept of *Idem*- and *Ipse*-identities should be applied in the technical design of the processing. This includes a technical design that enables the data subject to control the personal identities with access rights as part of the principle of transparency, Art. 5 para. 1 a), 12, 15 GDPR. In order to reach a high level of identity protection it would be reasonable to provide access e.g. to the profiles as *Ipse*-parts of the personal identity. This enables the data subject to gain information and knowledge about existing profiles in order to exercise control on the identities. The reason is that the data subject might not be aware about the impact of the profiles to the personal preferences [15].

The data subject has the opportunity of an iterative control on personal identities and the right to agree or disagree with a profile of the identity. Such a mechanism as "*identity management by design*" would make personal identities dynamic and negotiable. It would be desirable that the "*identity management by design*" mechanism would become the "best practice" version from a bundle of measures by determining the appropriate state of the art. This approach goes beyond the traditional identity management referring to access management by identification or authentication. The "*identity management by design*" should include a mechanism that allows the iterative negotiation of personal identities. Consequently, the mechanism of "*identity management by design*" serves the fundamental transparency requirement under Art. 5 para. 1 a) GDPR. With the transparency of personal identities created by the "*identity management by design*" mechanism the self-determination can be exercised effectively. With the information about the generated profiles the data subject can decide whether to agree to this *Ipse*-part of the personal identity or disagree. The decision of the data subject on the personal identities is extended by the rights of the data subject pursuant to Art. 15–21 GDPR.

In particular, a "dashboard" as proposed by *Raschke/Küpper/Drozd/Kirrane* would be a reasonable solution [28]. With this "dashboard" the data subject is enabled to manage the rights such as the right to information, the consent and the rights of the data subject pursuant to Art. 15–21 GDPR. In order to protect personal identities, it would be desirable to extent such a "dashboard" with the transparency of personal identities and the iterative control over the *Ipse*- and *Idem*-parts of personal identity. Such a "dashboard" could also raise awareness and be applied as a tool for risk minimization based on Art. 32 para. 2 GDPR.

In general, the mechanism "*identity management by design*" would ensure that the *Ipse*-parts of identities are kept dynamic. This is possible by providing the transparency of the identities and by keeping the identities negotiable. For this the mechanism of "*identity management by design*" a technical mediator should be included in order to guarantee the negotiability of the *Ipse*-parts of personal identity.

5   Negotiable Personal Identities with a Technical Mediator

The need to negotiate personal identities presumes an environment for cooperation. The concept of cooperation is subject to the GDPR (5.1.). Furthermore, the relationship between the controller and the data subject has to be defined (5.2.). Then the resolution of the different interests in this relationship has to be analyzed in order to create a cooperation environment (5.3.). This could follow by the increase of the iterations in accordance with the "TIT for TAT"-strategy [2] and the transfer into a solution with a technical mediator.

5.1   Cooperation in the GDPR

The concept of cooperation is anchored in the GDPR. It has the function to build a trustful relationship in order to widen the possible solutions. Thus, cooperation is recognized as an important factor in creating value and potential [8]. According to Art. 31 GDPR the controller shall "cooperate" with the supervisory authority regarding the performance of its legal duties. Furthermore, Art. 33 para. 4 GDPR expresses the communicative exchange with the supervisory authority. In particular, the information in case of a breach of the data processing principles may be provided progressively to the supervisory authority. On this way the solution of the problem becomes a "shared mission" [7] between controller and supervisory authority. The potential conflict becomes a challenge of the controller and supervisory authority equally. Therefore, the stipulation of "cooperation" provides a procedure that allows self-regulation in the rapidly changing environment of information technologies [33]. Consequently, the promotion of cooperation is a recognized concept in the GDPR.

For the protection of personal identities, a cooperative procedure could be an essential part in the mechanism of *"identity management by design"*. Since cooperation creates value, a cooperative environment would be beneficial for the protection of personal identities. This mechanism of *"identity management by design"* could create an environment for diverse personal identities. In this respect, cooperation should be made useful for identity management.

5.2   Relationship Between Controller and Data Subject

The controller and the data subject have divergent starting positions with regard to the available information. In particular the relationship between the controller and the data subject is characterized by an asymmetry of the available information. After identifying the information asymmetry, the relationship between the controller and the data subject should be analyzed with the game theory. With applying the game theory the economic perspective in the interaction between controller and data subject can lead to further findings for effective identity protection. Finally, the conflict of interest between the data subject and the controller has to be classified in order to define an appropriate mechanism for conflict resolution.

Information Asymmetry. The preparation of the processing, the legitimization of the processing and the exercise of the data subject rights can be described as phases of the processing in the GDPR. The determination of phases of processing in the GPDR clarifies the different degrees of influence the controller and data subject have during the data cycle. In order to include interdisciplinary research results regarding the actions of the data subject and the controller in each phase the relevant regulations in the GDPR shall be demonstrated.

In the phase of preparing the processing, the decisions by the controller on the degree of implementing the principles of data processing based on Art. 5 para. 1 GDPR may already lead to an information asymmetry. This information asymmetry develops because the controller knows the details about the amount of collected personal data and the detection possibilities out of profiles. In particular the controller chooses the technology for processing based on the required state of the art in Art. 25 GDPR, which is unknown to the data subject. The controller might even apply persuasive technologies that should encourage the consent and high period of use by the data subject [10]. It is in the economic interest of the controller to attract many users and encourage the data subject to disclose a large amount of personal data. It is also in the economic interest of the controller to encourage the consent by choosing a broadly formulated purpose for the processing, Art. 5 para. 1 b) GDPR. This broad purpose for processing is legitimized by consent or other legitimacy reasons, Art. 6, 7 GDPR. However, this information about the processing is only accessible for the data subject by reading the privacy policy diligently. And in some cases, it is even likely that the privacy policies are written in a way, that precisely meets the legal requirements by Art. 12, 13 GDPR and the information about the actual scope of the processing is missing. It can even occur that the privacy policies are incompliant with the requirements of Art. 12, 13 GDPR or they are formulated in a manner beyond what is required [38]. This could be if the privacy policy is drafted in a very abstract way, allowing a high degree of interpretation, or the privacy policy is very long, so that the data subject is likely to be overwhelmed by the information. Such privacy policies reinforce the information asymmetry between the controller and the data subject, because the possibilities to understand the risks of the processing by taking the privacy policies into account are limited. This illustrates that already in the phase of preparing the processing, that the relationship between the controller and the data subject is characterized by the higher level of information about the processing of the controller.

Moreover, the information asymmetry can be reinforced by the fact that processing is legitimated with consent or other grounds of legitimacy based on Art. 6, 7 GDPR. This is particularly the case, if the data subject does not read the data protection provisions. With regard to general terms and conditions it was argued in the "myth of the opportunity to read" [4], that a rational consumer does not read the terms and conditions. This seems also applicable to privacy policies. The research of *Acquisti* [1] verified the dominant interest of data subjects in a direct use of the service, which is perceived as gratification. So the decision-making process of the data subject is based on the interest on gratification rather than a rational decision that reflects the advantages and disadvantages of consenting to a service. This is an important fact to consider, as the right of informational self-determination requires the rational consent to generate *Ipse*-parts of personal identity. Thus, the information asymmetry between controller and data subject is reinforced by the privacy policies and the gratification interest to directly use the service.

Furthermore, if the data subject rights based on Art. 15–21 GDPR are applied the controller is required to realize the right. Once the processed personal data has been made transparent to the data subject, e.g. the right to be forgotten based on Art. 17 GDPR can be claimed in order to delete an *Ipse*-part of the personal identity. With these data subject rights the information asymmetry can be compensated to some extend. But still the information asymmetry remains if the controller is reserved to fully disclose the processed information. In particular, the German Federal Court of Justice (Decision from August 27, 2020, No. III ZB30/20) recently ruled against Facebook, that it has to provide complete access to the Facebook account of the deceased daughter to the inheriting parents. This case illustrates the reluctance of data controller s to provide full access to the generated information on personal identities. So even by applying the data subject rights, the information asymmetry is likely not to be compensated. The controller still has the economic interest to keep a high amount of personal data and the generated profiles. In order to determine a mechanism for protecting personal identities the phases of data processing shall by analyzed from a game theoretical point of view.

Game Theory. The game theory allows the modeling of two players interacting with each other with different information about the game. The actions of the players depend on the opponent's previous action and can lead to a cooperative or defective action. It might occur that the opponent reacts reciprocal to cooperation with cooperation or reciprocal to defection with defection. Also the strategy-decision of a player can differ, so that the actions of the player refer to the first action of the game and ignore the last action of the opposing player to avoid reciprocal actions. The development of actions based on the information about the previous action changes with each iteration. Also the complexity of the game increases with the amount of iterations. In summary, the game theory consists of players, actions, payouts and information ("Players, Actions, Payoffs and Information-PAPI") with the assumption that the players act in order to maximize their output by rational choice [29]. The game theory in a business context refers to the outcome of financial loss or profit. In data protection law the personal information is subject to the actions of the data subject e.g. with providing the consent to the controller that certain personal information can be processed. In terms of game theory, these actions relate to the public good of personal information [13]. The public good of personal information is characterized by the fact that it cannot be consumed and is available to everyone. The public good of personal information is maintained by a high degree of cooperation and it is challenged by a high degree of defection. In order to protect the public good of personal information, it is of interest to reach a high amount of cooperation between the controller and the data subject.

The iterations between the controller and the data subject are prescribed by the GDPR. Thus, the phases of preparing the processing, the phase of legitimizing the processing and the phase of the data subject rights shall be subject to the game theoretical modeling. The phase of preparation for processing can be dominated by the economic interest of the controller to make profit through a limited investment into the state of the art (Art. 25 GDPR) of the processing. Such an action can be classified as defection by the controller. In particular, the controller might apply persuasive technologies that should seem for the data subject cooperative, but after diligent consideration, they serve the controller to encourage a quick consent [10]. Thus, these technologies seem as cooperation, but are actually a manipulated defective action by the controller. Moreover, the privacy policies are likely to be more in the interests of the controller rather than fully disclosing the true extent and risks of the processing [37]. However, this defective action by the controller can lead to the consent by the data subject due to the interest on gratification, as shown with *Acquisti* [1] above. This action by the data subject can be classified as cooperation due to the trust in the lawfulness of the processing. If the data subject makes use of the data subject rights, the controller might choose a defective action on this request by realizing the data subject right in an unsatisfactory manner. Overall it can be summarized that the controller is likely to act in a defective manner, which conflicts with the interest of the data subject to cooperate on the public good of personal information. This conflict of interest between the controller and data subject regarding public good of personal information remains through the phases of data processing. Since this conflict is at the expense of the public good of personal information and the protection of personal identities, the conflict shall be characterized in order to identify a mechanism for resolution.

Classification of Conflict. The conflict of interest regarding the protection of personal identities between the controller and data subject has to be characterized. In order to reach a high level of protection for the public good of personal information a mechanism should be defined that leads to a high degree of cooperative actions. In order to specify a mechanism for a high degree of cooperation, attention should be drawn to the theory of conflict. The model of conflict escalation by *Friedrich Glasl* might allow the determination of a possible mechanism to solve the conflict of interest [11]. Taking the nine stages of conflict escalation by *Glasl* [11] into account, the conflict is characterized by the second stage of "debate and polemic", so that each party wants to assert its point of view. In this stage of the conflict it can easily escalate further and end up in a *"win-lose"* solution at the expense of the public good of personal information. So a mechanism has to be identified in order to prevent further escalation. Such a mechanism should promote cooperation and sanction defective actions.

Consequently, the resolution of the conflict of interest between the controller and the data subject should include an environment of cooperation. This could be implemented by a mechanism for identity management that enables the parties to iteratively communicate and influence the identities in a cooperative manner. In particular, the handling of *Cookie*-consent includes such an iterative communication with the controller as the data subject can choose, which *Cookie* should be activated each time a website is accessed. This iterative communication enables the data subject to manage the personal identities for each website context. Thus, for each website context the data subject has the chance to manage the *Ipse*-parts of the personal identity by deciding whether they should be generated or not. Such iterative process allows the new formation of the relationship between the controller and the data subject. However, the data subject is still left in uncertainty regarding the profiles as *Ipse*-parts of the personal identity generated after the consent. The right of transparency based on Art. 15 GDPR might be a reasonable step to visualize the generated profiles and identities. In many cases, however, the data subject will have to bear the transaction costs for requesting the transparency on the generated profiles and personal identities. And such a request could lead to unsatisfactory disclosure of information by the controller regarding the profiles and personal identities. After all, the economic interests of controller s make cooperation with the data subject difficult, as the Facebook case above has shown. Therefore, communication with a high degree of iterations should serve as a mechanism to resolve the conflict of interest to a *"win-win"*-solution. This should promote cooperation and protect the public good of personal information.

Conclusively, an *"identity management by design"*-mechanism could include a technical mediator that strengthens the position of the data subject. With a technical mediator the data subject gets the chance to influence the personal identities effectively. The controller could be held to implement a technical mediator in order to cooperate and ensure the protection of personal identities. Such a technical mediator would serve the public good of personal information and make defective actions more difficult. Thus, a technical mediator could provide a resolution of the conflicting interests between the controller and data subject by facilitating a cooperative environment.

5.3 Resolution with a Technical Mediator

The resolution of the conflict between the controller and data subject requires an environment that promotes cooperation. In game-theoretical models it was established that certain strategies encourage or discourage cooperation. In order to characterize the technical mediator, the environment for cooperation has to be defined. After defining the cooperative environment, the requirements of a technical mediator should be determined. With this technical mediator the personal identities should become negotiable and serve the notion of dynamic *Ipse-* and static *Idem-* identities.

Establishing a Cooperative Environment. The protection of personal identities in their *Ipse*-part requires an iterative and cooperative process. This process would widen the chances for pluralistic content of personal identities in their dynamic *Ipse*-part. A process with a high degree of iteration leading to cooperation was described by *Axelrod* in "The Evolution of Cooperation" [2] with the "TIT for TAT"-strategy.

This "TIT for TAT"-strategy describes that the chosen action whether to cooperate or to act defectively depends on the previous action. As the "TIT for TAT"-strategy starts with cooperation and punishes defective action with defection, it promotes cooperation [2]. It has the tendency to lead after several iterations to cooperation [2]. The advantage of the "TIT for TAT"-strategy is that it generates the reputation of cooperation [2]. In addition the "TIT for TAT"-strategy has the effect of blocking defective action [2]. Thus, the process for establishing a cooperative environment for dynamic personal identities needs a high degree of iteration and as a first step cooperation. This first step of the iterative process should be initiated by the controller by providing an *"identity management by design"* mechanism. With this mechanism the controller invites the data subject to cooperate. The *"identity management by design"* mechanism would allow the data subject to determine the different *Idem-* and *Ipse*-parts of identity. On this basis of a first cooperative action the chances to promote and maintain cooperation are high. A technical mediator could also be applied to promote cooperation by implementing a high degree of iteration and creating the necessary space for the realization of the fundamental rights in Art. 7, 8 CFR and protect the public good of personal information.

Technical Mediator. The process of mediation is one method of alternative dispute resolution with the aim of creating value in a controversial conflict. With the European Mediation Directive, the specific requirements of the mediation process are regulated. In particular, it is defined that mediation is a structured process on a voluntary basis, to reach a settlement of the conflict with the assistance of a mediator, Art. 3 a) Mediation Directive [6]. This mediation process is lead by the third party of a mediator, who is guiding the parties in an effective, impartial, solution abstinent and competent manner, Art. 3 b) Mediation-Directive. Also the law recognizes technical mechanisms for mediation with the concept of online mediation [30]. This technical mechanism for mediation provides a multi-level communication process [3, 27], that allows the iterative exchange of interests promoting cooperation [32]. As the process of mediation in the online-version also provides the ethical standards of impartiality and voluntarily this can be adopted for the identity protection with a technical mediator. The process of mediation promotes cooperation of the parties by providing a high degree of iteration in order to reach a settlement. Since the mediator typically asks the parties to bring their personal interests into the process, the probability of cooperation increases.

These characteristics of mediation should be adopted for the protection of dynamic personal identities. The openness of the outcome of a mediation process enables the negotiation of personal identities to lead to pluralistic results. Thus, the mediation process enables dynamic identities and should be subject to a technical mechanism. Such a mechanism could be implemented by providing an *"identity management by design"* mechanism. This mechanism should include the values of a mediator that has to be impartial, solution abstinent and provide the parties an effective, structured process on a voluntarily basis to negotiate the personal identities. In particular, a technical mediator could be implemented with a specific interface design that allows the data subject to access the profiles of the identity. After having access to the personal identities, the data subject gets the opportunity to agree or disagree in order to negotiate the *Ipse*-parts of the personal identity. With the opportunity to choose between different *Cookie*-preferences, there is already a mechanism on a minimum level in the sense of *"identity management by design"*. Furthermore, an *"identity management by design"* mechanism should provide the circumstances to effectively agree or disagree and make use of the data subject rights.

In addition a technical mediator could be a crucial element to also provide protection against discrimination. The technical mediation would include the characteristics of a mediator being neutral and non-discriminatory. So the *"identity management by design"* mechanism would need instructions that guarantee dynamic, but non-discriminatory personal identities. These instructions should be embodied by a technical mediator. The technical mediator should recognize the race, origin and political orientation of a data subject and provide protection against discriminatory profiles. With such a technical mediator in an *"identity management by design"* mechanism discriminatory personal identities could be excluded from the generated profiles according to Art. 9 GDPR.

Thus, the *"identity management by design"* mechanism serves the contextual integrity of the data subject and provides an effective protection of dynamic identities. From a technical point of view this concept could be implemented with a "dashboard" as proposed by *Raschke/Küpper/Drozd/Kirrane* [28]. With this "dashboard" the data subject is enabled to manage the rights in particular the right to information, the consent and the rights of the data subjects pursuant to Art. 15–21 GDPR. In order to protect personal identities in an online-context it would be desirable to extent such a "dashboard" with the transparency of personal identities in their *Ipse-* and *Idem*-parts. This would be possible by applying the access right based on Art. 15 GDPR. With such a mechanism, the iterative control on profiles as *Ipse*-parts of identities could raise awareness and enable the data subject to exercise the right to self-determination. In general, the GDPR already contains the rules to provide an iterative process in order to negotiate personal identities. This iterative process is defined in the GDPR by the phase of preparing the processing, the justification and the phase in which the rights of the data subject can be exercised (Fig. 2). This iterative process of negotiating personal identities is one possibility for an *"identity management by design"* mechanism that could be applied from a technical point of view.

The requirement to technically protect personal identities in their *Ipse-* and *Idem-* parts serves the implementation of the right of informational self-determination. Also the requirement of an *"identity management by design"* mechanism would be an incentive to controller s to review existing technical and organizational measurements. This would be a major step to solve the conflict of interest between the controller and the data subject with a mechanism promoting cooperation. If the *"identity management by design"* mechanism is implemented it could also be applied as a tool for risk minimization based on Art. 32 para. 2 GDPR. Furthermore the *"identity management by design"* mechanism could be matter of documentation and reduce the accountability of the controller, Art. 5 para. 2 GDPR.

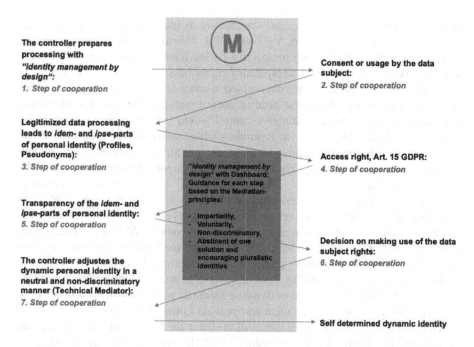

Fig. 2. Model of a *"identity management by design"*-concept with a technical mediator.

5.4   Technical Mechanism for Dynamic Identities

The *Idem-* and *Ipse-*parts of personal identities require a mechanism in order to negotiate the personal identities. The concept of cooperation is part of the GDPR and therefore can also be applied for the protection of personal identities. The relationship between the controller and the data subject is characterized by information asymmetry. This information asymmetry already exists in the phase of the preparing the processing and continues after the data subject rights are exercised. The information asymmetry is also a part of a conflict of interest between the controller and the data subject. The conflict was analyzed by applying the game theory, which lead to the differentiation between cooperative and defective actions by the parties. With this analysis it was shown that the protection of the public good of personal information and personal identities requires a cooperative environment. Such an environment can be provided with an *"identity management by design"* mechanism that includes a technical mediator. The technical mediator would guarantee an iterative process that allows the negotiation of personal identities. With this process, the right of informational self-determination can be effectively exercised so that the personal identities in their *Idem-* and *Ipse*-parts can be realized. For this the mechanism of *"identity management by design"* should include a technical mediator.

6   Conclusion

The *"identity management by design"* mechanism as proposed would meet the principle of transparency based on Art. 5 s. 1 a) GDPR. This mechanism would provide the data subject with an overarching perspective on the *Idem-* and *Ipse*-parts of personal identities. With the access and transparency rights based on Art. 13, 15 GDPR the generated personal identities of the data subject become accessible and negotiable. This enables the data subject to exercise iterative control regarding the *Ipse-* and *Idem*-parts of personal identities. Such an iterative control would provide further protection for users against generated profiles, as it would enable further self-determination in the online-context. This would require to make the pluralistic identities in the online-context accessible. With the technical method to provide transparency about the identities could be a "dashboard". Such a "dashboard" would serve the protection of personal identities according to the fundamental rights based on Art. 7, 8 CFR. With this technical mechanism for protection, the personal development would be enabled in the online-context in the same way as in the offline context. With an *"identity management by design"*-mechanism including a technical mediator the personal identities become legitimized by an iterative procedure. With a technical mediator, the process of mediation in its capacity of adding value may serve to protect identity. This procedure would directly reflect the concept of dynamic identities in the fundamental rights from Art. 7, 8 GRCh for the online context and provide further protection.

Thus, such a procedure with a technical mediator for the data subject would fulfill the concept of "legitimacy by procedure" [23]. In order to provide an effective incentive for controller the term *"identity management by design"* could be added into the wording of Art. 25 GDPR. Given its regulatory nature, this might lead to a higher acceptance than adding the term *"identity management by design"* in the existing recital 78. Since the definition of personal data based on Art. 4 para. 1 GDPR contains the notion of "dynamic identities", a corresponding technical protection of personal identities is a necessary paradigm shift in data protection law. Furthermore, the obligation for a cooperative *"identity management by design"* would balance the use of persuasion technologies in the era of Big Data. In conclusion the mechanism of *"identity management by design"* with a technical mediator would provide an ethical and human rights-based environment for the development and determination of personal identities.

References

1. Acquisti, A.: Privacy in electronic commerce and the economics of immediate gratification. In: Proceedings of the 5th ACM conference on Electronic commerce, pp. 21–29. ACM (2004)
2. Axelrod, R.: The Evolution of Cooperation. Basic Books, New York (2006)
3. Barnett, J., Treleaven, P.: Algorithmic dispute resolution—the automation of professional dispute resolution using AI and blockchain technologies. Comput. J. **61**, 399–408 (2017)
4. Ben-Shahar, O.: The myth of the 'opportunity to read' in contract law. In: ERCL, pp. 1–28 (2009)
5. Bernsdorff, N., Borowsky, M.: Die Charta der Grundrechte der Europäischen Union – Handreichungen und Sitzungsprotokolle, Baden-Baden (2002)
6. Directive 2008/52/EC of the European Parliament and of the Council of 21 May 2008 on certain aspects of mediation in civil and commercial matters (2008)
7. Dürig, M., Fischer, M.: Cybersicherheit in Kritischen Infrastrukturen. Datenschutz und Datensicherheit - DuD **42**(4), 209–213 (2018). https://doi.org/10.1007/s11623-018-0909-1
8. Eidenmüller, H.: Ökonomische und spieltheoretische Grundlagen von Verhandlung/Mediation. In: Breidenbach/Henssler (Hrsg.), Mediation für Juristen, pp. 31–55 (1997)
9. Erikson, E.H.: Identität und Lebenszyklus – Drei Aufsätze, vol. 27, pp. 150. Auflage, Berlin (2015)
10. Fogg, B.J.: Computers as persuasive social actors. In: Persuasive Technology: Using Computers to Change What We Think and Do, vol. 94, pp. 89–120 (2003)
11. Glasl, F.: Konfliktmanagement – Ein Handbuch für Führungskräfte, Beraterinnen und Berater, vol. 12, p. 236. Auflage, Bern (2020)
12. Fuster, G.G.: The Emergence of Personal Data Protection as a Fundamental Right of the EU, Cham, Heidelberg, pp. 256, 266–271 (2014)
13. Hermstrüwer, Y.: Informationelle Selbstgefährdung – zur rechtsfunktionalen, spieltheoretischen und empirischen Rationalität der datenschutzrechtlichen Einwilligung und des Rechts auf informationelle Selbstbestimmung, München, p. 158 (2016)
14. Hildebrandt, M.: Smart technologies and the end(s) of law – novel entanglements of law and technology, Cheltenham, USA (2015)
15. Hildebrandt, M.: Profiling and AmI. In: Rannenberg, K., Royer, D., Deuker, A. (eds.) The Future of Identity in the Information Society. Springer, Heidelberg (2009). https://doi.org/10.1007/978-3-642-01820-6_7
16. Hornung, G.: Die digitale Identität – Rechtsprobleme von Chipkartenausweisen: Digitaler Personalausweis, elektronische Gesundheitskarte. JobCard-Verfahren, Baden-Baden (2005)
17. Jarass, H.D.: Kommentar, Charta der Grundrechte der EU, München, Art. 7 GRC (2016)
18. Keupp, H.: Identitätskonstruktionen – Das Patchwork der Identitäten in der Spätmoderne, Reinbek bei Hamburg, vol. 215, pp. 99–103 (1999)
19. Kieck, A.: Der Schutz individueller Identität als verfassungsrechtliche Aufgabe – Am Beispiel des geschlechtlichen Personenstands, Berlin (2019)
20. Koops, E., De Vries, K., Hildebrandt, M.: D7.14b: idem-identity and ipse-identity in profiling practices, FIDIS report 21, pp. 28–33, April 2009
21. Korsgaard, C.M.: Self-constitution – agency, identity, and integrity, Oxford, pp. 35–37 (2009)
22. Lippmann, E.: Identität im Zeitalter des Chamäleons – Flexibel sein und Farbe bekennen, 2. Auflage, Göttingen/Bristol (2014)
23. Luhmann, N.: Legitimation durch Verfahren, 10. Auflage, Frankfurt am Main (2017)

24. Marsch, N.: Das europäische Datenschutzgrundrecht, Tübingen, vol. 209, p. 77 (2018)
25. Maschmann. In: Kühling, Buchner (Hrsg.) Kommentar, DS-GVO, BDSG, München, Art. 88 DSGVO, pp. 14–16 (2018)
26. Nissenbaum: Privacy as contextual integrity, Wash. L. Rev., p. 119 (2004)
27. Pretschner, A., Walter, T.: Negotiation of usage control policies - simply the best? In: Third International Conference on Availability, Reliability and Security, pp. 1135–1136. IEEE (2008)
28. Raschke, P., Küpper, A., Drozd, O., Kirrane, S.: Designing a GDPR-compliant and usable privacy dashboard. In: Hansen, M., Kosta, E., Nai-Fovino, I., Fischer-Hübner, S. (eds.) Privacy and Identity Management. The Smart Revolution. Privacy and Identity 2017. IFIP AICT, vol. 526, pp. 221–236. Springer, Cham (2018). https://doi.org/10.1007/978-3-319-92925-5_14
29. Rasmusen, E.: Games and Information – An Introduction to Game Theory, 4th edn., pp 182–185. Oxford Press, Malden (2009)
30. Regulation (EU) No 524/2013 of the European Parliament and the Council of 21 May 2013 on online dispute resolution for consumer disputes (2013)
31. Ricœur, P.: Oneself as Another. Chicago Press, Chicago (1994)
32. Schelling, T.C.: The Strategy of Conflict. Oxford Press, Oxford (1969)
33. Spindler, G.: Persönlichkeitsschutz im Internet - Anforderungen und Grenzen einer Regulierung – Gutachten F zum 69. Deutschen Juristentag. In: Verhandlungen des 69, p. 212. Deutschen Juristentages, München (2012)
34. The Guardian. www.theguardian.com/news/series/cambridge-analytica-files. Accessed 08 Jan 2020
35. Turkle, S.: Leben im Netz – Identität in Zeiten des Internet, Reinbek bei Hamburg (1999)
36. Watzlawick, P., Beavin, J.H., Jackson, D.D.: Menschliche Kommunikation – Formen, Störungen, Paradoxien, 13. Auflage, Bern (2016)
37. Windley, P.J.: Digital identity – unmasking identity management architecture (IMA), Beijing (2005)
38. Zander, T., Steinbrück, A., Birnstill, P.: Game-theoretical model on the GDPR – market for lemons? In: JIPITEC, p. 200 (2019)

Open About the Open-Rate?
State of Email Tracking in Marketing Emails and Its Effects on User's Privacy

Shirin Kalantari[✉]

imec-DistriNet, KU Leuven, Leuven, Belgium
`shirin.kalantari@kuleuven.be`

Abstract. While many suspected that commercial email communications would be obsolete by 2020, email still continues to prevail over other mediums in terms of bringing revenue. In order to take full advantage of this valuable channel, commercial emails are tagged with tracking measures that at the very least enable senders to obtain individual read receipts for their emails. The collection of these read receipts, referred to as the *open-rate*, is used to measure the success of the campaign. In this paper we investigate the implications of email tracking, as it is used for obtaining open-rates, on recipients' privacy. In addition, we demonstrate the prevalence of email tracking in marketing emails of 736 websites and provide suggestions for mitigating its privacy risk.

1 Introduction

While web traffic dominates our modern usage of Internet, email is another inevitable part of our online life. Many suspected that email would fade away by the advent of alternative technologies [6,37,42] but in reality, email still continues to be among the most fundamental building blocks of our online life. In addition to delivering day-to-day communications, emails are widely used for distributing marketing contents [20]. It is estimated that marketing emails account for 44% of all emails in a user's inbox [1]. Popularity of email for distributing marketing content is partly due to its high Return of Investment (ROI) rate. As a recent report suggests, marketers can expect an average ROI of €42 for every €1 they spend on email marketing [46].

Being a strategic channel in terms of bringing revenue, marketing emails often include analytics measures that enables marketers to measure the effectiveness of their email marketing strategy. Stimulating user engagement is considered as one of the main goals of email campaigns [46]. The campaign *open-rate* is a metric used to represent user engagement by indicating the proportion of the recipients who opened a certain marketing email.

Techniques for increasing campaign open-rates are highly sought after. Several email marketing businesses offer dedicated services for increasing open-rates.

© IFIP International Federation for Information Processing 2021
Published by Springer Nature Switzerland AG 2021
M. Friedewald et al. (Eds.): Privacy and Identity 2020, IFIP AICT 619, pp. 187–205, 2021.
https://doi.org/10.1007/978-3-030-72465-8_11

For example, the company, *phrasee*[1], offer personalized machine generated subject lines that promise to boost email open-rates. Similarly, various email marketing platforms offer *send time optimization* services [32,41] that personalize email delivery time to be the "optimum" time in which each recipient is most likely to open the email. In fact, even from an academic perspective, techniques are proposed for increasing campaign open-rates such as the research by Sahni et al. [44].

To calculate the open-rate of their email campaign, marketers take advantage of *HTTP requests for remote images to track their emails*. Therefore, instead of directly embedding images in the email message, they host images on a remote web server and include their URL address in the email message. At the moment when the recipient opens one of these emails, a series of HTTP requests are initiated by the email client for loading these remote images. These HTTP requests carry the information required for tracking email open-rates in three forms: *meta-data*, *headers*, and *URL parameters*. While meta-data and headers are generic to all HTTP requests, URL parameters are chosen by the sender and can be *personalized* to carry identifying information about the recipient. A primitive (yet still widely used) example for such personalization is a remote image that uses the recipient email address as part of its URL.

The information carried in HTTP *meta-data*, *headers*, or *URL parameters* allow senders to infer more than just the campaign open-rates. Especially, with personalized parameter the HTTP requests act as *individual read receipts* for emails enabling senders to obtain fine grained information about a user's interaction with their email such as time of opening in addition to devices and software used for opening the email. Concerns about the privacy implications of email tracking using personalized URLs has been raised since 1995 [45] and previous academic works revealed the prevalence of this method of tracking in marketing emails [4,11,21,30].

In this paper we aim to provide a comprehensive overview of marketing email eco-system. We demonstrate the prevalence of email tracking techniques in a corpus of 237,741 marketing emails that we collected from 736 websites. Based on this corpus we try to give some additional insights about email tracking techniques and also highlight some misapprehension regarding email tracking techniques.

2   Background

Email started out very simple, the Simple Mail Transfer Protocol (SMTP) can only carry textual messages that are represented by US-ASCII. In 1991, Multipurpose Internet Mail Extensions (MIME) relaxed this restriction by defining algorithms that encode the email message to US-ASCII. Although the first motivation for using MIME was to support European characters in email [39], its introduction also enabled sending emails with richer text formatting such as HTML. With HTML, email messages are no longer restricted to textual content as they could contain well-designed messages with integrated multimedia contents that render consistently across different email clients.

---

[1] https://phrasee.co/.

In addition to having styling and richer text formatting, an HTML email often contains references to remote resources. These resources are loaded by the email client, when the recipient opens the email. Email tracking is inherently linked to emails with HTML content, which consequently generates HTTP requests for all embedded resources. This HTTP request leaks information in three forms: *meta-data*, *headers*, and *URL parameters*. In this section we give an overview of email marketing eco-system and the protocols used in email, further elaborate on each of the three forms of HTTP tracking and discuss the effectiveness of existing countermeasures in stopping them.

2.1 Overview of the Email Marketing Eco-system

Main Entities: The main entities that drive the email marketing ecosystem are:

- *Campaign owners:* These are the businesses that reach their audience via email to deliver services. For example news services that send headlines, news digest and briefs via email and e-commerce platforms that promote sale campaign or transactional emails. The end users either explicitly subscribe to newsletters or receive transactional emails as part of the services they are using (e.g., social media updates, online purchase confirmation, reminders, etc.). The campaign owner might want to include a number of third parties into their campaign emails to improve their services or to monetize their audiences. For example they might integrate advertisement partners such as Facebook or Instagram Ads; email optimization services such as mailing list sanitization tool *ZeroBounce*[2] or subject line personalization service *phrasee*; marketing platforms such as *Salesforce*[3] or *Google Analytics*[4].
- *Email Service Providers (ESPs):* While sending emails is very important for campaign owners, it is not part of their core business. As a result, they involve ESPs to manage and send out their campaign emails. The ESP manages the mailing list, provides email templates, and most importantly sends out the campaign emails[5]. In addition, an ESP provides integration tools, allowing marketers to seamlessly integrate third parties into their marketing platform. The ESP Mailchimp offers more than 250 integration tools to its customer.[6]
- *Mailbox providers:* Each email address is registered with a mailbox provider. It offers email hosting for users to send, receive and store their email messages. Gmail and Yahoo! are examples of widely used mailbox providers. Additionally, mailbox providers offer email security services such as spam filtering, malware detection, and transport layer encryption to protect users from malicious content.

---

[2] https://www.zerobounce.net/.
[3] https://www.salesforce.com/.
[4] https://analytics.withgoogle.com/.
[5] Mailchimp, Selligent, and Campaign Monitor are examples of well-known ESPs.
[6] https://mailchimp.com/integrations/.

- *Email Clients:* Also called Mail User Agents (MUAs), email clients are software such as Thunderbird and Microsoft Outlook that recipients use to open, read and interact with their emails.

Email Delivery and Protocols: Figure 1 is an overview of key components and protocols that are used in sending and retrieving an email. To send an email the ESP submits it over SMTP to the marketers' (i.e., email marketer) Mail Transfer Agent (MTA) who is in charge of transmitting emails and relaying each email to its recipient network via SMTP (step 1). Before routing an email, each MTA performs certain checks like validating email message format, spam filtering, and malware detection on the email. If the email fails the checks, MTA sends a bounce message with a status code, like those described in RFC 3463 [49], to the ESP (step 2&3). Finally, the email arrives at the final MTA, which is the recipient's mailbox provider. Afterward, the recipient can use an email client to retrieve the newly arrived email via email access protocols such as POP3 or IMAP (step 4). Before rendering the email, the email client performs a *preprocessing* step to sanitize the email message (step 5).

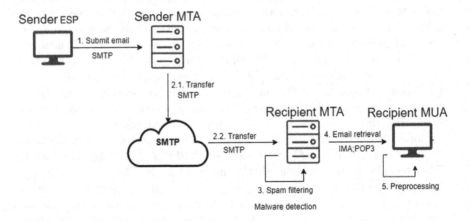

Fig. 1. Overview of software and protocols used in sending marketing emails.

Email Marketing Guidelines: For campaign owners, *deliverability* and *consistent rendering* of their emails are of outmost important. These two factors are directly affected at two points in the email transportation process: *spam filtering performed by the MTA (step 3)* and *preprocessing by the email client (step 5)*:

- *Spam filtering:* Compliant with the spam filtering guidelines that is enforced by mailbox providers and MTAs, ensures that each email gets delivered to its intended recipients and spam emails are filtered out. CAN-SPAM Act [16] is an example of such regulations that is currently in place in the US. Getting the recipient's consent in form of confirmation email and providing an opt-out option, through an unsubscribe link or List-Unsubscribe header [2], are among the basic requirements for sending bulk and transactional emails. To classify an email as spam, most spam filters use the text of the email message [5,43]. A technique that spammers use to circulate these textual filters is a so-called *image spam* in which spammers format their whole messages inside images [5, 25]. Figure 2 is an example of an image spam email. Thus, including embedded images in an email alerts spam filters that the email might contain an image spam. Gmail use optical character recognition (OCR) techniques to extract the text from an image and run their spam filters on it [19]. Email service providers advise against embedded images[7] and recommend external images instead [22,33,36].

– *Preprocessing by the email clients:* Consistent rendering is another important concern for email marketers which is affected by the *HTML preprocessing step of email clients.* In the preprocessing step, based on email client policy, some HTML tags are removed (*HTML stripping*) and certain elements are overwritten (*HTML overwriting*) [27]. The HTML stripping removes HTML tags that cause serious attacks in email. For example, <script> tag is strictly removed by all email clients. This is due to the *Reaper exploit* that was discovered in 1998 by Carl Voth [51] and demonstrated that by running javascript, an attacker can wiretap email communications. Some email clients also remove external CSS files since they open an attack surface that can be exploited to change the content of an email. The exploit called *Ropemaker* enables a malicious attacker to change the content of an email after it is sent, just by changing the content of the external CSS that is used inside an email [17]. In the HTML overwriting step the email client overwrites parts of the HTML email for example, to block remote contents the email client change the URL of remote images to prevent the HTML rendering engine from automatically requesting them (see Fig. 3 as an example of HTML overwriting which prevents remote images from automatically loading). It should be noted that email clients *make different choices* about HTML stripping and overwriting. For example, Apple email clients such as Apple Mail and iOS Mail block images by HTML overwriting but do not block remote CSS files (no <link> stripping or overwriting) [7], Thunderbird blocks images but does not remove remote CSS (no <link> stripping) which exposes recipients to attacks such as Ropemaker when they choose to load remote contents. Campaign owners format their email templates with an eye on these differences, and they use ESPs' testing services to ensure that their email renders properly across different email clients.

---

[7] There are two methods for embedding images in emails: data URI and Content-ID (CID). With data URI, the src attribute of an <img> include the 'immediate data' [34]. CID images come as attachments to emails and the image src attribute reference to the MIME Content-ID of the attachment [34].

Fig. 2. Examples of image spams taken from the study by Ketari et al. *A Study of Image Spam Filtering Techniques* [25]

2.2   Remote Resources and HTTP Requests

The HTTP requests for remote resources are the seeds of email tracking. However, it could be argued that remote resources are unavoidable in marketing emails. Marketing emails are in nature call-to action and they depend on the linkability of the HTML links. For displaying images, while embedded alternatives exist that do not require a HTTP request, their usage is discouraged as they affect deliverability of the email. In this part we take a closer look at privacy implication of HTTP requests in email and discuss the effectiveness of existing countermeasures in stopping them. As already mentioned an HTTP request carries three categories of information that are interesting for trackers: *meta-data, HTTP headers and personalized URL tokens*. An HTTP request can be generalized in the following form:

$$\texttt{GET request-URL [request-header]}^{*}$$

Meta-data: Since HTTP is an application layer protocol, it depends on transport layer protocols such as TCP/IP. These protocols reveal meta-data information about the email client. For instance, the IP address, ports and packet size. Xu et al. [52] demonstrate that by combining IP address and other tracking methods, long term surveillance attacks can be launched upon recipients revealing their geolocation information and their email reading habits. Information about recipients' timezone can also be inferred based on meta-data. This is used by ESPs to deliver emails according to users' timezone [8,31].

HTTP Headers: The `request-header` is one or more HTTP headers that the email clients attach to the request to help the server provide a tailored response. HTTP headers are used for email tracking. Englehardt et al. [11] demonstrated that email clients send the `Cookie` along with the HTTP requests which enables the sender to link the requests with the recipient's web profile. Bender et al. [3] show that `User-Agent` header is used by sender to infer information about the recipient's device to deliver advertisement accordingly.

Personalized URL Tokens: The `request-URL` in the representation above, is the address of the remote resource. In email, it can also be personalized to contain identifying information about the recipient. This could be any string that map to the recipient email address at the server side. Englehardt et al. [11] considered the email address of the recipient, or a combination of hashing and encoding functions applied on it. They considered these tokens as Personally Identifying Information (PII) and looked for cases where they are shared with third parties. Haupt et al. [21] and Maass et al. [30] use multiple subscription to find personalized URLs, by comparing the URL structure of emails sent to multiple users.

2.3 Countermeasures

Blocking Remote Contents: This countermeasure is deployed in every modern email client, either by default or through user settings. To block remote contents, the email client changes the URL of remote resources in the HTML overwriting step which prevents the rendering engine from automatically requesting them. Figure 3 is an example of HTML overwriting to block remote images in Outlook web. While blocking remote contents stops all HTTP-based tracking, it imposes negative effects on the user experience. Especially since some email clients take a rough approach to blocking remote contents. For example, blocking remote contents also implies *blocking embedded images* in several email clients such as Yahoo! [22]. Note that loading embedded images does not require any HTTP requests, though it can trigger image spam emails and can be used to expose recipients to a sophisticated phishing attack [26,35]. Currently the only email client that provide more fine-grained content blocking is ProtonMail[8], which offers a multi-level option for loading embedded and remote images as shown in Fig. 4.

Disabling HTML: Most email clients allow users to disable HTML as a countermeasure against email tracking [48]. If the HTML part never gets rendered, there will be no HTTP requests. The email client then ignores the `text/html` MIME parts and will use the `multipart/alternative` text parts. According to MIME specification in RFC 2046, *"... the content of the various parts are interchangeable"* [15]. However, this is under the assumption that the senders do provide alternative MIME parts for their emails.

---

[8] https://protonmail.com/.

```
<!-- Before HTML overwritting -->
  <tr>
    <td bgcolor="#474747" style="line-height:0px;">
      <img alt=" " src='http://contentz.mkt3495.com/ra/2018/2521/04/19768701/8188897.gif'/>
    </td>
  </tr>

<!-- After HTML overwritting -->
  <tr>
    <td bgcolor="#474747" style="line-height:0px;;">
      <img alt=" " blockedimagesrc='http://contentz.mkt3495.com/ra/2018/2521/04/19768701/8188897.gif'/>
    </td>
  </tr>
```

Fig. 3. HTML overwriting in Outlook web, the **src** attribute of the image is overwritten.

Fig. 4. Providing a multi-level option for loading embedded and external image in ProtonMail.

Content Proxies: This is the most effective, existing countermeasure for minimizing the risks of email tracking. Content proxies are currently only deployed by Google [18] and Yandex and can fully mitigate tracking based on *meta-data* and *HTTP headers*. The proxy make the HTTP requests for remote contents in email and serve the response back to the email client. The request has the meta-data and the HTTP headers of the proxy and reveals nothing about the recipient. However, content proxies do not change the URL of the requests. Hence, they *cannot protect against tracking using personalized tokens.*

Browser Extensions: There are several browser extensions that aim to prevent email tracking by identifying and blocking beacons images in the email. Beacons are images in the size of a few pixels that incorporate third parties into email. Two examples of plugins that block pixels are *Ugly Mail*[9] and *Trocker*[10]. Using advertisement blocking extensions also mitigate some of the privacy risks of email tracking as it blocks all the requests to known third party trackers [11].

---

[9] https://uglyemail.com/.
[10] https://trockerapp.github.io/.

3   Data Collections

3.1   Collecting Newsletter Corpus with Multiple Subscription

To illustrate how the prevalence of URL personalization in marketing emails, we set up a mail server and collected a corpus of commercial newsletter emails by subscribing with multiple identities to each newsletter service. In order to find newsletters forms we crawled Alexa top 10K sites[11]. We adapted the crawler specification of Englehardt et al. [11] to subscribe with multiple email addresses to each newsletter. This multiple subscription enables us to find personalization tokens by comparing the URL structure of emails sent to multiple users.

The crawler and mail server communication is summarized in Fig. 5. A web server is set to act as the intermediary between the crawler and the mail server. First, the crawler searches each site for a subscription form (step 1). Once a potential subscription form is found, the crawler requests a new email address from the web server along with information about the website in which this email address is going to be submitted (step 2). The web server generates a unique email address for this site and registered this email address on the mail server (step 3). The web server then sends the newly generated email address to the crawler to submit it to the subscription form. In order to subscribe with multiple email addresses to each newsletter, step 2–4 are then repeated.

When the subscription form has been submitted, the website will often send a *confirmation email* to the specified email address. This email contains a *confirmation link* and only after this link is clicked, the subscription is considered finalized and newsletter emails start to arrive. Confirmation emails intend to reduce the risk of newsletter emails being identified as spam. By clicking on the *confirmation link*, the entity in possession of that email address confirms that (s)he is willing to receive further emails from this sender. The confirmation link extraction scheme is specified in the next section. Once the mail server finds the confirmation link, it submits it to the web server so that the crawler can find it and click on it.

3.2   Email Preprocessing

For each incoming email, the mail server extracts the HTML message by retrieving the MIME part `text/html`. It stores the images, links, and checks whether the email include an embedded image. It stores links to external files (`<link>`), checks if there are any `<script>` tag in the HTML structure and also searches for URLs within `<style>` tag.

To extract the text part of an email, the mail server stores both the text alternative part and the text extracted from the HTML part. It also extracts some meta-data related to the email header.

To find the confirmation link, the mail server searches the *first incoming email* of each inbox (i.e., email address. It extracts all `<a>` tags from the HTML

---

[11] From Alexa top 1 Million list used in [11] available at https://github.com/citp/ email_tracking/blob/master/crawler_mailinglists/data/top-1m.csv.

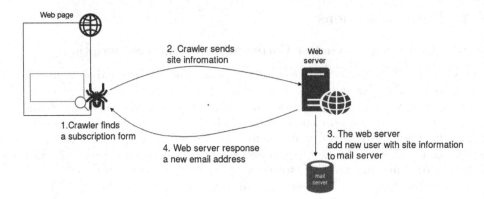

Fig. 5. Crawler communicates with our web server.

message and checks if the text of the tag contains one of the keywords *confirm, validate, finalize, subscribe, activate, step*. If no such link is found, it checks if the URL in the `href` attribute contains one of these keywords. In case no link is found, the mail server is going to adapt a bottom-up approach for finding the confirmation link: for each link in the email, it is going to search for the keyword in the text of the enclosing HTML element (see Fig. 6).

The mail server also checks every incoming email for implementation of anti-spam practices. It first searches for evidence of *email address sharing*. It checks whether the sender email address has the same domain name as the website on which the email address was registered. Providing opt-out options is also checked using the `List-Unsubscribe` header, and the unsubscribe link within the HTML message. For finding the unsubscribe link the same approach as finding confirmation link is repeated, using keywords *opt-out, unsubscribe, opt out* and *unsub*.

```
<td align="center">
    You are receiving this newsletter because you subscribed to the The Spruce Daily newsletter.
    <span class="hide">
        <br />
    </span>If you wish to unsubscribe, please
        <a href="http://link.about.com/oc/5ac171b7fbd297138a6288df7pcr4.1b1d/d3671e0d&page=spruce">
            click here
        </a>
</td>
```

Fig. 6. An unsubscribe link found by searching the text of the parent element of `<a>` tag.

3.3   Identifying Personalized Parameters

We identify personalized URLs parameters using *differential testing*. In this method multiple email addresses are subscribed to the same newsletter. Personalized URL parameters are identified by comparing the URL structure of the same campaign email that is sent to these different inboxes. To do so we perform the following steps:

- We first identify email addresses that are subscribed to the same site.
- For websites on which multiple users are subscribed we calculate the cosine similarity of pairwise emails. We use the text extracted from the HTML part, to calculate text similarity. These steps avoids comparing emails that are subjected to A/B testing. If the similarity of two emails is more than 95%, we consider them to be the same campaign email.
- When two emails are identified as identical, we compare the URL structure of their images and links based on their order of appearance in HTML structure.
- We then compare the two URLs. If they are different in a substring of 5 or longer, we consider them personalized. We assume that such string has enough entropy to identify the recipient.

4   Results

In total our crawler made 187,886 subscription attempts (and, hence, so many requests for a new email address on the mail server). The crawler might have filled in a contact form, or a comment section. 6,160 users received at least two emails during the period. The mail server was running between 2018/04/01 and 2018/06/10. During this period, we received 237,741 newsletter emails from 736 websites.

External Images and Links Are the Most Common Remote Contents in Email: Analyzing the prevalence of remote resources in our corpus shows that links and images together account for 97.25% of remote resources in newsletter emails.[12] However, in terms of privacy risks of images are more hazardous since they are made without user involvement as soon as the client renders an email.

Marketing Emails Follow Anti-spam Regulation and Guidelines: The corpus confirms that anti-spam practices are followed by email marketers:

- No instances of email address distribution were detected (i.e., each inbox received emails only from the website on which it was registered).
- An unsubscribe link is found in 87.58% of all emails. In addition, the `List-Unsubscribe` header is used in 89.48% of emails.

---

[12] HTML `<a>` tag account for 52.26% and `<img>` tag for 44.99%.

URL Personalization is Very Common: Almost every marketing email in our corpus contains images or links with personalized URLs. For 58% of senders, the personalized token was persistently used in all the emails they sent (for the remainder the URL parameter changes in different emails). Our dataset indicates no instances of URL personalization for other remote resources such as CSS files.

Distinction Between Third Party and First Party is Blurry in Email: Previous studies consider the distribution of third-parties in emails as indication of email tracking [4,11,23,30]. In these studies, the URL of third-party contents *use a different domain name* than the email sender, or the website on which the email address was registered. Most web tracking protections use domain blacklisting for identifying tracking content. However, our corpus shows that this distinction does not always hold in email as we find instances of *third-party advertisement using the first-party domain*.

```
<a href="http://li.stltoday.com/click?[..]&e=jeanpatrice.mlynek535@apesianik.com&p=903464" rel="nofollow">
   <img src="http://li.stltoday.com/imp?[..]&e=jeanpatrice.mlynek535@apesianik.com&wc=&p=903464"/>
</a>
```

Fig. 7. A LiveIntent advertisement and its HTML code snippet which users a subdomain of the sender *stltoday.com*.

We find 14 senders that use their own domain to serve third party advertisement. These advertisements are served by LiveIntent[13], a Supply Side Platform (SSP) that enables publishers to receive revenue by managing their advertising space inside their emails. LiveIntent is among trackers that receive the highest number of PII information in the paper by Englehardt et al. [11]. LiveIntent advertisements are served through a so-called LiveTag that uses a dedicated subdomain of the email marketer to serve the advertisement. Figure 7 is an example of a LiveIntent advertisement that uses a subdomain of the sender, *stltoday.com*. To find the advertisement element, we use the general HTML and URL structure of LiveTag [28]: find everu `<a>` element that has an `<img>` tag as its immediate

---

[13] https://www.liveintent.com/.

child in the HTML structure, check if URLs in the `src` and the `href` attributes of these elements contain the corresponding query parameters of a LiveTag ($p=$, and either $e=$ or $m=$). In addition, for each of these senders we rendered one email and manually verified whether the identified tag is serving an advertisement. Table 1 illustrates the results. To check whether these images could get blocked by current countermeasures, we checked the domains in Table 1 in trackers list of the ad-blocker Disconnect.me[14], and EasyList[15]. None of these domains are among the online trackers that will be blocked by ad-blockers that are using these lists.

Table 1. The domain names that were used to serve LiveIntent advertisement.

Domain	Advertisement URL	Presence in email
al.com	eads.al.com	59.61%
alternet.org	li.alternet.org	49.69%
cleveland.com	eads.cleveland.com	62.27%
dealnews.com	c3.dealnews.com	96.38%
nj.com	eads.nj.com	61.38%
nola.com	eads.nola.com	58.33%
philly.com	li.philly.com	79.10%
realtor.com	li.realtor.com	17.24%
seriouseats.com	li.seriouseats.com	17.14%
stltoday.com	li.stltoday.com	40.08%
tigerdirect.com	li.tigerdirect.com	88.76%
timesofisrael.com	nl.timesofisrael.com	89.62%
townhall.com	li.townhall.com	14.53%
travelocity.com	content.travelocity.com	20%

5 Discussion

5.1 Privacy Concerns of Email Tracking

The result shows that using personalized parameters is common in marketing emails which enables them to obtain an HTTP-based read receipt for their emails. It is reasonable to compare this form of email tracking with norms of obtaining read receipts in similar applications. This is in-line with the contextual definition of privacy [38] that uses informational privacy norms for assessing privacy risks. Email standards provision protocols for obtaining read receipt emails

---

[14] https://github.com/disconnectme/disconnect-tracking-protection.
[15] https://easylist.to/easylist/easylist.txt.

through Message Disposition Notification (MDN) [47]. Different privacy concerns of MDN have been discussed in RFC 8098 for example it emphasizes on obtaining user consent before sending MDNs: *"[...] While Internet standards normally do not specify the behavior of user interfaces, it is strongly recommended that the user agent obtain the user's consent before sending an MDN. [...] The purpose of obtaining user's consent is to protect user's privacy. The default value should be not to send MDNs."* [47]. For this reason, email clients use a very explicit user interface before sending an MDN report.

Another application that involves sending read receipts are mobile messaging applications. Email has been compared with messaging applications quite often in the web and in academic research [13,50]. Table 2 shows policy of popular messaging apps in regard of read receipt. Unlike email, in messaging applications user often have control over sending read receipt and can reject them.

Table 2. Popular messaging apps and their policy regarding read receipts.

Application	Read receipt	Disabling read receipt
WhatsApp	✓	✓
Messenger	✓	✗
Skype	✓	✓
Telegram	✓	✗
Hangout	✗	✗
iMessage	✓	✓

Obtaining read receipts in email protocols and messaging applications is *unambiguous* and comes with *explicit interface* and *fair denial consequences*:

1. *Unambiguous:* In both MDN protocol and messaging applications, a read receipt is exactly what the name suggests: it indicates whether the recipient has opened a message. The same cannot be said about HTTP-based read receipts in email since remote contents are loaded *every time the email is opened.* Moreover, each request contains fine-grained meta-data such as the exact time at which the email was read, devices and software that were used and the location of the recipient.
2. *Explicit interface:* Read receipts use a clear and explicit user interface in messaging applications (e.g. a double blue check mark next to the message) and in MDN protocol (see Fig. 8). However, the user survey of Xu et al. [52] revealed that the majority of participants had no awareness about the information leaks of loading remote contents in email.
3. *Fair denial consequences:* Recipients can reject sending MDN and disable read receipts in most messaging applications without sacrificing functionality. However, to prevent HTTP-based read receipts a user should either block remote contents, or disable HTML emails which both have a significant negative impact on the user experience.

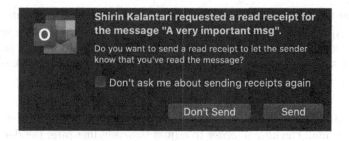

Fig. 8. Obtaining a read receipt through the MDN protocol in Outlook.

While most of the discussions in this paper are around marketing emails, note that the same techniques for obtaining read receipts can be and *are being used* in day-to-day, conversational email communications. There are several email tracking services targeting personal email communications for example, the renowned modern email client *Superhuman*[16] includes tracking pixels in every outgoing email and shows the read status of sent emails, *MixMax*[17], *Streak*[18] and *Yesware*[19] offer browser extensions for integration of email tracking services to popular email clients such as Gmail or Outlook. The privacy implications of email tracking for personal email communication is even greater, since it conveys additional information as illustrated in the following example by M. Davidson [10]:

"An ex-boyfriend ... pens a desperate email Subject: "I've been thinking about us". He sends it to his former partner. She reads it when she gets to work in Downtown Los Angeles at 9am. She reads it again before dinner with friends in Pasadena at 7pm. She reads it again at home in Santa Monica ... She decides not to answer the email ... [but] her email is always communicating, and it's sharing info she does not want to send and doesn't even know she is sending." [10].

While in this paper we mainly focus on privacy implications of email tracking for obtaining privacy invasive HTTP-based read receipts, note that email tracking is also a stepping stone to pervasive online tracking. Although performed by hackneyed techniques, email tracking is very effective to persistently track users over time and across devices. In fact, there are a number of online tracking businesses that are built around email tracking, promoting it as *the solution for cookie-less tracking across devices* [9,12,29]. Moreover, email tracking often includes third parties which receive yet more data about the users such as newsletters they are subscribed to, online services they are using, and their email reading habits. This information is valuable to spammers for *personalizing* their phishing and spamming attacks. Adding personalized context to phishing attacks amplifies its impact, as shown in the recent *Emotent* phishing campaign,

---

[16] https://superhuman.com/.
[17] https://www.mixmax.com/.
[18] https://www.streak.com/.
[19] https://www.yesware.com/.

which is at the moment of writing among the *"top malware threats affecting Europe"* [14]. Furthermore, there are businesses interested in sneaking into users' inboxes to gain business insights from their bulk emails. In 2017 *Unroll.me*, a free service that allows users to manage their newsletter subscriptions, sold parts of its users' data to Uber [24].

Senders' Justification: Adjusting Sending Rate. It is argued that some senders use email tracking in order to adjust their sending rate. Bender et al. [3] subscribed multiple email addresses to different newsletters but exhibited *different email reading behavior* including different email reading/opening frequencies for each account. Their findings confirm that email marketers respond to the user's behavior and adjust their sending frequency, i.e., they send fewer emails to less-active inboxes.

However, this practice mainly serves to the interest of sender as it aims to prevent users from reporting their emails as spam, which jeopardizes their reputation and delivery rate. Note that for recipients there is a difference between receiving fewer emails and unsubscribing from a newsletter. Unsubscribing from email communications has strict legal bindings that often protects the recipient such as mandating the sender to delete all the user data. In contrast, when a sender reduces sending frequency or even stops sending emails, the user data remains within the system. Instead of infecting emails with tracking tokens to steadily monitor users' interactions senders should put user in control and allow them to adjust their preferences.

5.2   Toward Mitigation: Multi-level Content Blocking

While blocking remote contents can stop HTTP-based tracking, it is a rough approach with heavy impact on user experience. De Paula et al. [40] emphasis on providing multi-level countermeasures that enable users to choose different levels of risks according to their tasks. Similarly, the privacy concerns of email tracking could be reduced by involving the user. For example, giving users the option to only load certain images in email (e.g., only loading the banner of a newsletter). While this would not fully mitigate email tracking risks, it could minimize the scope of tracking. Despite its simplicity, practical implementation of a multi-level countermeasures is still missing in most email clients.[20]

6   Conclusion

In this paper we demonstrate the prevalence of email tracking in a corpus of 237,741 marketing emails. Our results illustrate that marketers are strictly following email communication guidelines by providing opt-out options and obtaining consent for sending emails. Though these guidelines have not progressed as

---

[20] As mentioned in Sect. 2.3, ProtonMail is the only email client that we could find which provides a multi-level blocking for remote and embedded images.

the email eco-system evolves and do not protect users against the current methods of email tracking. As work in progress, we aim to assess the implications of email tracking with respect to European General Data Protection Regulation and ePrivacy directive.

References

1. The Direct Marketing Association (UK) LTD.: Consumer email tracker 2019 (2019). https://dma.org.uk/uploads/misc/consumer-email-tracker-2019---v5.pdf. Accessed 15 Dec 2020
2. Baer, J., Neufeld, G.: The use of URLs as meta-syntax for core mail list commands and their transport through message header fields. RFC 2369, July 1998
3. Bender, B., Fabian, B., Haupt, J., Lessmann, S., Neumann, T., Thim, C.: Track and treat - usage of e-mail tracking for newsletter individualization. In: Twenty-Sixth European Conference on Information Systems (ECIS 2018), Portsmouth, UK, June 2018
4. Bender, B., Fabian, B., Lessmann, S., Haupt, J.: E-mail tracking: status quo and novel countermeasures. In: Proceedings of the Thirty-Seventh International Conference on Information Systems (ICIS), Dublin, Ireland, December 2016
5. Biggio, B., Fumera, G., Pillai, I., Roli, F.: Image spam filtering using visual information. In: 14th International Conference on Image Analysis and Processing (ICIAP 2007), pp. 105–110, September 2007. https://doi.org/10.1109/ICIAP.2007.4362765
6. Brandon, J.: Why email will be obsolete by 2020, April 2015. https://www.inc.com/john-brandon/why-email-will-be-obsolete-by-2020.html. Accessed 15 Dec 2020
7. CampaignMonitor: The ultimate guide to CSS. https://www.campaignmonitor.com/css/. Accessed 15 Dec 2020
8. Clare, V.: Introducing time zone sending (2017). https://www.campaignmonitor.com/blog/new-features/2017/04/introducing-time-zone-sending/. Accessed 15 Dec 2020
9. Conversant: Five building blocks of identity management. https://www.conversantmedia.com/hubfs/US%20Conversant/IMAGE%20ILLUSTRATIONS %20and%20VIDEOs/Resource-center-assets/PDFs/Five_Keys_to_Identity_ Resolution_24Apr2019.pdf. Accessed 15 Dec 2020
10. Davidson, M.: Superhuman is spying on you (2019). https://mikeindustries.com/blog/archive/2019/07/superhuman-is-spying-on-you. Accessed 15 Dec 2020
11. Englehardt, S., Han, J., Narayanan, A.: I never signed up for this! Privacy implications of email tracking. Proc. Priv. Enhanc. Technol. **2018**(1), 109–126 (2018)
12. Epsilon: The way the cookie data crumbles: people-based profiles vs. cookie-based solutions (2019). https://www.epsilon.com/hubfs/Cookie%20Crumbles.pdf. Accessed 15 Dec 2020
13. Ermoshina, K., Musiani, F., Halpin, H.: End-to-end encrypted messaging protocols: an overview. In: Bagnoli, F., et al. (eds.) INSCI 2016. LNCS, vol. 9934, pp. 244–254. Springer, Cham (2016). https://doi.org/10.1007/978-3-319-45982-0_22
14. Europol: Internet Organised Crime Threat Assessment (IOCTA) 2020. European Union Agency for Law Enforcement Cooperation (Europol) (2020)
15. Freed, N., Borenstein, N.: Multipurpose internet mail extensions (MIME) part two: media types. RFC 2046, November 1996. https://tools.ietf.org/html/rfc2046

16. FTC.gov: can-spam act: a compliance guide for business. https://www.ftc.gov/tips-advice/business-center/guidance/can-spam-act-compliance-guide-business. Accessed 15 Dec 2020
17. Gardiner, M.: Ropemaker email security weakness - vulnerability or application misuse? https://www.mimecast.com/blog/2017/08/introducing-the-ropemaker-email-exploit/. Accessed 15 Dec 2020
18. Gmail: turn images on or off in gmail. https://support.google.com/mail/answer/145919. Accessed 15 Dec 2020
19. Google Workspace Admin Help: use optical character recognition to read images. https://support.google.com/a/answer/6358855. Accessed 15 Dec 2020
20. Handley, A., et al.: B2B content marketing benchmarks, budgets, and trends-North America (2019). https://contentmarketinginstitute.com/wp-content/uploads/2019/10/2020_B2B_Research_Final.pdf. Accessed 15 Dec 2020
21. Haupt, J., Bender, B., Fabian, B., Lessmann, S.: Robust identification of email tracking: a machine learning approach. Eur. J. Oper. Res. **271**(1), 341–356 (2018). https://doi.org/10.1016/j.ejor.2018.05.018
22. Hodgekiss, R.: Embedded image support in HTML email (2019). https://www.campaignmonitor.com/blog/email-marketing/2019/04/embedded-images-in-html-email/. Accessed 15 Dec 2020
23. Hu, H., Peng, P., Wang, G.: Characterizing pixel tracking through the lens of disposable email services. In: 2019 IEEE Symposium on Security and Privacy (SP), pp. 365–379 (2019)
24. Isaac, M., Lohr, S.: Unroll.me service faces backlash over a widespread practice: selling user data (2017). https://nyti.ms/2pYH0Eb. Accessed 15 Dec 2020
25. Ketari, L.M., Chandra, M., Khanum, M.A.: A study of image spam filtering techniques. In: 2012 Fourth International Conference on Computational Intelligence and Communication Networks, pp. 245–250 (2012)
26. Klevjer, H.: Phishing by data URI (2012). https://doi.org/10.13140/2.1.4088.0007
27. Litmus: why do some email clients show my email differently than others? https://help.litmus.com/article/158-why-do-some-email-clients-show-my-email-differently-than-others. Accessed 15 Dec 2020
28. LiveIntent: how to implement LiveTags (2020). https://support.liveintent.com/hc/en-us/articles/360001247043-How-to-Implement-LiveTags-. Accessed 15 Dec 2020
29. LiveIntent: overview of custom audiences (2020). https://support.liveintent.com/hc/en-us/articles/204889644-Overview-of-Custom-Audiences. Accessed 15 Dec 2020
30. Maass, M., Schwär, S., Hollick, M.: Towards transparency in email tracking. In: Naldi, M., Italiano, G.F., Rannenberg, K., Medina, M., Bourka, A. (eds.) APF 2019. LNCS, vol. 11498, pp. 18–27. Springer, Cham (2019). https://doi.org/10.1007/978-3-030-21752-5_2
31. MailChimp: use Timewarp. https://mailchimp.com/help/use-timewarp/. Accessed 15 Dec 2020
32. MailChimp: insights from MailChimp's send time optimization system (2014). https://mailchimp.com/resources/insights-from-mailchimps-send-time-optimization-system/. Accessed 15 Dec 2020
33. MailPoet: why we don't allow embedded images. https://docs.mailpoet.com/article/26-embedding-images-in-emails-bad-idea. Accessed 15 Dec 2020
34. Masinter, L.: The "data" URL scheme. RFC 2397, August 1998. https://tools.ietf.org/html/rfc2397

35. Maunder, M.: Wide impact: highly effective gmail phishing technique being exploited. https://www.wordfence.com/blog/2017/01/gmail-phishing-data-uri/. Accessed 15 Dec 2020

36. Mitchell, T.: Everything you know about email content filtering is wrong. https://blog.returnpath.com/everything-you-know-about-email-content-filtering-is-wrong/. Accessed 15 Dec 2020

37. Nisen, M.: The future of work won't include email (2013). https://www.businessinsider.com/why-email-should-become-obsolete-2013-1. Accessed 15 Dec 2020

38. Nissenbaum, H.: Privacy in Context: Technology, Policy, and the Integrity of Social Life. Stanford University Press, Stanford (2009)

39. Partridge, C.: The technical development of internet email. IEEE Ann. Hist. Comput. **30**(2), 3–29 (2008)

40. de Paula, R., et al.: In the eye of the beholder: a visualization-based approach to information system security. Int. J. Hum Comput Stud. **63**(1), 5–24 (2005). https://doi.org/10.1016/j.ijhcs.2005.04.021

41. Roberts, C.: Announcing send time optimization (2017). https://www.campaignmonitor.com/blog/new-features/2017/05/announcing-send-time-optimization/. Accessed 15 Dec 2020

42. Rogers, A.: As workplace communication evolves, email may not prevail, February 2017. https://www.forbes.com/sites/ciocentral/2017/02/15/as-workplace-communication-evolves-email-may-not-prevail/. Accessed 15 Dec 2020

43. Sahami, M., Dumais, S., Heckerman, D., Horvitz, E.: A Bayesian approach to filtering junk e-mail. In: Learning for Text Categorization: Papers from the 1998 Workshop, Madison, Wisconsin, vol. 62, pp. 98–105 (1998)

44. Sahni, N.S., Wheeler, S.C., Chintagunta, P.: Personalization in email marketing: the role of non-informative advertising content. Mark. Sci. **37**(2), 236–258 (2018). Providence, R.I

45. Strom, D.: The hidden privacy hazards of HTML email. https://strom.com/awards/192.html. Accessed 15 Dec 2020

46. The Direct Marketing Association (UK) LTD.: marketer email tracker 2019 (2019). https://dma.org.uk/uploads/misc/marketers-email-tracker-2019.pdf

47. Tony, H., Alexey, M.: Message disposition notification. RFC 8098, February 2017. https://tools.ietf.org/html/rfc8098

48. TorBirdy: towards a tor-safe Mozilla thunderbird reducing application-level privacy leaks in thunderbird (2011). https://trac.torproject.org/projects/tor/attachment/wiki/doc/TorifyHOWTO/EMail/Thunderbird/Thunderbird+Tor.pdf. Accessed 07 Sept 2020

49. Vaudreuil, G.: Enhanced mail system status codes. RFC 3463, January 2003. https://tools.ietf.org/html/rfc3463

50. Vella, H.: Interview: messaging apps take on work email. https://www.raconteur.net/hr/messaging-apps-take-on-work-email. Accessed 15 Dec 2020

51. Voth, C.: Reaper exploit. http://web.archive.org/web/20011005083819/www.geocities.com/ResearchTriangle/Facility/8332/reaper-exploit-release.html. Accessed 15 Dec 2020

52. Xu, H., Hao, S., Sari, A., Wang, H.: Privacy risk assessment on email tracking. In: IEEE INFOCOM 2018 - IEEE Conference on Computer Communications, pp. 2519–2527, April 2018. https://doi.org/10.1109/INFOCOM.2018.8486432

Privacy Respecting Data Sharing and Communication in mHealth: A Case Study

Michael Pleger$^{(\boxtimes)}$ ⓘ and Ina Schiering$^{(\boxtimes)}$ ⓘ

Ostfalia University of Applied Sciences, Wolfenbüttel, Germany
{mic.pleger,i.schiering}@ostfalia.de

Abstract. The increasing usage of mobile devices within the health-care domain and the social sector requires a closer look on privacy and security aspects of those systems. Major data breaches have been made public in recent years, which resulted in privacy issues for unaware users, ranging from loss of control over their data, to identity theft cases, up to discrimination because of political, religious or sexual orientation. To this aim, privacy enhancing technologies enabling privacy-preserving communication and data sharing are investigated in the context of an mHealth solution.

Keywords: mhealth · Data sharing · Attribute-based encryption · Privacy enhancing technology · Zero knowledge

1 Introduction

Mobile technology like wearable devices and mobile phones, for example, utilize existing communication technologies to provide a vast amount of unique services, all within a single device. While these devices are used for personal health-monitoring, they can be accounted as digital, mobile health solutions (*mHealth*).

Safety and security concerns of mHealth applications have been broadly addressed [11,14,15,24,27], where, among others, unencrypted data gets transmitted to remote servers without notifying the user of their purpose and without compliance with data regulations applicable for mHealth apps, e.g. GDPR [5]. In several contexts, mHealth applications need to gather health related data from patients or vulnerable people, which are considered as special categories of data according to Article 9 GDPR. To protect such data from unwanted access (both locally on a device, as well as remotely stored on servers) cryptographic methods like encryption can be generally used. While a secure communication channel to a remote server might protect the transmission itself, it leaves data stored on a remote server completely unencrypted. To protect such data against unauthorized access and prevent data breaches, it should be stored encrypted as well. End-to-end encryption can be managed to complete such task, but requires a generally more complex approach concerning key management and distribution.

© IFIP International Federation for Information Processing 2021
Published by Springer Nature Switzerland AG 2021
M. Friedewald et al. (Eds.): Privacy and Identity 2020, IFIP AICT 619, pp. 206–225, 2021.
https://doi.org/10.1007/978-3-030-72465-8_12

The aim of this paper is to investigate privacy patterns and privacy enhancing technologies for privacy preserving communication and data sharing in the context of an existing mHealth solution. Within the healthcare domain such data typically is highly sensible due to their nature in providing insides for professional assessments. Reports of medical- or physical conditions, vital signs or blood-level measures are information that should be protected and limited to eligible personal. As an example, if a doctor receives a radiograph from a hospital stay of one of his patients (e.g. a public figure), it does contain identifying information (e.g. the patients full name, birth date, date of x-ray, etc.). What happens, if such scan would be leaked to the public, since it could have significant, unclear consequences for the patients. Therefore the communication between the doctor and clinic should be secured, as well as the access to such data within the clinic limited without proper authentication. Furthermore the electronic data storage should be encrypted as well. Within a mHealth-domain, on the other hand, if the patient is using a wearable self-monitoring devices (e.g. a fitness tracker) that collects vital signs (step count, heart rate) over a period of time and shares these information with the devices manufacturer for processing, there is typically not such a strict data protection requirement. It is not uncommon to buy such devices with a privacy policy attached, that requires the publication of personal data towards the manufacturer or application provider, in order to use the device itself, since often times the data processing is done on remote servers due to the limited capabilities these devices face.

The selection process for privacy enhancing technologies (PETs), based on the given requirements in the selected use case, as well as the intended purpose with such PETs, is provided within the methodology section of this publication. The analysis focuses on selected approaches addressing untrustworthy service providers and the risk of data breaches at the service provider level respectively. Hence, which privacy patterns can be utilized to improve privacy in data sharing towards untrustworthy platform providers in the context of an mHealth application.

Two prototypes, based on the analysis, were developed to further evaluate the usability by less technological skilled people. After that the shortcomings for both prototypes are then be provided within the discussion section, along with a brief overview of further technologies, that could be utilized to improve the privacy aspects of data sharing within mHealth.

2   Background

Smartphone based mHealth applications and *Assistive Technologies* (AT) enable users to monitor their own vital-signs and e.g. allow them to provide data to physicians remotely for quality and improvement assessments without the need of personal, eye-to-eye contact [14]. This technology enables users to engage in healthcare related activities on their phones rather than using traditional, stationary personal computer systems, while being flexible in their location [19]. Smartphone based mHealth applications provide various types of services, e.g.

tracking behavior for developmental disorders, information and treatments on cognitive disorders, as well as mood, eating and sleep disorders among others [15,19,27], which can be very useful for patients at home.

The downside of this technology has been continually picked up by ongoing discussions regarding user's privacy, since (mHealth) applications tend to collect and share significant amounts of data to provide their services, even if the purpose of such collections is not always disclosed [11,24,27]. Common identifiers like name, age, weight and address might be collected, which according to data protection regulations, can be classified as *Personally Identifiable Information* (PII). Furthermore, depending on the application and what service it provides, the collection of fitness data (including location data), medical results or personal images, treatment plans or -schedules might be necessary.

While users could be enlightened about the usage of such data through privacy policies on an informational level (e.g. what data is collected, where is the data processed, who is processing the data and with whom is the collected data being shared), this would not protect the data itself on a computational level, e.g. when the data is stored on a server or within a database. This needs to be addressed with technical means, like data encryption, -separation and access-structures within the realm of ICT, or information and communications technology.

To set the scope regarding privacy within mHealth in the context of this paper, a typical use case will be provided as follows (see Illustration in Fig. 1). Whenever patients require services from within the healthcare domain, they generally are required to provide personal identifiable information (PII) like name and address, age, their social security number, healthcare account number or other highly sensitive data like blood type or medical conditions, in order to receive services by healthcare professionals. For example, if a cognitive impaired patient requires assistance to achieve daily tasks (e.g. to stock up groceries), through a mobile health application instead of a caregiver or personal care assistant, sensible information like time schedules, preferences and what items have been bought could be gathered by that application. This could leave the patient vulnerable to information loss, since the item list could also contain prescriptions, which could disclose the patients medical conditions. On the contrary, using an application instead of a human assistant might increase the anonymity in regards to the patient, which could be beneficial (depending on the conditions).

As a generalization, the issues for privacy can be seen by mHealth solutions and -services that do not have access to larger, established medical solutions and electronic health record systems, to process the patients data in a privacy preserving way. Instead, smaller or dedicated service providers are used to process and exchange information with the healthcare domain, which could expose sensible personal identifiable information to a broader scale.

Such data required by healthcare professionals, which contains sensitive information, is then often being processed through dedicated software applications, in order to provide services to the patient. Since healthcare professionals often times rely on software developed by third parties, they do not have (and should

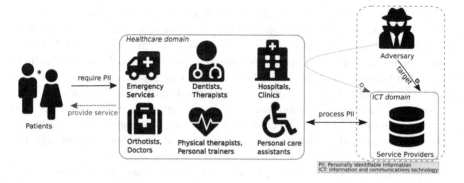

Fig. 1. Generalized data processing flow in mHealth, where healthcare professionals require third party providers for their services. In such case adversaries typically target service providers within the ICT domain directly

not require) the knowledge of how such personal information are been processed or stored. What they require is the sole outcome of the data processing, therefore their understanding of information processing can be seen limited, since these are typically not tech-savvy users. For example, rehabilitation centers and personal care assistants are specialized to provide a service (e.g. consultations) to their patients and utilize applications to fulfill their tasks.

A distinction has to be made between healthcare (and electronic health) and mHealth. While the former is based on professional healthcare and -systems (e.g. patient management software within clinics, clinical or laboratory software, etc.) the latter one often times refers to mobile applications, that tend to assist or self-monitor instead of treat them. Such applications are, for example, Apple Fitness, Google Fit, FitBit or Strava.

In regards to mHealth applications on mobile devices (and the increasing availability of such), healthcare professionals tend to have difficulties with what kind of application should be recommended to patients. Since a vast amount of these applications have not been created by medical experts, healthcare professionals, like doctors, have to evaluate applications by themselves to validate their functions. If the application's functions vindicate the intended purpose, without proper validation of the safety and security mechanism (or certification thereof), massive privacy and security risks need to be addressed.

While a healthcare professional might be able to validate the purpose of such mHealth applications, this does not hold true for the data protection against service providers, in regards to unauthorized access, while maintaining the user's control over the data. Furthermore it might be non-trivial to use systems that deliver strong privacy implementations without advanced training.

As context for the investigation presented here, an mHealth application called *RehaGoal* is considered. It has been developed to provide treatment capabilities to patients with an impairment of executive dysfunction, which could be received either through an accident or a congenital disease. Such an impairment could result in patients being unable to perform consecutive tasks on their own. For example, if someone is asked to water all plants in a specific room, a healthy person would water each plant successively through a pattern (e.g. start from left and go to right) until each plant has been watered sufficiently. This behavior would not be the case for a person diagnosed with executive dysfunction, where the motion to stop and reflect the acted behavior might be unavailable for such person. This could result in watering all plants multiple times in a row, until the motion to stop is either remembered or the person is notified by external means (e.g. another person). To change or treat such false behavior, the concept of *Goal-Management Training* has been used to define therapies for affected patients.

Individual therapies can be provided in a supervised environment, with assisted interactions between patients and therapists (e.g. in a clinical setting). It could also be used individually in a private environment, whenever personal interactions with healthcare professionals might not be feasible or possible (e.g. during a pandemic) [20].

Fig. 2. Representation of the RehaGoal application to support people with cognitive disabilities during daily activities

Developed as a hybrid, cross-platform web-application with a strong focus on mobile devices (e.g. smartphones, see Fig. 2), its intended purpose is to assists patients in completing a defined goal, by serving a sequential list of single tasks as a workflow. Users are able to create, execute, schedule or share workflows inside the application. Workflows can be designed with a graphical editor by placing task-blocks on a virtual canvas. Workflow tasks are typically modeled on a textual basis, but images can be added for increased accessibility as well. RehaGoal users can be differentiated into two roles: *patients* and *therapists*. The latter typically designs workflows for each patient individually on a stationary device (e.g. a desktop computer or notebook) by splitting an intended goal into sub-goals or -tasks. Patients on the other hand can be considered as the main users, which run the application on smartphones or other mobile devices like tablets to execute workflows in the context of a given therapy.

Although no vital data of patients are collected, the individual workflows might include names of persons or addresses, required doses of medicals for a given therapy or photos might show people and the personal environment of patients. Also, only the fact that a person uses the app on his/her mobile device allows conclusions, that the user has a certain disease or impairment (thus this can be seen as metadata).

An important requirement for neuropsychological trials and usage of the app afterwards in rehabilitation scenarios is the ability to exchange workflows between patients and therapists. While each patient might receive individual treatments and intensities with the application, it could occur that pre-defined workflows are applicable to multiple patients. Furthermore, if the application is rolled out through small to large scale therapy institutions (e.g. clinics), the ability to distribute workflows is required. Sharing can be done either locally through an export on the device or alternatively the data exchange can be realized via a remote server. A visualization of that requirement can be seen in Fig. 3, which illustrates the life-cycle for workflows, which where designed by therapists and provided to patients. The inner arrows picture a local file exchange, while the outer ones attached with the cloud symbols represent the server method. In case the rehabilitation is commenced within a larger institution (or e.g. patients with severe impairment), a mutual handler can be utilized to assist patients to load and start their workflows, or schedule multiple workflows for a given therapy and provide feedback to the therapist. While in this context, patients, therapists and the mutual handler are not considered as tech-savvy, the use of an secure and privacy respecting data exchange solution must be very simplistic. A workflow export, that requires a unique password to be defined, which has to be communicated through a secure channel and entered prior to importing, can be seen as to cumbersome and not suitable for deployment. Furthermore, the protection against unauthorized access and control over the data by the user should not be relayed to the end user, but instead be mitigated through information processing means within the application itself.

During the development process of the RehaGoal application both privacy and accessibility were accredited of utmost importance. Therefore *Privacy by Design* principles have been incorporated, which were based on *privacy design strategies* (PDS) [2] in conjunction with the definition of *privacy protection goals* (PPG) [9]. Furthermore the concept of data minimization was adhered to, wherever possible [6]. The RehaGoal application has been utilized during neuropsychological intervention-studies to evaluate whether the usage of *Assistive Technology* can improve the participation of patients with cognitive impairments [20].

A central characteristic of mHealth scenarios is that the organizations are typically therapists or physicians, working in relatively small practices, hospitals or rehabilitation facilities, which are (in general) not able to host software services. Hence external service providers would be typically needed, thus it is important to analyze Privacy by Design approaches concerning untrusted platform service providers.

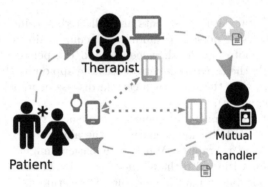

Fig. 3. Workflows created by therapist are shared either directly with patients, or in case of a larger deployment (e.g. within an institution) via a mutual handler that can assist in importing, scheduling or executing workflows for impaired patients

Standard security measurements would be authentication of users in combination with a role and right model, network encryption and the use of pseudonyms instead of usernames, allowing an identification. Though access to the cloud based database is limited by authentication, a data exchange solution should not solely be used to protect data from unintended access. Unlinkability is, in addition, an important goal. In the RehaGoal context, user accounts on the remote server are based on pseudonyms generated by therapist rather than the patient's name and do not contain addresses or other highly sensitive information.

To protect against unauthorized access through server- or database breaches, as well as rogue platform service providers (e.g. system administrator) and furthermore to hide potential metadata, workflow encryption should be used. But this requires further evaluation on how such an encryption scheme could be both, designed and implemented, because the selection depends on regulations and the perspective. A straightforward solution would be the encryption of any data by the users themselves, including the key management and -exchange. Although this solution would provide secure means regarding the remote server, it lacks the ability to be scaled up efficiently. Larger businesses or institutions (e.g. healthcare clinics or hospitals) could require the usage of a remote server-oriented workflow exchange with an elaborated role-based access model, where therapists and doctors of different departments can treat patients in unison.

Since the RehaGoal application (and the therapies thereof) can be situated within the mHealth domain, the following distinctions will be made to reflect stakeholders, with the data protection terminology defined in the GDPR. In this context data subjects will be referenced as users (patients and therapists), which provide data to the RehaGoal application by e.g. generating and executing workflows. A remote server will be provided by an platform service provider, which can be seen as a processor of the provided data, since these servers are being used for workflow file exchanges. The development and research group of the RehaGoal application can be seen as both, data controller and -processor as well, since usage-metrics might be collected in case patients have joined selected neuropsychological studies.

3   Related Work

To address and promote privacy friendly solutions, Colesky et al. [3] documented a collection of privacy pattern for multiple categories, e.g. control of data, minimization or enforcement of policies. Theses have been classified based on previous work of Colesky et al., where privacy design strategies have been extended with privacy tactics intended to address privacy issues, by *Privacy by Design* during the development process. Further research has been commenced to characterize such privacy patterns [16] and on how these patterns could be applied to the healthcare domain [1]. Since authentication and encryption are necessitated for secure data sharing in mHealth, the usage of such patterns [8] is evaluated.

While proper encryption standards to protect data communications on the internet have been developed and used for a long time [13], they generally require an elaborated key distribution and -management scheme. Those communications rely on a trust-model that is based on certificates and public key cryptography. To mitigate the trust-model, newer technologies like Blockchain, advanced by crypto-currencies, have been introduced and used to authenticate and store data online [4,12]. A shift from Single-Factor-Authentication (SFA) to Two-Factor-Authentication (2FA) or even Multi-Factor-Authentication (MFA) has increased the security aspects of such processes [23].

On the other hand, processing encrypted data within the cloud can be achieved by advanced cryptographic schemes, like homomorphic encryption, which permits a limited evaluation of encrypted data without the need for a decryption key [7]. Attribute-based encryption (ABE) extends asynchronous encryption, based on public/private keys and incorporates an access structure within the encrypted data itself, mitigating the need for elaborated key distribution schemes [8]. This concept has been extended with approaches for distributed [21] and decentralized [18] implementations.

To protect sensitive information in a privacy preserving manner, intervention studies typically rely on methodologies that combine pseudonymization and encryption schemes to reduce e.g. linkability between data sets [10,22]. Polymorphic encryption and Pseudonymisation (PEP) by Verheul et al. [26] is a novel approach suitable for such applications, based on a similar idea of ABE where the decryption relies on policies rather then fixed keys.

4   Methodology

Patients and therapist of RehaGoal, or users of any mHealth solution in general, use an application to fulfill an intended purpose (e.g. to execute a treatment plan or monitor their vital signs). The user's knowledge, in regards to information security and data privacy, can not be expected in this domain and should, in a best case scenario, only contribute to the validation that an application or policy preserves the users privacy. Since complex applications, that require user interactions to set privacy settings, tend to be difficult to get used to, they should provide a user centered privacy setting by default. Otherwise this behavior could burden users with overwhelming settings of which they do not know the ramifications for, require advanced training or would raise the user acceptance threshold, using the application in general.

To identify, which privacy patterns or privacy enhancing technologies could be utilized to improve privacy in data sharing, specifically against untrustworthy platform providers, an overview of suitable solutions had to be created. Figure 4 illustrates four steps, that have been established. The initial step (*Identify*) was to gather an overview of data sharing solutions, based on common proposals, current research and best practices. This selection was not limited to the mHealth domain and listed, among others, file exchange through messages (e-mail), peer-to-peer solutions (P2P), network based file shares (e.g. Network File Share [NFS], Server Message Block [SMB]) or role-based access structure concepts on private and public clouds.

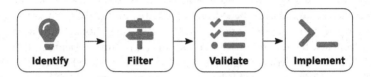

Fig. 4. Established steps, that have been performed to generate an overview of sharing solutions (1), narrowed down to a subset based on privacy design strategies (2), adjusted to the requirements by the RehaGoal use case (e.g. low-powered mobile devices) (3) and realization of prototypes to evaluate the functionality and conduct usability studies (4).

The second step (*Filter*) was conducted to narrow down the subset of solutions based on their classification within the privacy design strategies, with emphasis to minimize trust towards platform providers. For example, in this step solutions that utilize a peer-to-peer network have been excluded, since this scheme only provides a mean to transport data (with package validation), but does not provide further means to protect the actual data itself. Furthermore, this solution does not provide a reasonable mean to delete already shared data, reducing the intervenability in case users do want to remove their data, significantly. Therefor only solutions that utilize a (de-)centralized client/server architecture where processed further. Within the RehaGoal use case, one requirement was the protection of sensible health data, that should adhered to on an end-to-end basis. This means that only patients and e.g. their therapists should be able to decrypt the shared data respectively. The utilization of service providers for remote data sharing should only require the storage of data by those. Data processing should not be outsourced from the mHealth application itself. Following that, shared data should not provide any insight for service providers into how users workflows look like, or what they intend to solve.

The third step (*Validate*) imposed further requirements to the filtered subset. All proposed solutions are required to be used on low-powered, mobile devices. Furthermore, solutions should be, if possible, utilize established web-standards and assessed cryptographic libraries, since the usage is intended for a production environment. The mHealth solution should be usable by users with medical conditions or impairments. This means that the need for a key management (in case data is encrypted) should be easy to use without the need for users to choose complex (e.g. secure) passphrases for each data exchange. The need for advanced user training should also be avoided. Instead the application and their processes should be as self-explanatory as possible. And lastly workflows need to be shared with multiple recipients or re-used with others. Since cryptographic computations on mobile devices are rather costly (e.g. battery usage, wait time), they should not be encrypted for each individual separately. Instead an encryption scheme able to encrypt once (for either all or an intended group instead) should be considered. This process generated an overview of suitable privacy enhancing technologies and data sharing schemes, that are listed in Table 3.

After that was the realization (*Implement*) of selected concepts within RehaGoal, in order to evaluate the functionality for both users and service providers, the computational costs and resources requirements. This step provided artifacts that can be used to conduct usability studies in the future.

While this provided the general steps that have been passed through, the following text will provide more context on the filtering and validation process.

Privacy by Design is generally focused on design principles and tends to be difficult to be overcome from a software development standpoint. In order to select suitable privacy patterns, which provide the ability to preserve privacy within a data sharing scheme, especially towards platform service providers, a general filtering process has been commenced. The selection process had two phases:

The first phase identified applicable privacy patterns for data sharing on a conceptual level. Specifically patterns should be intended to improve data confidentiality for RehaGoal users, along with reduced linkability features for the platform service provider. Based on the privacy design strategy tags, that have been used within the catalog provided by Colesky et al. [3], a pre-selection of suitable privacy enhancing technologies had been commenced. The selection has then been cross-referenced with the classification matrix identified by Lenhard et al. [16], to focus on data oriented categories, namely *MINIMIZE, AGGREGATE, SEPARATE* and *HIDE*. Table 1 lists the included privacy design strategies, based on Colesky et al. [2] with the reasoning and an example as how they can be applied in the stated use case.

Process oriented categories have largely been excluded, since privacy towards service providers should be addressed, rather than the user's means to *ENFORCE, DEMONSTRATE, CONTROL* or *INFORM* (see Reasoning in Table 2). Lastly the results had been compared to Aljohani et al.'s findings [1], who identified privacy patterns in a similar mHealth use case on a larger, nationwide scale. Since the RehaGoal application is focused on individual deployments

Table 1. Overview of the included privacy design strategies with their intentions and implications for the given use case

Included PDS	Reasoning
HIDE	Since this improves both unlinkability and confidentiality, the strategy seemed most promising. For example by encrypting the workflow data before sharing it with the platform service provider, a general obfuscation could be accomplished
CONTROL	This strategy allows users to have the ability to choose who can process or access their personal data. By encrypting workflow data through the *HIDE* strategy and the management of related encryption keys by the RehaGoal users themselves, this could provide useful means to improve the intended purpose
SEPARATE	Tries to prevent correlation between data as much as possible by either distribution or isolation. Since the remote server is intended to be realized as a single instance the isolation tactic could be utilized to process (store and provide) workflow data without access or correlation to further information (e.g. content of other workflows of each user)

for e.g. rehabilitation centers with limited resources, up to larger institutions with role-based access structure, the up-scaling aspects of the suitable PETs had to be addressed as well.

Within the second phase of the selection process, the privacy patterns have been evaluated with existing privacy enhancing technologies (PET). In contrast to privacy design strategies, which are renowned as guidelines in the complete development life cycle, PETs can be seen as solving "only one specific privacy

Table 2. Excluded privacy design strategies

Excluded PDS	Reasoning
DEMONSTRATE INFORM CONTROL ENFORCE	Privacy design strategies that focus on Transparency and Intervenability have largely been excluded from analysis, since these focus on privacy regarding users rather then platform service providers
MINIMIZE	Requires the minimal data collection and procession to fulfill an intended request with a specific purpose limitation. Since only workflows should be exchanged between users, this strategy could not been used in this instance
ABSTRACT	The strategy's intention is to limit details by grouping or summarizing data together. Similar to MINIMIZE, this is not applicable in the given use case

problem in already implemented software" [1]. To enhance applications that gather raw outcome measurements, containing sensitive or personal information, an anonymization function could be used to remove or replace such information prior to distribution. An aggregation function could also be seen as a PET, since e.g. data can be grouped together to provide insight while still managing to mask individuals personal information.

5 Analysis

The following section will provide an overview of which patterns have been implemented within an mHealth application, to increase the privacy aspects in regards to an untrusted platform service provider. Both are designed to enhance the functionality of a remote server sharing concept, where therapists and patients are able to share workflow data securely. Note that the mentioned remote server is configured in a privacy preserving way. To achieve this all logging functionalities have been disabled or limited. For example if a client requests a resource of this server, typically the IP address gets captured in the log file of the web server. In our case this type of logging has been removed. Therefore the server can only store the connection details while the connection is established. After the transmission has ended, no information about what was exchanged can be restored. In regards to data storage, the only identifier that is actually stored within the database along with the encrypted data is the pseudonym of the user, that belongs the data. But since the pseudonyms are generated out of scope of the server (and the service provider respectively), no identifying information (quasi-identifier, or combinations of non-identifiers) can be gained. Table 3 lists three selected concepts together with the privacy design strategy, which their usage represents. As mentioned previously, many novel and experimental cryptographic schemes like *Homomorphic encryption* (HE) and *Polymorphic Encryption and Pseudonymisation* (PEP) exist, but their implementations were not be considered for this use case deployment yet, because only data storage and not the processing thereof is required here. Further details on what these technologies do, or what they imply to improve privacy, will be discussed later on.

Based on the overview provided by Colesky et al. [3], the concepts *Private Link* and *Encryption with user-managed keys* have been chosen. Both have been classified within the selected strategies in the first phase. Furthermore *Attribute-based encryption* has been selected as a holistic approach to secure data sharing within RehaGoal. In contrast to the first two PET's, this concept provides further privacy improvements, not only for platform service providers, but also to RehaGoal users by providing enhanced intervenability due to the role-access structure embedded in ABE schemes. To differentiate the concepts and their intended purpose, they will be sectioned into individual or general deployments for *Private Link* and *Encryption with user-managed keys*. On the other hand *Attribute-based encryption* will be listed within deployments with existing role-based structures.

Table 3. Overview of the selected privacy PET's classified within the privacy design strategy terminology by Colesky et al. (*excluded due to the experimental state)

PET	Privacy design strategy
Private Link	HIDE
Encryption with user-managed keys	CONTROL
Attribute-based encryption	SEPARATE, HIDE, CONTROL
Homomorphic encryption*	ABSTRACT, HIDE
Polymorphic Encryption and Pseudonymisation*	SEPARATE, HIDE, CONTROL

5.1   For Individual or General Deployments

A privacy enhancing technology, which has been adopted broadly and can typically be found within applications like cloud storage services and social media platforms, is called *Private Link*. If, for example, a user intends to upload a video to their social media profile, without releasing it to the general public, they could mark it as private or unlisted, such that the platform or service will generate a link to that resource and provide that link to the user. Accessing such will only be possible with knowledge to that particular link. Further examples can be partially found in cloud-based file exchange services (e.g. Nextcloud, Dropbox or Google Drive), where users can selectively share files by generating a unique link.

The privacy aspects of this PET are associated with the *HIDE* strategy, whereas the purpose is to limit the access to only those who received such a link. This PET enables users to selectively disclose a shared resource with a number of recipients, as long as such private link is retained secret.

With a valid link created, the data owner can share the secret with every person he or she intends to. Since this privacy PET is based on a shared secret it has to be transmitted between other users. Figure 5 shows the general life cycle of this PET, where the controller returns a private link, which can then be send to individuals through any communication channel (email, direct message, etc.) to access the resource.

In order to prevent unintended recipients from accessing the resource, a link should not be guessable and therefore be unique or randomly generated. This mechanism can be extended by adding limitations to the private link implementation, e.g. a time constraint for the link validity or that the link only provides a specific version of the resource.

By combining the aforementioned PET with *Encryption with user-managed keys*, access-control can be gained for RehaGoal users to improve intervenability. The basic concept demands that users are responsible to generate and manage their own, strong encryption keys used to encrypt data, prior to storing or transferring it to the data controller. The process consists of three stages, illustrated in Fig. 6, beginning with the user generating secret encryption keys, which will,

Fig. 5. *Private Link* pattern; access to shared resources is only available through a unique, private address, rather than a public registry or website-index

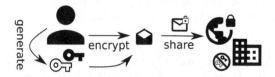

Fig. 6. To increase users authority over who can access data *Encryption with user-managed keys* can be used in conjunction with the *Private Link* pattern to encrypt information prior of sharing it

in turn, be used to encrypt any data intended to be stored or transmitted. Once shared with the data controller, these can not access the encrypted information, since the keys are only accessible by the user.

The combination of the enhancing technologies *Private Link* and *Encryption with user-managed keys* provided enhanced privacy aspects for user data shared with platform service providers in RehaGoal. Figure 7 shows the process of how workflow sharing has been implemented with this solution. The `RehaGoal-GUI` as the applications user interface provides the feature to share workflows remotely. The data of each selected workflow will be processed by the `ExchangeService`, which will then call the `EncryptionService` to generate a random, unique encryption key. This key will be return together with the encrypted workflow data to the ExchangeService. After posting the encrypted workflow data to the `RemoteServer` and receiving a valid URL, the `ExchangeService` will finally return the ExchangeURL with the decryption key appended by a fragment identifier. This ensures that once the URL is clicked, the content behind the fragment identifier will not be transmitted to the `RemoteServer`, but rather be processed within the `RehaGoal-GUI` (or any web-browser) itself.

5.2   Deployments with Existing Role-Based Structures

In the realm of data sharing with multiple users, a functional encryption mechanism should be considered, where data can be encrypted once and decryption is enabled for all users with a secured access structure. Such an encryption scheme,

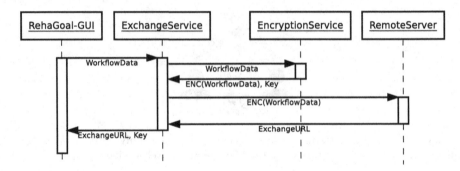

Fig. 7. Sequence diagram of the implemented prototype where data is stored remotely fully encrypted without access to the decryption key for the remote server

introduced by Sahai et al. [25] in 2005 is called *Attribute-based encryption* (ABE). It was extended into key-policy and ciphertext-policy schemes by Goyal et al. [8] in 2006. While multiple kind of attribute-based encryption schemes exist, they are typically distinguished between key-policy (KP-ABE) and ciphertext-policy (CP-ABE) based schemes. Within the former system, policies are related to the private key of the user, while the attributes are linked to the ciphertext. Therefore retrieval of the plaintext is only possible for users, which fulfill the policy with their private keys. In contrast to KP-ABE, in a ciphertext-policy attribute-based encryption scheme, the user's private key contains the attributes instead of the ciphertext. Vice versa the ciphertext contains the policy, hence user attributes have to fulfill the policy of the ciphertext.

The basic concept consists out of an attribute authority, which provides private keys for each user and public parameters relevant for the encryption. Users can encrypted data using public parameters and specify an access policy within the ciphertext. Such policy consists out of attributes which define a Boolean formula. As an example for RehaGoal, the following attributes have been defined by the attribute authority (among others): Role Organization, Studies. If a user wants to encrypt a message for two different subjects: once for all members of the organization A and secondly that only therapists from the organization B should be allowed to decrypt the message. A policy could therefore be represented as follows: "Organization: A" OR ("Organization: B" AND "Role: Therapist"). Users not matching those attributes will not have permission to decrypt and access the data. Figure 8 shows the process for both, valid and invalid, user attributes.

This ABE scheme improves data privacy for RehaGoal users in multiple ways. The concept lets users choose which attribute (e.g. user role) is required to decrypt data. Due to the encryption, it also hides any sensitive workflow information towards the platform service provider, similar to *Encryption with user-managed keys*. Furthermore does it provide means to separate data between multiple platform service providers, since Attribute-based encryption can also be deployed on a decentralized basis. Also this solution provides abilities for

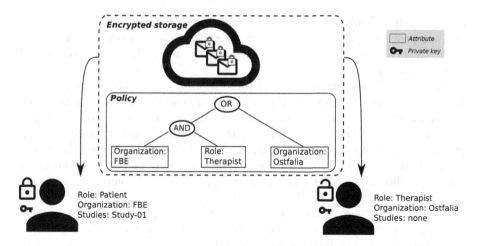

Fig. 8. Basic principle of a ciphertext-policy ABE scheme in RehaGoal, where user attributes are correlated with the policy of an encrypted object. If the policy is fulfilled the plaintext can be decrypted by the user's private key

advanced key management, which is required by Attribute-based encryption schemes. For example, in case authorized therapists do change their occupation, and it is required to revoke the deployed key, mechanisms introduced by Lewko et al. [17] could be used.

6 Discussion

Appropriate data sharing schemes should be chosen, depending on the scale of which data sharing is required. Both proposed solutions provide decent means to improve privacy in mHealth applications. Attribute-based encryption provides a very powerful and feature-rich solution, based on functional encryption by managing a fine-grained access policy. This mitigates both, security and privacy concerns, significantly. Major drawbacks of Attribute-based encryption are the lack of available web-based standard libraries, as well as functional attribute-revocation systems within a ciphertext policy based scheme. Hence, the revocation of a private key (e.g. a patients who left a therapy) will be difficult for distributed and decentralized schemes and the mitigation of that fact should be further investigated.

On the other hand, *Private Link* in conjunction with *Encryption with user-managed keys* improved the privacy with significant less complexity. It provides privacy by being virtually transparent to the RehaGoal user itself. But the principle drawback of the *Private Link* pattern is obvious: once the address (ExchangeURL with fragment identifier and content) is publicly available (e.g. listed on a website, registry, index or within a social media posting) the confidentiality of the resource, in regards to who has access to it, is basically lost. The responsibility to manage the encryption keys offsite through the user however, proposes other challenges for a deployment. Since the platform service provider can not provide any key management for those keys, in case the user looses access to them (and has not yet shared the keys), decryption will be prohibited and the content be lost.

In regards to the performance of those solutions, it highly depends on the capabilities of those devices. Without a user intervention study, it is unknown how much the computational overhead will impact users on a daily basis (e.g. battery drain, wait time, etc.). But since these prototypes are intended to evaluate the proposal of a secure data sharing scheme (given the use case), this has so far not been a critical performance indicator. Especially for larger deployments this should be addressed in a follow up evaluation, possibly paired with an user acceptance study.

In case any of these solutions will be used, where the platform service provider does not have access to the encrypted information itself, metadata like file names, timestamps or system information can still be gathered and processed, since these are typically not encrypted, which might posses minor privacy risks.

Another privacy preserving concept, *Homomorphic encryption* where encrypted data can be processed through platform service providers, without a prior decryption, has not been considered. While *Homomorphic encryption* does not fit within the selected use case, since only data storage is required here, it does provide strong privacy implications. Especially for mHealth providers this technology could be used to analyze sensitive information of patients on a larger scale, e.g. to collect trends within groups of patients without ever loosing control over their data. Reference implementations and libraries are already available. *Homomorphic encryption* has also not been considered within RehaGoal, because it is a web-based application which uses web standards and libraries, whereas no reviewed or audited cryptographic libraries for HE have been released at the time of this writing.

In contrast to *Homomorphic encryption*, where reference implementations exists, *Polymorphic Encryption and Pseudonymisation* has also not been selected in this use case. Similar to ABE, the concept of PEP encrypts data in a polymorphic way, which means that the decryption keys could be formed, depending on relevant attributes, which could be managed by the users. This allows for a larger privacy protection gain, but requires a rather complex system, for which currently only experimental libraries exist.

Further subject of evaluation should be a user acceptance study with different UI designs, in order to see if users actually desire to know, or set the encryption key themselves (e.g. with a password-derived function), or if the encryption scheme is even perceived when utilizing small scale deployments.

7   Conclusion

Several solutions, based on privacy patterns for data sharing, have been examined in an mHealth application context. Those solutions have been introduced and conceptualized within this paper, to provide a basis for the implementation of prototypes. Since these prototypes are part of a complex mHealth system, it is not possible to provide the whole source code under an open license, but it will be considered to publish single modules with a focus on secure data sharing.

The implemented approaches, utilizing privacy enhancing technologies, already improved the privacy of the system, by prohibiting access to (meta-) data during data exchange and -storage for service providers and hence allowing more control. Especially usability aspects and specific requirements concerning role-based access control, in the context of mHealth applications, need to be further investigated. Future prototype evaluations should also investigate resource consumption, as well as required computation time, the amount of storage needed for individual transactions and how additional measurements, like padding of the data, would provide protection against re-identification attacks within the server.

References

1. Aljohani, M., Hawkey, K., Blustein, J.: Proposed privacy patterns for privacy preserving healthcare systems in accord with Nova Scotia's personal health information act. In: Tryfonas, T. (ed.) HAS 2016. LNCS, vol. 9750, pp. 91–102. Springer, Cham (2016). https://doi.org/10.1007/978-3-319-39381-0_9
2. Colesky, M., Hoepman, J.H., Hillen, C.: A critical analysis of privacy design strategies. In: 2016 IEEE Security and Privacy Workshops (SPW), pp. 33–40 (2016). https://doi.org/10.1109/SPW.2016.23
3. Colesky, M., et al.: Patterns. https://privacypatterns.org/patterns/
4. Dang, N.T., Nguyen, V.S., Le, H.-D., Maleszka, M., Tran, M.H.: Sharing secured data on peer-to-peer applications using attribute-based encryption. In: Nguyen, N.T., Hoang, B.H., Huynh, C.P., Hwang, D., Trawiński, B., Vossen, G. (eds.) ICCCI 2020. LNCS (LNAI), vol. 12496, pp. 619–630. Springer, Cham (2020). https://doi.org/10.1007/978-3-030-63007-2_48
5. European Parliament: General data protection regulation (GDPR). https://eur-lex.europa.eu/legal-content/EN/TXT/PDF/?uri=CELEX:32016R0679
6. Gabel, A., Ertas, F., Pleger, M., Schiering, I., Müller, S.: Privacy-preserving metrics for an mHealth app in the context of neuropsychological studies. HEALTHINF **5**, 166–177 (2020). https://doi.org/10.5220/0008982801660177
7. Gentry, C.: Fully homomorphic encryption using ideal lattices. In: Proceedings of the 41st Annual ACM Symposium on Symposium on Theory of Computing - STOC 2009, p. 169. ACM Press (2009). https://doi.org/10.1145/1536414
8. Goyal, V., Pandey, O., Sahai, A., Waters, B.: Attribute-based encryption for fine-grained access control of encrypted data. In: Proceedings of the 13th ACM Conference on Computer and Communications Security, CCS 2006, pp. 89–98. Association for Computing Machinery (2006). https://doi.org/10.1145/1180405.1180418
9. Hansen, M., Jensen, M., Rost, M.: Protection goals for privacy engineering. In: 2015 IEEE Security and Privacy Workshops, pp. 159–166 (2015). https://doi.org/10.1109/SPW.2015.13
10. Hillen, C.: The pseudonym broker privacy pattern in medical data collection. In: IEEE Trustcom/BigDataSE/ISPA, vol. 1, pp. 999–1005 (2015). https://doi.org/10.1109/Trustcom.2015.475

11. Huckvale, K., Prieto, J.T., Tilney, M., Benghozi, P.J., Car, J.: Unaddressed privacy risks in accredited health and wellness apps: a cross-sectional systematic assessment. BMC Med. **13**(1), 214 (2015). https://doi.org/10.1186/s12916-015-0444-y
12. Kan, J., Kim, K.S.: MTFS: Merkle-tree-based file system. In: IEEE International Conference on Blockchain and Cryptocurrency (ICBC), pp. 43–47 (2019). https://doi.org/10.1109/BLOC.2019.8751389
13. Khanezaei, N., Hanapi, Z.M.: A framework based on RSA and AES encryption algorithms for cloud computing services. In: IEEE Conference on Systems, Process and Control (ICSPC 2014), pp. 58–62 (2014). https://doi.org/10.1109/SPC.2014.7086230
14. Kotz, D.: A threat taxonomy for mHealth privacy. In: Third International Conference on Communication Systems and Networks (COMSNETS 2011), pp. 1–6 (2011). https://doi.org/10.1109/COMSNETS.2011.5716518
15. Larson, R.S.: A path to better-quality mHealth apps. JMIR mHealth Health **6** (2018). https://doi.org/10.2196/10414
16. Lenhard, J., Fritsch, L., Herold, S.: A literature study on privacy patterns research. In: 43rd Euromicro Conference on Software Engineering and Advanced Applications (SEAA), pp. 194–201 (2017). https://doi.org/10.1109/SEAA.2017.28
17. Lewko, A., Sahai, A., Waters, B.: Revocation systems with very small private keys. In: 2010 IEEE Symposium on Security and Privacy, pp. 273–285. IEEE (2010). https://doi.org/10.1109/SP.2010.23
18. Lewko, A., Waters, B.: Decentralizing attribute-based encryption. In: Paterson, K.G. (ed.) EUROCRYPT 2011. LNCS, vol. 6632, pp. 568–588. Springer, Heidelberg (2011). https://doi.org/10.1007/978-3-642-20465-4_31
19. Luxton, D.D., McCann, R.A., Bush, N.E., Mishkind, M.C., Reger, G.M.: mHealth for mental health: integrating smartphone technology in behavioral healthcare. Prof. Psychol. Res. Pract. **42**, 505–512 (2011). https://doi.org/10.1037/a0024485
20. Müller, S.V., Ertas, F., Aust, J., Gabel, A., Schiering, I.: Kann eine mobileanwendung helfen abzuwaschen? Zeitschrift für Neuropsychologie **30**(2), 123–131 (2019). https://doi.org/10.1024/1016-264X/a000256. Hogrefe AG
21. Müller, S., Katzenbeisser, S., Eckert, C.: Distributed attribute-based encryption. In: Lee, P.J., Cheon, J.H. (eds.) ICISC 2008. LNCS, vol. 5461, pp. 20–36. Springer, Heidelberg (2009). https://doi.org/10.1007/978-3-642-00730-9_2
22. Neubauer, T., Heurix, J.: A methodology for the pseudonymization of medical data. Int. J. Med. Inf. **80**, 190–204 (2011). https://doi.org/10.1016/j.ijmedinf.2010.10.016
23. Ometov, A., Bezzateev, S., Mäkitalo, N., Andreev, S., Mikkonen, T., Koucheryavy, Y.: Multi-factor authentication: a survey **2** (2018). https://doi.org/10.3390/cryptography2010001
24. Papageorgiou, A., Strigkos, M., Politou, E., Alepis, E., Solanas, A., Patsakis, C.: Security and privacy analysis of mobile health applications: the alarming state of practice. IEEE Access **6**, 9390–9403 (2018). https://doi.org/10.1109/ACCESS.2018.2799522
25. Sahai, A., Waters, B.: Fuzzy identity-based encryption. In: Cramer, R. (ed.) EUROCRYPT 2005. LNCS, vol. 3494, pp. 457–473. Springer, Heidelberg (2005). https://doi.org/10.1007/11426639_27

26. Verheul, E.R., Jacobs, B., Meijer, C., Hildebrandt, M., de Ruiter, J.: Polymorphic encryption and pseudonymisation for personalised healthcare. IACR Cryptology ePrint Archive 2016, 411 (2016)
27. Vrhovec, S.L.R.: Challenges of mobile device use in healthcare. In: 39th international convention on information and communication technology, electronics and microelectronics (MIPRO), pp. 1393–1396 (2016). https://doi.org/10.1109/MIPRO.2016.7522357

Privacy-Preserving Analytics for Data Markets Using MPC

Karl Koch[1](✉), Stephan Krenn[2](✉)(iD), Donato Pellegrino[3](✉),
and Sebastian Ramacher[2](✉)(iD)

[1] Graz University of Technology, Graz, Austria
karl.koch@iaik.tugraz.at
[2] AIT Austrian Institute of Technology, Vienna, Austria
{stephan.krenn,sebastian.ramacher}@ait.ac.at
[3] TX Tomorrow Explored, Helsinki, Finland
donato@tx.company

Abstract. Data markets have the potential to foster new data-driven applications and help growing data-driven businesses. When building and deploying such markets in practice, regulations such as the European Union's General Data Protection Regulation (GDPR) impose constraints and restrictions on these markets especially when dealing with personal or privacy-sensitive data.

In this paper, we present a candidate architecture for a privacy-preserving personal data market, relying on cryptographic primitives such as multi-party computation (MPC) capabl e of performing privacy-preserving computations on the data. Besides specifying the architecture of such a data market, we also present a privacy-risk analysis of the market following the LINDDUN methodology.

Keywords: Data market · Multi-party computation · Privacy analysis

1 Introduction

For the last decades, the amount of data generated, processed, and shared has been ever-increasing [29]. Especially personal data has become more and more interesting [12]. One of the trends in this area is fitness and health data as more and more people are using fitness trackers, e.g. Garmin's connect [21] or Apple's Health app [4], where the collected data can then be used in clinical research [33]. Relatedly, machine learning-based approaches facilitate the development of small sensors for measuring bodily functions of chronically ill patients. As an example, diabetes patients needing to draw blood multiple times a day, benefit from novel, noninvasive monitoring methods of their blood sugar levels [37]. Very recently,

This project leading to this publication has received funding from the European Union's Horizon 2020 research and innovation programme under grant agreement No 871473 ("KRAKEN").

M. Friedewald et al. (Eds.): Privacy and Identity 2020, IFIP AICT 619, pp. 226–246, 2021.
https://doi.org/10.1007/978-3-030-72465-8_13

location data collected by mobile network operators have become of interest to help combat the COVID-19 pandemic [9,34].

However, personal data is highly sensitive and regulations such as the General Data Protection Regulation (GDPR) have to be taken into account when collecting, transmitting, storing, or processing the data. Therefore, these regulations present unique challenges in the design of data markets offering any kind of personally identifiable data. To profit from the opportunities as an individual (e.g., by sharing fitness data with insurance companies for better premiums) or for the common good (e.g., for limiting the outbreak of pandemics or clinical research), these challenges have to be overcome first, as otherwise misuse of the data could lead to discrimination, e.g., on the job market or by insurance companies [3].

More and more data markets are tackling these challenges via cryptographic means offering a wide variety of differing privacy guarantees. Mediacalchain [1] among many others facilitates the exchange of medical data end-to-end secured. Agora [26] goes a step further and offers a data market place for privacy-sensitive data built from functional encryption (FE) [7] where data consumers are able to buy evaluations of certain functions on user data. Thereby only the results of the evaluation are exchanged without the need to transfer the original data sets. Besides proposing the specific FE-based architecture, Koutsos et al. also provide a security model for confidentiality of processed data and consider payments in their analysis. However, the security model does not consider confidentiality of the data against the broker. Similarly, MyHealthMyData [31] offers FE-based analytics with the focus on medical data while providing confidentiality of the data throughout the system. Enveil [2] is a platform for outsourced computation using fully homomorphic encryption (FHE), but also offers possibilities for consumers to perform some analytic functions on the data. Wibson [20] provides a smart contract based market place focusing on different privacy aspects, namely the privacy of seller's and buyer's identity.

Brokerage and Market Platform for Personal Data (KRAKEN). The H2020 project KRAKEN [27] develops a data market for privacy-sensitive data. To achieve that, the project "aims to enable the sharing, brokerage, and trading of potentially sensitive personal data, by returning the control of this data to citizens (data providers) throughout the entire data lifecycle" [27]. KRAKEN mainly builds upon three pillars: (i) a data market place, (ii) self-sovereign identity (SSI) [17], and (iii) a toolbox of cryptographic primitives for privacy-preserving computation to achieve that. The market place acts as a broker between data providers and consumers. SSI is used to manage authentication, authorization, and, e.g., key management between data consumer and producer. Privacy-preserving cryptographic protocols and primitives including secure multi-party computation (MPC) are used to enable privacy-preserving analytics.

1.1 Contribution

In this paper, we propose and analyse a candidate architecture for the KRAKEN personal data marketplace that provides privacy-preserving distributed analytics features through the usage of MPC. The KRAKEN platform ensures user privacy and security of the overall system by relying on the decentralization of its core subsystems, SSI-based user management, and MPC-based processing of data. KRAKEN does not provide user data to the buyers. The core goal is to link buyers and sellers on the basis of metadata and policies, and enable data transfer between them in a privacy-preserving and decentralized manner. Thereby, KRAKEN closes the gap left open in Agora. Our contribution is twofold:

Architecture. We describe a candidate architecture of the KRAKEN platform in detail, thereby explaining the necessary cryptographic background, suggesting instantiations of the building blocks to be used, and justifying any necessary design choices. The platform is designed in a way that allows for computations over inputs from potentially many different data sources in a single computation to allow for, e.g., statistics over many users.

Privacy Analysis. To validate the privacy requirements of the architecture, data flow diagrams and a privacy analysis based on LINDDUN [16] are presented. This analysis considers all the privacy goals of KRAKEN, defines the related threats, and proposes mitigation strategies.

2 Preliminaries

The following sections give the necessary background on cryptographic building blocks, self-sovereign identities, and the LINDDUN methodology.

2.1 Cryptographic Building Blocks

Besides standard primitives such as encryption, our cryptographic architecture relies on a set of advanced privacy-preserving cryptographic mechanisms, which we will briefly introduce in the following. We want to stress that practically efficient solutions and instantiations are available for each of these building blocks.

Group Signatures. Group signatures, initially introduced by Chaum and van Heyst [14] allow a party to sign a message on behalf of a group. That is, the verifier receives cryptographic guarantees that a member of the group indeed signed the message, yet he does not learn the identity of the actual signer. To achieve this goal, a *group manager* generates a group public key gpk as well as a master secret key msk. Now, when a user U joins the group, she engages in a protocol with the group manager to receive her secret key sk_U which she uses for signing messages, while the verifier only needs access to gpk to verify the validity of signatures.

It is worth noting that in group signatures, signer privacy is not absolute: in order to avoid abuse, a dedicated *inspector* holding a inspection secret key *isk* is able to revoke anonymity and reveal the originator of a signature. For the remainder of this paper we assume that all inspector public keys are generated in a way that no entity knows the corresponding secret key (e.g., by setting the public key to the hash value of a public nonce), as the inspection feature is not required in our scenario. The resulting primitive is then akin to Intel's Enhanced Privacy ID (EPID) scheme [8], which also allows for signing messages on behalf of a group without anonymity revocation functionality. Recently, Kim et al. [25] proposed the first group signature scheme supporting batch verifications, which significantly speeds up the verification process in case of many signatures.

Zero-Knowledge Proofs of Knowledge. A zero-knowledge proof of knowledge (ZKPoK) is a two party protocol between a *prover* and a *verifier*, which achieves two intuitively contradictory goals: it allows the prover to convince the verifier that she knows a secret piece of information, while at the same time revealing no further information than what is already revealed by the claim itself.

Such protocols were first introduced by Goldwasser et al. [22], and are a central building block for many privacy-preserving applications such as anonymous credential systems [11,13], voting schemes [23], e-cash [10], or group signatures. In recent years, zero-knowledge succinct non-interactive arguments of knowledge (SNARKs) [5] achieving very high efficiency have gained significant attention.

Secure Multi-party Computation. Since its introduction by Yao [39], secure multi-party computation (MPC) has developed to an important building block for a variety of privacy-preserving applications. It allows a group of nodes to jointly evaluate a function on their inputs without revealing the inputs to the other nodes or any trusted third entity. Two major branches of MPC exist: while techniques based on garbled circuits are more efficient for bitwise operations [39], integer arithmetic can be computed highly efficiently using secret sharing based mechanisms [6,36] due to the algebraic properties of these schemes. Especially during the last decade, research has come up with practically efficient protocols which have also been deployed in real-world scenarios and products [15,19,24].

2.2   Self-Sovereign Identity

The Self-Sovereign Identity (SSI) [17,32] model describes an identity management concept which grants the owners of digital identities complete control over their data. The goal of SSIs are ensuring the security and privacy of users' identity data, full portability of the data, no central authorities, and data integrity.

2.3   LINDDUN Methodology

LINDDUN [16] is a threat modeling methodology for systematically analyzing privacy threats in software architectures. Threats are analyzed along the categories linkability, identifiability, non-repudiation, detectability, disclosure of information, unawareness, and non-compliance. On top of the threat analysis, it offers mitigation strategies to handle the identified threats. The analysis consists of the following, cf. also Fig. 1:

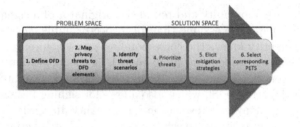

Fig. 1. Overview of the LINDDUN methodology [28].

(1) First, a data-flow diagram (DFD) is created detailing all involved entities, processes, trust boundaries, data stores and data flows.

(2) In the second step, the DFDs are mapped to the threat categories and for each element of the DFD potential threat categories are identified.

(3) Third, the identified threats are refined and documented. Also, assumptions that are made in the architecture are documented.

(4) Fourth, the threats are prioritized based on their risk.

(5) Next, mitigation strategies are defined, taking into account the risks that have been associated to each threat.

(6) Finally, effective countermeasures are selected by mapping the defined mitigation strategies to suitable privacy-enhancing technologies.

3   KRAKEN Architecture

As discussed by Koutsos et al. [26], a data market has to at least satisfy data privacy and output verifiability which are defined as follows:

Data privacy: No party can learn any information about on the data of the data owners. Only the result of computations on the data is known to the data consumers.[1]

Output verifiability: Authenticity of the data and results has to be ensured, i.e., falsified or incorrect results cannot be sold to a consumer.

Note that in contrast to Koutsos et al. [26] we omit *atomicity of payments*, which requires that data owners are correctly reimbursed, as for simplicity we do not (yet) consider per-access payments at this stage, but assume that data owners are compensated through a lump sum when uploading their data. However, we consider it important that data owners stay in control of their data, and therefore request that data owners need to be able to define for which (types of) computations their data may be used, and which computations are considered to privacy-invasive by the data owner.

---

[1] Note that in contrast to our definition, Agora allows data brokers, i.e. the market place, to learn the results as well.

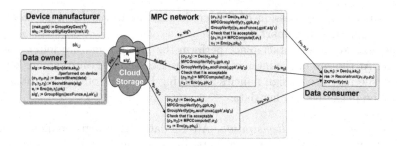

Fig. 2. KRAKEN cryptographic architecture overview.

We will discuss one a candidate architecture of the KRAKEN market place. The core idea of this architecture is centered around the use of MPC for privacy-preserving computation on data, group signatures to ensure data authenticity while preserving anonymity, and SNARKs for output verifiability. In our architecture we consider the following actors:

Device manufacturers produce devices that collects sensitive data. All devices contain a signing key for a group signature scheme where the group is managed by the manufacturer. Devices sign the data using their key.

Data owners use devices from the device manufacturer to collect sensitive data. The owner defines a family of functions which are allowed for performing computation on the data.

Data consumers define the functions that should be used for the analysis of the data. They are in possession of a public-key encryption key.

Computation nodes perform the analysis as defined by the data consumer on the data of the data owner using a secret sharing-based MPC protocol. They are in possession of a public-key encryption key. These computation nodes can be run by cloud computing providers that offer "computation as a service", various participants of the market place including the data owners and consumers, or by operator of the market place.

KRAKEN market place handles the registration of data owners and consumers and manages listings of available data sets. The information is stored on an internal blockchain and database.

Cloud storage provider offers storage to data owners without the need for registration.

An overview of the data processing is depicted in Fig. 2. We will now discuss the three typical data flows.

User Registration. We start with the registration of a data owner and data consumers on the market place which is centered around credentials from a SSI system. In this step we assume that they obtained their credential from an identity provider before, as this is a step only performed once independent of the registration at the market place.

(1) The user is in possession of SSI credentials and uses them to create an account on the data market place.
(2) The user and the market place perform the group signature joining procedure. At the end of the interaction, the user obtains a group signing key sk'_U that she may use to sign policies specifying the types of computations that may be performed on her data.

Data Pre-processing and Registration. After a data owner registered on the market place, she is able to register her data for subsequent analysis in the market place. To do so, the data owner performs the following steps:

(1) The data owner collects data produced by her device, which is signed also by the device's group signature signing key sk_U.
(2) The data owner produces shares of the data and associated signature, using a secret sharing scheme compatible with the deployed MPC protocol, resulting in shares σ_i, $i = 1, 2, 3$ – one per MPC node.
(3) Using the public key pk_i of MPC node i, the data owner encrypts σ_i.
(4) The data owner signs the encrypted shares and an acceptable family of functions using their group signature key sk'_U.
(5) The data owner sends all information, i.e. encrypted shares, acceptable family of functions, and the signature under sk'_U, to a cloud storage provider of their choice.
(6) The data owner registers the offering on the market place and informs the market place on the location of the encrypted secret shares.

For simplicity, in the proposed architecture, we assume that data owners are reimbursed by the market place via a lump sum when registering their data, and no further payments will take place on a per-usage basis.

Analysis. A consumer uses the market place to find data sets that are of interest and negotiates their use via the market place. During the negotiation, the consumer declares the function to be evaluated on the data. Once an agreement is reached, the evaluation is performed as follows:

(1) The market place informs the computation nodes of the function to perform and the location of the data items.
(2) The computation nodes fetch the encrypted secret shares and signatures from the cloud storage.
(3) After receiving all encrypted shares and signatures and the function f, the computation nodes first verify, for each data item, the signature on the data evaluation policy, and that f is an eligible function with respect to this policy. They then decrypt the shares, jointly verify the shared signatures, and start the MPC protocol to compute f on the data.
(4) The shares obtained as result of the computation, are then encrypted with respect to the consumer's public key, pk_C.
(5) The nodes provide a ZK-PoK/SNARK that they computed the function f on the received data and that the obtained signature verified on the inputs.

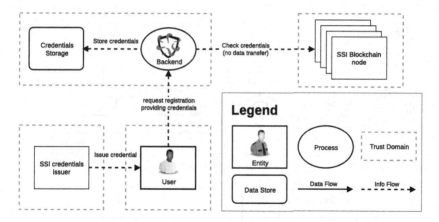

Fig. 3. DFD for the user action of registering.

(6) The nodes send the encrypted results and the proof to the consumer.
(7) The consumer decrypts the shares of the result and combines them to obtain the result of the evaluation. The consumer also verifies its correctness by checking the proofs sent by the nodes.

Similarly to before, in the current architecture we assume that consumers pay the market place, but no (direct or indirect) payment from the consumer to the data owner takes place. Further suggestions for a more fine-granular reimbursement concept can be found in Sect. 5.

4   LINDDUN Analysis of KRAKEN

We now present the LINDDUN analysis for KRAKEN's architecture. In the analysis, we focus on three user actions: (1) Register user, (2) Register availability of data, and (3) Perform data analysis.

We start with the DFDs. For reasons of clarity and comprehensibility, we split the data flow into two categories. First, a *real data flow*, which contains (parts of) personal data from data owners; such as encrypted shares or an analytics result. Second, an *info flow*, for other types of data flow; such as registering availability of data or invoicing data analysis. Figure 3 visualizes the DFD for the user action of registering a user. Figure 4 visualizes the DFD for the user actions of registering availability of data and performing data analysis.

4.1   Threat Tables

We use the LINDDUN mapping template [16] to map the DFD elements to the seven threat categories: Linkability, Identifiability, Non-repudiation, Detectability, Disclosure of information, Unawareness, Non-compliance. In the LINDDUN mapping template, entities are affected only by linkability, identifiability and

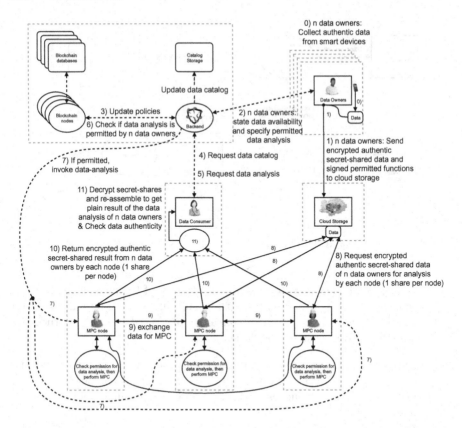

Fig. 4. DFD for the user actions of registering data and performing data analysis. The legend is as in Fig. 3.

unawareness threats, while the other DFD elements are affected by every threat except unawareness. We consider processes, flows and entities internal to trust domains not affected by any privacy threat from outside due to the fourth assumption. Data Flows and Info Flows are not affected by Non-compliance threat as the communications are secured with TLS. The Non-compliance threat does not affect Data Stores as well as they are implemented with the data-minimization principle. Also processes are not affected by the Non-compliance threat as no sensitive information (user personal data) is handled by them; in the case of MPC nodes the second assumption rules out the privacy threat.

Table 1 shows the threat table of our 1st user action, performing user registration. Table 2 shows the threat table of our 2nd user action, performing registration of data availability. Table 3 shows the threat table of our 3rd user action, performing data analysis.

Table 1. LINDDUN's threat table of the 1st user action, performing user registration. An ✗ in a cell indicates a privacy threat for the corresponding threat target. Cells labeled by "Ax" are no threats because of the indicated assumptions.

DFD Elements	Threat Target	Privacy Threats						
		L	**I**	**Nr**	**De**	**Di**	**U**	**Nc**
Data Store	Credentials Storage	✗	✗					
Info Flow	Issue credentials	✗	✗	✗	✗	A3		
	Request Registration	✗	✗	✗	✗	A3		
	Check credentials	✗	✗	✗	✗	A3		
	Store credentials							
Process	Backend							
Entity	User							
	SSI credentials issuer	A1	A1	A1	A1	A1	A1	A1
	SSI Blockchain							

4.2 Threat Elicitation

After having identified the elements of the DFD sus ceptible to privacy threats, the next step is to describe them in detail. In our scenario we make four assumptions, which we present and briefly discuss in the following.

Assumption 1. The SSI's credential issuer is a trusted entity. If the KRAKEN backend colludes with the credential issuer, the KRAKEN backend gets to know not only the SSI identity, but also the users' real identity. The assumption of an honest SSI's credential issuer, gives us the guarantee that the KRAKEN backend cannot link SSI identities to real identities.

While this assumption might look overly strong at first glance, it could be achieved by designing the issuer as a distributed party deploying threshold cryptography, or, on a policy-level, through regular audits. Furthermore, by informing users about this requirements, they can also check for, e.g., legal relationships between these two entities, before revealing any personal data.

Assumption 2. At least one MPC node is honest. For MPC, we can use protocols which give security guarantees although all parties bar one are malicious. We refer to these kind of protocols as *fully-malicious protocols*. Thus, with this assumption and the respective protocols, no MPC node either gets to know the underlying data, nor the analysis result. Furthermore, due to this assumption and the provided policies by the data owners, we do not need to worry about the case, that MPC nodes compute without authorization, since the honest MPC node aborts the computation, which leads to a global termination of the computation.

To minimize the impact of this assumption, the hosts of the MPC nodes should be carefully selected in order to minimize intended collusions among them or their simultaneous corruptions. A possible approach might be to include more

Table 2. LINDDUN's threat table of the 2nd user action, performing registration of data availability. An *✗* in a cell indicates a privacy threat for the corresponding threat target. Cells labeled by "Ax" are no threats because of the indicated assumptions.

DFD Elements	Threat Target	Privacy Threats						
		L	I	Nr	De	Di	U	Nc
Data Store	Catalog Storage	✗	✗					
	Cloud Storage	✗	✗					
Info Flow	collect authentic data from smart devices							
	send encrypted authentic secret-shared data to cloud storage and signed permitted functions	✗	✗	✗	✗	A3		
	state data availability and specify permitted data analysis	✗	✗	✗	✗	A3		
	Update data catalog							
	Update policies							
Process	Backend							
	Blockchain nodes							
Entity	Data Owner						✗	
	Data Consumer							
	Cloud Storage							

than the required three computation nodes in the ecosystem, and letting the user choose which nodes to support when encrypting her data. Note that a selected node can still get corrupted, but it might be less likely. Though, after all, (1) the probability that all nodes get corrupted might decrease too, and (2) all nodes need to get corrupted to leak sensitive data when using a fully-malicious protocol.

Especially for highly sensitive data, one of these nodes might even be deployed at the data owners. Thereby, the honest node is in control of the data owner and hence leaking sensitive data is low.

Assumption 3. Each communication between actors of different trust domains is secured using transport-layer security (TLS). When two actors of different trust domains communicate, this assumption guarantees that no content is leaked during transit. Only the communication's metadata can still leak, like the IP addresses of the source and target. Secure communication protocols are heavily deployed in many scenarios, and can be considered state-of-the-art.

Assumption 4. Anybody who gains access to any of trust boundaries is considered to have the same possibilities as the corrupted entity itself, and trust boundaries are implemented in a secure way. If someone hacks into a any of trust domains, the intruder (normally) gets access to the corresponding data stores, processes, and data flow. Hence the intruder has full control over the trust domain's system.

Table 3. LINDDUN's threat table of the 3rd user action, performing data analysis. An ✗ in a cell indicates a privacy threat for the corresponding threat target. Cells labeled by "Ax" are no threats because of the indicated assumptions.

DFD Elements	Threat Target	Privacy Threats						
		L	**I**	**Nr**	**De**	**Di**	**U**	**Nc**
Data Store	Catalog Storage	✗	✗					
	Cloud Storage			✗	✗			
	Data Consumer							
Info Flow	4) Request data catalog	✗	✗	✗	✗	A3		
	5) Request data analysis	✗	✗	✗	✗	A3		
	7) Invoke data analysis	✗	✗	✗	✗	A3		
Data Flow	8) Request enc. auth. se-sha. data	✗	✗	✗	✗	A3		
	9) Exchange se-sha. data	✗	✗	✗	✗	A3		
	10) Return enc. analysis result	✗	✗	✗	✗	A3		
Process	6) Check permission of data analysis							
	9) Check permission & Perform MPC					A2		A2
	11) Decrypt analysis result & Check authenticity							
Entity	Cloud Storage							
	MPC Nodes							
	Data Consumer							

To a major extent, this is rather a simplification than an assumption, as it significantly simplifies the analysis. We do not need to distinguish between insider attacks (e.g., a system administrator), and an external attack (e.g., an attacker partial gaining control over an entity), but we assume that once a trust boundary is violated, the entire entity is fully controlled by the adversary.

Mapping LINDDUN's Privacy Threats to the DFDs. In this section the threats identified using the threat tables are described in detail.

Threat 1 (Linkability in one or more storages). An insider of KRAKEN links data coming from the catalog, credentials, policies or purchases storages.

Assets, stakeholder, threats: Linking different users or different information of the same user could lead to gain more information about users than expected.
Primary misactor: An internal user that has access to the data storages of the backend and/or of the internal blockchain.
Basic flow: (1) The insider gains specific information by querying the data store. (2) The obtained set of information can be linked.
Preconditions: The user has updated the system with some informations or is at least registered.
DFD elements: Credentials storage, Catalog storage, Policies storage, Purchases storage, Cloud storage.

Remarks: This threat could lead to identification. When applied to the credentials storage, the probability is much lower as credentials have a high level of minimization of information.

Threat 2 (Identifiability in one or more storages).   An insider of KRAKEN identifies one or more users in a set of data coming from one or more storages.

Assets, stakeholder, threats: The identity of the user must be unknown in the KRAKEN.

Primary misactor: An internal user that has access to the data storages of the backend and/or of the internal blockchain.

Basic flow: (1) The insider gains specific information by querying one or more data stores. (2) The obtained set of information can be linked and can lead to identification of one or more users.

Preconditions: The user has updated the system with some information or is at least registered.

DFD elements: Credentials storage, Catalog storage, Policies storage, Purchases storage, Cloud storage.

Threat 3 (Detectability of data existence).   The user uploads the data on the cloud without publishing on KRAKEN, revealing the existence of data.

Assets, stakeholder, threats: The detection of the existence of the data must take place at the will of the user.

Primary misactor: The cloud or an external actor.

Basic flow: The misactor checks periodically the cloud storage until the data is uploaded.

DFD elements: Cloud storage

Threat 4 (Detectability in communication between different trust domains).   An internal/external actor can detect user actions by listening to requests.

Assets, stakeholder, threats: The detectability of user actions is not expected outside of the scope of the interested actors.

Primary misactor: A skilled internal/external actor that has access to the network of the user and can inspect user's packets.

Basic flow: (1) The misactor intercepts packets between a user and KRAKEN. (2) Whenever a packet is sent, an action has been detected.

DFD elements: All the data flows between two different trust domains.

Remarks: This threat disclosure of information is not expected as the communication happens through TLS.

Threat 5 (Linkability of IP addresses in communication between different trust domains). An internal/external actor can link different events to the same user by listening to user's requests.

Assets, stakeholder, threats: Any information that can be gained by linking user actions are not expected to be known by anyone except the user.

Primary misactor: A skilled internal/external actor that has access to the network of the user and can inspect user's packets.

Basic flow: (1) The misactor intercepts packets between a user and KRAKEN. (2) Whenever a packet is sent, IP addresses are collected. (3) The misactor links packets with the same IP.

DFD elements: All the data flows between two different trust domains.

Remarks: This threat disclosure of information is not expected as the communication happens through TLS.

Threat 6 (Linkability of IP addresses in communication between different trust domains leads to identifiability). An internal/external actor can identify users by linking different events to the same IP by listening to user's requests.

Assets, stakeholder, threats: User's identity and any information that can be gained by linking user actions are not expected to be known by anyone except the user.

Primary misactor: A skilled internal/external user that has access to the network of the user and can inspect user's packets and knows or can link to an IP address the user's identity.

Basic flow: (1) The misactor intercepts packets exchanged between a user and KRAKEN. (2) Whenever a packet is sent, IP addresses are collected. (3) The misactor links packets with the same IP. (4) The gained information, together with any information that can link the IP to a user (e.g., insecure traffic with other systems) leads to the identification of the user.

DFD elements: All the data flows between two different trust domains.

Threat 7 (Non-repudiation of encrypted data). The cloud storage cannot repudiate that encrypted data is available.

Primary misactor: Data stores which do not handle data access properly.

DFD elements: Cloud storage (data store; user action (UA) 2/3).

Threat 8 (Non-repudiation of communication between different trust domains). An entity cannot repudiate that he sent a message to another entity within a different trust domain.

Primary misactor: An external user that has access to the network of the user and can inspect user's packets.

DFD elements: All data flows between two different trust domains.

Threat 9 (Unawareness of the data owner). First, a data owner provides data for which he is not allowed, such as by national law. Second, a data owner does not take care of the defined analysis policies/permissions, such that a consumer could learn something about the owner based on the analysis result. For example, if an owner allows an analysis without any other owners in addition (aggregated analysis), then, e.g., an average would reveal the actual data.

Table 4. Threat prioritization depending on likelihood and impact.

Likelihood	Impact	Priority		Likelihood	Impact	Priority		Likelihood	Impact	Priority
low low medium	low medium low	low		low medium high	high medium low	medium		medium high high	high medium high	high

Table 5. Overview of threat prioritization. Threats that are not effective due to our assumptions are not included in the table.

Threat	Likelihood	Impact	Priority
Linkability in one or more storages	medium	medium	medium
Identifiability in one or more storages	low	high	medium
Detectability of data existence	medium	low	low
Detectability in communication between different trust domains	low	low	low
Linkability of IP addresses in communication between different trust domains	low	medium	low
Linkability of IP addresses in communication between different trust domains leads to identifiability	low	high	medium
Non-repudiation of encrypted data	low	low	low
Non-repudiation of communication between different trust domains	low	low	low
Unawareness of the data owner	low	high	medium
Non deletion of data in cloud storage	low	low	low

Primary misactor: A data owner making data available.
DFD elements: Data owner (entity; UA 2).

Threat 10 (Non-deletion of data in cloud storage). The data owner is not aware that the cloud storage is in possession of his data.

Primary misactor: A cloud storage not deleting user's data.
Basic flow (1) The data owner requests the cloud storage to delete his data. (2) The cloud storage doesn't delete the data. (3) The data owner is not aware that the data is stored on the cloud storage.
DFD elements: Data owner (entity; UA 2).

4.3   Prioritizing Threats

For the prioritization of the threats, first a likelihood and impact value is assigned to every threat identified in the threat table. Both values are taken from low, medium, and high indicating a low to high likelihood and impact, respectively. The likelihood value depends on the joint evaluation of difficulty and outcome of performing the specific action, while the impact value depends on threatened assets where identifiability and disclosure of information are high impact, linkability is medium and Non-repudiation, Detectability, Unawareness, Non-compliance are low. Table 4 shows how threats are prioritized depending on likelihood and impact values.

Table 5 gives an overview of the prioritization of the identified threats. In the following, we give a brief justification for each threat.

Linkability in one or more storages. In this threat the likelihood value is medium as even if the misactor needs to be an insider, exploiting more than one storages leads to better outcomes in trying to link user's data. The impact is medium as the threatened asset is the linkability of user's data, that if combined with identifiability reveals which users performed certain actions.

Identifiability in one or more storages. The likelihood value is low as the misactor would need more information other than the ones contained in the KRAKEN system to identify one or more users. The impact is high as the threatened asset is the identity of users that is considered high priority asset.

Detectability of data existence. The likelihood is medium as the threatened information is public by default. The misactor could be an external user without any specific capability that needs to know by other means that the specific data is destined to KRAKEN. In the case where the misactor is the cloud storage that may know the identity of the user, the cloud storage would still need to know by other means that the specific data is destined to KRAKEN. In a hospital scenario, If a patient decides to adopt the hospital's cloud system, the hospital could make assumptions on the content of the dataset by linking the detection of the dataset existence with information related to the patient. However, this situation is highly unlikely as the user can choose any cloud system without relying on the hospital's one. The impact is low as the data is always encrypted, existence of data may be detected, but the data itself does not leak.

Detectability in communication between different trust domains. The likelihood value is low as the misactor is an external skilled individual that has access to the network of the user or to the KRAKEN network. The impact is low as the threatened asset is the detectability of user actions, which is considered a low-priority asset.

Linkability of IP addresses in communication between different trust domains. This threat depends on the same actions and actor needed to perform the previous one, so the likelihood is the same. The impact is medium as the threatened asset is the linkability of user's data, that if combined with identifiability reveals which users performed certain actions.

Linkability of IP addresses in communication between different trust domains leads to identifiability. This threat depends on the same actions and actor needed to perform the previous one, so the likelihood is the same. The impact is high as the threatened asset is the identity of users that is considered high priority asset.

Non-repudiation of encrypted data. As cloud-storage providers usually use unguessable file links, the likelihood for this threat is low. The impact is low as one cannot identify the receiver of the ciphertext recover its content.

Non-repudiation of communication between different trust domains. Similar as for detectability of communication, likelihood and impact are low.

Unawareness of the data owner. The likelihood value is low as the personal data provided belongs to the user and therefore it is her own interest to provide data that does not affect her in terms of non compliance with regulations. Moreover (for the second case) the outcome of publishing the analysis of a dataset without a pool of other user's datasets would not be appealing for a possible buyer. The impact is high as the threatened asset is the personal information of users that is considered high priority asset.

Non deletion of data in cloud storage. The likelihood value is low as the outcome of performing this action would lead the cloud storage to have an encrypted dataset that is not possible to consume in any way. Because of Assumption 2, the cloud storage cannot collaborate with the MPC nodes to unveil the data as at least one of them is honest. The impact is low as the threatened asset is the unawareness of users that is considered low priority.

4.4 Mitigating Threats

For every threat in non low priority, we propose a set of mitigations expressed in the following list:

Linkability in one or more storages. To mitigate the threat on the SSI storage side, on registration phase the system can request to the user the minimum set of credentials required to allow the user to get registered and do not lead to linkability/identification. To mitigate the threat on the other storages, the system can display a suggestion to user saying to non include any identifiable information before the publication of any product.

Identifiability in one or more storages. This threat depends on the previously described threat "Linkability in one or more storages", the mitigation applied in that threat mitigate consequently also this one.

Linkability of IP addresses in communication between different trust domains leads to identifiability. To avoid the misactor to understand that the communication is happening with KRAKEN, avoiding linkability and resulting identifiability, we propose onion routing like Tor [18].

Unawareness of the data owner. The mitigation can be implemented on the user's frontend side in two complementing ways. First, the system provides thorough documentation that explains potential risks when offering certain data sets for data analytics. Second, based on the type of data and the acceptable function families, privacy metrics [38] are displayed to make the user aware of any risks. Thereby, the system is able to warn the user, e.g., before allowing the computation of an average but where the user's input is the only considered data set.

4.5   Privacy Analysis Outcome

We adopted an iterative approach in the design of the architecture that used the LINDDUN privacy analysis to identify threats and plan the changes for the iterations. It's worth mentioning the most relevant changes that this approach generated. The DFDs (Figs. 3 and 4) highlight the differences in information and data flow. This division in typology of data flows has been key leading us to construct an architecture where personal data is exchanged solely between data owner and consumer, without passing through centralized parties unencrypted.

Another key element derived from the analysis is the use of group signatures. Public keys of the users represent a risk for identification of the user or could be linked to other actions. For this reason we decided to adopt group signatures to allow the user to sign data and permitted functions on behalf of a group. In this way the user can demonstrate to be part of the users of KRAKEN and can sign data and functions anonymously while retaining authenticity.

Finally, we identified a set of threats that do not imply architectural changes, but instead have to be considered in a development context. These threats and their mitigations affect single elements of the architecture: the Credentials storage, Catalog storage, Policies storage, Purchases storage, Cloud storage, and the Data owner. A set of changes need to be implemented in these elements to address the mitigations. In particular, we applied a principle of data minimization in the context of the backend and the blockchain storages, while in the user software development, we considered a set of tools to be provided to the Data owner for documentation, analytics, and threat detection purposes.

5   Conclusion and Future Work

In this paper, we presented a privacy-preserving data market platform and analysed its privacy-guarantees following the LINDDUN methodology. The proposed solution allows users to sell data without any disclosure of information in regards to the data itself. The LINDDUN analysis revealed threats related to linkability and disclosure of information that could have a relevant impact, however these threats have a low likelihood and the system's methodologies in collecting information related to those threats is implemented in a way that highly minimizes the collected information. The LINDDUN analysis does not reveal any threat related to disclosure of information of the owners data sets.

The proposed architecture is based on cryptographic mechanisms, and in particular secure multi-party computation (MPC). With that approach, a data consumer is able to obtain privacy-preserving data analysis results from data owners, while the consumer receives only the analysis result. Furthermore, our marketplace does neither learn the owners' data content nor the analysis result, but only metadata. As opposed to Agora [26], where the broker, their market place, gets to know the analysis result. Our security guarantees in terms of privacy analysis, however, depend on the assumption that at least one MPC node behaves honestly. A possible future work would be on realising a trust measurement to drive the choice of MPC nodes. Another possible field of research would go towards moving the MPC computations on data owners. The obstacle to overcome in this case would be the problem of user availability during the computation, as users typically do not have constantly running servers available.

The architecture (cf. Section 3) only considers lump sums to reimburse the data owner. However, it might be practically more preferable to get paid *per usage*, i.e., whenever one's data is actually used in a computation, resulting in additional privacy challenges. A straightforward solution might be to add an exchange service. This service would then be able to link usages of a user's data, thereby being able to profile a user, especially when collaborating with a data consumer. Thus, such a service would need to be highly trusted akin to traditional banks in a physical world. An alternative approach could be to leverage privacy-friendly crypto currencies like Monero [35] or z.cash [30]. To further increase trust in the system, the MPC nodes could publish cryptographic yet privacy-preserving proofs which data was used for which computation, such that a user could audit that she was indeed paid for every computation involving her data. The precise format of such auxiliary outputs of the MPC nodes is currently being investigated.

References

1. Medical chain: Whitepaper 2.1 (2018). https://medicalchain.com/Medicalchain-Whitepaper-EN.pdf
2. Enveil: Encrypted Veil (2020). https://www.enveil.com/
3. Allen, M.: Health Insurers Are Vacuuming Up Details About You - And It Could Raise Your Rates (2020). https://www.propublica.org/article/health-insurers-are-vacuuming-up-details-about-you-and-it-could-raise-your-rates
4. Apple-Inc.: A more personal Health app. For a more informed you (2020). https://www.apple.com/ios/health/
5. Bitansky, N., Canetti, R., Chiesa, A., Tromer, E.: From extractable collision resistance to succinct non-interactive arguments of knowledge, and back again. In: ITCS, pp. 326–349. ACM (2012)
6. Bogdanov, D., Niitsoo, M., Toft, T., Willemson, J.: High-performance secure multi-party computation for data mining applications. Int. J. Inf. Sec. **11**(6), 403–418 (2012)
7. Boneh, D., Sahai, A., Waters, B.: Functional encryption: a new vision for public-key cryptography. Commun. ACM **55**(11), 56–64 (2012)
8. Brickell, E., Li, J.: Enhanced privacy ID from bilinear pairing for hardware authentication and attestation. In: SocialCom/PASSAT, pp. 768–775. IEEE (2010)
9. Bruni, A., Helminger, L., Kales, D., Rechberger, C., Walch, R.: Privately Connecting Mobility to Infectious Diseases via Applied Cryptography. IACR Cryptology ePrint Archive 2020, 522 (2020)
10. Camenisch, J., Hohenberger, S., Lysyanskaya, A.: Balancing accountability and privacy using e-cash (Extended Abstract). In: De Prisco, R., Yung, M. (eds.) SCN 2006. LNCS, vol. 4116, pp. 141–155. Springer, Heidelberg (2006). https://doi.org/10.1007/11832072_10
11. Camenisch, J., Lysyanskaya, A.: An efficient system for non-transferable anonymous credentials with optional anonymity revocation. In: Pfitzmann, B. (ed.) EUROCRYPT 2001. LNCS, vol. 2045, pp. 93–118. Springer, Heidelberg (2001). https://doi.org/10.1007/3-540-44987-6_7

12. Chandler, S.: We're giving away more personal data than ever, despite growing risks (2020). https://venturebeat.com/2019/02/24/were-giving-away-more-personal-data-than-ever-despite-growing-risks/
13. Chaum, D.: Blind signatures for untraceable payments. In: CRYPTO, pp. 199–203. Plenum Press, New York (1982)
14. Chaum, D., van Heyst, E.: Group signatures. In: Davies, D.W. (ed.) EUROCRYPT 1991. LNCS, vol. 547, pp. 257–265. Springer, Heidelberg (1991). https://doi.org/10.1007/3-540-46416-6_22
15. Cybernetica: Sharemind MPC (2020). https://sharemind.cyber.ee/sharemind-mpc/
16. Deng, M., Wuyts, K., Scandariato, R., Preneel, B., Joosen, W.: A privacy threat analysis framework: supporting the elicitation and fulfillment of privacy requirements. Req. Eng. **16**(1), 3–32 (2011)
17. Der, U., Jähnichen, S., Sürmeli, J.: Self-sovereign identity - opportunities and challenges for the digital revolution. CoRR abs/1712.01767 (2017)
18. Dingledine, R., Mathewson, N., Syverson, P.F.: Tor: the second-generation onion router. In: USENIX, pp. 303–320. USENIX (2004)
19. Duality Technologies Inc: Duality (2020). https://dualitytech.com/
20. Fernandez, D., Futoransky, A., Ajzenman, G., Travizano, M., Sarraute, C.: Wibson protocol for secure data exchange and batch payments. CoRR abs/2001.08832 (2020)
21. Garmin-Ltd.: connect: Fitness at your fingertips (2020). https://connect.garmin.com/
22. Goldwasser, S., Micali, S., Rackoff, C.: The knowledge complexity of interactive proof-systems (extended abstract). In: STOC, pp. 291–304. ACM (1985)
23. Groth, J.: Non-interactive zero-knowledge arguments for voting. In: Ioannidis, J., Keromytis, A., Yung, M. (eds.) ACNS 2005. LNCS, vol. 3531, pp. 467–482. Springer, Heidelberg (2005). https://doi.org/10.1007/11496137_32
24. Ion, M., et al.: Private intersection-sum protocol with applications to attributing aggregate ad conversions. IACR Cryptology ePrint Archive 2017, 738 (2017)
25. Kim, H., Lee, Y., Abdalla, M., Park, J.H.: Practical dynamic group signature with efficient concurrent joins and batch verifications. IACR Cryptology ePrint Archive 2020, 921 (2020)
26. Koutsos, V., Papadopoulos, D., Chatzopoulos, D., Tarkoma, S., Hui, P.: Agora: a privacy-aware data marketplace. IACR Cryptology ePrint Archive 2020, 865 (2020)
27. KRAKEN Consortium: The Project — KRAKEN (2020). https://www.krakenh2020.eu/the_project/overview
28. linddun.org: LINDDUN privacy engineering (2020). https://www.linddun.org/
29. Marr, B.: How much data do we create every day? The mind-blowing stats everyone should read (2020). https://www.forbes.com/sites/bernardmarr/2018/05/21/how-much-data-do-we-create-every-day-the-mind-blowing-stats-everyone-should-read/
30. Miers, I., Garman, C., Green, M., Rubin, A.D.: Zerocoin: anonymous distributed e-cash from bitcoin. In: IEEE S&P, pp. 397–411. IEEE (2013)
31. Morley-Fletcher, E.: MHMD: my health, my data. In: EDBT/ICDT Workshops. CEUR Workshop Proceedings, vol. 1810. CEUR-WS.org (2017)
32. Mühle, A., Grüner, A., Gayvoronskaya, T., Meinel, C.: A survey on essential components of a self-sovereign identity. Comput. Sci. Rev. **30**, 80–86 (2018)
33. Muoio, D.: Fitbit launches large-scale health study to detect a-fib via heart rate sensors, algorithm (2020). https://www.mobihealthnews.com/news/fitbit-launches-large-scale-consumer-health-study-detect-fib-heart-rate-sensors-algorithm

34. Muoio, D.: Google mobilizes location tracking data to help public health experts monitor COVID-19 spread (2020). https://www.mobihealthnews.com/news/google-mobilizes-location-tracking-data-help-public-health-experts-monitor-covid-19-spread
35. Noether, S., Mackenzie, A.: Ring confidential transactions. Ledger **1**, 1–18 (2016)
36. Shamir, A.: How to share a secret. Commun. ACM **22**(11), 612–613 (1979)
37. Todd, C., Salvetti, P., Naylor, K., Albatat, M.: Towards non-invasive extraction and determination of blood glucose levels. Bioengineering **4**(4), 82 (2017)
38. Wagner, I., Eckhoff, D.: Technical privacy metrics: a systematic survey. ACM Comput. Surv. **51**(3), 57:1–57:38 (2018)
39. Yao, A.C.: Protocols for secure computations (extended abstract). In: FOCS, pp. 160–164. IEEE (1982)

Towards Models for Privacy Preservation in the Face of Metadata Exploitation

Marine Eviette[✉] and Andrew Simpson

Department of Computer Science, University of Oxford, Wolfson Building,
Parks Road, Oxford OX1 3QD, UK
marine.eviette@cybersecurity.ox.ac.uk, andrew.simpson@cs.ox.ac.uk

Abstract. It is well understood that today's society generates enormous volumes of data, with much of that data being used to drive the emerging digital data economy. However, due to dataveillance and related concerns, the magnitude and specificity of this data has given rise to well documented privacy concerns. Amongst these concerns is the unregulated collection of online metadata. Despite being commonly used, metadata is a term that few understand. Yet its richness, prevalence and collection has serious implications for many. In this paper we describe initial work with regards to a means of allowing users to control access to metadata pertaining to them, with a view to addressing these implications. To do so, we leverage the work of the Solid data decentralisation project and build upon the notion of Category-Based Access Control.

1 Introduction

Ubiquitous computing has given rise to vast quantities of data, with some sources suggesting that 2.5 quintillion bytes of data are being created on a daily basis[1]. These enormous volumes of data have been used to fuel a growing data economy, with many companies taking advantage of the opportunities that can flow from leveraging fine-grained consumer personalisation. In concert with these opportunities there are challenges—most obviously in the guise of threats to privacy in the context of a market where personal data is traded as a commodity. The acknowledgment of such threats has led to an evolution of privacy guidelines and requirements in the online space, driven by manifestations of data management legislation such as the EU's General Data Protection Regulation (GDPR)[2].

Despite increasing concerns over data management with reference to privacy and human rights, the topic of *metadata* has remained relatively unexplored. (In the context of this paper we consider metadata to be any data serving to provide contextual or otherwise additional information about other data.) While the definition of online metadata has remained relatively constant, the information to which it pertains has become far more complex, its volume has become greater,

---

[1] https://www.domo.com/learn/data-never-sleeps-5.
[2] https://gdpr-info.eu.

© IFIP International Federation for Information Processing 2021
Published by Springer Nature Switzerland AG 2021
M. Friedewald et al. (Eds.): Privacy and Identity 2020, IFIP AICT 619, pp. 247–264, 2021.
https://doi.org/10.1007/978-3-030-72465-8_14

and its specificity has, for many, become more worrisome. Online metadata is routinely overlooked since it is often generated without users' explicit consent and awareness due, in part, to the unfavourable online conditions of dark patterns [1,2], privacy-averse designs [3], and general privacy fatigue [4]. As a result, there is often unregulated collection of such metadata, which can have troubling, and potentially disastrous, implications for an individual's privacy.

A single instance of metadata is often trivialised as being harmless, since, in isolation, it may not compromise an individual's privacy. However, it is well understood that, when aggregated with other instances of metadata, sensitive details may be inferred or reidentification may occur. This is akin to the problem of *jigsaw re-identification* [5] in the context of publicly available data, though, in this case, the reidentification may be undertaken by data custodians, data brokers, or third-party organisations. Notably, the issues of concern extend far beyond reidentification due to the magnitude of metadata collection and consequent analysis in the online realm. To this end, we find that the breadth, pervasiveness and implicitness of metadata has led to online browsing habits shaping an extremely detailed trail of online activities via the passive *digital footprints* [6] that are unknowingly left behind. Such digital footprints that are accumulated by means of dataveillance have led to inferences on identity elements that expose user identity while rendering these users powerless in the management of their personal privacy.

At present, there is no single unifying method to identity management as it relates to this problem. As such, we leverage solutions to related problems to give rise to formal models of access control with a view to applying them to metadata and identity management. In doing so, we build upon the work of the Solid data decentralisation project[3], which aims to preserve personal privacy on a decentralised Web via Access Control Lists. We hope that, by building upon the Solid project's foundation, we may be able to formalise our specific problem.

It is worth noting that, while the access control 'problem' is well defined and well understood [7], things become more complicated when we start to consider broader privacy concerns: considerations of beneficiary and ownership can cause complex issues [8], not least because it is often the case that, despite (for example) legal obligations, the data-holder will not typically have a vested interest in the protection of privacy.

Deviation from 'traditional' policy requirements has seen the introduction of a variety of novel approaches to access control. For example, in [9] Fernandez *et al.* report upon a framework for secure data collection whereby users are able to specify data management rules through the extension of the *Category-Based Access Control* metamodel [10]. Category-Based Access Control (CBAC) adopts a foundational notion of access control, by considering notions of categories in order to provide flexible access control concepts, which can be specialised for particular needs. In particular, the logical foundations of this approach enable the analysis and verification of policy properties. We argue that utilising such an approach should enable one to reason about the problem at hand. Thus, we

---

[3] https://solidproject.org.

present a model of CBAC in terms of the Z notation [11,12], the mathematical language of which is based upon typed set theory and first-order predicate logic. In addition, the schema language of Z allows us to combine aspects of a model in a way that makes reuse and composition of aspects relatively straightforward and also allows us to reason about evolution of states.

The choice of Z was influenced, in part, by the fact that its notation is relatively straightforward to understand and that its underlying logical structures have much in common with those of relational databases. In addition, it has been used previously in describing models of access control (see, for example, [13]).

Given the foundations provided by the CBAC framework and the Solid decentralisation project, we frame our research problem thus:

How can we leverage a Solid-style approach to data ownership together with formal models of data access to aid in the protection of data subjects' privacy, so as to mitigate inference-driven identity exposure from metadata collection?

2   Background and Motivation

2.1   Metadata and Dataveillance

Metadata, in this era of pervasive computing, has become infrastructural [14] in the manner in which it invisibly supports almost all interactions in the online realm, leaving a distinct digital trail for any given user. This digital trail is made up of *digital footprints* [6] from user interaction. Digital footprints can be thought of as identifying features that are used to infer elements or attributes of an identity, or are themselves identity elements or attributes, where identity elements are defined to be single pieces of information that are indicative of an identity [15].

These digital footprints consist of two types: those of a *passive* nature, such as metadata, and those which might be described as *active*, such as a Facebook post or a tweet. Passive digital footprints are comprised primarily of metadata created unintentionally by user activities without the user's explicit consent or knowledge. Collection of this passive data is particularly disconcerting due to the nature of online surveillance, or *dataveillance* [16].

The phenomenon of dataveillance has, in part, motivated the race for storage, analysis and creation of large data volumes whilst simultaneously degrading user privacy and exerting control in intimate settings. Moreover, dataveillance has played a pivotal role in the inference of identity or digital personas, where, as early as the 1990s, there were indications of organisations' ability to create digital personas [17].

Today, dataveillance's role in big data has become drastically more pervasive, and, hence, so too have these inferred digital personas. In fact, in this surveilled online environment, with continuous monitoring in the form of metadata, many truthful identity elements can be inferred without the user needing to explicitly express them online [18], which exposes users' identity information.

With regards to identity management in the offline space, the multiplicity of identity is naturally explored through context, where a single individual's identity is made up of numerous aspects that they may choose to reveal. This allows individuals to refrain from sharing certain details or identifiers outside of settings that they deem appropriate. Similarly, the contexts in the online space reflects one's self-presentation whereby individuals are free to choose how they wish to express themselves to others across a multitude of platforms. However, as it pertains to metadata in the online space, this multiplicity struggles to adapt to a persistent, non-forgetting terrain that often lacks context despite the aggressive aggregation and sharing. This is epitomised by revelations that a unique persona can always be inferred for individuals, regardless of the differing personas maintained by these individuals across the online space.

Given that this problem is only set to worsen as technology becomes further intertwined with individuals' lives with, for example, the increased ubiquity of the IoT and 'smart' devices, the generated metadata agglomeration will only further expand. Therefore, regulation and access control mechanisms are needed in this area to divert privacy violations that threaten human rights and to ensure the metadata collected is not easily exploitable.

2.2   Data Ownership

The definition of privacy is an all-encompassing, ever-evolving, fluid notion that has enjoyed (and continues to enjoy) many definitions [19]. The varying definitions for privacy can, in part, be seen as a result of discrepancies between individuals' own conceptions, the varying cultures of belonging, and economic and lawful practices. Despite these variances, privacy is viewed by many as an important factor in human life—to some, a human right—and "[over] 130 countries have constitutional statements regarding the protection of privacy" [20].

As far as we are concerned in this paper, privacy can be viewed as

A limitation on access to self

(This is reminiscent of earlier philosophical definitions, such as those of [21] and [22].)

Defining privacy in this fashion allows us to move towards formulating the problem in terms of *access control*: if we consider self as a collection of data objects, we can begin to see how access control may be applied to this problem. However, while it may be a nice intellectual exercise to reason about access to data objects as a method of protecting individuals' privacy, there is a clear roadblock in the form and nature of today's Internet, whereby users typically have no control over their own data and, consequently, no control over managing access to it.

Of course, data ownership has long been a source of debate [23,24]. Initial hopes for the Web narrated a vision of radical decentralisation and freedom [25], yet its incredible growth has been plagued with centralisation, so that, decades later, we see a significant proportion of traffic on the Web flowing through a comparatively minuscule set of corporations.

The disadvantages of such centralisation follow a similar path to the pitfalls of corrupt central entities, such as corrupt governments and companies, whereby we find the Web today ripe with surveillance, data breaches, privacy loss and manipulation. Indeed, a "few large companies now own important junctures of the Web, and consequently a lot of the data created on [it]" [26]. Thus, while individuals largely remain the source of their data, this does not translate into automatic data ownership. Of course, the complexities of data ownership become even more complex when one considers, for example, transfer of data to third parties, analysis information of data aggregates from various sources, etc.

2.3 An Alternative Approach

A number of projects (including those described by [27] and [26]) have begun to investigate methods for users to retain (or regain) ownership, as well as consequent control, of their data, through the introduction of decentralised architectures that can be implemented on top of the current Internet.

The Web, as originally formulated, was intended to facilitate easy data sharing between researchers across the Internet in a largely decentralised manner. However, the Web today, as we have argued, tends towards centralisation, with data being controlled and processed by a small number of large companies. To counter the resultant privacy dilemmas, the inventor of the Web, Tim Berners-Lee, and colleagues began work on Solid [28]—a distributed data decentralisation project that seeks to enable information sharing in a privacy-preserving manner.

In the Solid approach, data generated by a user is written to their own individual 'pods' (with a pod being 'personal online data store'). These pods may be hosted wherever the user chooses, and the user can then authorise granular access of the pod to other parties as they please. This means that authenticated applications are allowed to request data, assuming that the user has given the particular application permission.

At this point, it is worth noting that other solutions (such as those described in [29] and [30]) offer approaches to decentralised access control via blockchain technology. However, our motivations—including the consideration of aggregation of metadata and the automatic evolution of access control policies—have led us to conclude that developing a solution based on the Solid approach is appropriate for our needs.

For managing control over data, Solid utilises Web Access Control (WAC) Lists. These Web Access Control Lists have much in common with the Access Control Lists generally used in Discretionary Access Control [31] policies.

Users and groups are attached to URIs, or WebIDs; resources are identified by URLs that may refer to web documents or resources. To handle permissions, these latter resources are accompanied by a set of Authorisation statements that describe:

- which agents have access to the resource, and
- what type, or mode, of access the given agent has.

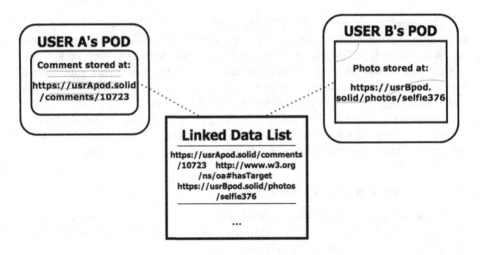

Fig. 1. Links between users' data

These Authorisations are placed into separate WAC documents called Access Control List Resources (ACLs) with the permissions of the ACL resource stored in a *Linked Data* [32] format. Linked Data can be described as typed links that enable explicit connections to be made when necessary. Thus, we may have links between different users' data pods, as depicted in Fig. 1.

By adapting the Solid philosophy and principles, there is scope for reasoning about the 'metadata problem' in terms of access control—due to the fact that a fundamental tenet of Solid is that users control access to their own data.

Crucially, though, Solid by itself will be insufficient. With regards to metadata, it is almost inevitable that the pods will not be a sufficient method of protection (as it is usual for metadata to appear 'harmless'). Metadata typically becomes useful as a result of inferences from aggregations. As such, Solid provides the intellectual foundations upon which we build, but we need to go further in terms of reasoning about access. It is the notion of Category-Based Access Control (CBAC) [10] that allows us to do that.

3 CBAC

There is undeniably a trend with regards to the development of novel access control models to handle use cases that are perceived to be new and/or unique. Often these novel approaches have much in common with each other or with previous approaches. An alternative to re-inventing the wheel on a regular basis is to consider a more general, 'primitive' notion upon which new models can be built. The meta-model for Category-Based Access Control (CBAC) [33] is such a notion.

Category-Based Access Control (CBAC) was developed to provide flexible access control concepts that can be specialised for particular needs [33]. With regards to our problem of interest, CBAC has the potential to provide the foundations for a model that allows one to reason about autonomous changes to permissions.

In CBAC, permissions are assigned to categories of users (as opposed to users); this, in turn, allows permissions to be associated with categories. Categories can be defined on the basis of, for example, roles and resources, as well as attributes and geographical constraints so that permissions can change when a user attribute or geographical location changes, without intervention from an administrator. This would be decidedly beneficial in our case regarding thresholds for data aggregation and inferences, whereupon a permission can be withdrawn.

The CBAC meta-model works on interactions between the following sets [10]:

- A countable set C of categories, where c_0, c_1, etc. denote arbitrary category identifiers.
- A countable set P of principals, where p_0, p_1, etc. denote principals.
- A countable set A of named atomic actions, where a_0, a_1, etc. denote arbitrary action identifiers.
- A countable set R of resource identifiers, where r_0, r_1, etc. denote arbitrary resources.
- A countable set S of situational identifiers, where s_0, s_1, etc. denote possible situations that may occur in the system.
- A countable set E of event identifiers, where e_0, e_1, etc. denote possible events that may happen in the system.

With respect to *permissions* and *authorisations*:

- A permission is an ordered pair $(a, r) \in A \times R$, consisting of an action, $a \in A$, and a resource, $r \in R$.
- An authorisation is a triple, $(p, a, r) \in P \times A \times R$, which associates a permission with a principal, $p \in P$.

Continuing, the meta-model of [10] details the following relations:

- Principal–category assignment: $PCA \subseteq P \times C$, where $(p, c) \in PCA$ if, and only if, the principal $p \in P$ is assigned to the category $c \in C$.
- Permission–category assignment: $ARCA \subseteq A \times R \times C$, where $(a, r, c) \in ARCA$ if, and only if, action $a \in A$ on resource $r \in R$ can be performed by principals associated with the category $c \in C$.
- Authorisations: $PAR \subseteq P \times A \times R$, where $(p, a, r) \in PAR$ if, and only if, the principal $p \in P$ can perform the action $a \in A$ on the resource $r \in R$.

In the following, we shall use 'syntactic sugar' of the form $pca\,(p, c)$, $arca\,(a, r, c)$ and $par\,(p, a, r)$ to capture these concepts.

Subsequently, Barker [10] determines that the set of *par* (p, a, r) facts that hold with respect to the specification of a particular access control policy may be expressed in first-order terms thus:

$$\forall p : P; \ a : A; \ r : R \bullet \exists c : C \bullet$$
$$par(p, a, r) \Leftrightarrow pca(p, c) \wedge arca(a, r, c)$$

A further relationship, ρ, captures the notion of the existence of a relationship, such as inclusion, holding between categories:

$$\forall p : P; \ a : A; \ r : R \bullet \exists c, c' : C \bullet$$
$$par(p, a, r) \Leftrightarrow pca(p, c) \wedge \rho(c, c') \wedge arca(a, r, c')$$

Although the model does not consider aspects such as sessions, delegations, denial of permissions or conflict resolution strategies, it is noted that, from this initial basis, these notions can naturally be accommodated [10]. This has been illustrated in practice by the aforementioned contribution of Fernandez *et al.* [9].

4   A Formal Model

As a first step, we have developed a formal model of the Category-Based Access Control meta-model, $\mathcal{M}$ [10], in terms of the Z schema language [11,12]. The intention is that we should be in a position to leverage and build upon this model as we move forward. As well as providing the necessary formal foundations, Z schemas provide a degree of flexibility—allowing us to add or remove optional elements (such as situational and event identifiers) in a relatively straightforward fashion. In this section we present key aspects of the formal model.

4.1   Types and Relations

Our interpretation of the meta-model $\mathcal{M}$ captures the key components of the original presentation as faithfully as possible. For example, the original characterisation gives rise to six *basic types*: C, the set of categories; P, the set of principals/users; A, the set of actions; R, the set of resources; S, the situational identifier set; and E, the event identifier set. (These last two are optional for any particular instantiation.)

Thus, we have the following declaration:

$$[C, P, A, R, S, E]$$

As already discussed, we may consider permissions and authorisations thus:

- A permission is an ordered pair (a, r) consisting of an action $a \in A$ and a resource $r \in R$.

- An authorisation is a triple (p, a, r) that associates the constituent parts of a permission with a principal $p \in P$.

We define the sets *Perm* (for permissions) and *Auth* (for authorisations) thus:

$$Perm == A \times R$$
$$Auth == P \times Perm$$

In the previous section, we discussed three relations: principal–category assignment, permission–category assignment, and authorisations. We capture these in our Z model thus.

$$PCA == P \leftrightarrow C$$
$$ARCA == C \leftrightarrow Perm$$
$$PAR == P \leftrightarrow Perm$$

Here, $P \leftrightarrow C$ captures the set of all possible relations between the set P and the set C (i.e. the set of all sets of pairs appearing in the Cartesian product $P \times C$)—with *PCA* being an abbreviation for this collection. The sets of relations, *ARCA* and *PAR*, are defined similarly: the former captures relations of type $C \leftrightarrow Perm$; the latter captures relations of type $P \leftrightarrow Perm$.

4.2   The *MModel* Schema

The schema *Instance* captures the 'current' categories, principles and permissions of the system under consideration and is defined thus.

Instance
$permset : \mathbb{F}\ Perm$
$principalset : \mathbb{F}\ P$
$catset : \mathbb{F}\ C$

Here, *permset* is a finite set of elements of type *Perm*; *principalset* is a finite set of elements of type P; and *catset* is a finite set of elements of type C.

The *MModel* schema is then defined as follows.

```
┌─ MModel ──────────────────────────────────────────────
│  Instance
│  pca : PCA
│  arca : ARCA
│  par : PAR
├───────────────────────────────────────────────────────
│  dom pca ⊆ principalset
│  ran pca ⊆ catset
│  dom arca ⊆ catset
│  ran arca ⊆ permset
│  dom par ⊆ principalset
│  ran par ⊆ permset
│  par = pca ⨾ arca
└───────────────────────────────────────────────────────
```

The inclusion of *permset*, *principalset* and *catset* via the *Instance* schema allows different instances of the metamodel to operate on different combinations of permissions, principals and categories. The sets *pca*, *arca* and *par* capture principal–category assignment, permission–category assignment and authorisations respectively.

The constraints are direct derivatives of the rules placed upon the sets as defined in the original model. The first six constraints simply restrict the domains and ranges of the *par*, *arca* and *par* relations (via constraints that leverage the dom and ran operations). The final constraint captures the fact that the *par* relation can be viewed as the relational composition of *pca* and *arca*: a pair (p_1, p_2), for some $p_1 \in P$ and some $p_2 \in Perm$, appears in *par* if, and only if, there is some $c \in C$, such that $(p_1, c) \in pca$ and $(c, p_2) \in arca$.

4.3   Support for Modularity

To support modularity, we utilise two schemas. The first, which is concerned with the attributes of the *Instance* schema, is defined thus:

```
┌─ SetupRetained ───────────────────────────────────────
│  ΔMModel
├───────────────────────────────────────────────────────
│  catset' = catset
│  principalset' = principalset
│  permset' = permset
└───────────────────────────────────────────────────────
```

This schema is used in operations that are concerned only with the relations *arca*, *par* and *pca*.

The second such schema, *ModelRetained*, is used in operations that are concerned only with the sets of categories, principles and permissions.

```
┌─ ModelRetained ──────────────────────────────────
│ ΔMModel
├──────────────────────────────────────────────────
│ par' = par
│ arca' = arca
│ pca' = pca
└──────────────────────────────────────────────────
```

4.4 Example Operations: Permissions

In category-based access control (CBAC), permissions are not assigned to individuals users, but, instead, to categories of users. These categories can then be changed as necessary.

As a means of illustrating operations on our model, we present operations that are specifically concerned with explicit changes to the set of permissions (as opposed to operations concerned with changes made by category or principal assignments).

We start by defining a schema, *UpdatePerms*:

```
┌─ UpdatePerms ────────────────────────────────────
│ ModelRetained
├──────────────────────────────────────────────────
│ catset' = catset
│ principalset' = principalset
└──────────────────────────────────────────────────
```

To any given instance of the model we want to be able to define a starting set of permissions on the set of actions and resources. As such, we utilise a schema, *AllocatePerms* to allocate a chosen set of permissions to the particular instance:

```
┌─ AllocatePerms ──────────────────────────────────
│ UpdatePerms
│ allocation? : F₁ Perm
├──────────────────────────────────────────────────
│ permset = ∅
│ permset' = allocation?
└──────────────────────────────────────────────────
```

$allocation? : \mathbb{F}_1\ Perm$

The operation *AddPerms* allows the set of permissions to be augmented:

```
┌─ AddPerms ───────────────────────────────────────
│ UpdatePerms
│ allocation? : F₁ Perm
├──────────────────────────────────────────────────
│ permset ≠ ∅
│ permset ∩ allocation? = ∅
│ permset' = permset ∪ allocation?
└──────────────────────────────────────────────────
```

The operation *RemovePerms* captures the notion of permissions being removed via this route:

$\text{\textit{RemovePerms}}$
$\Delta MModel$
$allocation? : \mathbb{F}_1 \, Perm$

$permset \neq \emptyset$
$allocation? \subseteq permset$
$permset' = permset \setminus allocation?$
$par' = par \rhd allocation?$
$pca' = pca$
$arca' = arca \rhd allocation?$
$principalset' = principalset$
$catset' = catset$

Here, $\rhd$ is the range co-restriction operator: in this case, all elements of the set *allocation?* are removed from the ranges of both *par* and *arca*. These updates are necessary as the removal of permissions from *permset* can impact upon both *par* and *arca*.

4.5 Example Operations: Principals

In CBAC, for users to be granted permissions, they must first be assigned to categories. This results in operations on principals typically involving the set *pca* and, at times, *par*. As such, the schema *UpdatePrincCat* ensures the set *arca* remains unchanged.

$\text{\textit{UpdatePrincCat}}$
$SetupRetained$

$arca' = arca$

In order to assign a principal to a particular category, we consider two cases. The first such case is in which a principal is being assigned to category that does not have any assigned permissions (i.e. for a category c, it is the case that $c \notin dom \, arca$). The second such case is in which a principal is being assigned to a category that already has assigned permissions (i.e. for a category c, it is the case that $c \in dom \, arca$). As such, the schema *AllocatePrincCat* involves an **if** clause with respect to the set of authorisations added to *par*.

```
┌─ AllocatePrincCat ─────────────────────────────────────────
│  UpdatePrincCat
│  p? : P;  c? : C
│  v : 𝔽 Auth
├────────────────────────────────────────────────────────────
│  p? ↦ c? ∉ pca
│  v = if c? ∈ dom arca
│      then {m : arca | first m = c? • (p?, second m)}
│      else ∅
│  pca' = pca ∪ {p? ↦ c?}
│  par' = par ∪ v
└────────────────────────────────────────────────────────────
```

To handle the complementary case—removal of a principal from a given category—we define *RemovePrincCat*. In order to remove a principal from a category, we must consider whether the category has assigned permissions: if the category has no assigned permissions, the only change made is to the set *pca*; otherwise, the set *par* may also change (as reflected by the *IF* clause).

```
┌─ RemovePrincCat ───────────────────────────────────────────
│  UpdatePrincCat
│  p? : P;  c? : C
│  d : 𝔽 C;  v : ℙ Auth;  pe : Perm
├────────────────────────────────────────────────────────────
│  p? ↦ c? ∈ pca
│  c? ↦ pe ∈ arca ∨ c? ∉ dom(arca)
│  d = {n : pca | first n = p? ∧ second n ≠ c? • second n}
│  v = {m : arca |
│          first m = c? ∧ second m ∉ ran(d ◁ arca) • (p?, second m)}
│  par' = if (pe ∈ ran(d ◁ arca) ∧ v = ∅)
│         then par
│         else par \ v
│  pca' = pca \ {p? ↦ c?}
└────────────────────────────────────────────────────────────
```

4.6   Example Operations: Categories

Categories are, by definition, at the heart of CBAC. Categories can be characterised as a class of entities that share some property.

In our model, the set of categories, *catset* captures the categories that exist in the current system. The schema *AddCat* allows us to add categories:

```
┌─ AddCat ──────────────────────────────────────────
│ ModelRetained
│ c? : 𝔽₁ C
├───────────────────────────────────────────────────
│ c? ∩ catset = ∅
│ permset′ = permset
│ principalset′ = principalset
│ catset′ = catset ∪ c?
└───────────────────────────────────────────────────
```

The schema *RemCat* is concerned with removing categories. Category removal needs to handle the cases where: the category has principals previously assigned; the category has no assigned principals; and the category has permissions assigned to it and, as such, can be found in *arca*.

```
┌─ RemCat ──────────────────────────────────────────
│ ΔMModel
│ c? : C
│ pe : 𝔽 Perm
├───────────────────────────────────────────────────
│ c? ∈ catset
│ pe = if c? ∈ dom arca
│       then {m : permset | c? ↦ m ∈ arca}
│       else ∅
│ pca′ = pca ⊳ {c?}
│ arca′ = {c?} ⊲ arca
│ par′ = par ⊳ pe?
│ permset′ = permset
│ principalset′ = principalset
│ catset′ = catset \ {c?}
└───────────────────────────────────────────────────
```

Within a given category, members are associated with permissions that have been assigned to the category. As such, operations on categories often involve the sets *arca* and *par*. Thus, we define a schema, *UpdateCatPerms*, which ensures that *pca* remains unchanged:

```
┌─ UpdateCatPerms ──────────────────────────────────
│ SetupRetained
├───────────────────────────────────────────────────
│ pca′ = pca
└───────────────────────────────────────────────────
```

We may consider the assignment of permissions to categories (as found in the set *arca*), where we consider how assignment of permissions applies to a category that does not have any assigned principals, i.e. for a category c, it is the case that $c \notin \mathrm{ran}\, pca$. Here, we reason that the only set to be updated is *arca* and so $v = \emptyset$. We may also consider the handling of category–permission assignment when the category already has assigned principals, i.e. for a category c, it is the case that $c \in \operatorname{ran} pca$. Here, $arca$ is updated, as is the set of authorisations: par must change to reflect an assignment of permissions to principals found in the given category.

$$
\begin{array}{l}
\hline
\quad CategoryPerms \underline{\hspace{6cm}} \\
\;\; UpdateCatPerms \\
\;\; c? : C; \; pe? : Perm \\
\;\; v : \mathbb{P}\, Auth \\
\hline
\;\; c? \mapsto pe? \notin arca \\
\;\; v = \{m : pca \mid second\ m = c? \bullet (first\ m, pe?)\} \\
\;\; arca' = arca \cup \{c? \mapsto pe?\} \\
\;\; par' = par \cup v \\
\hline
\end{array}
$$

The next schema provides a method to remove permissions from a category and update the authorisation set, par. In the first case, we deal with the removal of permissions from a category that does not have any principals assigned to it, and as a result, the only set to change is $arca$. This is in contrast to the case where the category has principals assigned to it. This difference is reflected in the need to update the authorisation set, par, if these permissions are the sole result of membership of the category in question, i.e. for a category c_1, it is the case that $\forall pe : arca\,(c_1) \bullet pe \notin \operatorname{ran}(\{c_1\} \lhd arca):$.

$$
\begin{array}{l}
\hline
\quad RemoveCatPerms \underline{\hspace{6cm}} \\
\;\; UpdateCatPerms \\
\;\; c? : C; \; pe? : Perm; \; v? : \mathbb{P}\, Auth \\
\hline
\;\; (v? = \emptyset \wedge c? \notin \operatorname{ran}(pca)) \\
\;\; pe? \in permset \\
\;\; c? \mapsto pe? \in arca \\
\;\; arca' = arca \setminus \{c? \mapsto pe?\} \\
\;\; par' = par \setminus v? \\
\hline
\end{array}
$$

The following schema encapsulates an update or 'swap' on the permissions found within a category. Here, for a category, c_1, with $c_1 \mapsto perm_1 \in arca$, if we wish to 'swap' the permission $perm_1$ with $perm_2$ so that we have $c_1 \mapsto perm_2 \in arca$, we can define this for a category with or without principals. In the case of a category without principals, we see changes to $arca$ only; for the other case, we see changes to both $arca$ and par.

$$
\begin{array}{|l}
\underline{\quad SwapCatPerms \underline{\hspace{8cm}}} \\
\quad UpdateCatPerms \\
\quad c? : C \\
\quad pe?, qe? : Perm \\
\quad v, d, w : \mathbb{P}\, Auth \\
\hline
\quad c? \mapsto qe? \in arca \\
\quad c? \mapsto pe? \notin arca \\
\quad v = \{m : pca \mid second\ m = c? \bullet (first\ m, qe?)\} \\
\quad d = \{n : v;\ s : pca;\ t : arca \mid \\
\qquad\qquad first\ n = first\ s \wedge second\ s = first\ t \wedge second\ s \neq c? \bullet \\
\qquad\qquad (first\ n, second\ t)\} \\
\quad w = \{m : pca \mid second\ m = c? \bullet (first\ m, pe?)\} \\
\quad arca' = (arca \setminus \{c? \mapsto qe?\}) \cup \{c? \mapsto pe?\} \\
\quad par' = ((par \setminus v) \cup d) \cup w
\end{array}
$$

5 Conclusion

We have presented a preliminary model of the Category-Based Access Control (CBAC) meta-model in terms of the schema language of Z. The model enables one to reason about potential extensions, to account for, for example, the dynamic, contextual nature of privacy as it relates to metadata.

Our problem of interest relates specifically to the issue of metadata collection as it applies to personal data, consent and dataveillance. As we have discussed, metadata collection informs the identity profiles companies create for their users [18].

This threat to users' privacy is entwined with the issue of data ownership on the Internet, where we see that users rarely have explicit ownership of their own data. To address this, we have identified a possible stepping stone in the form of the Solid proposal. The Solid proposal, as has been outlined, focuses on access control for users' data pods, whereby individuals may authorise granular access of their data as they please.

Our next task is to build upon our initial model to capture the Solid proposal's Web Access Control Lists. Subsequently, we will be in a position to build upon it, focusing on the specific problems faced due to collation of metadata. By reasoning about user data pods, we will be able to implement our own privacy notions that handle the complexities of inferences from metadata—allowing us to make further progress with respect to our main research question.

Acknowledgments. The authors would like to thank the anonymous reviewers for their helpful and constructive comments. Marine Eviette's research is funded by the EPSRC via the Centre for Doctoral Training in Cyber Security at the University of Oxford.

References

1. Fritsch, L.: Privacy dark patterns in identity management. In: Open Identity Summit (OID), 5–6 October 2017, Karlstad, Sweden., pp. 93–104. Gesellschaft für Informatik (2017)
2. Mathur, A., et al.: Dark patterns at scale: findings from a crawl of 11k shopping websites. Proc. ACM Hum. Comput. Interact. **3**, 1–32 (2019)
3. Bösch, C., Erb, B., Kargl, F., Kopp, H., Pfattheicher, S.: Tales from the dark side: privacy dark strategies and privacy dark patterns. Proc. Priv. Enhancing Technol. **2016**(4), 237–254 (2016)
4. Choi, H., Park, J., Jung, Y.: The role of privacy fatigue in online privacy behavior. Comput. Hum. Behav. **81**, 42–51 (2018)
5. Al-Azizy, D., Millard, D., Shadbolt, N., O'Hara, K.: Deanonymisation in linked data: a research roadmap. In: World Congress on Internet Security (WorldCIS-2014), pp. 48–52. IEEE (2014)
6. Lewis, K.: Three fallacies of digital footprints. Big Data Soc. **2**(2), 2053951715602496 (2015)
7. Benantar, M.: Access Control Systems: Security, Identity Management and Trust Models. Springer Science & Business Media, Berlin (2005)
8. Tschantz, M.C., Wing, J.M.: Formal methods for privacy. In: Cavalcanti, A., Dams, D.R. (eds.) FM 2009. LNCS, vol. 5850, pp. 1–15. Springer, Heidelberg (2009). https://doi.org/10.1007/978-3-642-05089-3_1
9. Fernández, M., Kantarcioglu, M., Thuraisingham, B.: A framework for secure data collection and management for Internet of Things. In: Proceedings of the 2nd Annual Industrial Control System Security Workshop (ICSS 2016), pp. 30–37. ACM (2016)
10. Barker, S.: The next 700 access control models or a unifying meta-model? In: Proceedings of the 14th ACM Symposium on Access Control Models And Technologies (SACMAT 2009), pp. 187–196. ACM (2009)
11. Spivey, J.M.: The Z Notation: A Reference Manual. Prentice Hall, New Jersey (1992)
12. Woodcock, J., Davies, J.: Using Z: Specification, Refinement, and Proof. Prentice-Hall Inc., Upper Saddle River, NJ, USA (1996)
13. Power, D.J., Slaymaker, M.A., Simpson, A.C.: On formalising and normalising role-based access control systems. Comput. J. **52**(3), 303–325 (2009)
14. Metadata. Springer, Cham (2016). https://doi.org/10.1007/978-3-319-40893-4_9
15. Hodges, D., Creese, S., Goldsmith, M.: A model for identity in the cyber and natural universes. In: 2012 European Intelligence and Security Informatics Conference, pp. 115–122. IEEE (2012)
16. Clarke, R.: Information technology and dataveillance. Commun. ACM **31**(5), 498–512 (1988)
17. Clarke, R.: The digital persona and its application to data surveillance. Inf. Soc. **10**(2), 77–92 (1994)
18. Van Dijck, J.: Datafication, dataism and dataveillance: big data between scientific paradigm and ideology. Surveill. Soc. **12**(2), 197–208 (2014)
19. Parent, W.A.: Privacy, morality, and the law. Philos. Public Aff. 269–288 (1983)
20. Privacy International. What is privacy, October 2017. https://www.privacyinternational.org/explainer/56/what-privacy
21. Garrett, R.: The nature of privacy. Philos. Today **18**(4), 263–284 (1974)
22. Gavison, R.: Privacy and the limits of law. Yale Law J. **89**(3), 421–471 (1980)

23. Van Alstyne, M., Brynjolfsson, E., Madnick, S.: Why not one big database? principles for data ownership. Decis. Support Syst. **15**(4), 267–284 (1995)
24. Foshay, N., Mukherjee, A., Taylor, A.: Does data warehouse end-user metadata add value? Commun. ACM **50**(11), 70–77 (2007)
25. Barlow, J.P.: A declaration of independence for cyberspace (1996). https://www.eff.org/cyberspace-independence
26. Zyskind, G., Nathan, O., Pentland, A.: Enigma: decentralized computation platform with guaranteed privacy. arXiv preprint arXiv:1506.03471 (2015)
27. Van Kleek, M., Smith, D.A., Shadbolt, N., et al.: A decentralized architecture for consolidating personal information ecosystems: the webbox. In: Proceeding Workshop on Personal Information Management (PIM), pp. 177–189 (2012)
28. Sambra, A.V., et al.: Solid: a platform for decentralized social applications based on linked data. Technical report, Technical Report, MIT CSAIL & Qatar Computing Research Institute (2016)
29. Ouaddah, A., Abou Elkalam, A., Ait Ouahman, A.: FairAccess: a new blockchain-based access control framework for the internet of things. Secur. Commun. Netw. **9**(18), 5943–5964 (2016)
30. Nofer, M., Gomber, P., Hinz, O., Schiereck, D.: Blockchain. Bus. Inf. Syst. Eng. **59**(3), 183–187 (2017)
31. Sandhu, R.S., Samarati, P.: Access control: principle and practice. IEEE Commun. Mag. **32**(9), 40–48 (1994)
32. Bizer, C., Heath, T., Berners-Lee, T.: Linked data: the story so far. In: Semantic Services, Interoperability and Web Applications: Emerging Concepts, pp. 205–227. IGI Global (2011)
33. Barker, S.: Personalizing access control by generalizing access control. In: Proceedings of the 15th ACM Symposium on Access Control Models and Technologies, pp. 149–158 (2010)

Author Index

Printed in the United States
by Baker & Taylor Publisher Services